Please see Circ. Desk for accompanying disc.

GAY SHAME

GAY

SHAME

DAVID M. HALPERIN & VALERIE TRAUB

The University of Chicago Press   CHICAGO AND LONDON

DAVID M. HALPERIN is the W. H. Auden Collegiate Professor of the History and Theory of Sexuality at the University of Michigan. He is the author of several books, including *Saint Foucault: Towards a Gay Hagiography* (Oxford University Press, 1995) and, most recently, *What Do Gay Men Want? An Essay on Sex, Risk, and Subjectivity* (University of Michigan Press, 2007). VALERIE TRAUB is professor of English and women's studies at the University of Michigan, where she chairs the Women's Studies Department. She is the author of *Desire and Anxiety: Circulations of Sexuality in Shakespearean Drama* (Routledge, 1992) and *The Renaissance of Lesbianism in Early Modern England* (Cambridge University Press, 2002).

The University of Chicago Press, Chicago 60637
The University of Chicago Press, Ltd., London
© 2009 by The University of Chicago
All rights reserved. Published 2009
Printed in the United States of America

17 16 15 14 13 12 11 10 09   1 2 3 4 5

ISBN-13: 978-0-226-31437-2 (cloth)
ISBN-13: 978-0-226-31438-9 (paper)
ISBN-10: 0-226-31437-5 (cloth)
ISBN-10: 0-226-31438-3 (paper)

Library of Congress Cataloging-in-Publication Data

Gay shame / [edited by] David M. Halperin and Valerie Traub.
    p. cm.
    Includes bibliographical references and index.
    ISBN-13: 978-0-226-31437-2 (cloth : alk. paper)
    ISBN-10: 0-226-31437-5 (cloth : alk. paper)
    ISBN-13: 978-0-226-31438-9 (pbk. : alk. paper)
    ISBN-10: 0-226-31438-3 (pbk. : alk. paper) 1. Gay and lesbian studies. 2. Gays—
Attitudes. 3. Homosexuality—Political aspects. 4. Queer theory. I. Halperin, David M.
1952– II. Traub, Valerie, 1958–
HQ75.15.G53 2008
306.76'6—dc22

                                                        2007049301

♾ The paper used in this publication meets the minimum requirements of the American National Standard for Information Sciences—Permanence of Paper for Printed Library Materials, ANSI Z39.48–1992.

CONTENTS

COMMUNITIES OF SHAME

ACKNOWLEDGMENTS

Gay Shame emerged out of a conference at the University of Michigan. Many people at the university contributed time, money, and encouragement to support both the original conference and the volume which is based on it. So we have a lot of people to thank.

The conference and this book benefited alike from the generous support of the Dean of the College of Literature, Science, and the Arts, and the Office of the Vice President for Research at the University of Michigan. The conference was also supported by the Associate Dean for Interdisciplinary Initiatives at the Rackham Graduate School, the Department of English Language and Literature, the Department of Romance Languages and Literatures, the Program in Comparative Literature, and the Program in Women's Studies. Two additional sponsors deserve our warm gratitude. Under the directorship of Daniel Herwitz, the Institute for the Humanities embraced the happy accident of our being fellows in 2002–2003 to provide the conference with exceptional administrative assistance; Eliza Woodford, in particular, responded to our constant requests with energy, graciousness, and fortitude. In addition to financially underwriting the conference, the Institute for Research on Women and Gender has provided an institutional home for the Lesbian-Gay-Queer Research Initiative, the unit at the University that sponsored the conference, as well as a grant for the preparation of the manuscript of this volume. We particularly thank Colin Johnson and Abby Stewart for helping to bring LGQRI into being, and Carol Boyd and Peggy Burns for their ongoing support of this program area.

Suraj Patel, our conference coordinator, was indefatigable in his enthusiasm, dedication, insight, and sensitivity to participants' needs; we thank him for taking this project on so entirely and so competently while completing his senior year at the University of Michigan. For visual enhancement of our project, we would like to thank Brian Hussey and Jayne Hamilton, as well as Patrick Moore, Brennan Gerard, and Catherine Opie. We are particularly grateful to Tim Retzloff and Julie Herrada, who created a library installation from the Labadie Collection; Holly Hughes, for associating her performance piece, "After a Fashion," with the conference; and Gayle Rubin, for DJing the final dance at the conference.

Staff at the Women's Studies Program provided much valued assistance in helping with manuscript preparation; we would particularly like to thank Shelley Shock and Sandra Vallie. We would also like to thank Chad Thomas, Lamont Egle, Laura Ambrose, Marjorie Rubright, and Dashini Jeyathurai for help with many aspects of the manuscript.

It has been a pleasure to work with the University of Chicago Press. We extend our special appreciation to Doug Mitchell, our editor, who believed in this project and supported it from the beginning; also, to Mary Gehl, for smoothing our way to publication.

Most of all, we would like to thank our contributors, who often took time out from their own work to address a difficult, volatile, and elusive topic, and who rose marvelously to the occasion.

D. M. H.
V. T.
Ann Arbor, Michigan
December 3, 2005

GAY SHAME

[DAVID M. HALPERIN AND VALERIE TRAUB]

Beyond Gay Pride

Ever since the Stonewall Riots of 1969 and the era of gay liberation they inaugurated, "gay pride" has been the rallying cry of a broad social movement for sexual freedom. It has also been the driving political force behind the emergence of the interdisciplinary fields of lesbian and gay studies and, more recently, queer theory. Liberation, legitimacy, dignity, acceptance, and assimilation, as well as the right to be different: the goals of gay pride require nothing less than the complete destigmatization of homosexuality, which means the elimination of both the personal and the social shame attached to same-sex eroticism. Since 1969 the lesbian and gay movement has made remarkable global progress toward its goals, leading to such once undreamt-of achievements as the visible integration of queer folk into mainstream popular culture and the formal, public recognition of same-sex partnerships. At the same time, gay pride has generated considerable dissatisfactions of its own among some of the very people it has aimed, or claimed, to benefit. Despite everything it has accomplished, and perhaps because of everything it has accomplished, the gay pride movement has given rise to a surprising array of discontents.

It was in this context that we decided, some years ago, to interrogate the continued usefulness of gay pride. We wanted to find out what it would be like to do queer politics and queer studies otherwise. In this case, "otherwise" seemed necessarily to imply some degree of renewed engagement with a category that represents, by definition, the very opposite of "pride," at once its emotional antithesis and its political antagonist: namely, the category of shame.[1] Gay pride has never been able to separate itself entirely from shame, or to transcend shame. Gay pride does not even make sense without some reference to the shame of being gay, and its very successes (to say nothing of its failures) testify to the intensity of its ongoing struggle with shame.

We started, accordingly, to identify topics that the imperative of gay pride had tended to place off-limits to legitimate inquiry, or had simply repressed—shameful topics, that is, or topics gay pride itself might make us ashamed to investigate. And we tried to imagine a queer community founded not only in collective affirmations of pride but also in residual experiences of shame. We wondered if it would ever be possible to create a queer sociality that could take account of those incorrigible, inwardizing impulses that drive sexual pariahs to want to have nothing to do with one another. Originating as they seem to do in the shame of social rejection, those inveterate queer tendencies to disassociation and disidentification offer the greatest resistance to group cohesiveness, coalition building, political alliance, emotional and social support, erotic bonding, mutual appreciation, and queer solidarity. Even from the perspective of a gay pride agenda, it is important to confront those antisocial queer tendencies, because they pose some of the most insurmountable obstacles to the realization of gay pride. And in fact gay pride has never managed entirely to overcome the mutual hostility and self-imposed isolation of the shamed. Perhaps, then, the time has come to consider some alternate strategies for the promotion of queer sociality.

With those aims in mind, we decided to bring together a number of scholars, critics, activists, archivists, writers, performers, journalists, and artists—some of whom turn out to be the same individuals—and we asked them to explore these issues. The result was an international conference that took place at the University of Michigan in Ann Arbor on March 27–29, 2003. We called it Gay Shame. The present volume builds on that conference by grouping together some of the material presented at it and by supplementing that material with other contributions designed to address the conjunction of shame, queerness, identity, and pride.

What are the residual effects of shame on lesbian and gay subjectivity in the era of gay pride? What affirmative uses can be made of shame and related affects, now that not all queers are condemned to live in shame? Are there important, nonhomophobic values related to the experience of shame that gay pride does not or cannot offer us? Can we do things with shame that we cannot do with pride? What are the similarities and differences between gay shame and ethnic shame, or racial shame, or disabled shame? Are there significant divergences between the shame of being a gay man and the shame of being a lesbian? Between the shame of being bisexual or transgendered and the shame of being lesbian or gay? How does the possibility of reclaiming gay shame enable us to create new forms of community as well as new opportunities for inquiry into lesbian-gay-queer history and culture? Is gay shame the new gay pride? Or does the turn to shame represent neither a rejection of pride nor a retooled version of it, but something else?

Those are the broadest questions that we wanted to address. We believe that some answers emerge from the material collected in this volume—despite its great diversity and the conflicting approaches, assessments, and viewpoints contained in it. Even if it turns out that gay shame is not about to displace or replace gay pride—and we are the last people in the world who would want it to do that—we still consider that the issues explored in this volume have the potential to effect a major redefinition and reconceptualization of lesbian-gay-queer studies and politics. In any case, we wish to provide an additional impetus to the radical transformations that are already taking place within some queer communities and that hold out the promise of an affirmative queer future unrestricted by the increasingly exhausted and restrictive ethos of gay pride.

I

As the organizers of the conference and the editors of this volume, we find ourselves in a curious position. For reasons we will explain in a moment, we conceived the conference in such a way as to make the prospect of publishing the proceedings unlikely, if not impossible. The collection we have assembled is therefore not your usual conference publication. Nor was it meant to be. So we need to explain what it is, and why it is the way it is.

The conference had a number of subsidiary purposes. Some of them relate to our own institutional situation at the University of Michigan. Others have to do with developments over the past fifteen years within the field of lesbian-gay-queer studies. Yet others have to do with more recent developments in queer politics, performance, and culture. And still others derive from the current disciplinary shape and practice of queer theory itself. All of them have had a share in determining the contents as well as the form of this volume. So let us be explicit about them.

One of our aims was simply to stage a major international event in lesbian-gay-queer studies at the University of Michigan, where we both teach. No public event on such a large scale had ever taken place at the University of Michigan with the university's full sponsorship and support, and no significant conference in the field had been held at the university since 1975. And yet the university could boast an extraordinary concentration of scholars and critics, archivists and staff, students and faculty, administrators and activists engaged in various forms of reflection on sex, gender, sexuality, identity, subjectivity, history, and politics. The University of Michigan has long been a lively site of lesbian-gay-queer intellectual and political life. That much is attested by the thirty-five-year history of the current Office of Lesbian Gay Bisexual and Transgender Affairs (now called the Spectrum Center), by the long-standing activity of faculty pressure groups, and by the expanding Labadie Collection of social protest documents at the university library, as well as by the creation in 2000 of an LGBT studies minor in the Women's Studies Department, the establishment in 2001 of the Lesbian-Gay-Queer Research Initiative at the Institute for Research on Women and Gender, and the launch in 2006 of a graduate certificate in LGBTQ studies through the Women's Studies Department.

The Midwest can certainly be inhospitable to queers. Robert McRuer's reflections, in this volume, on his experience of returning home to southeastern Michigan convey that all too vividly. But it is also true that the University of Michigan has proven to be remarkably hospitable, especially lately, to queer community organizing and queer scholarship. We wanted to make productive use of its resources and to celebrate the unique opportunities for queer research and interdisciplinary collaboration that the university encourages, supports, and rewards. We also wanted to promote a wider dialogue about the current state of queer politics and queer theory, both among members of the local community in and around Ann Arbor and among different generations of scholars in the fields of lesbian, gay, bisexual, and transgender studies.

In particular, we wanted to examine the notion of shame, which had been a leitmotif in critical writing within those overlapping fields for more than a decade at the time we began our work on the conference but had never received sustained analytic attention from a large group of researchers gathered together in one place. In 1993, in the first article in the first issue of the first volume of *GLQ: A Journal of Lesbian and Gay Studies*, Eve Kosofsky Sedgwick argued that queer identity and queer resistance are both rooted in originary experiences of shame. For Sedgwick, therefore, shame provided the conceptual link necessary to understanding the relation between queer identity and queer performativity: "asking good questions about shame and shame/performativity," she concluded, "could get us somewhere with a lot of the recalcitrant knots that tie themselves into the guts of identity politics—yet *without* delegitimating the felt urgency and power of the notion of 'identity' itself."[2] That was a startling, upsetting, and courageous challenge, especially at a time when more than two decades of gay pride had culminated in the militant, in-your-face defiance of Queer Nation; when the queer movement seemed to be farthest removed from the long, sad, odious, and embarrassing history of gay shame as well as from the snares of identity politics; and when queer theorists and queer activists alike were mounting an assault on gay and lesbian identity as old-fashioned, assimilationist, reactionary, delusional, and phantasmatic, as if the habit of making an identity out of queer sexuality was what lesbians and gay men ought to feel most ashamed of themselves for doing. In that context, Sedgwick asked us to rethink pride, identity, performativity, and queerness in relation to the volatile dynamics, both individual and collective, of shame.

Over the next ten years Sedgwick went on to elaborate her thinking in a series of essays, and her formulations proved to be widely influential as well as highly controversial. She succeeded in putting shame on the agenda of queer studies throughout the latter half of the 1990s without, however, securing for that notion any generally acknowledged solidity, clarity, or coherence. We reprint in this volume, with her kind permission, Sedgwick's latest reformulation of her groundbreaking 1993 *GLQ* article as she provided it in her 2003 book, *Touching Feeling*.

One of the most potent effects of Sedgwick's inquiries into shame was to permit and legitimate the rediscovery and exploration of earlier monuments of lesbian and gay culture irretrievably compromised, according to the criteria of post-Stonewall gay pride, by their queasy-making saturation in experiences of shame—such as Radclyffe Hall's novel *The Well of Loneliness* or the writings of Jean Genet. To be sure, the credit for this queer revisionism does not belong to Sedgwick alone. One of the achievements of the antiassimilationist queer culture of the early 1990s was to bring about the rehabilitation of pre-Stonewall queer outlaws—from Leopold and Loeb to Gertrude Stein to Liberace—whose criminality, pathology, sinfulness, flamboyance, brutality, homophobia, or sexual and gender deviance had made them inimical to the ethos of gay pride, repulsive to liberated, self-respecting lesbians and gay men of the post-Stonewall era, and resistant to inclusion within affirmative histories of homosexuality.

What made such figures newly attractive to the queer movement was the scandal they continued to represent to conventional social values, their unfitness for sociality (gay or straight), their inaptitude for "serving the state" (the test André Gide applied to the antihero of his 1902 novella, *The Immoralist*). They had not been bought off by gay pride; they had lived too early to have been tempted to purchase social respectability at the price of conformity and assimilation. Queer culture of the early 1990s was all about the rejection of heteronormativity, the refusal to conform to social norms deemed irreparably heterosexual and heterosexist; it gravitated toward those figures whose mode of homosexual existence was premised on the impossibility of social acceptance and integration, and therefore on the impossibility of gay pride. As Dennis Allen, Jaime Hovey, and Judith Roof note in their commentary on queer activism in this volume, the approach developed in the early 1990s was to insist that queer difference "is irreducible" and therefore that the social and political claims queers make on the rest of the world are not "merely a recognition of gay difference or of the political and personal validity of this difference but, finally, a recognition of the impossibility of sameness itself." By reclaiming these pre-Stonewall queer pariahs, the queer movement marked its rejection of assimilation, along with what it had perceived as the increasingly sanitized, staid, politically vacuous, and generally boring official gay culture of self-affirmation.[3]

As David Caron points out in his own contribution to this volume, "The recent development of scholarly interest in the pre-Stonewall era . . . is less a matter of archaeology than a search for viable forms of queerness as alternatives to standardized, and standard-enforcing, gayness." This programmatic reclamation of pre-Stonewall styles of queer cultural resistance is neatly captured by the title Douglas Crimp gives his study of Andy Warhol and early queer underground culture: "Queer before Gay." Crimp forges a direct link between Sedgwick's inquiry into shame and his own attempt to recover queer cultural values from an era before the ascendance of gay pride. He makes the connection clear in an essay called "Mario Montez, For Shame," a reading of Andy Warhol's film *Screen Test #2*. Because of the way it connects Sedgwick's theoretical discussion of shame with the queer turn against pride, and because of the questions it raises about the utility of a return to notions of shame, Crimp's essay could easily have served as the keynote address for the Gay Shame conference at Michigan—if, that is, he hadn't already just published it in a 2002 festschrift for Sedgwick. We were grateful to Douglas Crimp for allowing us to use his essay instead as a focal point for one of the opening sessions of the conference, and we are grateful to him for permitting us to reprint the essay here.

A third purpose of the Gay Shame conference was to bring the intellectual current in queer studies that had given new prominence to the category of gay shame into direct dialogue with a newer impulse in queer activism that went by that very name: Gay Shame. Crimp himself makes the connection explicit in his essay on Warhol. The impulse to counter gay pride has not been limited to the academy. Celebrations of Gay Shame took place before and after the turn of the third millennium in a number of cities in North

America and Europe. Typically, as in Brooklyn, where they are claimed to have originated in 1998, these celebrations were scheduled on the same weekend as Gay Pride, on the days before and after the official parade, and were designed to provide an alternative to it.[4] The point of such celebrations has varied. In San Francisco, Gay Shame Awards ceremonies were held in May 2002 and June 2003: their aim was to call attention to, and to shame, members of the local gay and lesbian communities who had sold out their queer comrades to profit, property values, or electoral popularity. Elsewhere, the point has been not to promote a sense of shame at gay misdeeds, but rather to affirm aspects or practices of homosexuality that seem increasingly marginal to the official celebrations of lesbian and gay identity tailored to the civic and political requirements of gay pride.

For the growing numbers of people who have come to feel alienated from gay pride and who have had increasing difficulty finding a place for themselves in its civic pageants, with their contingents of gay policemen, lesbian mothers, business leaders, corporate employees, religious devotees, athletes, and politicians, Gay Shame offers a refuge, a site of solidarity and belonging. It willingly embraces those queers whose identities or social markings make them feel out of place in gay pride's official ceremonies: people with the "wrong" bodies, sadomasochists, sex workers, drag queens, butch dykes, people of color, boy-lovers, bisexuals, immigrants, the poor, the disabled. These are the queers that mainstream gay pride is not always proud of, who don't lend themselves easily to the propagandistic publicity of gay pride or to its identity-affirming functions. In the context of gay pride celebrations, the presence of such marginal, or overtly sexual, populations can be a cause of shame. Gay Shame festivals strive to capitalize on that dynamic—and to reverse it. As with much gay-lesbian-queer activism, erotic self-assertiveness finds expression in the generalized performativity of the participants in Gay Shame celebrations as well as in specific performances by artists. Finally, and most important, what many of the celebrations of Gay Shame have in common is their explicit opposition to the takeover of gay pride marches and festivals by large gay organizations, corporate sponsors, city hall, and the gay bourgeoisie. In this sense, Gay Shame represents an effort to construct a new grassroots queer collectivity founded on principles of resistance to normalization.

In staging a conference on gay shame, we wanted to bring together these currents in politics, performance, activism, and theory. We wanted to unite those engaged in both the academic and the activist reclamation of gay shame (sometimes they are the same people), as well as others working in a variety of critical, cultural, and artistic contexts. We wanted to get them to discuss how they understood shame, what the category of shame meant to them, what the significance of shame was in their own work, and how they understood the relation of shame to the contemporary situation of queer militancy. What were the differences and correspondences among the various usages of "gay shame" in these diverse locations? How did the theme of gay shame play among different populations? We didn't know whether anything useful would come of this. But we wanted to find out, and we thought it was worth a try.

The reaction against the lesbian and gay establishment is nothing new, after all. Not only had it been a theme in queer culture for some time—the slogan "It's a movement, not a market" has been in circulation since the early 1990s—but it also inspired the work of the various writers and critics anthologized by Mark Simpson in his 1996 collection *Anti-Gay* (which in turn led directly to the "post-gay" phenomenon). We were pleased that Mark Simpson himself was willing and able to participate in the Gay Shame conference. We wanted particularly to uncover the connections, if there were any, between the Gay Shame activist movement and those earlier repudiations of gay respectability, to learn whether gay shame meant the same thing in critical writing since Sedgwick as it did in this new social movement, and, if not, how its meanings varied and what the consequences were of those slippages among the different significations of gay shame. We didn't have a particular vision in mind that we hoped would emerge from these encounters and discussions. We simply wanted them to happen, so that we could discover what shame has meant and what it continues to mean across a range of intellectual, artistic, and political positions. Our aim was to set in motion a conversation about their synchronicity and convergence.

One thing the cultural currents we have just reviewed have in common is the permission they give us to explore experiences of shame that have not totally disappeared from the lives of queer people with the allegedly newfound possibility of gay pride. Gay shame confers potential legitimacy and acceptability on the discussion of issues that don't make gay people feel proud, that even proud gay people aren't always proud of. In this sense, gay shame is continuous with gay pride, insofar as the success of gay pride now makes it possible to address realities that may not present a "positive image" of gay people. Because of gay pride, we have become proud enough that we don't need to stand on our pride.

We no longer have to be defensive about aspects of gayness or of the social experience of gayness that don't easily conduce to the production of propaganda on behalf of gay people, that don't argue unambiguously that gay is good. We have become proud enough that we are now unashamed of our shame, proud enough to confront the things about homosexuality that still have the power to make us feel embarrassed or abject. Just as Gay Shame activists in Brooklyn sought to create a new community on the grounds of shame, a new community of the shamed, drawn from those whom official Gay Pride would prefer to ignore—whether because of their income level, gender identification, body type, race, nationality, or sexual practices—so queer studies is taking up topics that aren't necessarily calculated to make gay people feel affirmed.

The relatively recent transformation of homosexuality from a sexual perversion into a social identity and the post-1969 political requirements of gay pride have tended to militate against public discussion of a number of uncomfortable topics pertaining to the intersection of sexuality, gender, identity, and subjectivity. Just as leading lesbian and gay political organizations continually struggle to present to the world a dignified and respectable image of homosexuality, so lesbian and gay researchers have often been reluctant to delve into topics that risk offering new opportunities for the denigration and demonization of homosexuality. Without consciously engaging in a publicity campaign on behalf of lesbians and gay men, practitioners of queer studies, alert to the themes and the discursive operations of homophobia, tend to avoid subjects that seem to vindicate antigay prejudice or that simply do not lend themselves to the requirements of gay self-affirmation.

Some fear that unencumbered inquiry into the inner life of homosexuality will disclose elements they don't like. Others worry, with good reason, that the results of free and uncensored analysis will be used against lesbians and gay men. This has led to an unofficial and informal ban on the investigation of certain unsettling or undignified aspects of homosexuality, specifically questions of emotion or affect, disreputable sexual histories or practices, dissident gender identities, outdated or embarrassing figures and moments from the lesbian-gay-queer past. That ban has never been complete or total, but it has been palpable, and the Michigan conference on gay shame was intended to lift it.

No one involved in the conference wished to return gay people to a state of shame about their sexuality or its emergence onto the scene of public visibility. But it was the premise of the conference that the risk of shame should not prevent us from exploring any aspect of queer life, no matter how embarrassing or discreditable. Indeed, the very exemption from the imperative to affirmation might itself turn out, we thought, to be bracingly affirmative. And so we took advantage of the rubric of gay shame to explore a number of taboo topics.

Gay male gym culture, as well as the concerted production and display of beautiful bodies, has contributed significantly to public demonstrations of gay pride. After more than a century of scientific efforts to correlate deviant sexual desire with abnormal or deficient body types, not to mention the age-old association of same-sex desire with masculine lack and female monstrosity, it is eminently understandable that the culture of gay pride should have generated an attachment to able-bodiedness and morphological normativity. It is similarly unsurprising that gay pride should have entailed the performance, indeed the hyperperformance, of masculinity by gay men. In this context, nothing is more shameful than having the wrong kind of body. Lesbian culture may have developed a more generous appreciation of a range of body types, but embarrassment and abjection at inhabiting the wrong kind of body continues defensively to shape lesbian representation in at least some instances, as any viewer of the television series *The L-Word* can testify. In order to resist such impulses, to explore the persistence of shame in the era of gay pride, and to examine the particular sorts of shame that cluster around body morphology, we decided to make the category of disability a major focus of the conference.

Accordingly, we arranged with Abby Wilkerson and Robert McRuer, the editors of an award-winning issue of *GLQ* on the intersection of queer studies and disability studies, to organize and present a panel on queer/disabled shame. All the presenters on that panel—Wilkerson, McRuer, Terry Galloway, Dylan Scholinski, and Tobin Siebers—have allowed us to publish their work. We are happy to present the panel here (with individual contributions somewhat altered) in its entirety. Some of those contributions—paintings by Scholinski, a transgender activist artist, and a performance by Galloway produced by her Micky Faust collective—appear on the DVD that accompanies this volume.

Other taboo issues that the rubric of gay shame allowed us to explore also figure in this collection. Deborah Gould, writing about the earliest responses to HIV/AIDS by gay and lesbian communities, captures the multiple relations to shame that her subject reveals. (Leo Bersani's recent claim that "AIDS was not mentioned in any of the talks . . . at a 2003 conference called Gay Shame at the University of Michigan" is therefore false.[5]) Although from the very start of the epidemic some gay community members reacted courageously and heroically to the terrifying, isolating, and stigmatizing threat of HIV/AIDS, not all gay social actors, especially in the early days, covered themselves with glory. Given the long association in Western culture between homosexuality and disease, and the relatively recent and still incomplete efforts to depathologize same-sex desire, the advent of HIV/AIDS was deeply shaming, especially to the gay men who bore the initial brunt of its depredations in the industrialized world. Just when gay pride seemed finally to have triumphed, a new and fatal disease threatened to demolish it. Gould examines the role that shame played in early political responses to HIV/AIDS. But her engagement with shame is not limited to its role as a historical actor. She also has to confront her own shame, as a queer historian, in writing an inglorious chapter in the history of gay AIDS response.

Through its specific focus on the recent past, Gould's essay dramatizes some larger questions about the intimate and uneasy relationship between queer histories of shame and the potential shame of queer history. How should a queer historian write about nonheroic, or downright shameful, parts of the queer past? Is it permissible to write a community history that is not one of triumph or glory but of shame? Can such a history continue the work of community building? How does a queer historian handle the parts of queer history that queers nowadays would prefer to forget? How does the historian's own shame affect the kind of history she writes? Is it possible to write about the historical force of shame without being flooded by shame oneself? And is it possible to build an acceptable queer history on people and events from which lesbian and gay readers nowadays might prefer to dissociate themselves?

In her contribution to this volume, Heather Love approaches these issues by reversing the historical dynamic. She wonders about how to deal with those historical figures who would prefer to dissociate themselves from us. She questions the queer historian's appropriation of personalities from the past who, whatever their sexual or erotic lives, would have wanted nothing to do with the lesbians and gay men today who claim them as their ancestors. According to Love, when contemporary queer writers undertake to resituate those remote figures in a redemptive history (which would accord them the political, moral, and sexual validation they supposedly wanted but could not achieve in their own lifetimes), they may actually be trying to escape, or to deny, the loneliness and loss that make them need to recuperate the queer past in the first place. In the historian's dream of effecting what Love calls an "emotional rescue" of pre-Stonewall queers, it is not clear who is rescuing whom, or from what: despite, or because of, their gay pride—which, by repressing their actual neediness, serves to conceal from them the reality of its scope and intensity—queer historians may be in greater need of rescue than the object of historical recovery. In this way Love explores the play of desire, rejection, and shame in queer historiography. She asks whether it is possible to write a nontriumphalist queer history, a history based on the disidentification of historical subjects from the identity or subject position of the queer historian.

We invited a panel of historians to comment on Deborah Gould's and Heather Love's remarks. We are pleased to include here some observations on the historicity of shame by Helmut Puff. We are also grateful for the rejoinder by George Chauncey, who interrogates the usefulness of shame as a category of historical inquiry.

Perhaps the last sacred cow of queer theory is the category of "activism." We invited a number of those responsible for putting on the Gay Shame festivities in Brooklyn and San Francisco to take part in the conference, and we gave them an hour-long panel with which to do whatever they liked. But we also wanted to address the issues of activist burnout, alternatives to activism, and generational tensions around the very category of activism, which is increasingly viewed by many young queers as the source of a kind of moral priggishness and condescension toward them on the part of the ACT UP generation. So we included a panel called "Fuck Activism?" at which Emma Crandall spoke about her uneasy relationship to the notion of activism and to the identity of activist. Her eloquent remarks about the forms of everyday underground activism pursued by those who take part in the queer punk culture of Ann Arbor were accompanied by a video that she had made for the occasion; we are delighted to include the revised version, "Totally Kickball or the Philosophy of Activity-ism" (a Flush Forward Production) on the DVD that accompanies this volume.

Crandall was followed by Judith Roof and Jaime Hovey, whose reflections on the viability of queer activism in the current era also took the form of a video work, "Enactivism: The Movie," produced with Dennis Allen. We gratefully include it on the DVD as well, along with a subsequently elaborated commentary by the three filmmakers, this time in textual form, in the printed volume. As enactments of enactivism, both contributions convey the sense that new modes of queer activism "will involve pixels more often than picket signs."

What would gay shame be without sex? Although questions of sexuality were never far from the forefront of the topics discussed at the conference, two presentations dealt specifically with shameful or potentially shaming dimensions of queer eroticism. Amalia Ziv reviewed recent works of lesbian erotica that feature imaginary scenarios of sex between lesbians and gay men and that create through such scenarios a powerful vehicle of sexual excitement for some queer women. Suggesting that shame is an affect that "blights all erotic potential," whereas humiliation is "one of the mainstays of S/M eroticism," Ziv traced the sources of the sexual excitement produced by these texts to the psychic processes of lesbian subject formation, and she did not hesitate to grapple with the sticky problem of "traditional female masochism."

Ellis Hanson gave new life to the ancient association between pedagogy and pederasty by inquiring into the queer connections between shame and teaching, especially as they are relayed through the sublime and repulsive body of the professor in the lesbian/gay studies classroom. He found in Plato's *Symposium* as well as in the writings of the feminist critic Jane Gallop what queer theory had, in his view, hitherto lacked: namely, an adequate, which is to say unashamed, analysis of pedagogy as "erotic dominance and submission at its most refined, and vice versa."

Leo Bersani offered a brief and polemical appreciation of both of these adventurous, speculative forays and the audience's reaction to them. We are pleased to be able to include his remarks in this volume.

The presentations by Ziv and Hanson, as well as several others, produced their own shame responses. Indeed, they were designed specifically to do so. And exchanges among participants during the discussion periods at the conference often dramatized the continuing operations of shame and shaming. A number of contributions to this volume return to the scene of those exchanges and offer varying descriptions of them (we will have more to say about this in a moment). Interactions at the conference thereby illustrated, dramatically if not always intentionally, some of the most pressing issues raised by the topic of gay shame itself. As Heather Love put it, "While the capacity of shame to isolate is well documented, its ability to bring together shamed individuals into meaningful community is more tenuous." Or, in the formulation of David Caron, "An identity thus defined by its own negation through an identification mediated by disconnectedness and difference cannot produce communities simply on the basis of a shared positive trait."

Disagreement and conflict among the participants at the conference enacted the contagious communicability of shame and tested the ability of shame to generate, in actual practice, a workable redefinition of queer sociality. Each reader of this volume will draw independent, and probably different, conclusions about the extent to which shame can function productively as a solvent of identities, as a source of resistance to normalization, or as a means of stabilizing subject positions and consolidating discursive privileges.

The final purpose of the conference was to de-discipline queer studies, to resist its increasing professionalization and routinization, and to return

queer studies to a community practice, one that benefits from the most po-
rous of boundaries between universities and artists, journalists, cultural
workers, street activists, local cultures, and broader social movements. It is
this last goal that explains the form of the conference and the peculiar features of the present volume.

Once upon a time, namely in the 1980s, when the first European and
North American conferences in lesbian and gay studies took place, that
emergent field was electrified by a rare and intense intellectual and political
excitement. One had the sense that things long thought or experienced
but never before named were being identified, defined, described, analyzed, talked about in public, made sense of, and shared. The differences
between sex and gender as well as their inextricability; the uncertain fron-
tier between homosexuality and homosociality; the epistemology of the
closet; the discursive and social operations of homophobia; the (il)logic of
lesbian and gay inscription; the performativity of sex and gender norms;
the functioning of heteronormativity; the constructedness of sexuality; the
intersection of race, gender, and sexuality; the strategies of lesbian and gay
male representation: between 1983 and 1995, all these notions were given
rich and vivid meaning.

In the same period, six enormous interdisciplinary conferences were
held in the United States, as well as three in Amsterdam. A transformation
took place in the world of knowledge. The teaching of lesbian-gay-queer
studies secured a foothold in the academy in North America, the United
Kingdom, and the Netherlands.

The tenor of those early conferences was noticeably different from that
of standard academic conferences, where participants are routinely heard
to complain in the corridors, in the intervals between panels, "I don't know
how I managed to survive that last session" or "I'm dreading having to go
back into the room." There was no problem motivating interested parties,
inside or outside the academy, to listen to what was being said at the pioneering conferences in lesbian and gay studies, even if there was often conflict or disagreement among members of the audience. It seemed as if the
world was being newly discovered, or rediscovered, and nobody was exactly
desperate to locate the exit.

In recent years, by contrast, conferences in lesbian-gay-queer studies,
with some exceptions, have become as routine and predictable as any other
academic conferences. The speakers featured are mostly the same. The academic star system operates smoothly and produces the usual combination
of adulation and resentment. The same theoretical gestures are repeated;
the same authorities are cited; the same conceptual and political moves are

made; the topics and the language in which they are treated lose individual distinction. As the field becomes more integrated into the institutions of higher learning, the element of political insurgency fades. Instead of transforming what counts as knowledge and revolutionizing academic practice so as to accommodate a different set of relationships among truth, power, authority, desire, and identity, those who enter the field today often seem less interested in changing the university than in benefiting from what the university has to offer. One effect of the very success of this once-insurgent movement has been to give the field a new disciplinarity. Instead of working with students to create possibilities for critical reflection that have never previously existed, professors are now obliged to *train* students in queer theory as if it were any other established field.

The assimilation of lesbian/gay studies to "queer theory" has a lot to answer for in this respect. Despite its virtue of attending to the complexities of identity and identification and its provision of inroads into disciplines and fields of study previously impervious to lesbian/gay studies, queer theory in its ascendancy has also radically narrowed the scope and transformative power of queer critique. By privileging the theoretical register of queer studies, queer theory has restricted its range of applicability and scaled down its interdisciplinary ambitions. The first step in this process was for the "theory" in queer theory to prevail over the "queer," for "queer" to become a harmless qualifier of "theory," which enabled queer theory to be folded back into the standard practice of literary and cultural studies, without impeding academic business-as-usual. The next, and crucial, step was to despecify the lesbian, gay, bisexual, transgender, or transgressive content of queerness, thereby abstracting "queer" and turning it into a generic badge of subversiveness, a more trendy, nonnormative version of "liberal" or "oppositional." Finally, queer theory, being (supposedly) a theory instead of a discipline, and therefore posing no threat to the monopoly of the established disciplines, could be incorporated into each of them and then "applied" to topics in already established fields. Queer theory did not require the creation of independent, and expensive, academic departments or programs. The practice of queer studies was thereby recuperated by the academic establishment, adapted to its formal division into traditional departments and fields, and incorporated into its disciplinary routine, producing many of the discontents we have described.

It is of course impossible to turn the clock back to 1983, nor would we want to do so. It is similarly impossible to undo or to ignore the disciplinary shape that queer studies has taken during the interval. Although we regret the increasing distance between the academic practice of queer studies and the lesbian-gay-queer movement, because we believe that both are significantly impoverished by the loss of mutual contact and exchange, we also cannot deny it, nor can we undo it—not by ourselves, at least. Nonetheless, in organizing the Gay Shame conference, we tried in various ways to work against the current disciplinarity of queer studies and to overcome its isolation from broader social movements. That required a number of concrete innovations and alterations in the standard form and practice of the lesbian-gay-queer studies conference.

First of all, we raised sufficient funds to ensure that all conference events (including the final dance party) would be free and open to the public, and we publicized the conference widely outside the academic community. We could not afford to fund transportation to the conference for all those interested in attending, but when several interested persons indicated to us that their ability to secure the funding necessary to attend was conditional on a space on the conference program, we opened up the program to them without asking them to tell us what they intended to say. Participants in the conference came, accordingly, from the Ann Arbor and Detroit areas, from around the United States, as well as from Canada, Europe, and the Middle East.

Next, because Douglas Crimp had already published a short paper that was well suited to our conference, and because for the reasons just mentioned we had no intention of including in the proceedings anything resembling a keynote address, we decided to begin the first full day of the conference with a communal discussion of his paper. In order to enable everyone to take part in the discussion on an equal basis, on the previous evening (the opening night of the conference) we showed *Screen Test #2*, the Andy Warhol film analyzed in Crimp's essay. We also distributed copies of Crimp's ten-page essay to all conference participants in advance and to all members of the audience during the showing of the film. By those means, everyone at the conference was given access to all the materials necessary to assess Crimp's interpretation of the Warhol movie and its relationship to shame, when the topic became the focus of our collective discussion at the start of the following day—a discussion that took the place of the keynote address we wished to avoid. The screening of *Screen Test #2* was followed by a performance by Vaginal Davis, whose own experimental filmmaking continues and in interesting ways revises Warhol's film-production practices.

The next morning, we did not invite Crimp to speak. Rather, we asked Elisabeth Ladenson, who is not a specialist on Warhol but who, we believe, brings the right combination of intelligence, daring, ingenuity, lucidity, and disengagement to the topic, to lead a discussion of Crimp's essay, with Crimp on hand to answer any questions the participants cared to put to him. The ensuing dialogue between Crimp and the audience proved to be a defining moment for the conference as a whole, as several of the essays in this volume testify.

Although we brought to Ann Arbor a number of distinguished scholars from a variety of disciplines (African American studies, American studies, anthropology, history, literature, musicology, sociology, theater, women's studies), we did not invite them to give papers. We wanted them to participate in freewheeling discussions, for which we reserved substantial amounts of time, and, as a spur to those discussions, we arranged for panels of well-known and not-so-well-known personalities to give brief comments on what they had heard. In fact, we invited almost no one to give papers, we scheduled no concurrent sessions, and with occasional exceptions we asked only nonacademics, graduate students, or those who had just completed their dissertations to make formal presentations (and we let no speaker go on for longer than thirty minutes). We also encouraged presentations other than verbal ones.

Accordingly, the conference featured the visual art of Dylan Scholinski, performance art, and video productions, as well as reflections on performance by Holly Hughes and Joan Lipkin. Two movies were made expressly for presentation at the conference. Emma Crandall's "Totally Kickball" was part of a multimedia presentation that included her reading of her own text. "Enactivism: The Movie," created by Dennis Allen, Jaime Hovey, and Judith Roof, was presented by Hovey and Roof in Allen's absence (he was unable at the last moment to attend). Video documentation of some of the Gay Shame activist events was also shown, as were two brief (and hilarious) video works by Terry Galloway, who also performed an excerpt from her new performance piece "Tough." This last piece, subsequently filmed, is, along with "Totally Kickball" and "Enactivism," included on the DVD that accompanies this volume.

University of Michigan librarian Julie Herrada and library supervisor Tim Retzloff (now a doctoral student in American history at Yale) curated an exhibit, "Shamefully Gay," made up of archival materials, largely print media, drawn from the university library's Labadie Collection. The exhibit remained on display for a couple of months in the lobby of the Harlan Hatcher Graduate Library; it is also included in this collection, some of it in the printed volume and the rest on the DVD. And a block of seats was set aside for conference participants at a performance of a new theatrical work created and directed by Holly Hughes, "After a Fashion," which put center stage the queer insights and impressive talents of Hughes's students in the University of Michigan's Department of Theater and School of Art and Design.

Having arranged for the first evening of the conference to conclude with a spectacular drag performance and film showing by Vaginal Davis, we were delighted that the conference culminated in Hughes's theater piece and in a "Shamelessly Retro" queer dance party devised and DJed by Gayle Rubin. In this way, embodied performance framed and set the terms for our collective engagements with shame and deliberately raised the stakes for all artistic and critical interventions at the conference. Far from structuring the conference around a distinction between (academic) scholarship and (nonacademic) performance, we attempted to promote a fusion between the two.

Without asking academics to work outside their areas of competence or out of their depth, we pressed for a critical/artistic practice on the part of all participants that could combine reflection and performance. Even standard academic conferences have a performative dimension, after all: most academic papers simply come off as failed performances. By restricting our participants' allotted time for speaking, by promoting general discussion, and by instituting a forum on a paper led by someone other than its author, we did our best to elicit from all the contributors and the audience original, ephemeral, improvisational performances.

And because, as a result, visual, video, archival, and dramatic material played such an important role at the conference, we have taken the unprecedented step of publishing the conference proceedings in a mixed-media format so as to make as much of this material as possible available for publication and distribution. Some of the most provocative and suggestive explorations of gay shame that this collection has to offer will be found on the DVD.

Part of what motivated our emphasis on performance was the recognition that performance and performativity have played a constitutive role in both collective and individual experiences of gay shame. From Eve Sedgwick's theorizing of queer performativity as an effect of shame to Douglas Crimp's use of Sedgwick to describe the affective dynamics of Mario Montez's film performances, from David Caron's description of his shameful identification with Marlene Dietrich to Ellis Hanson's enactment of pedagogical embarrassment, shame has often been defined in relation to public spectacle and theatrical performance. In order to draw out the specifically theatrical dimensions of shame, we have included an interview with the British writer, historian, director, and actor Neil Bartlett, whose repertoire as a gay performance artist and producer has exploited the rich vein of shame and embarrassment in theatricality itself. Drawn particularly to forms of theater in which characters do bad things and suffer for them, Bartlett traces the genesis of his gay aesthetic to his own identification as a fairy and drag queen, while arguing that all theater is—from its personnel to its plots to its effects on the audience—intrinsically queer.

Given all this emphasis on performance, we did not initially imagine that it would be possible to publish the proceedings of the conference. How do you represent an experiment in critical thought organized around off-the-cuff commentary, discussion, and performance? And so it did not occur to us that "Gay Shame" would ever take the form of a published collection, even a mixed-media one. But, as we quickly discovered at the start of the first full day of the conference, it turns out to be a lot harder to de-discipline queer studies than we had imagined. Discussion was sometimes slow in getting started, especially in the presence of an audience numbering two hundred people. But, more important, academics are reluctant, even in a community event, to let go of their texts. As Elisabeth Ladenson unashamedly puts it, in her own contribution to this volume, "I was . . . skeptical in general at the idea that academics could be induced not to give formal papers, as well as apprehensive in particular, because delivering formal conference papers is the one skill I have managed over the course of my career so far to master to some degree." A number of participants, even those who were invited to speak very briefly at roundtables and panels, produced extended and carefully formulated statements.

That may have been frustrating for us, but it is lucky for those who did not attend the conference: it will give them something to read. It was only when we noticed how many texts the conference had in fact generated, despite our best efforts, that we realized a conference publication might be possible. And so we set out to assemble those texts. We also succeeded in encouraging a number of conference participants who had faithfully executed our instructions, and not written down anything at all, to transcribe what they had said or wanted to say, or to assemble some of the thoughts the conference had provoked, or to comment on the proceedings. We also collected additional material as we learned more about the work that others have been doing on shame.

What we've published, then, ranges from short and very informal thought pieces to in-depth analyses of problems posed by texts, histories, theories, practices, and particular sexual identities and communities. Because we continue to resist the disciplinary imperative to produce a compilation of formal papers, some of the texts are fragmentary or brief, lack footnotes, and bear the traces of oral presentation. Some contributions are transcripts of statements that were actually delivered at the conference or refer directly to what happened there, because the points made in them would be lost if those interventions were to be entirely cut off from the performative contexts for which they were created. But we have also encouraged contributors to stand back from the actual events of the conference and give their remarks the most general possible expression.

Although this volume is not intended to represent formal conference proceedings, neither is it designed as a memento or souvenir or documentary record of the actual conference as it took place, either for those who missed it or for those who were there. The conference itself happened once; it is over. We have reconstituted here some of its themes and have tried to elaborate on them, both in this introductory essay and in the selection and organization of the contributions. We have tried to collect work that documents the intellectual ferment produced by our collective reflections on the topic of gay shame—without, however, aiming to achieve any sort of closure on the issue—and we have made an effort to keep the contents of the book lively and informal. We've placed a premium on analytic originality rather than academic decorum, and we hope the result will be a collection that will have an impact on queer cultures as well as on academic and critical discourse. While submitting to the minimal requirements of the academic publishing industry, we have tried to preserve some of the improvisational experimentation of the conference, to convey a sense of thought in process, to emphasize the innovative gesture rather than the completed argument.

II

What is the political efficacy of shame for gay-lesbian-queer people? Is gay shame, as George Chauncey tentatively concedes in this volume, "a problem that is good to think with?" Is it, as Judith Halberstam has argued elsewhere, merely "A White Gay Male Thing"?[6] Or are the "bottom values" of shame and debasement, as Kathryn Bond Stockton has now insisted, privileged sites of communion—or "switchpoints"—between black and queer identities?[7] Could shame be an organizing principle of queer politics, or is it mainly a vehicle for the articulation of personal issues by stigmatized individuals?

Some of the themes and questions that arose at the conference follow the contours of dialogues and debates that have preoccupied the lesbian-gay-queer movement for years. Other issues surfaced directly out of what happens when we begin to talk about shame. Several participants struck a cautionary note about the usefulness of shame as an analytical rubric—and the events that transpired during the conference may have reinforced their suspicions. After all, the discussions at the conference sometimes seemed to oscillate between efforts to claim shame for oneself, to possess it as a personal property, and the determination to wield it against others. In his contribution to this volume, Michael Warner warns us, accordingly, to differentiate among the various meanings of shame and to attend to its changing implications in different social and historical settings. If they demonstrate nothing else, both the conference and this volume testify eloquently, for better or for worse, to the continuing productivity and unpredictable operations of shame.

Many of our contributors comment on the interiorizing or inwardizing emphasis in current work on shame—what Frances Negrón-Muntaner does not hesitate to call, in the interview by Rita Gonzalez adapted for this collection, its "narcissism." They note the insistent preoccupation of gay shame theorists with the formation of the individual human subject and the way such a preoccupation licenses the production and proliferation of self-authorizing personal narratives. Another effect of this emphasis seems to be a recurrent privileging of infancy and youth as constitutive sites of shame. Yet another is the persistent methodological recourse to psychoanalytic concepts (or, in Sedgwick's case, to psychology and affect theory). Can we, as Sedgwick proposes, detach the therapeutic and individualistic view of shame—in which shame is something to "work through" or "move beyond"—from the project of analyzing it as an affective structure? Can we make transformative use of it? Or should we rather, as Ellis Hanson urges, try to see what happens when we linger in untransformed experiences of it?

If shame, at least in the modern world, is an individualizing affect, it is not only that. As a "structure of feeling," shame also gives rise to what Crimp calls "collectivities of the shamed." Essays by many of our contributors emphasize the social dimensions of shame, not just its isolating or individualizing tendencies. They testify to the various social energies and collective mobilizations of desire, emotion, and identity that infuse shame with its peculiar powers—to motivate or to debilitate, as the case may be. Don Kulick and Charles Klein draw a striking parallel between the techniques used by individual *travesti* (Brazilian transgendered prostitutes) to extort money from their clients through the threat of public humiliation and the communal pressure tactics employed by Brazilian AIDS activists to achieve social recognition and rights for marginalized and underserved populations. Shame in this instance becomes a strategy for achieving sexual citizenship.

Deborah Gould's analysis of how power relationships are "exercised through and reproduced in our feelings" suggests how shame in its psychic functioning impedes, as well as motivates, community formation. This focus on the social formations of shame, however, can also seem to preclude analyzing the psychic structures that, as Sedgwick and Crimp in particular have suggested, generate shame's most potent effects. Leo Bersani's disheartened appraisal, at the conference and in this volume, of what is lost by failing to "consider shame in its psychic dimensions" leads him to ask, "In what sense is shame"—as a psychic phenomenon—"an isolating factor that blocks the thinking and the formation of politically viable communities?"

Amalia Ziv takes up precisely this issue, deftly employing psychoanalytic insights to unpack lesbian cross-sex fantasies (as Bersani himself acknowledges). She argues that "Oedipal desire, transformed into identification, may provide one of the trajectories of lesbian identity formation" and that "residual Oedipal investments are incommensurable with the lesbian identity to which they give rise and disavowed by it." In contrast, Eve Sedgwick treats shame as an affect precisely in order to describe subjectivity and identity formation in terms other than the psychoanalytic.

A different though perhaps compatible approach might be to look at shame as a formal property of discourse. One of the more interesting things to come out of our collective reflections on the shame of performance, spectatorship, and pedagogy is an appreciation of the role of irony in mediating shame's public expression. The confluence of these essays raises the question of how well or how easily tonalities of discourse translate across racial and gendered divides. And if, as some of our contributors maintain, shame is less an object, a thing to be claimed or reclaimed, than a dynamic, then it is not only a matter of psychology or politics but aesthetics. The most elegant articulation of shame's relationship to aesthetics and irony has been D. A. Miller's work on sexuality and form, whether in the case of the Broadway musical or Jane Austen's style. Because this work is difficult to excerpt, being formally complete in its own right, we have not tried to reproduce any of it here, but we refer the reader to Miller's two books, *Place for Us* and *Jane Austen, or The Secret of Style*.[8]

Whatever its psychic or formal determinants, the experience of shame, both individual and collective, has a lot to do with the vicissitudes of particular social groups. For that reason, it is intimately and irremediably tied, at this historical moment, to the politics of identity. The direct relevance of shame to specific groups, the demand for representation by such groups, and the identity policing that often accompanies such demands were all in evidence at the Gay Shame conference. In the final hours of the gathering (during what was billed as an open discussion), the proceedings took on a ritualistic character as several speakers castigated the conference, the conference organizers, and the University of Michigan for its multiple failures of inclusion: of bisexuals, of sex workers, of local activists, of undergraduates, of people of color. Members of each group had, in fact, been involved, some of them centrally, but evidently not enough to satisfy the desire for inclusiveness. Accordingly, audience members stood up to voice complaints about the perceived exclusion of their own identity position. Each of them authorized his or her comments from the standpoint of that position, then confessed, in a personal narrative, his or her own experience of shame, and finally attempted to reattach that shame to others. The techniques of shaming were deployed with considerable rhetorical force, and they did not fail to garner applause. As the discourses of shame took on increasingly didactic and moralizing dimensions, the analytical and critical reflection on shame that the conference intended to enable risked being brought to a halt by the tactical redeployment of shame itself.

This experience would seem, on the one hand, to make all the more imperative our collective exploration of Sedgwick's proposal that we ask "good questions about shame" if we ever hope to get at the "recalcitrant knots that tie themselves into the guts of identity politics." It also suggests, on the other hand, that there is still much analytical and political work to be done in order to think through both the efficacy and the inefficacy of identity *as* politics—and also to determine whether the social operations of shame can take us beyond identity as politics or whether, on the contrary, they will bind us to it by multiplying the risks to our own authority that we incur as soon as we question identity as a mode of political empowerment.

Many of the contributors to this volume honor identity as a crucial ground of experience, a source of social knowledge, and a basis for activism. Many of them, however, do not assume that knowledge can authorize itself primarily or exclusively by making reference to that term—that is, by invoking the speaker's membership in a group. Some kind of balance is being sought in a number of the contributions to this volume between the acknowledgment of identity as one source of embodied knowledge and the search for a model of knowledge in which identity figures as a mediated, contingent, and problematic (rather than self-evident) way of defining both the individual and the group. It would seem that, for at least some of our contributors, identity is not a sufficient ground for the articulation of experience. At the same time, the recognition that shame operates as a solvent and not as the basis of identity may induce a kind of panic about legitimation, representation, power, and politics.

The most contentious dialogue about the relations between shame and identity politics focused on the politics of race, including whiteness. It took place before, during, and after the conference itself. After the announcement of the conference went out, Lawrence La Fountain-Stokes (who has since become our colleague at the University of Michigan) wrote "An Open Letter to Douglas Crimp," which he e-mailed to us and many of the participants. We reprint it here, as it arrived by e-mail in a plain-text version without diacritics or Spanish-language accents, with La Fountain-Stokes's kind permission:

AN OPEN LETTER TO DOUGLAS CRIMP
March 22, 2003
Highland Park, New Jersey

Dear Douglas:
I have just finished reading your essay "Mario Montez, For Shame." On the one hand, I want to thank you for a thought-provoking piece which I believe will be very useful to me in furthering my understanding of shame and the terms "pato" [duck], "loca" [mad woman] and "maricon," used in Puerto Rico and the Hispanic Caribbean as a synonyms for "queer," and in general in my work on queer Puerto Ricans and Latinos in the United States. I am also thankful because you remind me and all of your readers that Mario Montez was Latino, specifically Puerto Rican. I confess that I actually learned this first at a CLAGS conference on autobiography several years ago, from Ondine Chavoya and the Chicana filmmaker Rita Gonzalez, after watching her wonderful "The Assumption of Lupe Velez," an homage to Montez and to "Lupe," the 1966 film by the experimental New York-based queer Puerto Rican filmmaker Jose Rodriguez Soltero. In fact, your essay and Frances Negron Muntaner's recent work on Holly Woodlawn remind all of us of the profoundly Puerto Rican character of some of Warhol's film production and of his Factory world. Over all, I think that your understanding of queer shame is a valuable contribution.

And herein my question for you, perhaps my complaint, my own accusation of "For Shame!" Perhaps I have missed something, but as far as I can tell, race and ethnicity (as well as colonialism, for that matter) are all but invisible in your essay. Invisible, that is, in the sense that I could not perceive your analysis of them; for they are ever-present, an invisible normative whiteness and assertiveness of empire which blanket everything except the shamed (brown? powder-white?) body of Mario Montez. And that is particularly true (again, please correct me if I am mistaken) as we read your theoretical elaboration, your long list of white queer scholars and intellectuals, white artists, whites, for shame: Eve Sedgwick (reading Henry James, of all people), Andy Warhol, Jack Smith, Ronald Tavel (the person I confess I know the least about), George Plimpton, Andrew Sullivan, Michael Warner, Douglas Crimp. So that for me the shame of Mario Montez becomes that of Franz [sic] Fanon, faced by a child who stares at him in horror, the shame of Gloria Anzaldua and Cherrie Moraga and Audre Lorde, of those Puerto Ricans

and other diasporic people of color shamed every day for being a subjugated and racialized people, and particularly, the shame of the Puerto Rican queer. My shame, perhaps.

Nowhere is this more evident than in the passage you quote (speaking about Ronald Tavel): "I enjoyed working with him," Warhol wrote, "because he understood instantly when I'd say things like, 'I want it simple and plastic and white.' Not everyone
can think in an abstract way, but Ronnie could" (67). It is an association of whiteness
and Warhol that makes me think, for example, of Jose Munoz's insightful analysis in
his book "Disidentifications" of the complex relationship between Warhol and Jean-
Michel Basquiat.

I understand there is to be a discussion of your essay at the upcoming conference on
Queer Shame at the University of Michigan, Ann Arbor, to be held March 27–29, 2003.
I will unfortunately not be unable to attend, as it coincides with the Latin American
Studies Association meeting in Dallas. I wish you and all of the participants fruitful sessions. The questions I leave for you are the following: How do you read the intersection
of race and ethnicity in Mario Montez's shame? How does the colonial gaze fit into your
scheme? What is there of Puerto Rican in his shame, other that the passing reference to
a stereotypical Latin machismo and Catholic religiosity?

I hope my comments are of use to you and the conference participants.

Sincerely yours,
Lawrence M La Fountain-Stokes
Assistant Professor,
Department of Puerto Rican and Hispanic Caribbean Studies
Department of Women and Gender Studies
Rutgers University, New Brunswick

Frances Negrón-Muntaner, in a subsequent collective e-mail (also in
plain text), supported La Fountain-Stokes's observation about the inextricability of Puerto Rican identity and shame:

Thank you for forwarding me your "Open Letter to Douglas Crimp."

I would like to take this opportunity to support your central argument concerning
Puerto Ricans and shame.

In my upcoming book, Boricua Pop: Puerto Ricans and the Latinization of
American Culture, I make the argument that Puerto Rican identity is an identity that
remains socially constituted in shame for at least two complex reasons.

One, the fact that Puerto Ricans are colonial subjects of the U.S., and often, seemingly "consensual" colonial subjects, complicates our national identity in ways that are
evident in virtually all public articulations of identity, from the Puerto Rican Pride Parade to the love of boxers and beauty queens, from Dame Edna to anti-colonial politics.

In a sense, Puerto Ricans constitute a "queer" nation, in the sense that it has imagined itself in cultural not in state terms, and has largely rejected dominant (virile) definitions of nationhood as the product of an epic past supported by military might.

Two, the often brutal way that Puerto Ricans were (and still are) racialized and humiliated as colonial migrants in urban centers like New York further constituted Puerto Rican identity in shame. This was no longer the shame of the Puerto Rican (male, white) elites arguing for a dignified political status in Congress, but the shame of the Puerto Rican majority, looking at contempt in the face. Any superficial look at how Puerto Ricans have been historically represented and treated in major U.S. cities points to how shame is the stuff our ethno-national identity continues to be made of.

Given this context, it would be impossible to speak about Mario Montez, a man who lived in New York during a very precarious time for Puerto Ricans, without taking into consideration his Puerto Ricanness. In fact, in my chapter about Holly Woodlawn, I briefly speak about how both Woodlawn's and Montez's performance styles— "warm" and "empathetic"—were indebted to their socially constituted identities as queer Puerto Ricans. In this sense, shame is both a sign for our limited political agency as "national" subjects and the source for much of our cultural richness—a complicated matter indeed.

I think that there is much to be gained from further dialogue between queer and/or Puerto Rican theorizations of shame. I hope that this letter continues a much-needed debate.

Thank you for promoting this discussion,
Frances Negron-Muntaner

Negrón-Muntaner has since elaborated on the relation of shame to ethnonationalism, with specific reference to Crimp's paper and the Gay Shame conference as a whole, in an interview with Rita Gonzalez in an issue of *Signs*; we print here a new version of that interview, revised expressly for this volume, with many thanks to Negrón-Muntaner for her collegiality and collaboration.

We also reprint an essay by Taro Nettleton, "White-on-White: The Overbearing Whiteness of Warhol Being," in which the author argues that despite Warhol's purported intent to project himself and his stars into celebrity through the transcendence of particularity, "access to self-abstraction was unevenly distributed" in the Warhol Factory: "some members of the Factory were not allowed to transcend their embodied particularities." "Once the register is shifted from gender and sexuality to race," Nettleton observes, "the relative malleability of or freedom from embodied particulars comes to a grinding halt."

This work by Negrón-Muntaner and Nettleton helps to round out Crimp's treatment of Warhol, which had been undertaken with a quite particular and limited purpose, one that was often lost from sight when Crimp's essay became the theoretical and critical point of departure for the entire Gay Shame conference. Although as the organizers of the conference we do not regret using Crimp's work and Warhol's film to launch what we intended to be a textually based and theoretically sophisticated discussion of gay shame, we do regret that our choice led others to expect from Crimp's short essay a complete and definitive account of both Warhol and gay shame instead of what it actually offered, namely a daring and inventive expansion of some hints from Sedgwick about the relations among sexuality, shame, and identity. Though some of our contributors still feel the need to critique Crimp's silences, many others find his suggestions powerfully enabling of their own analyses, and all consider his work a significant, indeed authoritative elaboration of a theme originally sounded by Sedgwick.

During the conference itself, tensions arose around the treatment of race in three interrelated ways: the neglect of the concept of race in the analyses of some of the presenters; the theoretical and historical question of the intersection of racial identity, queer identity, gender, and shame; and the inclusion, or rather noninclusion, of people of color among the participants. It is clear that the racialization of shame is an integral aspect of sexual communities, racial and ethnic communities, and current critical discourse. A panel dedicated to exploring how and why this is so would have immeasurably enriched our discussions. Some participants felt that the absence of such a panel severely compromised the proceedings, and we have been taken to task for this, in print, by two of the conference participants, Judith Halberstam and Hiram Perez, as well as by the editors of the special 2005 issue of *Social Text* in which Halberstam's and Perez's essays appear.[9]

All those writers criticize us specifically for our failure to ensure the adequate representation of people of color, and they criticize the conference for the way discourses of race circulated at it. (We must, however, correct their assertion that "it was a conference that included only one queer person of color out of forty invited participants."[10] In fact, we invited five queer people of color to participate.) We do wish the conference had included more people of color, and although we quite deliberately refused to inquire in advance about the topics that any of the presenters would address, we nonetheless regret that we did not create formal opportunities for a focused dialogue on race and shame.

We regret it all the more because of the particular way that issues of racialization played out during the conference itself. In one of the few invited papers, Ellis Hanson accompanied his theorization of queer pedagogy with the projection, onto a screen next to him, of a sequence of images from a pornographic photo spread in the magazine *Latin Inches* featuring a Puerto Rican man named Kiko in various stages of nudity and sexual arousal. Some of these images are reproduced in Hanson's contribution to this volume. Refusing (for reasons that he lays out in the essay published here) to explain the purpose behind the projection of these photographs or their relationship to his analysis of the erotics of pedagogy, Hanson produced a performance that many in the audience found incomprehensible and offensive. During the controversy that ensued, Hanson acknowledged that his intention was in part to cause discomfort and embarrassment and thereby to provide an incitement for the community's simultaneous enactment of and reflection on (his? its? our?) shame.

What followed did not take a very pedagogical form. And it was as predictable as it was unsettling. Unwilling to resist the pull of a role that has all too often been constructed for people of color, Hiram Perez dedicated his time on the final panel to detailing the racist offense of Hanson's presentation. We extended an offer to Perez to contribute to this volume and to include the remarks he said he had prepared for the conference but had set aside in order to register his indignation. Perez indicated, however, that to accept our invitation would be to compromise his intention to respond to what had transpired. He has since published an account of his experience at our conference in a special issue of *Social Text*, as we have noted, where one can also find an analysis by Judith Halberstam of the gendered and racial limitations of gay shame discourses.[11]

A quite different appraisal of Hanson's paper and the outrage it provoked at the conference figures centrally in the essay that Jennifer Moon, who participated in one of the panels at the conference, has contributed to this volume. She agrees on the terms of the offense but differs in the lessons she draws from it, as well as in the strategies and remedies by which she would wish to deal with the connections among gay shame, whiteness, masculinity, and racialization. After anatomizing the racial politics of the conference, Moon argues that gay shame is a subject cultivated by white gay men but displaced and projected onto people of color. She suggests that Perez's "justifiable outrage illustrates some of the potential problems with identity politics, and particularly with its relationship to shame as a vehicle for queer mobilization." For Moon, the beauty of shame as a political tool is that it has the potential to connect queers across differences in race, age, and class, and to redirect attention away from internal antagonisms within

the gay community toward the real enemy: religious and social conservatives. Implicit in her essay is an analysis of the peculiar relevance and usefulness of shame to the political and cultural projects of white gay men,
an explanation of how shame should have come to be, just at this point in
time, the vehicle for the white gay male critique of gay pride and of white
gay male privilege.

Frances Negrón-Muntaner, by contrast, observes that "as contradictory
[and culturally 'productive'] as shame can be, being socially constituted by
shame is not desirable for most people who are so hailed. . . . It seems to me
that only the privileged can advance this proposition." Invoking a distinction between "disgrace-shame" and "discretion-shame," Negrón-Muntaner
goes on to point out that "when shame is constitutive of an ethnic group,
of the group's poetics of identification, we are faced with a different object
than that of queer theory. For instance, it is individual queers, rather than
the gay community, that are most frequently the subject of shame. In the
Puerto Rican case, it is the *boricua* subject as part of a colonized group that
is constituted in shame by symbolic, economic, and racist violence."

The question lingers, then: how can we adequately address and account for a host of specificities—of race, of gender, of class, of ethnicity,
of nationality, of able-bodiedness, of sexual practice—and describe their
different, irreducible, and variable connections with the politics of shame
while preserving the potential of shame to cut across experiences and categories of identity?

That is one of the questions that motivates Barry Adam's comparative analysis of gay male communities in Toronto and Cuba. Adam argues that the
concept of gay shame is useful because it "reminds us that signing on to social relationships infused by the norms of the global marketplace is not the
only possibility." It might therefore be possible to deploy shame in order to
create a queer politics that is less totalizing and tyrannical, a politics that
can allow for the isolating force of shame without capitulating to it. Such a
politics would self-consciously embrace a multiplicity of lesbian-gay-queer
emotions, impulses, and political gestures.

Adam's cautiously optimistic assessment of shame's potential to generate new political collectivities seems all the more urgent after the presentation by Gay Shame activists at the conference. Beginning with the charac-
terization of the Gay Shame conference itself as an academic rip-off of the
innovative energy of activists—or, in the words of Stephen Kent Jusick, as a
"Gay Sham"—the presenters went on to assert a proprietary claim over the
ownership of gay shame, insisting that it was their own invention, and de-

fended their rights to define its purpose and meaning. They have since re-peated these views of the conference in print.[12] We invited Jusick to lay out his thinking more fully in this volume, but after some initial hesitation he declined.

During the conference it became clear that a gulf separates at least some of the aims and strategies of Gay Shame activism from the interrogation of shame in the academy. If Sedgwick's intervention consists in hypothesizing the utility of shame as a source of transformational energy within the self that can be redirected and mobilized on behalf of the queer community, the activists responsible for Gay Shame celebrations do not hesitate to mobi-lize shame as a political tactic to be used against other queers. Distributing copies of the zine *Swallow Your Pride: A Queer Hands-On Tool for Do-It-Yourself Activism* and showing video footage of some Gay Shame activities, Mattilda (aka Matt Bernstein Sycamore), Stephen Kent Jusick, Oakie Treadwell, and other members of the Gay Shame movement surveyed the range of events and issues that the movement had taken up, and they forcefully articulated the principal political values the movement aims to actualize. At the same time, they seemed unaware that discourses of gay shame had pre-dated the beginnings of their own activity in June 1998, and they did not attend the sessions of the conference at which that earlier history was elaborately re-viewed and discussed. For that reason, their assertion of ownership rights over gay shame was not readily accepted by many conference participants.

Some in the audience did experience the activists' denunciations of the academy as a call to arms and as a welcome reminder of how complacent, bourgeois, and accommodationist queer academics have become. Others thought their attempt to privilege activism over the academy was facile and self-serving. Yet others bemoaned the activists' refusal to acknowledge the impact of academic queer theory on the queer and transgender movements, or were insulted by the activists' tendency to treat as apolitical those in the audience who had in fact done much pioneering political work, or objected to the reactionary cultural politics of speakers who styled themselves as radicals. In any case, the outcome was not a happy one. The activists closed off the possibility of dialogue with some of the very academics who would have been most likely to embrace their politics.

So, at least, we believe. For a different portrait of this encounter ("No one at the University of Michigan physically attacked us, yet . . ."), the reader can consult the version that Mattilda has published.[13]

The activist appropriation of a discourse of shame is nothing new. It was, for instance, a common tactic of the antinuclear movement of the

1970s and 1980s. In confrontations with the police, senior women did not hesitate to launch the reprimand "Shame on you!" at the officers who were arresting them for their acts of civil disobedience. Exploiting their moral authority as mothers and grandmothers (even if they were neither), these women harnessed the powerful affects associated with the Imaginary and the pre-Oedipal in a classic maternal gesture of shaming discipline. Are affects such as those the ones we mean to evoke when we deploy shame as a source of political leverage against other queers? What are the psychic structures that invest what Sedgwick calls the "transformational grammar of 'Shame on you!'" with its emotional and moral power? And are those psychic structures ones that can be redeployed successfully, or ethically, or with principled consistency, by a queer or progressive politics?

Even if our answer to those questions is yes, we still need to ask what specific effects those redeployments of shame are likely to produce, or do produce, and whether they bring about their desired ends. In *Blush: Faces of Shame*, Elspeth Probyn, distinguishing "between a politics resulting from feeling shame and a politics that actively seeks to cause shame in those seen as the enemy," noted how tricky such a distinction is, "because often groups spring up around sites of experienced shame, which then coalesce into fields where those assumptions and rules are used to shame others." "After all," she went on to observe, "if historically women and queers have been made to feel ashamed and as a consequence have become more attuned to detecting the shame of others, it makes a certain sense that the subordinated may have more nuanced skills at shaming than the privileged." And so she asked, "How do you voice your own shame *and* a collective one without shaming again the objects of that shame? . . . How can shame be used not as moral reproach but as a goad for action?"[14] The point, then, is not to ban shame as a political weapon. The use of a shaming tactic does not necessarily symptomatize a lack of critical self-awareness. But the question remains: what, specifically, concretely, in a particular context, does the redeployment of shame achieve?

In order to pursue that question, we need to back up and ask—remembering Negrón-Muntaner's cautionary remarks about the relative privilege implicit in any move to aestheticize shame or to luxuriate in the experience of being shamed—for whom exactly shame is an active, productive, or even possible category of identification. Indeed, we might need to back up further and revise the obvious question "Who is shamed?" and ask instead, as Tobin Siebers does, "Who gets to feel shame?" Analyzing the constraints on the sexual existence of people with disabilities, Siebers links the conditions of possibility for feeling shame with access to agency, with the individual's ability to meet the defining criteria of liberal human subjecthood.

In *Queer Attachments: The Cultural Politics of Shame* (Ashgate, 2007), Sally Munt explores the contagious dynamics of gay shame, analyzing not only its power to abject and deform, but to produce unpredicted, self-affirming forms of sociality. Paying particular attention to the way shame informs and links queer, Irish, and working-class identities in cultural phenomena as diverse as eighteenth-century aesthetics and New York City's Saint Patrick's Day parades, Munt lobbies for a more historicized understanding of gay shame.

Some of our other contributors similarly caution against falsely universalizing the subject of shame, calling our attention instead to the specifics of shame as they apply to particular races, classes, genders, or geographic locations. Some of them also problematize the phenomenological focus on childhood as the originary scene of shame in the work of Sedgwick and Crimp. For others, shame adheres to specific geographies (the suburbs of Detroit, small-town Ohio), to specific fantasies (lesbians having sex with gay men), or to cross-sex identifications (the male desire to be Marlene Dietrich or Maria Montez). A number of contributors consider identification and cross-identification, instead, to be the means by which to battle shame.

We need to ask, then, how particular identity formations—such as Nadine Hubbs's identification as a classical musician and a "working-class dyke from the cornfields, dark Catholic in a land of fair Lutherans"—contribute to the potential productivity of shame as well as how they may diminish that productivity, reducing the utility of shame as a means of self-actualization or as a transformational political strategy. If shame has specific, and widely differing, uses for different racialized groups, it may also have widely differing uses for different social classes. Is shame merely anger in middle-class clothing, as Esther Newton suggested at the conference?

And what about gender? Elspeth Probyn has argued that because women have been associated with the realm of feeling, feminists have reason to examine the production of shame—including its deployment within the feminist movement.[15] She has had less to say about the specificity of lesbian shame. In our volume, however, Jennifer Moon observes that the question of lesbians' relation to shame was repeatedly invoked and then deferred throughout the conference discussions. What did our failure to sustain a discussion about lesbians' relation to shame say about its relevance to lesbian identity? Not unexpectedly, the butch lesbian figured most prominently in discussions of lesbian shame—significantly, no one ever raised the question of femme shame—but that does not settle the matter.

On the one hand, Judith Halberstam has argued that tomboys do not experience the same abjection (as children or adults) as do sissies.[16] On the other hand, Terry Galloway and Nadine Hubbs provide strikingly different assessments of what is involved in the desire, in Hubbs's words, "to be my own man." Jennifer Moon further asks whether the denial of butch lesbian shame "reifies masculinity as presence and femininity as lack." Butches "are supposed to feel ashamed," she observes, "and if they don't, it's because they've developed the self-confidence needed to protect themselves." In other words, the butch's transcendence of shame is just another testimony to the prestige that attaches to her successful performance of masculinity.

Whatever our eventual assessment of the particular relationship of butch identity to shame, Halberstam's suggestion that shame is a gendered form of sexual abjection—attached to normative femininity and thus something that lesbians and feminists necessarily resist and work through in order to become what they are—offers one powerful insight from which to theorize this asymmetry.[17] Indeed, it may be that women's unequal status renders them always already shamed, yet also, upon the assumption of feminist consciousness, more immune to shame than gay men, whose historical relationship to homosexuality has been mediated in part through the shaming category of effeminacy.

As Frances Negrón-Muntaner notes, however, this insight may depend on the assumption of a universal and relatively privileged female subject. From the standpoint of disability studies, Tobin Siebers hypothesizes that the asymmetrical relationships to shame among masculine women and effeminate men may derive "from the unequal social mobility and cultural access produced by the equation between femininity and disability." If that is true, then perhaps cross-gender queer identification and cross-gender queer sex may provide particularly useful points of entry to an understanding of the dynamics of shame—as the analyses of lesbian identification with gay male culture and sexual styles by Moon and Ziv suggest.

Indeed, the convergences in Moon's and Ziv's work on lesbian identification with gay men raise a broader question. What accounts for the differential production of knowledge about gay men and lesbians *by* gay men and lesbians? Despite the long and venerable history of gay men's complex re-lations with the category of femininity, gay male academic discourse has often been preoccupied with masculinity and with men, thereby mapping the gender of the writing subject onto the gender of the object of analysis. In other words, this discourse reproduces a relatively tight relation between identity and identification. Yet, as Moon and Ziv demonstrate, that is not particularly the case in writing by lesbians, which has produced influen-tial and pioneering studies of gay male bodies, sexualities, cultures, social practices, and representations, from drag queens to aesthetes, from S/M subcultures to HIV/AIDS.

Esther Newton's classic and inexhaustible *Mother Camp* can stand as a symbol for this tradition, which both preceded her research in the 1960s on female impersonators in America and has continued without interruption ever since.[18] Why do cross-gender identifications, when they are pursued analytically, move so consistently from women to men and not the other way round? Is there any way to resist the logic of this apparent cultural truism, whereby gay men are more interesting, both to themselves and to others, than lesbians?

This issue is not raised as an accusation. We don't believe that this asym-metry is necessarily or merely evidence of gay male indifference to lesbians or of the persistence among gay men of patriarchal attitudes. But given the difficulty the conference participants had in thinking consistently about the nexus of lesbian shame, we do want to ask: Why is it that gay male iden-tities, histories, and sexual practices seem so good for so many lesbians to think with? And what is it about lesbian identities, histories, and sex-ual practices that might limit their use-value for other conceptual prob-lems and other groups? Or is it the identities, histories, and sexual prac-tices of other groups that somehow prevent them from finding use-value in lesbian sexual culture? What does this have to do with what lesbians do, or don't do, in bed? What does it have to do with our particular history of female husbands and romantic friendships? And what does it have to do with the structures of visibility that organize our culture's recognition of sexuality in the first place? We're interested in these questions not because such asymmetrical commitments prove the primacy of gender and sexual identity over the potential flexibility of identifications, but because the ef-fect of these commitments is to produce a systematic patterning in modes of knowledge production. So it may be a clue to a larger phenomenon. Ap-proaching this issue as a theoretical and methodological question—and so depersonalizing it—might be one way to think through the reconfigura-tions of identity, desire, and shame we hope to pursue.

III

The differential relations to shame of specific groups are evident not only in the present, but also in the past. Because a historical consciousness about past identities, survival strategies, and modes of life provides a basis for evaluating the worth and efficacy of present-day discourses and politics, this volume pays sustained attention to historical matters. The importance of history is pointedly highlighted in the commentary on "Enactivism: The Movie," where the authors argue that activism is always historical and con-textual and, therefore, that effective activism will adapt itself strategically to specific contexts.

Gayle Rubin, in her contribution to this volume, cites an eloquent ex-ample of such an adaptation in the story of the disabled straight man whose invention of the silicone dildo unintentionally provided lesbians with de-cades of sexual ecstasy. His invention testified to the productive and un-foreseen possibilities for crossover applications of far-flung resistances to shame. It also implies the need, as Rubin says, for "a little humility" in our definitions of who can contribute to whose political progress.

The curators of the Labadie Collection exhibit also provide ample evi-dence of the variety of sites of queer activism, past and present, drawing on both underground and commercial materials in their survey of how non-normative queer representations managed to evade censorship in American popular culture.

The exhibit thereby supports George Chauncey's contention that the 1950s were not a dark age of shame from which we have now emerged. Carefully distinguishing between shaming processes and their effects, Chauncey insists that even during the height of state-sponsored homopho-bia in the United States some gay men managed to shrug off the shame that they knew they were supposed to feel.

As Chauncey and Warner both point out, we need to pay greater atten-tion to what "we mean by shame": how we define it, and on what basis, for whom, when, and where. And it may be useful to remember that although shame is a very old word (present in medieval and early modern Western cultures), its specific role as an internalized mechanism of discipline is a peculiarly modern invention—part of the "civilizing" process, as Chauncey and Helmut Puff note. Not only has the production of shame been uneven; not only has it taken different forms. Shame came into being under certain conditions of modernity.[19] Who knows what its future history may be?

Although shame turns out to be supremely mobile, it never seems to get all that far from home. It consistently conduces to the performance, or the reperformance, of the personal. "Shame is productive above all of first-person narrative," Elisabeth Ladenson reminds us. Sedgwick, who argues that "shame is itself a form of communication," positions shame securely in the realm of queer performativity: "Performance interlines shame as more than just its result or a way of warding it off, though importantly it is those things. Shame is the affect that mantles the threshold between introversion and extroversion, between absorption and theatricality, between performativity and—performativity."

Given the performative qualities of shame, it is hardly surprising that many of our contributors perform their relationship to shame through autobiographical art, video, or narrative. Scholinski's art comes directly out of his imprisonment in a psychiatric hospital. Wilkerson uses her experience of temporary disability caused by slipping on ice to mine the metaphor of slipping for the conceptual work of analyzing the social affinities that link disability and bisexuality. Hubbs offers her experience in and identification with the culture of an elite music school to reflect on how gay pride has always borne the weight of shame. Crandall candidly explores her own feelings of activist shame, theorizing from the ground up how conventional activism "fucks people" by its inclusions and exclusions, as well as how she and her friends are "fucking with activism" by inhabiting public space in unorthodox ways.

Ladenson and Caron both entitle their essays "Shame on Me," but their witty inversions of the conventional guilt trip have rather different aims. Whereas Ladenson probes the apparent cultural acceptability of claiming shame in the first person, Caron (like Hanson) suggests that assuming the mantle of shame—taking shame on—might be one means of refiguring one's own experience of humiliation. Caron's interest in how the practice of confessing a humiliating narrative achieves "the twofold status of parody" underscores the extent to which the trope of shame is useful not only for generating narrative but also, potentially at least, for generating community.

Telling a humiliating story, Caron writes, "momentarily deactivates the disciplinary power of confession and turns isolation into something like a membership card." Whether such membership then translates into a collective identity or a movement or any larger communal practice is a question that Moon takes up. Her critique of the role that personal anecdote and confession played at the Gay Shame conference itself returns us to our own activities (in organizing the conference, editing this volume, and writing this essay) as inescapable sites of shame—as well as pride.

Neither we nor our contributors have a completed theory of Gay Shame. We are not attempting to replace gay pride with gay shame, nor do we offer a manifesto for a new intellectual or political movement. It remains to be seen whether gay shame is a sufficiently flexible analytical framework to enable us to think through all the issues posed at the conference and in this volume. But we do believe that the material collected here, with its multiple provocations, challenges, defiances, discomforts, criticisms, polemics, contradictions, surprises, and embarrassments, could help to launch a far-reaching, long-range reconsideration of some established commonplaces of lesbian-gay-queer politics and theory.

Notes

1. For a recent survey of the culture of shame as it has been constituted in modern thought and literature, see Jean-Pierre Martin, *Le livre des hontes* (Paris: Seuil, 2006). For an invocation of the opposition between shame and shamelessness to frame an understanding of the politics of sexuality in the United States throughout the last few decades, see Arlene Stein, *Shameless: Sexual Dissidence in American Culture* (New York: New York University Press, 2006).

2. Eve Kosofsky Sedgwick, "Queer Performativity: Henry James's *The Art of the Novel,*" *GLQ* 1, no. 1 (1993): 1–16, at 14; italics in original.

3. One example of this urge to reclamation is Patrick Moore's *Beyond Shame: Reclaiming the Abandoned History of Radical Gay Sexuality* (Boston: Beacon Press, 2004), which seeks to lift the veil of shame that has descended over the early history (1969–81) of gay male sexual communities.

4. For the claim of origination, see Mattilda, aka Matt Bernstein Sycamore, "Gay Shame: From Queer Autonomous Space to Direct Action Extravaganza," in *That's Revolting! Queer Strategies for Resisting Assimilation,* ed. Mattilda (Brooklyn: Soft Skull Press, 2004), 237–62, especially 238. Mattilda cautions the credulous reader, however, that "'Objective' history is a cruel lie, and I'm not interested in perpetuating such viciousness" (237).

5. Leo Bersani, "Shame on You," in Bersani and Adam Phillips, *Intimacies* (Chicago: University of Chicago Press, 2008), 31–56, at 31.

6. Judith Halberstam, "Shame and White Gay Masculinity," *Social Text* 23, nos. 3–4 (Fall-Winter 2005): 219–33, at 220.

7. See Kathryn Bond Stockton, *Beautiful Bottom, Beautiful Shame: Where "Black" Meets "Queer"* (Durham, NC: Duke University Press, 2006), 2, 5.

8. D. A. Miller, *Place for Us [Essay on the Broadway Musical]* (Cambridge, MA: Harvard University Press, 1998), and *Jane Austen, or The Secret of Style* (Princeton, NJ: Princeton University Press, 2003).

9. Halberstam, "Shame and White Gay Masculinity"; Hiram Perez, "You Can Have My Brown Body and Eat It, Too," *Social Text* 23, nos. 3–4 (Fall-Winter 2005): 171–91.

10. David L. Eng, Judith Halberstam, and José Estaban Muñoz, "Introduction: What's Queer about Queer Studies Now?" *Social Text* 23, nos. 3–4 (Fall-Winter 2005): 1–17, at 12.

11. See n. 9.

12. See especially Mattilda, "Gay Shame," 253: "The Gay Shame conference, we explained, was *trickle down academia*, by which academics appropriate anything they can get their hands on—mostly people's lived struggles, activism, and identities—and claim to have invented them" (italics in original).

13. Mattilda, "Gay Shame," 252–54 (quotation at 254). A somewhat different version of the conflict between the Gay Shame activists and other participants in the Gay Shame conference, written by another eyewitness, which, however, draws heavily on Mattilda's views, has also made its way into print: see Heather Love's epilogue to her book *Feeling Backward: Loss and the Politics of Queer History* (Cambridge, MA: Harvard University Press, 2007). We have reservations about both published accounts.

14. Elspeth Probyn, *Blush: Faces of Shame* (Minneapolis: University of Minnesota Press, 2005), 76, 87, 101.

15. See n. 14.

16. Halberstam, "Shame and White Gay Masculinity," 226.

17. Ibid.

18. Esther Newton, *Mother Camp: Female Impersonators in America* (Chicago: University of Chicago Press, 1972).

19. Compare Martin in n. 1.

[D A V I D   M .   H A L P E R I N]

Why Gay Shame Now?

Note: What follows is a transcript of the statement with which I opened the first full day of the 2003 Gay Shame conference. For documentary purposes, I have retained the spoken form in which I originally delivered these remarks.

Before there was Gay Shame, there was already gay shame.

At 5 PM on Saturday, May 25, 2002, at Harvey Milk Plaza on Castro and Market Streets in San Francisco, the First Annual Gay Shame Awards ceremony was held, presided over by Mattilda (aka Matt Bernstein Sycamore) and Oakie Treadwell, who are present at this conference. In their publicity for this event, the organizers called it "a radical queer extravaganza":

This is the ceremony where we reward the most hypocritical gays for their service to the "Community" (that's the CEO's, the landlords, the cops, and the dot-com criminals who give "gay" a bad name). That's right—it's time to expose the evil-doers who use the sham of gay "pride" as a cover-up for their greed and misdeeds. We are now taking nominations for the Gay Shame Awards by email at gayshamesf@yahoo.com. Gay Shame requests that all participants and attendees dress to absolutely terrifying, devastating, ragged excess. The Gay Shame Awards will be a festival of resistance, a queer takeover of the bland, whitewashed gayborhood, a chance to express our queer identities in ways other than just buying a bunch of crap. Why feel proud when there's so much to be ashamed of? Gay landlords evicting people with AIDS. Gay cops beating up homeless queers. Gay Castro residents fighting a queer youth shelter. We are awaiting your nomination.

GAY SHAME is the radical alternative to consumerist "pride" crap. We are committed to fighting the rabid assimilationist monster of corporate gay "pride" with a devastating mobilization of queer brilliance. With GAY SHAME festivals of resistance erupting from New York to Stockholm, Toronto to Barcelona, GAY SHAME is rapidly becoming a worldwide phenomenon. This year in San Francisco, we will be taking on the Pride Parade—stay tuned for future calls to action.

The awards ceremony was attended by hundreds of people, some waving flags that read, "Queers against capitalism," others holding signs with such slogans as "Sex not greed."[1]

The year before, on Friday, June 22, and Sunday, June 24, 2001, a somewhat different version of Gay Shame was celebrated at Dumba in Brooklyn, New York. One of the organizers, Stephen Kent Jusick, is present at this conference. Flyers from the event identify Gay Shame 2001 as "a radical queer alternative to consumerist 'Gay Pride' celebrations. A day of fierce performers, speakers, art, film, and dance party." The slogans announcing this event included: "It's a movement not a market," "Equality through corporate sponsorship?!?," "Gay Pride My Ass!," and, last but not least, "Acceptance is just a horrid thought!" The organizers also produced a zine called *Swallow Your Pride!* Copies are available at this conference.

But before there was Gay Shame, there was already gay shame. In the fall of 1993, in the first article to appear in the first issue of *GLQ: A Journal of Lesbian and Gay Studies,* Eve Kosofsky Sedgwick published some thoughts on the matter in "Queer Performativity: Henry James's *The Art of the Novel.*" Despite its unpromising title, Sedgwick's essay actually advances a powerful argument to the effect that queer identity and queer resistance are both rooted in originary experiences of shame. "If queer is a politically potent term, which it is," Sedgwick wrote, "that's because, far from being capable of being detached from the childhood scene of shame, it cleaves to that scene as a near-inexhaustible source of transformational energy." Invoking a psychological literature about the origins of shame in the affective life of the individual, Sedgwick claimed that shame is "identity-constituting": it is "a bad feeling that does not attach to what one does, but to what one is." Of course, you can do things that bring shame on you, but shame, according to Sedgwick, "can only be experienced as global and about oneself," even if it is occasioned by something accidental or inessential. "One therefore *is* some-*thing,* in experiencing shame," and one's very personality or character is "a record" of the history of the ways that the emotion of shame has structured one's relations to others and to oneself. Whence Sedgwick drew the following radical conclusion: "therapeutic or political strategies aimed directly at getting rid of individual or group shame, or undoing it," such as Gay Pride, "have something preposterous about them: they may 'work' . . . but they can't work in the way they say they work. . . . The forms taken by shame are not distinct 'toxic' parts of a group or individual identity that can be excised; they are instead integral to and residual in the processes by which identity itself is formed. They are available for the work of metamorphosis, reframing, refiguration, *transfiguration*, affective and symbolic loading and deformation," but they can't simply be jettisoned or transcended. Shame, then, is what propels identities into the performative space of activism *without* giving those identities the status of essences.[2]

That argument about gay shame and its transformation into queer resistance picks up a theme already present in much early work in lesbian and gay studies, at least since Esther Newton's 1972 book *Mother Camp*.[3] Sedgwick, along with many other queer theorists, went on to elaborate that theme further in the course of the 1990s.[4] Many of these authors, including Esther Newton, are present at this conference. (Eve Sedgwick herself sends best wishes and regrets.)

But before there was gay shame, there was already gay shame. In 1986 Sarah Schulman published a novel called *Girls, Visions and Everything*. In it, a character by the name of Isabel Schwartz "had the idea to change the name [of Gay Pride Week] to Lesbian Shame Week with thousands of dykes crawling down Fifth Avenue. She was even proposing 'Lesbian Shame Awards.' 'It's a new concept in anti-trend t-shirts,' she said."[5]

Schulman's character was making a specific political point about the state of affairs in the 1980s, when "things had gotten frighteningly mellow" in official manifestations of gay visibility while "Ronald Reagan and the AIDS crisis had sobered people up to the fact that the long haul was far from over."[6] But her remark echoes the kinds of conversations I can recall having with my friends in Boston, in the early 1980s, when we were still new to gay pride, and still too close to our original, *untransformed* experiences of shame at our sexuality. We would come home from the parade, collapse from our heroic efforts to sustain unflinching pride in our homosexuality before a skeptical public over the course of an entire six hours, and wonder whether we could now go back to the relative comfort zone of sexual shame which we were used to inhabiting.

But before there was gay shame, there was already gay shame. Consider the following episode, described by Jean Genet in *The Thief's Journal*, first published in 1948. Genet is describing an event that he witnessed in Barcelona, Spain, in the faraway year of 1933. It could be described in all seriousness as a Gay Shame parade. I quote Genet:

Those whom she, who was one of their number, called the Sheilas, went in ceremonious procession to the site of a public urinal that had been destroyed. The rioters, during the street fighting of 1933, had ripped out one of the filthiest of the tearooms, but also one of the most beloved. It was close to the port and the barracks: the hot urine of thousands of soldiers was what had corroded the iron sheeting of which it was composed. When it was known to be dead and gone forever, then in shawls, in mantillas, in silk dresses, in wasp-waisted jackets the Sheilas—not all of them, but their chosen representatives in solemn delegation—came to lay on the site a wreath of red roses held together by a gauzy piece of crepe. The cortege left from the Parallelo, crossed the calle Sao Paolo, and went down the Ramblas de los Flores to the statue of Columbus. The fairies were perhaps about thirty in number, at eight o'clock in the morning, at sunrise. I saw them go by. I followed them from a distance. I knew that my place was in the midst of them, not because I was one of them, but because their shrill voices, their cries, their extravagant gestures seemed to me to have no other aim than to try and pierce through the layers of the world's contempt. The Sheilas were great. They were the Daughters of Shame.[7]

If this procession of the Sheilas can be called a Gay Shame parade, that's not because it is intended as a spoof of Gay Pride marches, or as a reproach to them, or as a protest against gay hypocrisy, or as a reminder of the sort of homosexuality that gay pride is no longer proud of and the sort of homosexuals that no decent gay man wants to be associated with; nor is it the result of gay pride fatigue, the lapse from a hollow, willful, and willfully enacted pride into a gay shame that had never abated anyway for very long. The Sheilas are not commentary; they are originals. Their procession represents, in some real sense, the original performative gesture of queer social defiance, a gesture that contributed to what we now call Gay Pride.[8]

The purpose of this conference is not exactly to demolish gay pride, even less to return us to a state of shame or to promote shame instead of pride. Rather, it is to inquire into those dimensions of lesbian, gay, and queer sexuality, history, and culture that the political imperatives of gay pride have tended to repress and that Gay Pride as it is institutionalized nowadays has become too proud to acknowledge. It is my belief that the only kind of gay pride that is endurable—and since my life has been transformed beyond imagination by gay pride, I'm not about to renounce it—the only kind of gay pride that is endurable is a gay pride that does not forget its origins in shame, that is still powered by the transformative energies that spring from experiences of shame. Without that intimate and never-forgotten relation to shame, gay pride turns into mere social conformity, into a movement (as Leo Bersani, one of the participants in this conference, once remarked) with no more radical goal than that of "trying to persuade straight society that [gay people] can be good parents, good soldiers, good priests."[9]

Gay pride makes sense to me only in relation to shame, and it is only by returning to confront what still has the power to make us ashamed that we can meaningfully continue the work of gay pride. For the Sheilas, to be queer was to be socially unredeemable, and therefore to be powerful. Shame made them great. It is my hope that we will learn from one another in the course of the next two days how to mobilize our shame in such a way as to renew the transgressive and transformative energies that power queer and alternative cultures. It is no doubt a triumph for gay pride that even George W. Bush cannot avoid appointing openly gay officials to his administration; but still, could there possibly be a better illustration of the Dumba slogan that "acceptance is just a horrid thought!"? To their credit, Genet's Sheilas are about as far from a job in the Bush administration today as they were in 1933. They still have a lot to teach us—about shame, and about pride.

Notes

1. The quoted text was downloaded from http://www.gayshamesf.org and circulated via the Internet; additional information derives from Laurel Wellman, "Hip Roast of Some Gay Hypocrites," *San Francisco Chronicle* (May 28, 2002), http://sfgate.com/cgi-bin/article.cgi?f=/c/a/2002/05/28/MN127156.DTL. The Second Annual Gay Shame Awards duly took place in San Francisco on Friday, June 27, 2003; they included "the *Walk of Shame*, a street protest originating at the LGBT Center and ending at 18th & Castro Sts. in the Castro," according to Gay Shame's Web site. Two days later, on June 29, 2003, six queer activists were arrested for protesting the inclusion of straight conservative city supervisor Gavin Newsom (later mayor of San Francisco) in the Gay Pride Parade; felony charges against them were later dropped, and they were released on the night of July 1, 2003.

2. Eve Kosofsky Sedgwick, "Queer Performativity: Henry James's *The Art of the Novel*," *GLQ: A Journal of Lesbian and Gay Studies* 1, no. 1 (1993): 4, 2-14.

3. Esther Newton, *Mother Camp: Female Impersonators in America*, 2d ed. (Chicago: University of Chicago Press, 1979).

4. See especially Eve Kosofsky Sedgwick and Adam Frank, "Shame in the Cybernetic Fold: Reading Silvan Tomkins," in *Shame and Its Sisters: A Silvan Tomkins Reader*, ed. Sedgwick and Frank (Durham, NC: Duke University Press, 1995), 1-28; Sedgwick, "Shame and Performativity: Henry James's New York Edition Prefaces," in *Henry James's New York Edition: The Construction of Authorship*, ed. David McWhirter (Stanford, CA: Stanford University Press, 1995), 206-39, 312-14; "Queer Performativity: Warhol's Shyness/Warhol's Whiteness," in *Pop Out: Queer Warhol*, ed. Jennifer Doyle, Jonathan Flatley, and José Esteban Muñoz (Durham, NC: Duke University Press, 1996), 134-43; and, finally, "Shame, Theatricality, and Queer Performativity: Henry James's *The Art of the Novel*," this volume, 49-62. Among the more distinguished explorations of shame and queer performativity in the latter half of the 1990s can be numbered D. A. Miller, *Place For Us [Essay on the Broadway Musical]* (Cambridge, MA: Harvard University Press, 1998), and Michael Warner, *The Trouble with Normal* (New York: Free Press, 1999).

5. Sarah Schulman, *Girls, Visions and Everything* (Seattle, WA: Seal Press, 1986), 109.

6. Ibid.

7. Jean Genet, *Journal du voleur* (Paris: Gallimard, 1949; repr. 2001), 72–73. I have adapted the excellent English translation by Bernard Frechtman (which is based on the original, unexpurgated edition of Genet's text, never reprinted and still unavailable in France or anywhere else) in order to bring out certain details in Genet's narrative. In the original, Genet refers to the fairies (*tapettes*) as *les Carolines*, which Frechtman translates, plausibly, as "the Carolinas": this, however, does not convey the flavor of the word in French. I have preferred to use a bit of Australian slang, which may express the right tone of amused contempt at the spectacle of a disreputable, vulgar femininity but admittedly cannot capture the grandiose (royalist) dimensions of the word in the Spanish context. See Jean Genet, *The Thief's Journal*, trans. Bernard Frechtman (New York: Grove Press, 1964), 65. This passage from Genet was chosen by Didier Eribon to open his magnificent book-length discussion of gay shame and metamorphosis in Genet, and I am indebted to him for calling my attention to the passage and for discussing it with me: see Didier Eribon, *Une morale du minoritaire: Variations sur un thème de Jean Genet* (Paris: Fayard, 2001), especially 9–11.

8. For an account of an earlier prototype of gay shame, see D. A. Miller, *Jane Austen, or The Secret of Style* (Princeton, NJ: Princeton University Press, 2003). This book, which appeared around the time that the Michigan conference on gay shame took place, can be read as a study of the preconditions and foundations of gay shame, as well as an analysis of the essence of its operations.

9. Leo Bersani, *Homos* (Cambridge, MA: Harvard University Press, 1995), 113.

PERFORMING SHAME

[EVE KOSOFSKY SEDGWICK]

Shame, Theatricality, and Queer Performativity

HENRY JAMES'S *THE ART OF THE NOVEL*

In the couple of weeks after the World Trade Center was destroyed in September 2001, I had a daily repetition of an odd experience, one that was probably shared by many walkers in the same midsouthern latitudes of Manhattan. Turning from a street onto Fifth Avenue, even if I was heading north, I would feel compelled first to look south in the direction of the World Trade Center, now gone. This inexplicably furtive glance was associated with a conscious wish: that my southward vista would again be blocked by the familiar sight of the pre–September 11 twin towers, somehow come back to loom over us in all their complacent ugliness. But, of course, the towers were always still gone. Turning away, shame was what I would feel.

Why shame? I think this was, in effect, one of those situations in which, as Silvan Tomkins puts it, "one is suddenly looked at by one who is strange, or . . . one wishes to look at or commune with another person but suddenly cannot because he is strange, or one expected him to be familiar but he suddenly appears unfamiliar, or one started to smile but found one was smiling at a stranger."[1] Not that an urban vista is quite the same as a loved face, but it isn't quite different, either: the despoiled view was a suddenly toothless face, say, or suddenly preoccupied, or suddenly dead—to say nothing, even, of the historical implications surrounding that particular change of landscape.

These flashes of shame didn't seem particularly related to prohibition or transgression. Beyond that, though it was I who felt the shame, it wasn't especially myself I was ashamed of. It would be closer to say I was ashamed *for* the estranged and denuded skyline; such feelings interlined, of course, the pride, solidarity, and grief that also bound me to the city. The shame had to do, too, with visibility and spectacle—the hapless visibility of the towers' absence now, the shockingly compelling theatricality of their destruction.

Recent work by theorists and psychologists of shame locates the proto-form (eyes down, head averted) of this powerful affect—which appears in infants very early, between the third and seventh month of life, just after the infant has become able to distinguish and recognize the face of its care-giver—at a particular moment in a particular repeated narrative. That is the moment when the circuit of mirroring expressions between the child's face and the caregiver's recognized face (a circuit that, if it can be called a form of primary narcissism, suggests that narcissism from the very first throws itself sociably, dangerously into the gravitational field of the other) is bro-ken: the moment when the adult face fails or refuses to play its part in the continuation of mutual gaze; when, for any one of many reasons, it fails to be recognizable to, or recognizing of, the infant who has been, so to speak, "giving face" based on a faith in the continuity of this circuit. As Michael Franz Basch explains, "The infant's behavioral adaptation is quite totally dependent on maintaining effective communication with the executive and coordinating part of the infant-mother system. The shame-humiliation re-sponse, when it appears, represents the failure or absence of the smile of contact, a reaction to the loss of feedback from others, indicating social iso-lation and signaling the need for relief from that condition."[2] The proto-affect shame is thus not defined by prohibition (nor, as a result, by repres-sion). Shame floods into being as a moment, a disruptive moment, in a circuit of identity-constituting identificatory communication. Indeed, like a stigma, shame is itself a form of communication. Blazons of shame, the "fallen face" with eyes down and head averted—and, to a lesser extent, the blush—are semaphores of trouble and at the same time of a desire to recon-stitute the interpersonal bridge.

But in interrupting identification, shame, too, makes identity. In fact, shame and identity remain in very dynamic relation to one another, at once deconstituting and foundational, because shame is both peculiarly contagious and peculiarly individuating. One of the strangest features of shame, but perhaps also the one that offers the most conceptual leverage for political projects, is the way bad treatment of someone else, bad treat-ment *by* someone else, someone else's embarrassment, stigma, debility, bad smell, or strange behavior, seemingly having nothing to do with me, can so readily flood me—assuming I'm a shame-prone person—with this sen-sation whose very suffusiveness seems to delineate my precise, individual outlines in the most isolating way imaginable.

Lecturing on shame, I used to ask listeners to join in a thought experi-ment, visualizing an unwashed, half-insane man who would wander into the lecture hall mumbling loudly, his speech increasingly accusatory and disjointed, and publicly urinate in the front of the room, then wander out again. I pictured the excrucation of everyone else in the room: each looking down, wishing to be anywhere else yet conscious of the inexorable fate of being exactly there, inside the individual skin of which each was burningly aware; at the same time, though, unable to stanch the hemorrhage of painful identification with the misbehaving man. That's the double movement shame makes: toward painful individuation, toward uncontrollable relationality.

The conventional way of distinguishing shame from guilt is that shame attaches to and sharpens the sense of what one is, whereas guilt attaches to what one does. Although Tomkins is less interested than anthropologists, moralists, or popular psychologists in distinguishing between the two, the implication remains that one *is something* in experiencing shame, though one may or may not have secure hypotheses about what. In the developmental process, shame is now often considered the affect that most defines the space wherein a sense of self will develop ("Shame is to self psychology what anxiety is to ego psychology—the keystone affect").[3] Which I take to mean, not at all that it is the place where identity is most securely attached to essences, but rather that it is the place where the *question* of identity arises most originarily and most relationally.

At the same time, shame both derives from and aims toward sociability. As Basch writes, "The shame-humiliation reaction in infancy of hanging the head and averting the eyes does not mean the child is conscious of rejection, but indicates that effective contact with another person has been broken. . . . Therefore, shame-humiliation throughout life can be thought of as an inability to effectively arouse the other person's positive reactions to one's communications. The exquisite painfulness of that reaction in later life harks back to the earliest period when such a condition is not simply uncomfortable but threatens life itself."[4] So that whenever the actor, or the performance artist, or, I could add, the activist in an identity politics, proffers the spectacle of her or his "infantile" narcissism to a spectating eye, the stage is set (so to speak) for either a newly dramatized flooding of the subject by the shame of refused return, or the successful pulsation of the mirroring regard through a narcissistic circuit rendered elliptical (which is to say: necessarily distorted) by the hyperbole of its original cast. As best described by Tomkins, shame effaces itself; shame points and projects; shame turns itself skin side out; shame and pride, shame and dignity, shame and self-display, shame and exhibitionism are different interlinings of the same glove. Shame, it might finally be said, transformational shame, *is performance*. I mean theatrical performance. Performance interlines shame as more than just its result or a way of warding it off, though, importantly, it is those things. Shame is the affect that mantles the threshold between introversion and extroversion, between absorption and theatricality, between performativity and—performativity.

Henry James undertook the New York edition of his work (a handsome twenty-four-volume consolidation and revision, with new prefaces, of what he saw as his most important novels and stories to date) at the end of a relatively blissful period of literary production ("the major phase")—a blissful period poised, however, between two devastating bouts of melancholia. The first of these scouring depressions was precipitated in 1895 by what James experienced as the obliterative failure of his ambitions as a playwright, being howled off the stage at the premiere of *Guy Domville*. By 1907, though, when the volumes of the New York edition were beginning to appear, James's theatrical self-projection was sufficiently healed that he had actually begun a new round of playwrighting and of negotiations with producers—eventuating, indeed, in performance. The next of James's terrible depressions was triggered, not by humiliation on the stage, but by the failure of the New York edition itself: its total failure to sell and its apparently terminal failure to evoke any recognition from any readership.

When we read the New York edition prefaces, then, we read a series of texts that are in the most active imaginable relation to shame. Marking and indeed exulting in James's recovery from a near-fatal episode of shame in the theater, the prefaces, gorgeous with the playful spectacle of a productive and almost promiscuously entrusted or "thrown" authorial narcissism, yet also offer the spectacle of inviting (that is, leaving themselves open to) what was in fact their and their author's immediate fate: annihilation by the blankest of nonrecognizing responses from any reader. The prefaces are way out there, in short, and in more than a couple of senses of out.

In them, at least two different circuits of the hyperbolic narcissism/ shame orbit are being enacted, and in a volatile relation to each other. The first of these, as I've suggested, is the drama of James's relation to his audience of readers. In using the term "audience" here, I want to mark James's own insistent thematization of elements in this writing as specifically theatrical, with all the implications of excitement, overinvestment, danger, loss, and melancholia that, as Joseph Litvak has argued in *Caught in the Act*, the theater by this time held for him.[5] The second and related narcissism/ shame circuit dramatized in the prefaces is the perilous and productive one that extends between the speaker and his own past. James's most usual gesture in the prefaces is to figure his relation to the past as the intensely charged relationship between the author of the prefaces and the often much younger man who wrote the novels and stories to which the prefaces are appended—or between either of these men and a yet younger figure who represents the fiction itself.

What undertaking could be more narcissistically exciting or more narcissistically dangerous that that of rereading, revising, and consolidating one's own "collected works"? If these, or their conjured young author, return one's longing gaze with dead, indifferent, or even distracted eyes, what limit can there be to the shame (of him, of oneself) so incurred? Equal to that danger, however, is the danger of one's own failure to recognize or to desire them or him. As Tomkins writes, "Likes disgust, [shame] operates only after interest or enjoyment had been activated, and inhibits one or the other or both. The innate activator of shame is the incomplete reduction of interest or joy. Hence any barrier to further exploration which partially reduces interest . . . will activate the lowering of the head and eyes in shame and reduce further exploration or self-exposure."[6] To consider interest itself a distinct affect and to posit an association between shame and (the [incomplete] inhibition of) interest makes sense phenomenologically, I think, about depression, and specifically about the depressions out of which James had emerged to write his "major novels"—novels that do, indeed, seem to show the effects of a complicated history of disruptions and prodigal remediations in the ability to take an interest. Into such depressions as well, however, he was again to be plunged.

The James of the prefaces revels in the same startling metaphor that animates the present-day popular literature of the "inner child": the metaphor that presents one's relation to one's own past as a relationship, intersubjective as it is intergenerational. And, it might be added, for most people by definition homoerotic. Often, the younger author is present in these prefaces as a figure in himself, but even more frequently the fictions themselves, or characters in them, are given his form. One needn't be invested (as pop psychology is) in a normalizing, hygienic teleology of healing this relationship, in a mawkish overvaluation of the "child"'s access to narrative authority at the expense of that of the "adult," or in a totalizing ambition to get the two selves permanently merged into one, to find that this figuration opens out a rich landscape of relational positionalities—perhaps especially around issues of shame. James certainly displays no desire to become once again the young and mystified author of his early productions. To the contrary, the very distance of these inner self-figurations from the speaking self of the present is marked, treasured, and in fact eroticized. Their distance (temporal, figured as intersubjective, figured in turn as spatial) seems, if anything, to constitute the relished internal space of James's absorbed subjectivity. Yet for all that the distance itself is prized, James's speculation as to what different outcomes might be evoked by different kinds of overture across the distance—by different sorts of solicitation, different forms of touch, interest, and love between the less and the more initiated figure—provides a great deal of the impetus to his theoretical project in these essays. The speaking self of the prefaces does not attempt to merge with the potentially shaming or shamed figurations of its younger self, younger fictions, younger heroes; its attempt is to love them. That love is shown to occur both in spite of shame and, more remarkably, through it.

Not infrequently, as we'll see, the undertaking to reparent, as it were, or "reissue" the bastard infant of (what is presented as) James's juvenilia is described simply as male parturition, James also reports finding in himself "that finer consideration hanging in the parental breast about the maimed or slighted, the disfigured or defeated, the unlucky or unlikely child—with this hapless small mortal thought of further as somehow 'compromising.'"[7] James offers a variety of reasons for being embarrassed by these waifs of his past, but the persistence with which shame accompanies their repeated conjuration is matched by the persistence with which, in turn, he describes himself as cathecting or eroticizing that very shame as a way of coming into loving relation to queer or "compromising" youth.

In a number of places, for example, James more or less explicitly invokes Frankenstein and all the potential uncanniness of the violently disavowed male birth. But he invokes that uncanniness in order to undo it, or at least do something further with it, by offering the spectacle of—not his refusal—but his eroticized eagerness to recognize his progeny even in its oddness: "The thing done and dismissed has ever, at the best, for the ambitious workman, a trick of looking dead if not buried, so that he almost throbs with ecstasy when, on an anxious review, the flush of life reappears. It is verily on recognising that flush on a whole side of 'The Awkward Age' that I brand it all, but ever so tenderly, as monstrous."[8] It is as if the ecstasy-inducing power of the young creature's "flush of life," which refers to even while evoking the potentially shaming brand of monstrosity, is the reflux of the blush of shame or repudiation the older man in this rewriting doesn't feel. Similarly, James writes about his mortifyingly extravagant miscalculations concerning the length of (what he has imagined as) a short story: "Painfully associated for me has 'The Spoils of Poynton' remained, until recent reperusal, with the awkward consequence of that fond error. The subject had emerged . . . all suffused with a flush of meaning; thanks to which irresistible air, as I could but plead in the event, I found myself . . . beguiled and led on." "The thing had 'come,'" he concludes with an undisguised sensuous pleasure but hardly a simple one, "the flower of conception had bloomed."[9] And he describes his revision of the early fictions both as his (or their?) way of "remaining *unshamed*" and as a process by which they have "all joyously and *blushingly* renewed themselves" (emphasis added).[10] What James seems to want here is to remove the blush from its terminal place as the betraying blazon of a ruptured narcissistic circuit, and instead to put it in circulation: as the sign of a tenderly strengthened and indeed now "irresistible" bond between the writer of the present and the abashed writer of the past, or between either of them and the queer little *conceptus.*

You can see the displacement at work in this passage from James's most extended description of his process of revision:

Since to get and to keep finished and dismissed work well behind one, and to have as little to say to it and about it as possible, had been for years one's only law, so, during that flat interregnum . . . creeping superstitions as to what it might really have been had time to grow up and flourish. Not least among these rioted doubtless the fond fear that any tidying-up of the uncanny brood, any removal of accumulated dust, any washing of wizened faces, or straightening of grizzled locks, or twitching, to a better effect, of superannuated garments, might let one in, as the phrase is, for expensive renovations. I make use here of the figure of age and infirmity, but in point of fact I had rather viewed the reappearance of the first-born of my progeny . . . as a descent of awkward infants from the nursery to the drawing-room under the kind appeal of enquiring, of possibly interested, visitors. I had accordingly taken for granted the common decencies of such a case—the responsible glance of some power above from one nursling to another, the rapid flash of an anxious needle, the not imperceptible effect of a certain audible splash of soap-and-water. . . .

"Hands off altogether on the nurse's part!" was . . . strictly conceivable; but only in the light of the truth that it had never taken effect in any fair and stately . . . re-issue of anything. Therefore it was easy to see that any such apologetic suppression as that of the "altogether," any such admission as that of a single dab of the soap, left the door very much ajar.[11]

The passage that begins by conjuring the uncanniness of an abandoned, stunted, old/young Frankenstein brood (reminiscent of the repudiated or abused children in Dickens, such as Smike and Jenny Wren, whose deformed bodies stand for developmental narratives at once accelerated and frozen by, among other things, extreme material want) modulates reassuringly into the warm, overprotected Christopher Robin coziness of bourgeois Edwardian nursery ritual. The eventuality of the uncanny child's actual exposure to solitude and destitution has been deflected by an invoked

domesticity. Invoked with that domesticity, in the now fostered and nurtured and therefore "childlike" child, is a new, pleasurable form of exhibitionistic flirtation with adults that dramatizes the child's very distance from
abandonment and repudiation. In the place where the eye of parental care
had threatened to be withheld, there is now a bath where even the nurse's
attention is supplemented by the overhearing ear of inquiring and interested visitors. And in the place where the fear of solitary exposure has been
warded off, there's now the playful nakedness of ablution and a door left
"very much ajar" for a little joke about the suppression of the "altogether."

This sanctioned intergenerational flirtation represents a sustained
chord in the New York edition. James describes the blandishment of his finished works in tones that are strikingly like the ones with which, in his letters, he has also been addressing Hendrik Anderson, Jocelyn Persse, Hugh
Walpole, and the other younger men who at this stage of his life are setting
out, with happy success, to attract him. Note in this passage (from the *Am-
bassadors* preface) that "impudence" is the glamorizing trait James attributes to his stories—impudence that bespeaks not the absence of shame
from this scene of flirtation, but rather its pleasurably recirculated after-
glow: "[The story] rejoices . . . to seem to offer itself in a light, to seem to
know, and with the very last knowledge, what it's about—liable as it yet is
at moments to be caught by us with its tongue in its cheek and absolutely no
warrant but its splendid impudence. Let us grant then that the impudence
is always there—there, so to speak, for grace and effect and *allure*; there,
above all, because the Story is just the spoiled child of art, and because, as
we are always disappointed when the pampered don't 'play up,' we like it, to
that extent, to look all its character. It probably does so, in truth, even when
we most flatter ourselves that we negotiate with it by treaty."[12] To dramatize
the story as *impudent* in relation to its creator is also to dramatize the lux-
urious distance between this scene and one of *repudiation*: the conceivable
shame of a past self, a past production, is being caught up and recirculated
through a lambent interpersonal figuration of the intimate, indulged mutual pressure of light differentials of power and knowledge.

James writes about the writing of *The American*, "One would like to woo
back such hours of fine precipitation . . . of images so free and confident and
ready that they brush questions aside and disport themselves, like the artless schoolboys of Gray's beautiful Ode, in all the ecstasy of the ignorance
attending them."[13] (Or boasts of "The Turn of the Screw": "another grain . . .
would have spoiled the precious pinch addressed to its end.")[14] Sometimes
the solicitude is ultimately frustrated: "I strove in vain . . . to embroil and
adorn this young man on whom a hundred ingenious touches are thus lav-

ished."[15] The wooing in these scenes of pederastic revision is not unidirectional, however; even the age differential can be figured quite differently, as when James finds himself, on rereading *The American*, "clinging to my hero as to a tall, protective, good-natured elder brother in a rough place,"[16] or says of Lambert Strether, "I rejoiced in the promise of a hero so mature, who would give me thereby the more to bite into."[17] James refers to the protagonist of "The Beast in the Jungle" as "another poor sensitive gentleman, fit indeed to mate with Stransom of 'The Altar [of the Dead],'" adding, "My attested predilection for poor sensitive gentlemen almost embarrasses me as I march!"[18] The predilective yoking of the "I" with the surname of John Marcher, the romantic pairing off of Marcher in turn with the equally "sensitive" bachelor George Stransom, give if anything an excess of gay point to the "almost" embarrassment that is, however, treated, not as a pretext for authorial self-coverture, but as an explicit source of new, performatively induced authorial magnetism.

James, then, in the prefaces is using reparenting or "reissue" as a strategy for dramatizing and integrating shame, in the sense of rendering this potentially paralyzing affect narratively, emotionally, and performatively productive. The reparenting scenario is also, in James's theoretical writing, a pederastic/pedagogical one in which the flush of shame becomes an affecting and eroticized form of mutual display. The writing subject's seductive bond with the unmerged but unrepudiated "inner" child seems, indeed, to be the condition of that subject's having an interiority at all, a spatialized subjectivity that can be characterized by absorption. Or perhaps I should say: it is a condition of his *displaying* the spatialized subjectivity that can be characterized by absorption. For the spectacle of James's performative absorption appears only in relation (though in a most complex and unstable relation) to the setting of his performative theatricality; the narcissism/shame circuit between the writing self and its "inner child" intersects with that other hyperbolic and dangerous narcissistic circuit, figured as theatrical performance, that extends outward between the presented and expressive face and its audience.

I should say something about what it is to hear these richly accreted, almost alchemically imbued signifiers in this highly sexualized way—and more generally, about the kinds of resistance that the reading I suggest here may offer to a psychoanalytic interpretive project. In her psychoanalytic works on James, Kaja Silverman declares herself (for one particular passage in one particular preface) willing to "risk . . . violating a fundamental tenet of James criticism—the tenet that no matter how luridly suggestive the Master's language, it cannot have a sexual import."[19] I'm certainly with her on that one—except that Silverman's readiness to hear how very openly sexy James's prefaces are is made possible only by her strange insistence that he couldn't have known they were. James's eroticized relation to his writings and characters, in her reading, is governed by "unconscious desire rather than an organizing consciousness"; "armored against unwanted self-knowledge," James is diagnosed by Silverman as having his "defenses" "securely in place against such an unwelcome discovery."[20] I am very eager that James's sexual language be heard, but that it not be heard with this insulting presumption of the hearer's epistemological privilege—a privilege attached, furthermore, to Silverman's uncritical insistence on viewing sexuality exclusively in terms of repression and self-ignorance. When we tune in to James's language on these frequencies, it is not as superior, privileged eavesdroppers on a sexual narrative hidden from himself; rather, it is as an audience offered the privilege of sharing in his exhibitionistic enjoyment and performance of a sexuality organized around shame. Indeed, it is as an audience desired to do so—which is also happily to say, as an audience desired.

To gesture at a summing up: The thing I least want to be heard as offering here is a "theory of homosexuality." I have none and I want none. When I attempt to do some justice to the specificity, the richness, above all the explicitness of James's particular erotics, it is not with an eye to making him an exemplar of "homosexuality" or even of one "kind" of "homosexuality," though I certainly don't want, either, to make him sound as if he isn't gay. Nonetheless, I do mean to nominate the James of the New York edition prefaces as a kind of prototype of, not "homosexuality," but queerness, or queer performativity. In this usage, "queer performativity" is the name of a strategy for the production of meaning and being, in relation to the affect shame and to the later and related fact of stigma.

I don't know yet what claims may be worth making, ontologically, about the queer performativity I have been describing here. Would it be useful to suggest that some of the associations I've been making with queer performativity might actually be features of all performativity? Or useful, instead, to suggest that the transformational grammar of "Shame on you" may form only part of the performative activity seen as most intimately related to queerness, by people self-identified as queer? The usefulness of thinking about shame in relation to queer performativity, in any event, does not come from its adding any extra certainty to the question of what utterances or acts may be classed as "performative" or what people may be classed as "queer." Least of all does it pretend to define the relation between queerness and same-sex love and desire. What it does, to the contrary, is perhaps offer some psychological, phenomenological, and thematic density and motivation to what I described in the introduction as the "torsions" or aberrances between reference and performativity, or indeed between queerness and other ways of experiencing identity and desire.

But neither do I want it to sound as though my project has mainly to do with recuperating for deconstruction (or other antiessentialist projects) a queerness drained of specificity or political reference. To the contrary: I suggest that to view performativity in terms of habitual shame and its transformations opens a lot of new doors for thinking about identity politics.

It seems very likely that the structuring of associations and attachments around the affect shame is among the most telling differentials among cultures and times: not that the entire world can be divided between (supposedly primitive) "shame cultures" and (supposedly evolved) "guilt cultures," but rather that, as an affect, shame is a component (and differently a component) of all. Shame, like other affects, in Tomkins's usage of the term, is not a discrete intrapsychic structure, but a kind of free radical that (in different people and also in different cultures) attaches to and permanently intensifies or alters the meaning of—of almost anything: a zone of the body, a sensory system, a prohibited or indeed a permitted behavior, another affect such as anger or arousal, a named identity, a script for interpreting other people's behavior toward oneself. Thus, one of the things that anyone's character or personality is is a record of the highly individual histories by which the fleeting emotion of shame has instituted far more durable, structural changes in one's relational and interpretive strategies toward both self and others.

Which means, among other things, that therapeutic or political strategies aimed directly at getting rid of individual or group shame, or undoing it, have something preposterous about them: they may "work"—they certainly have powerful effects—but they can't work in the way they say they work. (I am thinking here of a range of movements that deal with shame variously in the form of, for instance, the communal *dignity* of the civil rights movement; the individuating *pride* of "Black Is Beautiful" and gay pride; various forms of nativist *ressentiment*; the menacingly exhibited *abjection* of the skinhead; the early feminist experiments with the naming and foregrounding of anger as a response to shame; the incest survivors movement's epistemological stress on truth-telling about shame; and, of course, many many others.) The forms taken by shame are not distinct "toxic" parts of a group or individual identity that can be excised; they are instead integral to and residual in the processes by which identity itself is formed. They are available for the work of metamorphosis, reframing, refiguration, *trans-figuration*, of affective and symbolic loading and deformation, but perhaps all too potent for the work of purgation and deontological closure.

If the structuration of shame differs strongly among cultures, among periods, and among different forms of politics, however, it differs also simply from one person to another within a given culture and time. Some of the infants, children, and adults in whom shame remains the most available mediator of identity are the ones called (a related word) shy. ("Remember the fifties?" Lily Tomlin used to ask. "No one was gay in the fifties; they were just shy.") Queer, I'd suggest, might usefully be thought of as referring in the first place to this group or an overlapping group of infants and children, those whose sense of identity is for some reason tuned most durably to the note of shame. What it is about them (or us) that makes this true remains to be specified. I mean that in the sense that I can't tell you now what it is—it certainly isn't a single thing—but also in the sense that, for them, it remains to be specified, is always belated: the shame-delineated place of identity doesn't determine the consistency or meaning of that identity, and race, gender, class, sexuality, appearance, and abledness are only a few of the defining social constructions that will crystallize there, developing from this originary affect their particular structures of expression, creativity, pleasure, and struggle. I'd venture that queerness in this sense has, at this historical moment, some definitionally very significant overlap, though a vibrantly elastic and temporally convoluted one, with the complex of attributes today condensed as adult or adolescent "gayness." Everyone knows that there are some lesbians and gay men who could never count as queer and other people who vibrate to the chord of queer without having much same-sex eroticism, or without routing their same-sex eroticism through the identity labels lesbian or gay. Yet many of the performative identity vernaculars that seem most recognizably "flushed" (to use James's word) with shame consciousness and shame creativity do cluster intimately around lesbian and gay worldly spaces. To name only a few: butch abjection, femmitude, leather, pride, SM, drag, musicality, fisting, attitude, zines, histrionicism, asceticism, Snap! culture, diva worship, florid religiosity; in a word, *flaming*.

And activism.

Shame interests me politically, then, because it generates and legitimates the place of identity—the question of identity—at the origin of the impulse to the performative, but does so without giving that identity space the standing of an essence. It constitutes it as to-be-constituted, which is also to say, as already there for the (necessary, productive) misconstrual and misrecognition. Shame—living, as it does, on and in the muscles and capillaries of the face—seems to be uniquely contagious from one person to another. And the contagiousness of shame is only facilitated by its anamorphic, protean susceptibility to new expressive grammars.

These facts suggest, I think, that asking good questions about shame and shame/performativity could get us somewhere with a lot of the recalcitrant knots that tie themselves into the guts of identity politics—yet without delegitimating the felt urgency and power of the notion "identity" itself. The dynamics of trashing and of ideological or institutional pogroms, like the dynamics of mourning, are incomprehensible without an understanding of shame. Survivors' guilt and, more generally, the politics of guilt will be better understood when we can see them in some relation to the slippery dynamics of shame. I suggest that the same is true of the politics of solidarity and identification; perhaps those, as well, of humor and humorlessness. I'd also want to suggest, if parenthetically, that shame/performativity may get us a lot further with the cluster of phenomena generally called "camp" than the notion of parody will, and more too than will any opposition between "depth" and "surface." And can anyone suppose that we'll ever figure out what happened around political correctness if we don't see it as, among other things, a highly politicized chain reaction of shame dynamics?

It has been all too easy for the psychologists and the few psychoanalysts working on shame to write it back into the moralisms of the repressive hypothesis: "healthy" or "unhealthy," shame can be seen as good because it preserves privacy and decency, bad because it colludes with self-repression or social repression. Clearly, neither of these valuations is what I'm getting at. I want to say that at least for certain ("queer") people, shame is simply the first, and remains a permanent, structuring fact of identity: one that, as James's example suggests, has its own powerfully productive and powerfully social metamorphic possibilities.

Notes

This article was previously published in GLQ: A Journal of Lesbian and Gay Studies (vol. 1, 1993: 1-16) and in Touching Feeling: Affect, Pedagogy, Performativity (Duke University Press, 2003).

1. Silvan S. Tomkins, Shame and Its Sisters: A Silvan Tomkins Reader, ed. Eve Kosofsky Sedgwick and Adam Frank (Durham, NC: Duke University Press, 1995), 135.

2. Michael Franz Basch, "The Concept of Affect: A Re-Examination," *Journal of the American Psychoanalytic Association* 24 (1976): 765.

3. Francis J. Broucek, "Shame and Its Relationship to Early Narcissistic Developments," *International Journal of Psychoanalysis* 63 (1982): 369.

4. Basch, 765-66.

5. Joseph Litvak, *Caught in the Act: Theatricality in the Nineteenth-Century English Novel* (Berkeley: University of California Press, 1991).

6. Tomkins, 135.

7. Henry James, *The Art of the Novel* (Boston: Northeastern University Press, 1984), 80-81.

8. Ibid., 99.

9. Ibid., 124.

10. Ibid., 345.

11. Ibid., 337-38.

12. Ibid., 315.

13. Ibid., 25.

14. Ibid., 170.

15. Ibid., 97.

16. Ibid., 39.

17. Ibid., 310.

18. Ibid., 246.

19. Kaja Silverman, "Too Early/Too Late: Subjectivity and the Primal Scene in Henry James," *Novel* 21, nos. 2-3 (1988): 165.

20. Ibid., 149.

[DOUGLAS CRIMP]

Mario Montez, For Shame

From shame to shyness to shining—and, inevitably, back, and back again: the candor and cultural incisiveness of this itinerary seem to make Warhol an exemplary figure for a new project, an urgent one I think, of understanding how the dysphoric affect shame functions as a nexus of production: production, that is, of meaning, of personal presence, of politics, of performative and critical efficacy.[1]

Eve Sedgwick's intuition, indicated here in one of her essays on queer performativity, might be more unfailing than she knew, since at the time she wrote this sentence she would have seen very little of what most bears it out—Andy Warhol's vast film production from the mid-1960s.[2] I want in this essay to consider one instance of Warhol's mobilization of shame as production, and in doing so I want to specify that urgency Sedgwick imagines such a project might entail, an urgency that compels a project of my own.[3] I should qualify "my own" by adding that this project heeds Sedgwick's axiom for antihomophobic inquiry: "People are different from each other." This is, of course, Axiom 1 from the introduction to *Epistemology of the Closet*, but I take it to be much more thoroughly axiomatic for Sedgwick's writing generally and what I've learned most from it: the ethical necessity of developing ever finer tools for encountering, upholding, and valuing others' differences—or better, differences and singularities—nonce-taxonomies, as she wonderfully names such tools. In one of the many deeply moving moments in her work, Sedgwick characterizes this necessity in relation to the "pressure of loss in the AIDS years"—years in which we sadly still live—"that the piercing bouquet of a given friend's particularity be done some justice."[4]

Thanks for inspiration, ideas, facts, and feedback to Callie Angell, Jonathan Flatley, Matthias Haase, Juliane Rebentisch, and Marc Siegel.

"Poor Mario Montez," Warhol writes in *Popism*,

Poor Mario Montez got his feelings hurt for real in his scene [in Chelsea Girls] *where he found two boys in bed together and sang "They Say that Falling in Love Is Wonderful" for them. He was supposed to stay there in the room with them for ten minutes, but the boys on the bed insulted him so badly that he ran out in six and we couldn't persuade him to go back in to finish up. I kept directing him, "You were terrific, Mario. Get back in there—just pretend you forgot something, don't let them steal the scene, it's no good without you," etc., etc. But he just wouldn't go back in. He was too upset.*[5]

Poor Mario. Even though Andy is full of praise for Mario's talents as a natural comedian, nearly every story he tells about him is a tale of woe:

Mario was a very sympathetic person, very benign, although he did get furious at me once. We were watching a scene of his in a movie we called The Fourteen-Year-Old Girl [*also known as* The Shoplifter *and* The Most Beautiful Woman in the World, *the film is now known as* Hedy], *and when he saw that I'd zoomed in and gotten a close-up of his arm with all the thick, dark masculine hair and veins showing, he got very upset and hurt and accused me in a proud Latin way, "I can see you were trying to bring out the worst in me."*[6]

I call my project, provisionally, "Queer before Gay." It entails reclaiming aspects of New York City queer culture of the 1960s as a means of countering the current homogenizing, normalizing, and desexualizing of gay life. In an essay initiating the project, on Warhol's classic 1964 silent film *Blow Job*, I wanted to contest the facile charge of voyeurism so often leveled at Warhol's camera.[7] It seemed to me important to recognize that there can—indeed must—be ways of making queer differences and singularities visible without always entailing the charge of violation, making them visible in ways that we would call *ethical*. In that essay, titled "Face Value" both to suggest that I meant to pay attention to what was on the screen (in this case, as in so many others, a face) and to gesture toward Emmanuel Levinas's ethics, I contrasted the self-absorption of the subject of *Blow Job* to what seemed to me its comic opposite, the utter self-consciousness of Mario Montez as he performs mock fellatio on a banana in *Mario Banana*, a single 100-foot-reel Warhol film of the same year as *Blow Job*.[8] On this subject of Mario's self-consciousness, Warhol writes, "He adored dressing up like a female glamour queen, yet at the same time he was painfully embarrassed about being in drag (he got offended if you used that word—he called it 'going into costume')."[9]

How certain the violation, then, when Mario was subjected by Warhol in *Screen Test #2* to being shamed precisely for his gender illusionism, or perhaps his gender *illusions*. Warhol—with his uncanny ability to conceal dead-on insight in the bland, unknowing remark—writes of that film in a parenthetical aside in *Popism*, "*Screen Test* was Ronnie Tavel off-camera interviewing Mario Montez in drag—and finally getting him to admit he's a man."[10] I call this "insight" because, although it doesn't really describe what takes place in the film at all, it nevertheless gets right to the point of what is most affecting, most troubling, most memorable about it—that is, Mario's "exposure"—a word that Warhol used, in its plural form, as the name of his 1979 book of photographs,[11] and the word Stefan Brecht chose to characterize Warhol's filmic method:

Warhol around 1965 discovered the addictive ingredient in stars. He found that not only are stars among the industrial commodities whose use-value is a product of consumer phantasy, a phantasy that publicity can addict to a given brand of product . . . , but that what addicts the consumer is the quality of stardom itself. . . . He set out to isolate this ingredient, succeeded, proceeded to market it under the brand name "Superstar,"— Warhol's Superstar. Superstar is star of extraordinary purity: there is nothing in it but glamour, a compound of vanity and arrogance, made from masochist self-contempt by a simple process of illusio-inversion. The commercial advantages of this product originated in its area of manufacture: the raw materials, any self-despising person, were cheap, and the industrial process simple: to make the trash just know he or she is a fabulous person envied to adoration. You didn't have to teach them anything. If the customers would take them for a star, they would be a star; if they were a star, the customers would take them for a star; if the customers would take them for a star the customers would be fascinated by them. Exposure would turn the trick. Here again Warhol's true genius for abstraction paid off: he invented a camera-technique that was nothing but exposure.[12]

Ostensibly just what its title says it is, *Screen Test #2* is the second of Warhol's screen test films of early 1965 in which Ronald Tavel, novelist, founding playwright of ridiculous theater,[13] and Warhol's scenarist from 1964 to 1967, interviews a superstar for a new part (*Screen Test #1*, which I haven't seen, stars Philip Fagan, Warhol's lover of the moment, who shared the screen with Mario in *Harlot*, Warhol's first sound film and the first in which Tavel participated).[14] In the case of *Screen Test #2*, Mario Montez is ostensibly being tested for the role of Esmeralda in a remake of *The Hunchback of Notre Dame*. He is shown throughout in a slightly out-of-focus close-up on his face, wearing (and often nervously brushing) a cheap, ratty dark wig. He also wears dangling oversize earrings and long white evening gloves. For a long time at the film's beginning, he ties a silk scarf into his wig, using, it seems, the camera's lens as his mirror. After speaking the credits from off-screen, where he remains throughout the film, Tavel begins to intone, insinuate, cajole, prod, demand: "Now, Miss Montez, just relax . . . you're a lady of leisure, a grande dame. Please describe to me what you feel like right now."

"I feel," Mario begins his reply—and there follows rather too long a pause as he figures out what to say—"I feel like I'm in another world now, a fantasy . . . like a kingdom meant to be ruled by me, like I could give orders and suggest ideas."

Poor Mario. This kingdom is ruled by Ronald Tavel. It is he who gives orders and suggests ideas. At first, though, he indulges Mario's fantasy. He asks about his career to date, allowing Mario to boast of his debut as Delores Flores in Jack Smith's *Flaming Creatures*, his part as the handmaiden in Ron Rice's *Chumlum*, his starring role as the beautiful blonde mermaid in Smith's *Normal Love*, and his small part as the ballet dancer wearing hot-pink tights in the same film. Asked whether the critics were satisfied with his performances, he gives an answer fully worthy of his namesake in Jack Smith's famous paean, "The Perfect Filmic Appositeness of Maria Montez."[15] "It's a funny thing," Mario says with no guile whatsoever, "but no matter what I do, somehow it comes out right, even if it's meant to be a mistake. The most wonderful mistakes that I've done for the screen have turned out the most raging, fabulous performances."

Poor Mario. Now begins his humiliation. Tavel tells Mario to repeat after him, "For many years I have heard your name, but never did it sound so beautiful until I learned that you were a movie producer, Diarrhea." Mario is obliged to say "diarrhea" again and again, with various changes of inflection and emphasis. Then to lip sync as Tavel says it. "Mouth 'diarrhea' exactly as if it tasted of nectar," Tavel instructs. Mario obeys, blissfully unaware of where this game of pleasing a producer named Diarrhea will lead. He will gamely demonstrate his ecstatic response to "playing spin the bottle"—to masturbating, that is, by shoving a bottle up his ass (remember, though, we see only his face).[16] Mario will ferociously mime biting the head off a live chicken as he obeys Tavel's demand that he pretend he is a female geek. He will show how he'll manage, as Esmeralda, to seduce three different characters—captain, priest, Quasimodo—in *The Hunchback of Notre Dame*. He'll scream in terror and dance a gypsy dance with only his shoulders; he'll pout, sneer, and stick out his tongue; he'll cover the lower half of his face with a veil and show that he can be evil or sad using only his eyes. He'll repeat after Tavel, apparently as an exercise in stressing consonants, "I have just strangled my pet panther. Patricia, my pet panther, I have just strangled her, my poor pet. Yet I am not scratched, just a little fatigued."

Now and again Tavel gives encouragement: "That's fine, Miss Montez, thank you very much." "That was delightful, Miss Montez." "Thank you, Miss Montez, that was beautiful, that was perfect, and I think we are going to sign you on immediately for this role."

"How can I ever thank you?" Mario replies, so delighted as to make it obvious he's still hoodwinked. But the encouragement only sets Mario up for his fall, which comes near the end of the film's second thirty-three-minute reel. Mario has just cheerfully described the furniture in his apartment. Then it comes, as if out of nowhere.

"Now, Miss Montez, will you lift up your skirt?"

"What?" Mario asks, with a stunned look. He's clearly caught completely off guard.

"And unzipper your fly."

"That's impossible," Mario protests, shaken.

"Miss Montez," Tavel continues, "you've been in this business long enough to know that the furthering of your career depends on just such a gesture. Taking it out and putting it in, that sums up the movie business. There's nothing to worry about, the camera won't catch a thing. I just want the gesture with your hands. This is very important. Your contract depends on it." Following confused, helpless, silent stalling, Mario finally gives in, and the humiliation continues: "Look down, look down at it," he's commanded.

"I know what it looks like," is his petulant response.

"Zipper your fly half way up and leave it sticking out. That's good, that's good, good boy, good boy." When he refers to Mario this way, Tavel isn't calling attention to Mario's "true" gender; far worse that that, he's treating Mario like a dog. "Take a look at it, take a look at it please. What does it look like?"

Mario half-heartedly fights back, "What's it look like to you?"

"It looks fairly inviting, as good as any," Tavel answers, not with much conviction. "Will you forget about your hair for a moment. Miss Montez, you're not concentrating."

But Mario is defiant: "It's really senseless what you're asking me. I must brush my hair."

Mario finally seems able to put a stop to this couch-casting episode, and we breathe a sigh of relief. But Tavel has still one more ordeal in mind, and it's no doubt all the more painful for Mario because it follows upon the mockery of his cross-dressing. Remember that Warhol writes in *Popism* of Mario's embarrassment about doing drag. He goes on to explain that Mario "used to always say that he knew it was a sin to be in drag—he was Puerto

Rican and a very religious Roman Catholic. The only spiritual comfort he allowed himself was the logic that even though God surely didn't *like* him for going into drag, that still, if He really hated him, He would have struck him dead."[17] So, resisted by Mario in making him expose his sex, the ever-inventive Tavel moves on to a new torment. Showing Mario how to take a supplicating pose, with eyes and hands turned heavenward, he instructs him to say, and repeat, and repeat again, "Oh Lord, I commend this spirit into Thy hands." Poor Mario looks alternately bewildered and terrified, as though he feels he might truly be struck dead for such irreverence. Finally, though, Tavel has little time left to taunt his superstar. As Mario begins to acquiesce in giving the camera the cockteaser look Tavel wants, the film runs out. Just how tense the experience of watching Warhol's films makes us is revealed to us from the release that comes when the reel comes to an end, a moment always entirely unanticipated but occurring with astonishingly perfect timing.

Many of Warhol's films include similar scenes of extraordinary cruelty that are met with disbelief on the part of the performers, most famously when Ondine, as the pope in *Chelsea Girls*, slaps Ronna Page. "It was so for real," Warhol writes, "that I got upset and had to leave the room—but I made sure I left the camera running."[18] The moment that I'd found most discomfiting, up to seeing Mario's shaming in *Screen Test #2*, is when Chuck Wein, who's been taunting Edie Sedgwick through the whole of *Beauty #2*, but who's rarely a match for her sparkling repartee, suddenly hits the raw nerve of her relationship with her father. She looks more stunned than if she'd been literally hit, like Ronna. It isn't merely a look of incredulity, it's one of utter betrayal, a look that both says, *Surely you didn't say that*, and pleads, *How could you possibly say that? How could you so turn our intimacy against me? Would you really do this for the sake of a film? I thought we were just play-acting.*

George Plimpton captures the feel of such moments when he describes *Beauty #2* in Jean Stein's devastating book *Edie*:

I remember [Chuck Wein's] voice—nagging and supercilious and quite grating. . . . A lot of the questions, rather searching and personal, were about her family and her father. On the bed Edie was torn between reacting to the advances of the boy next to her and wanting to respond to these questions and comments put to her by the man in the shadows. Sometimes her head would bend and she would nuzzle the boy or taste him in a sort of distracted way. I remember one of the man's commands to her was to taste "the brown sweat," but then her head would come up, like an animal suddenly alert at the edge of a waterhole, and she'd stare across the bed at her inquisitor in the shadows. I re-

member it as being very dramatic . . . and all the more so because it seemed so real, an actual slice of life, which of course it was.[19]

How might we square these scenes of violation and shaming with what I'm describing as an ethical project of giving visibility—and I want also to say dignity—to a queer world of differences and singularities in the 1960s? What does the viewer's discomfiture at Warhol's techniques of exposure do to the usual processes of spectator identification?

To answer these questions, I need to take a detour through the present, whose sexual politics fuels my interest in this history in the first place.

Following New York's annual gay pride celebrations in 1999, the *New York Times* editorialized:

When police harassed gay patrons of the Stonewall Inn in 1969, the patrons stood their ground and touched off three nights of fierce civil disobedience—prominently featuring men in drag. . . . The building that once housed the Stonewall Inn on Christopher Street has earned a listing in the National Register of Historic Places, becoming the first site in the country to recognize the contributions that gay and lesbian Americans have made to the national culture. This also marks the gay rights movement's evolution from a fringe activity to a well-organized effort with establishment affiliations and substantial political clout.

Noting that the gay pride parade included Mayor Rudolph Giuliani and Fire Commissioner Thomas Von Essen, the *Times* concluded, "Things have come a long way since those stormy summer nights in 1969."[20]

The *Times*'s view marks the extent to which the various myths about Stonewall and the progress of gay rights have now become commonplace and official, even to the point of the newspaper's ritual nod to the prominence of drag queens among the Stonewall rioters. But we might be inclined to skepticism toward this bland narrative of progress through its unremarked report of the mayor's participation in the parade, because not since the days of Stonewall has queer nightlife in New York been so under attack by a city administration. Harassment and padlocking of gay clubs have again become commonplace in New York City. The response to this disjunction between the *New York Times*'s sense of our having come a long way and the experience of many of us in New York has been for queers to organize, for the past several years, during the time of the gay pride celebrations, a counter-event devoted explicitly to shame. Gay Shame's annual zine is called *Swallow Your Pride*.

These may seem like no more than the usual exercises in camp humor aimed at normalizing mainstream gay and lesbian politics. But given the place of shame in queer theory—and in earlier queer culture, if we can take what I've described in Warhol's *Screen Test #2* as in any sense representative of that culture—I think we would do well to take the idea seriously.

What's queer about shame, and why does it get posed against the supposedly shame-eradicating politics of gay pride?

For an answer, I turn to Eve Sedgwick's essay "Queer Performativity: Henry James's *The Art of the Novel*."[21] Schematically, Sedgwick suggests that shame is what makes us queer, both in the sense of having a queer identity and in the sense that queerness is in a volatile relation to identity, destabilizing it even as it makes it. Sedgwick finds in shame the link between "performativity and—performativity" (1993,6), that is, between the two senses of performativity operative in Judith Butler's enormously generative work *Gender Trouble*. Performativity 1: "the notion of performance in the defining instance theatrical," and Performativity 2: that of "speech-act theory and deconstruction," in which we find a "necessarily 'aberrant' relation" between a performative utterance and its meaning (1993, 2). In order to demonstrate this latter, Sedgwick departs from J. L. Austin's paradigmatic instance of the performative in *How to Do Things with Words*, that of the "I do," of "I do take thee to be my lawful wedded wife" (how ironic that this has become the very performative that the official gay and lesbian movement in the United States has expended all its recent energies and resources to be able to utter!). Sedgwick moves from Austin's "I do" to the more "perverse"— the "deformative," she also calls it (1993, 3)—"Shame on you." For which, I want to suggest, "for shame" works just the same, linguistically and performatively, except that, when written, it can also be read the way I'd like it to be read here: as advocating shame. I hope it will become clear as I proceed that favoring shame in the way I intend it is just the opposite of, say, conservative Catholic ideologue Andrew Sullivan's view that contemporary American society lacks sufficient shame. Sullivan's is a conventionally moralistic view of shame's function. Mine, I hope, is an ethico-political one.[22]

Shame, in Sedgwick's view, is equally and simultaneously identity-defining and identity-erasing; in Sedgwick's words, it "mantles the threshold between introversion and extroversion" (1993, 8). Moreover, shame appears to construct the singularity and isolation of one's identity through an affective connection to the shaming of another.

One of the strangest features of shame (but, I would argue, the most theoretically significant) is the way bad treatment of someone else, bad treatment by someone else, someone else's embarrassment, stigma, debility, blame or pain, seemingly having nothing to

do with me, can so readily flood me—assuming that I'm a shame-prone person—with
this sensation whose very suffusiveness seems to delineate my precise, individual out-
lines in the most isolating way imaginable. (1993, 14)

I want to reiterate this passage, since I think it gets to the crux of the matter.
In the act of taking on the shame that is properly someone else's, I simultaneously feel my utter separateness from even that person whose shame it
initially was. I feel alone with my shame, singular in my susceptibility to
being shamed for this stigma that has now become mine and mine alone.
Thus, my shame is taken on in lieu of the other's shame. In taking on the
shame, I do not share in the other's identity. I simply adopt the other's vulnerability to being shamed. In this operation, most important, the other's
difference is preserved; it is not claimed as my own. In taking on or taking
up his or her shame, I am not attempting to vanquish his or her otherness. I
put myself in the place of the other only insofar as I recognize that I too am
prone to shame.

But who is prone to shame? The answer, for Sedgwick, will necessarily be a bit tautological. A shame-prone person is a person who has been
shamed. Sedgwick associates the susceptibility to shame with "the terrifying powerlessness of gender-dissonant or otherwise stigmatized childhood." And therefore, if "queer is a politically potent term . . . that's because, far from being capable of being detached from the childhood scene
of shame, it cleaves to that scene as a near-inexhaustible source of transformational energy" (1993, 4).

In this power of transformation, performativity functions both theatri-
cally and ethically. Just as shame is both productive and corrosive of queer
identity, the switching point between stage fright and stage presence,
between being a wallflower and being a diva, so too is it simultaneously
productive and corrosive of queer revaluations of dignity and worth.

In his book about the banishment of sex from contemporary queer politics, *The Trouble with Normal*, Michael Warner argues that we need to "develop an ethical response to the problem of shame." "The difficult question is not: how do we get rid of our sexual shame?" Warner writes, "The
question, rather, is this: what will we do with our shame? And the usual response is: pin it on someone else."[23]

How does this work, performatively? Sedgwick explains:

The absence of an explicit verb from "Shame on you" records the place in which an I,
in conferring shame, has effaced itself and its own agency. Of course the desire for self-
effacement is the defining trait of—what else?—shame. So the very grammatical trun-
cation of "Shame on you" marks it as a product of a history out of which an I, now

withdrawn, is projecting *shame—toward another I, an I deferred, that has yet and with difficulty to come into being, if at all, in the place of the shamed second person.* (1993, 4)

Saying "Shame on you" or "For shame" casts shame onto another that is both felt to be one's own and, at the same time, disavowed as one's own. But in those already shamed, the shame-prone, the shame is not so easily shed, so simply projected: it manages also to persist as one's own. This can lend it the capacity for articulating collectivites of the shamed. Warner explains,

A relation to others [in queer contexts] begins in an acknowledgment of all that is most abject and least reputable in oneself. Shame is bedrock. Queers can be abusive, insulting, and vile towards one another, but because abjection is understood to be the shared condition they also know how to communicate through such camaraderie a moving and unexpected form of generosity. No one is beneath its reach, not because it prides itself on generosity but because it prides itself on nothing. The rule is: get over yourself. Put a wig on before you judge. And the corollary is that you stand to learn most from the people you think are beneath you. At its best, this ethic cuts against every form of hierarchy you could bring into the room. Queer scenes are the true salons des refusés, *where the most heterogeneous people are brought into great intimacy by their common experience of being despised and rejected in a world of norms that they now recognize as false morality.*[24]

The sad thing about the contemporary politics of gay and lesbian pride is that it works in precisely the opposite way: It calls for a visibility predicated on homogeneity, and on excluding anyone who does not conform to norms that are taken to be the very morality we should be happy to accept as the onus of our so-called maturity. It thus sees shame as conventional indignity rather than the affective substrate necessary to the transformation of one's distinctiveness into a queer kind of dignity. This is why the queer culture of the 1960s, made visible in Warhol's films, is so necessary a reminder of what we need to know now.

So I'll return, in closing, to the shaming of Mario Montez in *Screen Test #2.* As I mentioned before, I wanted, in my earlier essay on *Blow Job*, to contest the cliché of Warhol's filmic vision as voyeuristic. I argued there that formal features in Warhol's films—different formal features in different films, of course—worked to foreclose a knowingness about the people represented in them. Warhol found the means to make the people of his world visible to us without making them objects of our knowledge. The knowledge of a world that his films give us is not a knowledge of the other for the self.

Rather what I see, when, say, I see Mario Montez in *Screen Test #2*, is a performer in the moment of being exposed such that he becomes, as Warhol said, "so for real." But unlike Warhol we don't leave the room (nor, for that matter, I'd bet, did Warhol). Rather we remain there with our disquiet—which is, after all, what? It is our encounter, on the one hand, with the absolute difference of another, his or her "so-for-realness," and, on the other hand, with the other's shame, both the shame that extracts his or her "so-for-realness" from the already for-real performativity of Warhol's performers, and the shame that we accept as also ours, but curiously also ours alone. I am thus not "like" Mario, but the distinctiveness that is revealed in Mario invades me—"floods me," to use Sedgwick's word—and my own distinctiveness is revealed simultaneously. I, too, feel exposed.

Ronald Tavel, the brilliant, ridiculous scenarist—brilliant, indeed, at ridicule[25]—seemed to provide just exactly what Warhol wanted. "I enjoyed working with him," Warhol wrote, "because he understood instantly when I'd say things like, 'I want it simple and plastic and white.' Not everyone can think in an abstract way, but Ronnie could."[26]

Tavel repays Warhol's compliment:

This operation-theatre he brings us to and in which we at first resentfully feel ourselves to be the patient, suddenly actualizes as the real and traditional theatre: we are audience as always, suddenly alive and watching, horrified after amused, scholarly after ennuied. And alarmed. The "destructive" artist proves again the prophet and makes of his life a stunning cry, withal keeping his mask-distance of laughter and contempt. He emerges gentle from a warehouse of Brillo boxes, having stated his bleak vision, as social an artist as any 30s fiend could ask for.[27]

Tavel continues in the same essay, "The Banana Diary: The Story of Andy Warhol's 'Harlot,'"

The New American Cinema has taken the mask off rather than putting it on. . . . The souls of the beings we view are enlarged before us, even to the point of snapping out of character and blinking into the camera; an instant more and they would be waving at us. That these souls are wretched, which means our souls are wretched, has brought the accusation of brutality and sadism against the movement. Yet who among us, in his own life, escapes the complex of sado-masochistic chaos or finds his way about in a commodiousness less than brutal?[28]

It should be clear from this, I believe, that Tavel's purpose in *Screen Test #2* is to solicit from Mario exactly what we see: Mario's irresistible, resplendent vulnerability. We see his soul enlarged before us most conspicuously at those moments when Mario is overcome with shame, and when we become aware—painfully—of his shame as what Sedgwick calls a blazon. That blazon, which we share, might well proclaim a new slogan of queer politics: For Shame!

Notes

This was originally published in *Regarding Sedgwick: Essays on Queer Culture and Critical Theory*, ed. Stephen M. Barber and David L. Clark (Routledge, 2002).

1. Eve Kosofsky Sedgwick, "Queer Performativity, Warhol's Shyness, Warhol's Whiteness," in *Pop Out: Queer Warhol*, ed. Jennifer Doyle et al. (Durham: Duke University Press, 1996), 135.

2. Warhol withdrew his films from circulation in the beginning of the 1970s. After his agreement in 1982 to allow the Whitney Museum of American Art to research and present the films, the museum began showing them in installments, the first in 1988, the second in 1994. See *The Films of Andy Warhol: An Introduction* (New York: Whitney Museum of American Art, 1988), and Callie Angell, *The Films of Andy Warhol: Part II* (New York: Whitney Museum of American Art, 1994). *Screen Test #2*, the film discussed here, was restored in 1995 and screened in 1998.

3. The stakes of such a project comprise a portion of my argument in "Getting the Warhol We Deserve," *Social Text* 59 (Summer 1999): 49–66.

4. Eve Kosofsky Sedgwick, *Epistemology of the Closet* (Berkeley: University of California Press, 1990), 23.

5. Andy Warhol and Pat Hackett, *Popism: The Warhol Sixties* (New York: Harcourt Brace, 1980), 181.

6. Ibid, 91. Hedy Lamarr was notoriously litigious; thus, since Warhol's film, with a script by Ronald Tavel, was inspired by a real-life incident in 1966 in which Lamarr was charged with shoplifting (charges of which she was later cleared), the title was variously obfuscated. Lamarr was arrested at least twice more for shoplifting.

7. My work on Warhol's films owes an enormous debt to the careful work and intellectual generosity of Callie Angell, curator of the Warhol Film Project.

8. Douglas Crimp, "Face Value," in *About Face: Andy Warhol Portraits*, ed. Nicholas Baume (Hartford: Wadsworth Atheneum; Pittsburgh: Andy Warhol Muesum, 1990), 110-25.

9. Warhol and Hackett, 91.

10. Ibid., 124.

11. Andy Warhol, *Andy Warhol's Exposures* (New York: Andy Warhol Books/Grosset & Dunlap, 1979).

12. Stefan Brecht, *Queer Theater* (New York: Methuen, 1986), 113-14.

13. "In 1965, Tavel was the Warhol dramatist in residence. He did the scenarios for what were, except for *Harlot* and *Drunk*, Warhol's first sound movies: *Screen Test Number One, Screen Test Number Two, Life of Juanita Castro, Vinyl, Suicide, Horse, Bitch, Kitchen*. His Warhol scripts, directed by John Vaccaro 1965-7, also became the first plays of the Playhouse of the Ridiculous" (Brecht, 107; see also the footnote on p. 29).

14. There was no scenario for *Harlot*. The soundtrack consists of an off-screen conversation improvised on the spot by Tavel, Billy Name, and Harry Fainlight. The conversation

is reproduced in Ronald Tavel, "The Banana Diary: The Story of Andy Warhol's 'Harlot,'" in *Andy Warhol: Film Factory*, ed. Michael O'Pray (London: BFI, 1989), 86–92.

15. See J. Hoberman and Edward Leffingwell, eds., *Wait for Me at the Bottom of the Pool: The Writings of Jack Smith* (New York: Serpent's Tail, High Risk Books, 1977), 25–35. Originally published in *Film Culture* 27 (Winter 1962–63).

16. This moment of *Screen Test #2* suggests that the tour-de-force scene of Paul Morrissey's *Trash*—Holly Woodlawn's Coke-bottle masturbation scene—was a reused Tavel idea. For all that Morrissey professed to find Warhol's early films self-indulgent, dull, and pretentious, he nevertheless made much use of them for his own film making.

17. Warhol and Hackett, 91.

18. Ibid., 181. Warhol writes that "Ondine slapped 'Pepper,'" remembering Angelina "Pepper" Davis in the place of Ronna Page.

19. Jean Stein, ed., with George Pilmpton, *Edie: American Girl* (New York: Grove Press, 1994), 242.

20. "Stonewall, Then and Now," *New York Times*, 29 June 1999.

21. Eve Kosofsky Sedgwick, "Queer Performativity: Henry James's *The Art of the Novel*," *GLQ* 1, no. 1 (1993): 1–16. Hereafter page numbers cited in text.

22. "Readers who have paid attention to the recent, meteoric rise of shame to its present housewife-megastar status in the firmament of self-help and popular psychology . . . may be feeling a bit uneasy at this point. So, for that matter, may those used to reading about shame in the neo-conservative framework that treasures shame along with guilt as, precisely, an adjunct of repression and an enforcer of proper behavior. In the ways that I want to be thinking about shame, the widespread moral valuation of this powerful affect as *good* or *bad*, *to be mandated* or *to be excised*, according to how one plots it along a notional axis of prohibition/permission/requirement, seems distinctly beside the point" (Sedgwick, "Queer Performativity: Henry James's *The Art of the Novel*," 6).

23. Michael Warner, *The Trouble with Normal: Sex, Politics, and the Ethics of Queer Life* (New York: Free Press, 1999), 3.

24. Ibid., 35–36.

25. "The universal humiliation of all characters in this [ridiculous, queer] theatre gives it a repulsive air of viciousness, even cruelty, because it is absolute: the victims are accorded no basic dignity, no saving graces. We are not reassured of worthy or innocent motives of underlying rational seriousness. The characters are not just clownish or foolish but clowns and fools. They are not exactly funny. Isolated clown scenes, jokes and parodies that at first seem pure fun trouble us by their implications of profound ridiculousness. Some important, often protracted, actions are specifically and formally cruel humiliations: Bajazeth's enslavement in [*When*] *Queens* [*Collide*]/*Conquest* [*of the Universe*], the entire action of *Screen Test*, Lady Godiva's undressing (according to [John] Vacarro), in *Lady Godiva*, Victor's re-education in *Vinyl*. These humiliations bring this close to a theatre of the terrible. It takes a strong stomach to participate in their fun" (Brecht, 36). *Screen Test* and *Vinyl* are both films by Warhol whose scenarios by Tavel became plays performed by the Playhouse of the Ridiculous.

26. Warhol and Hackett, 91.

27. Tavel, 77–78.

28. Ibid., 85.

[TARO NETTLETON]

White-on-White

THE OVERBEARING WHITENESS
OF WARHOL BEING

Vacant, vacuous Hollywood was everything I ever wanted to mold my life into. Plastic. White-on-white.

Andy Warhol and Pat Hackett, *Popism*, 1980

Elvis was a hero to most,
But he never meant shit to me 'cause he was straight up racist,
The sucker was simple and plain,
Motherfuck him and John Wayne.

Public Enemy, "Fight the Power," 1989

In his essay "Warhol Gives Good Face: Publicity and the Politics of Prosopopoeia," Jonathan Flatley persuasively argues that the use of a Pop aesthetic allowed Andy Warhol to gain access to the public sphere and "bring himself and his friends inside it as active participants."[1] For Flatley, Warhol's Factory—which might be understood as Warhol's counter-Hollywood—and its products functioned as "queer versions of what Nancy Fraser has called *subaltern counterpublics*."[2] As such, the Factory as well as the Pop aesthetic allowed "outsiders" like Warhol and others from his milieu to "acquire a public persona . . . [and] participate in 'utopias of self-abstraction' that enable us to feel as if we have transcended our particularity."[3] However, it is

I am grateful for the feedback I received while working on this article, especially from Douglas Crimp and Simon Leung. Thanks also to Robert Summers for allowing me to deliver an earlier version of this piece at the conference "Queer[ing] Warhol: Andy Warhol's (Self-)Portraits," held at the California Musuem of Photography, University of California, Riverside. January 2002.

worthwhile to complicate our understanding of Warhol's counterpublic by recognizing that in terms of chromatic makeup, Andy got what he wanted. Just like the Hollywood he adored, his own public sphere pretty much retained a white-on-white cast. Using Flatley's essay as a starting point, I hope to show that the access to self-abstraction was unevenly distributed, even within Warhol's counterpublic.

An interview with Mario Montez in the 1968 Warhol issue of *Film Culture* suggests that some members of the Factory were not allowed to transcend their embodied particularities at all. In recounting an incident that occurred during the shooting of one of Warhol's films in which he starred, Montez expresses dissatisfaction with Warhol and claims that he sees through Warhol's antics: "I think he's trying to bring out the worst in me—like in the 14 YEAR OLD GIRL—I was holding a cigarette in a holder and he zoomed in on my arm so that you could see my huge veins."[4] What Montez sees in Warhol is certainly not a wish to facilitate Montez's self-abstraction, but rather an underhanded attempt to undermine any such attempt. Montez's suspicion that Warhol would much rather focus in on his "humiliating particularities" than his performance of self-abstraction is confirmed by Warhol's own account: "When he saw that I'd zoomed in and gotten a close-up of his arm with all the thick, dark masculine hairs and veins showing, he got very upset and hurt and accused me in a proud Latin way, 'I can see you were trying to bring out the worst in me.'"[5] Repeating Montez's account almost word for word, Warhol makes explicit that it was Montez's masculinity that he zoomed in on and that Montez's response to this incident was an expression of his Latinness.

How do we reconcile such an anecdote with Warhol's purported intentions to project himself and his stars into publicity through a transcendence of particularities? If "white-on-white" was all Warhol ever wanted, it might very well be that those who were not white were marginalized even within Warhol's counterpublic space. Warhol was never one to indicate any explicit political stance, and the politics of race were certainly no exception. Still, given the fact that most of his work involved photographing, rephotographing, filming, and silkscreening white people's faces, it seems politically counterproductive and perhaps even disingenuous to write about the heterogeneity of Warhol's milieu, corpus, or both without qualifying this heterogeneity on the basis of color.

More important, not to comment on the "whiteness" that pervades Warhol's works is to reproduce uncritically the ideological structure of our white, hegemonic society, which maintains implicitly and often explicitly

Figure 1. Andy Warhol, *Ladies and Gentlemen*, 1975. One from a portfolio of ten screen-prints on Arches Paper 43 ³/₄ × 28 ¹/₂ in. (111.1 ×72.4 cm.). Courtesy of Andy Warhol Foundation, Inc./Art Resource, New York. © 2003 Andy Warhol Foundation for the Visual Arts/ARS, New York.

that whiteness is a colorless ground that neither warrants nor requires de-scriptors. As Richard Dyer writes in *White*, "The idea of whiteness as neu-trality already suggests its usefulness for designating a social group that is to be taken for the human ordinary."[6] While the body of Warhol's work is multivalent in both medium and subject and consequently refuses any easy, overarching categorization, it is crucial that we recognize that the work is also defined through certain exclusions. I do not mean to say that such exclusions are absolute. Certainly, the whiteness of Warhol's work has its exceptions, such as Montez's brilliant screen persona or the acerbic wit of Dorothy Dean. Nevertheless, despite a small minority presence within Warhol's world, there is a hierarchy of lightness, and it is at the top of this hierarchy of melanin deficiency that we find Andy himself.

Andy Warhol, *Silver Screen*
Can't tell them apart at all.

David Bowie, "Andy Warhol," 1971

Quoting Michael Warner, Flatley points out that becoming public requires an effacement of embodied particularities and that this abstraction is easier for some—specifically, white, heterosexual males—than it is for others.[7] If that is the case, then, in being both male and white, Warhol had something in common with the image of the publicized body despite his sexuality. The paleness of Warhol's complexion and the attention he paid to his dermatological conditions are frequently noted in the literature on him. In *The Philosophy of Andy Warhol*, Warhol describes his skin-care routine to "B," explaining that the "flesh-colored acne-pimple medication that doesn't resemble any human flesh I've ever seen . . . comes pretty close to mine."[8] Warhol clearly has a sophisticated understanding of the ways in which whiteness functions in our culture. While realizing that the whiteness of the acne medication—one prescribed form of normativity—is abstract and for this very reason cannot be embodied, Warhol suffered a unique predicament by actually bearing this abstract whiteness in the flesh. With respect to color, the supposedly inherent gap between the public, abstract images of the self and the embodied private self simply did not exist for Warhol.

The extreme color of his complexion—for which Warhol was called "pasty-white," "albino," and all shades in between—was one that the Hollywood cinema painstakingly applied to the faces of its stars. Dyer explains the extreme procedures by means of which Hollywood created glowing white faces: "The solution [to the face appearing "black"] . . . was a 'dreadful white make-up' worn under carbon arc lights so hot that they made the makeup run, involving endless retouchings."[9] Even the seemingly whitest of actresses were evidently not white enough:

Marlene Dietrich recounted that Josef von Sternberg had worked out a way to deal with her "broad Slavic nose": a line of silver make-up down her nose and a tiny spotlight placed directly above it. This was a technique used with other women stars who had the same "problem": Claudette Colbert, Ginger Rogers, Hedy Lamarr, Barbara Stanwyck and many others.[10]

In 1962, Warhol reproduced these cinematic beauties in several of his *Female Movie Star Composites*. Their unfinished appearance suggests that they were meant to serve as studies or sketches for larger projects, rather than to function as individual pieces in themselves. But as sketches, they tell us something about Warhol's foundational understanding of the way these faces come to be. To make the composites, he crudely taped together various facial elements whose sources are identified only by their initials. One example edits together the hair and forehead of G. G. (Greta Garbo), the eyes of J. C. (Joan Crawford), the nose of M. D. (Marlene Dietrich), and lips and chin of S. L. (Sophia Loren).

That the various parts of the face can be identified by the mere initials of their respective owners elucidates the fact that these faces are at once instantly recognizable and entirely interchangeable. Despite the crude technology involved in their creation, seen within the context of Warhol's works, these composites reveal his unique understanding of fame and the public face of the star. The technique used in these composites—and the word itself—recalls police tactics of giving face to a suspect at large, suggesting Warhol's desire to capture the magic of fame that threatened to escape his grasp. The composites also reveal a desire to come up with a facial type. Given the quasi-forensic analysis performed in them, it's unlikely that the whiteness of all these faces would have eluded Warhol. What is likely, however, is that he understood whiteness to be a crucial part of their creation. In regard to the whiteness of the women who make up these composites, Warhol would probably have agreed with the Japanese novelist Tanizaki Junichiro, who once wrote: "The whiteness of the white woman . . . perhaps it is only a mischievous trick of light and shadow, a thing of the moment only. But even so, it is enough. We can ask for nothing more."[11]

In other words, Warhol recgonized the complexity of the function whiteness served within the public sphere and particularly in the utopian world of Hollywood cinema, as both a requirement for inclusion and an impossible ideal. By complexity, I mean to underscore that Warhol knew this kind of whiteness to be an effect, "a trick of light and shadow," rather than a biological fact. Furthermore, it would have been painfully clear to Warhol—whose own particular whiteness made him an outcast—that the whiteness idealized in the public sphere was meant to be abstract and not embodied. Thus he would have also known that the similarity of his com-

Figure 2. Andy Warhol, *Female Movie Star Composite*, ca. 1962, detail. Mechanical ink, photographs, and tape on paper. Dimensions unknown. Courtesy of the Andy Warhol Museum, Pittsburgh, PA, a museum of the Carnegie Institute. © 2003 Andy Warhol Foundation for the Visual Arts/ARS, New York.

plexion with that of the images he saw on the screen would not be sufficient for, if indeed it were not an outright deterrent to, his acceptance into the public sphere. For starters, his name, Andrew Warhola, would give away, to use Michael Warner's phrase, his "humiliating particularity"[12] by signifying an ethnic specificity. As Wayne Koestenbaum remarks in a recent biography, Warhol "dropped the ultimate *a* in his last name. The extra *a* was clunky, ethnic."[13] Despite nicely rhyming with Coca-Cola, the name of the product of which he was so fond, Andrew Warhola sounded too particular; it didn't have the neutrality of a name that could be broadly commercialized and disseminated. It was in part by dropping the graphically awkward little *a* that Warhol transfigured himself into an iconic and symmetrical capital A and thereby became more like the household names that were so widely admired as to not need spelling out—like S. L., M. D., G. G., or J. C.

Capital A, as Warhol designated himself in his *The Philosophy of Andy*

Warhol (From A to B and Back Again), is also *alpha*. "Alpha," as defined in the *Oxford English Dictionary*, is the "first or foremost in a series of related items," but also "the brightest star in a constellation." It was the security of this knowledge—that Warhol would always be the brightest star in the constellation of the Factory—that enabled him to withdraw the traditional forms of labor associated with authorship and simultaneously have his name resonate as the executive producer of all things bearing the Warhol stamp. As is well known, Warhol repeatedly declared "that his assistants did most of the work,"[14] and famously insisted in a 1967 interview with Gretchen Berg that "if you want to know all about Andy Warhol, just look at the surface: of my paintings and films and me, and there I am. There's nothing behind it."[15] Curiously, in spite of the separate presence of the "Warhol" that's being interviewed and the surface of the "Warhols" that the former tells Berg to go see, Warhol draws an impossible equation between "my paintings and films and me." The Warhol that is speaking is not so much denying his authorial function as expanding its range, so that it is no longer confined to the limits of his body. Depth or no depth, assistant or no assistants, it all comes to be contained under the Warhol umbrella. The seamless continuity between the surfaces of his body and his images, the products of his self-abstraction, recalls and indeed reproduces the fact of the "republican notion of virtue . . . designed exactly to avoid any rupture of self-difference between ordinary life and publicity. The republican was to be same as citizen and as man. . . ."[16] Warhol's reluctance to talk about his work and his professed disinterestedness and indifference are then as much a mastering of the "rhetorics of disincorporation"[17] as they are an act of withdrawal. His radical openness to the Factory milieu was premised on the privilege of being a universal, unmarked omnipresence: a silver screen within the counterpublic sphere of the silver-painted Factory.

If I'm to be your camera, then who will be your face?

R.E.M., "Camera," 1984

In creating portraits at the Factory, both silkscreened and filmed, Warhol served as the medium through which others took on a recognizable identity and became, in many cases, his superstars. Looking at the material processes that Warhol employed in giving his sitters a face, one might conclude that the operation not only "reproduced the star effect"[18] but involved a portioning off of Warhol's "magical" celebrity status—as well as his excessive pallor.

Warhol's silkscreen portraits were created through multiple stages of mediation. In creating or appropriating photographic images and reshooting them onto a silkscreen, Warhol increased their contrast. For the mostly white sitters who were treated to this process, an increase in contrast necessarily meant a noticeable increase in whiteness. If we look at the 1978 portrait of Liza Minelli and the 1980 portrait of Debbie Harry, for example, we see that the dramatic effect produced in these silkscreen portraits might be more accurately described as an obliteration of features than as an increase in contrast. Only the hairstyles distinguish the faces. In addition to the eyes and lips, which are the only features left to speak of, the face is marked by an overwhelming whiteness. "Giving face" here involves not only an efface-ment of particularities but a logic that explicitly equates such effacement with being made over and masked in whiteface. I agree with Flatley's as-sessment that in creating such celebrity portraits, Warhol "drew attention to the constructed, anonymous identity of all the stars"[19] and showed that celebrity is only an endless proliferation of sameness. However, I do not be-lieve—contrary to Simon Watney's reading of "the Warhol effect"—that the constructedness of celebrity suggests that *anyone* can be famous.[20]

In building an argument against this notion that, in Warhol's hands, anyone could become identical to the stars, we might start with his *Ladies and Gentlemen* portfolio. The treatment of the face in this 1975 portfolio of ten screenprinted portraits of African American drag queens contrasts sharply with the celebrity faces discussed above. If "giving face" through portraiture implies the recognizability of an individual, then this portfo-lio was doomed from the start, for the ladies and gentlemen pictured here have no proper names. Insofar as attaining fame and face necessarily in-volves getting, having, or making a name for oneself, these sitters will never be stars. Hence their anonymity is of an entirely different order than "the anonymous identity of all the stars." These ladies and gentlemen fail to be-come the *anybodies* who represent the abstract notion of celebrity. Instead, in the absence of specific names, they remain *nobodies*.

Beyond their lack of names, the most striking feature of the faces in these prints is their color. The fullness of nonwhite color in these prints alone offers a striking contrast to the celebrity portraits, a function that might initially be presumed to reflect the tonal difference of the sitters' skin. However, at least in one case, the colors are used to reconstruct the sit-ter in blackface. While this may seem to make sense as a counterpart to the mask of whiteface, we should recall that the whiteness of the whiteface in the celebrity portraits does not call attention to itself. Instead, it functions ideologically as unmarkedness. Given the historical precedent and political implication of blackface in U.S. popular culture, its reproduction in *Ladies and Gentlemen* is difficult to ignore, despite Warhol's failure to comment upon or to call attention to it. Furthermore, unlike the celebrity portraits, the colors in this series function as interference. Where in most Warhol portraits colors are used to differentiate the face from ground and to effectively "pop" the face into relief, in *Ladies and Gentlemen* the colors bleed across lines that distinguish face and ground, leaving the faces undifferentiated and, in some cases, nearly unidentifiable.

Moreover, the colors in *Ladies and Gentlemen* are shaped by roughly torn pieces of paper. While the use of abstractly shaped and vibrant colors was a feature of many of Warhol's later portraits, such as those of Rudolf Nureyev from the same year, the violence suggested by the torn pieces of paper is, as far as I know, unique to this series. Since the subject matter of the series is also unique within Warhol's works, one cannot help but draw a correlation between the subjects portrayed and the treatment they have received. In Warhol's hands, these African American faces are torn up and fail to cohere as legible faces. Such a consideration of the *Ladies and Gentlemen* portfolio suggests that access to an idealized abstraction was distributed asymmetrically, even within Warhol's counterpublic sphere. It is as if the relative malleability of or freedom from embodied particulars comes to a grinding halt once the register is shifted from gender and sexuality to race. Once racial difference becomes the subject, otherwise fluid categories coalesce in biological determination.

Perhaps Dorothy Dean, an African American woman who, according to Koestenbaum, was a "brilliant, Harvard-educated art historian and editor, and the only black woman to be an important part of Warhol's circle,"[21] understood all too well that whiteness was an integral part of becoming a Warhol superstar. Despite having organized the funding for and starring in *My Hustler* and appearing in *Afternoon, Space, Restaurant*, and *Prison*, Dean rarely figures in Factory photographs or in Warhol's written accounts of the period. In fact, in Jonas Mekas's 1970 Warhol filmography, Dean is credited only for her appearance in *My Hustler*.[22] According to the chapter-long and rather negative biography of Dean in Hilton Als's book *Women* and the three-page account in Koestenbaum's Warhol biography, she would have found it humiliating to be "unironically identified" as black.[23] Dean was also fired from the magazine *Essence* for suggesting that it feature Warhol in blackface on a cover. All this, together with the fact that she coined the nickname "Drella"[24]—a hybrid of Dracula and Cinderella—for Warhol, suggests an acute awareness on Dean's part of the significance of his paleness and most likely the paleness of almost everyone else around her at the Factory.

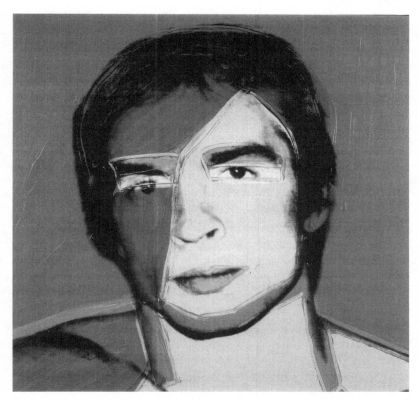

Figure 3. Andy Warhol, *Rudolf Nureyev*, 1975. Synthetic polymer paint and silkscreen ink on canvas. 40 × 40 in. (101.6 × 101.6 cm.). Courtesy of the Rudolf Nureyev Foundation and Andy Warhol Foundation, Inc./Art Resource, N.Y. © 2003 Andy Warhol Foundation for the Visual Arts/ARS, New York.

Als and Koestenbaum both remark that Dean was "unphotogenic," and Koestenbaum uses her supposed unphotogenic quality to undermine the very frame in which he introduces her when he writes that she was "another Factory player in the mid-1960s who evaded the camera's torture—if only because the camera ignored her."[25] Although the agency of the evasion slips from Dean to the camera or Warhol in the latter part of this sentence, I want to suggest a different reading. If Dean was as conscious of the effects of race within the Factory as the few facts above would seem to suggest, then she may have chosen to remain in the shadows as she did in *My Hustler*. Dean could very well have realized that as a black woman, being visually represented in the Factory would entail an "unironic" racial identification.

I believe that Warhol had a similar understanding too, for in *Popism* he includes an anecdote about a ball hosted by Truman Capote that pithily addresses the same issues I am suggesting that Dean contended with at the Factory. It is crucial to keep in mind, however, that recognition and understanding are quite different from engagement or action. Warhol writes: "I decided to grow along the sidelines, like a good wallflower, and as I was standing there, I heard a society lady remark, 'He's such a good dancer,' as she watched Ralph Ellison, the Negro author of *The Invisible Man* [sic]."²⁶ What I understand Warhol to be saying here is that the figure who is refused access to the public sphere is the same figure who must remain highly visible in an "unironic" identification. If this is the case, then Dean's self-(non) presentation can be read as a tactic of survival, rather than the victimization that Als suggests.²⁷

Dorothy Dean's occupation of the shadows within the brilliance of the Factory sheds significant light on the limits of abstraction allowed within Warhol's counterpublic sphere. Just as Pop offered Warhol an alternative relationship to mass culture, the figure of Dean allows us another way of looking at the myth of the Factory. Despite Warhol's understanding of the complex and problematic function of whiteness in the process of becoming public, the chromatic consistency of his portraits' subjects suggests a failure to critically engage such issues. In the face of such failure, we need to insist, *pace* Warhol, that if we are truly to reconfigure the public sphere in a meaningful way, we *have* to ask for something more than just white-on-white.

Notes

This article originally appeared in *Art Journal*, vol. 62 (2003): 14-23.

1. Jonathan Flatley, "Warhol Gives Good Face: Publicity and the Politics of Prosopopoeia," in *Pop Out: Queer Warhol*, ed. Jennifer Doyle, Jonathan Flatley, and José Esteban Muñoz (Durham, NC: Duke University Press, 1996), 102.

2. Ibid., 104.

3. Ibid., 104.

4. Gary McColgen, "The Superstar: An Interview with Mario Montez," *Film Culture* 45 (1968): 19.

5. Andy Warhol and Pat Hackett, *Popism* (San Diego: Harvest, 1980), 91.

6. Richard Dyer, *White* (New York: Routledge, 1997), 47.

7. Flatley, 104. Michael Warner, "The Mass Public and the Mass Subject," in *The Phantom Public Sphere*, ed. Bruce Robbins (Minneapolis: University of Minnesota Press, 1993), 239.

8. Andy Warhol, *The Philosophy of Andy Warhol (From A to B and Back Again)* (San Diego: Harvest, 1977), 9.

9. Dyer, 91.

10. Ibid., 42–43.

11. Tanizaki Junichiro, *In Praise of Shadows*, trans. Thomas J. Harper and Edward G. Seidensticker (New Haven, CT: Leete's Island, 1977), 33.

12. Warner, 239.

13. Wayne Koestenbaum, *Andy Warhol* (New York: Viking, 2001), 17.

14. Ralph Rugoff, "Albino Humor," in *Who Is Andy Warhol?* ed. Colin MacCabe (London: British Film Institute, 1977).

15. Gretchen Berg, "Nothing to Lose: An Interview with Andy Warhol," in *Andy Warhol Film Factory*, ed. Michael O'Pray (London: British Film Institute, 1989), 56.

16. Warner, 378.

17. Ibid., 382.

18. Flatley, 109.

19. Ibid., 109.

20. Simon Watney, "The Warhol Effect," in *The Work of Andy Warhol*, ed. Gary Garrels (Seattle, WA: Bay Press, 1989), 119.

21. Koestenbaum, 104–5.

22. Jonas Mekas, "The Filmography of Andy Warhol," in John Coplans, *Andy Warhol* (Greenwich, CT: New York Graphic Society, 1970), 146–56.

23. Koestenbaum, 105.

24. Ibid., 105.

25. Ibid., 104.

26. Warhol and Hackett, 196.

27. Hilton Als, *The Women* (New York: Farrar, Straus, Giroux, 1996), 67–117.

[RITA GONZALEZ]

Boricua Gazing

AN INTERVIEW WITH FRANCES NEGRÓN-MUNTANER

Born into a family of academics in San Juan, Puerto Rico, Frances Negrón-Muntaner is a filmmaker, writer, and critic whose work ranges from experimentally in-fused documentaries to journalistically enhanced academic writings. Negrón-Muntaner's cinematic and textual explorations map the contours of the Puerto Rican diaspora, from Jennifer López's butt ("Jennifer's Butt," 1997) to the Janus face of what she terms "ethnonational shame" and its counterpart, pride (Boricua Pop: Puerto Ricans and the Latinization of American Culture, 2004). *Among the films she has produced are* AIDS in the Barrio: Eso no me pasa a mí *(with Peter Biella, 1989),* Brincando el charco: Portrait of a Puerto Rican *(1994),* Puerto Rican ID *(1995),* Homeless Diaries *(1996), and* Regarding Vieques *(2008).*

Rita Gonzalez (RG): You're a filmmaker and academic scholar, a screen-writer, poet, and journalist, and you also cross all sorts of disciplinary lines as well. How do you negotiate what might be seen as the "discontinuity" of all your "boundary crossings," and how does this affect your filmmaking?

Frances Negrón-Muntaner (FNM): It is often the case that I approach a question across disciplinary boundaries. This discontinuity is a source of both creativity and despair. But I am comforted by the thought that the ultimate benefits of this method will become more evident in time and that, increasingly, I am not alone. These in-between spaces are shared by many other people (artists or not), those of us living on the edge between the "native"

An earlier version of this interview appeared in *Signs: Journal of Women in Culture and Society* 30, no. 1 (Autumn 2004): 1345–60; it has been abbreviated, expanded, and revised for the present volume.

neighborhoods we grew up in and the metropolitan cities of our adulthood, the carefully drawn academic disciplines that we learned in school and the chaos of contemporary experience, our grand dreams and the multiple limitations that shape our lives.

At another level, my textual practices appear as discontinuous in relation to established disciplines because I work out similar questions in different media. For instance, my interest in spectacle, the complex space of seeing and being seen that has been part of my last two books, *Boricua Pop* (2004) and *None of the Above* (2007), is also an important element of one of my new films, *Regarding Vieques* (2008). This film is a chronicle of the Vieques anti-Navy movement, partly as a televisual political phenomenon and partly as a battle of fictions over definitions of nationhood, national security, and citizenship. So, ultimately, the truth is fairly unglamorous: I can't help it.

RG: What is the argument of your book *Boricua Pop: Puerto Ricans and the Latinization of American Culture?*

FNM: *Boricua Pop* aims to understand why and to what effects attempts to socially value ourselves as Puerto Rican ethnonational subjects have so frequently been staged through cultural performances to offset shame. In bringing up shame as a matter of public concern, I am not, of course, arguing that every instance of exchange between *boricuas* can be primarily explained by analyzing shame. I am arguing that modern Puerto Rican ethnic and national *identity* has been historically staged by tropes of shame and displays of pride—not unlike Vieques.

RG: Ethnonational shame and pride derive from conditions of visibility and spectacle. How does the situation of "looking and being looked at"[1] that you consider in relation to *boricua* gazing differ from the binary that instigated feminist film theory?

FNM: Feminist film theory has tended to underscore the vulnerability of those who are being looked at in relation to those who are doing the looking. To the extent that Puerto Ricans are often represented as "effeminate" colonial subjects in the public sphere when we are visible, there are points of contact between my project and this feminist theorization. Yet one of my problems with feminist theory is that I can't see gender that straight. When one pays attention to multiplicity, the place of gender is relativized. Gender, class, and race can never be separated when theorizing "any" bodies, much less ethnic ones. In this sense, to suggest, as Judith Halberstam says, that "shame is . . . a gendered form of sexual abjection"[2] that women necessarily *work through* in order to become what they are ignores that shame is also linked to processes of racialization. As Norma Alarcón once observed, women do not become women only in relationship to men but also in relationship to other women.

So, in *Boricua Pop*, I experimented with several ways of addressing the simultaneity of a gendered, racialized, and class-specific location in concepts such as "racially engendered." I also repeatedly underscored how, for instance, Madonna is a different "woman" when consuming the ethnic other on the U.S. stage than when she is upholding *boricua* queerness on a Bayamón one. Ultimately, the whole truth is that I am a bad feminist subject.

RG: So, as a "bad feminist subject," perhaps you could map out your methodological concerns. How are you taking up cultural studies, postcolonial theory, queer and feminist studies in *Boricua Pop*?

FNM: I am more drawn to the *gesture* of queer critique than of feminist theory, because queer theory is less regimented as a theoretical practice, more unstable as a discipline, and by definition difficult to normalize. I am also not afraid to slip conceptually, to be found theoretically lacking, to let language seduce me into inconsistency or the "wrong" political posture. Theory for me is not a place to be whole, perfect, or flawless. On the contrary, it is a space to show my lacking selves—all of them—and connect with others like me.

Regarding specific bodies of theory, I am closest to cultural studies precisely because in practice it is sometimes even antidisciplinary. I have productive conflicts with postcolonial theory, beginning with its designation. In most of my work, for instance, I actually examine a colony that, if included in much of postcolonial analysis, would pose critical theoretical challenges to it. Not only is colonialism not in the past, temporally "post," but there are also peoples that have repeatedly chosen to remain a colony over other formal decolonizing options, complicating the matter politically. In addition, I think that it is counterproductive to "apply" theory that is produced in relation to a different context, say, India, as "evidence" in another context, such as Puerto Rico. Conceptual borrowing and comparative study are extremely conducive to sharpening analysis, but we can't just "apply" them.

RG: Shame, as you are using it, attends to multiplicities in spectacle, as well as to not seeing gender "straight." With regard to the latter, how have you determined what is useful in the varied queer discourses on shame?

FNM: Methodologically, *Boricua Pop* looks at the most conspicuous of Puerto Ricans—movie stars, artists, and entertainers—to see how their bodies are being shown and showing off. Through collecting the detritus of mass culture and elite national discourse, the book pieces together the public biographies of cultural performers to behold not only the role of shame in constituting *boricua* identity but also how seeing and being seen contribute—or not—to its attenuation. In retrospect, I see that I could have also looked at sports stars, crowds, and other moments of spectacularization, such as the activism of the 1970s in New York, but at the time my main concern was with pop-culture figures that were largely understudied yet were a common cultural reference among Puerto Ricans everywhere. My work as a filmmaker was also veering more in the direction of fiction, so I was increasingly interested in stars—how they are constructed and how they give body and/or deny voice to Puerto Rican spectators.

As my research progressed, I also found it important to accentuate that the specific ways that *boricuas* have been constituted by shame are not the same. The shame of the privileged, for instance, tends to be performed as "disgrace-shame," a sense of having done wrong by not living up to their own anticolonial principles, and/or being confused with Puerto Ricans of a lower status by others deemed equal or superior (more often than not, white Americans). The shame of the *boricua* majority (popular) is associated with what Carl D. Schneider calls "discretion-shame," an affect that delimits sacred spaces that are proscribed to us not only as Puerto Ricans but also as workers, blacks, women, queers, and/or migrants.[3] Interestingly, in making use of queer theory here, I often found the surface effects more productive than the core.

RG: That's an interesting turn of phrase. What are the "surface effects" that attract you?

FNM: The surface is made of the various textual inconsistencies around a matter. The core tends to be about what these "really" or ultimately mean. Because the core will, of necessity, be eventually declared void by new methodologies and different ways of constructing the object of study, it is the surface matter that often becomes more valuable to readers over time. In other words, I did not read Nietzsche for the "truth" about shame but to examine the line of inquiry, how he went about it. Also, to the extent that I can theorize queerness apart from other processes of subjection, queer theory alone is not as useful as an integrated analysis in which one does not take any single "identity" as an absolute center. In *Boricua Pop*, for instance, when writing about the performers Holly Woodlawn or Mario Montez, I found queer identity a less productive category than the appreciation of queer performativity on a much broader stage.

RG: What drew you to Woodlawn and Montez?

FNM: Ever since I saw Holly Woodlawn's performance in *Trash*, a 1970 film by Andy Warhol, I wanted to write something about her, particularly because she had been inexplicably ignored by Puerto Rican scholarship. In Woodlawn's performance, I found a space to think about ethnicity and shame, a relationship that I find so critical to understanding the twisted pleasures of *boricua* performativity. In walking on the wild side, I also encountered Mario Montez and became very intrigued by the fact that several observers underscored the beauty of Woodlawn and Montez's performance styles. Although both were framed in the context of camp practices, I think that their style was even more complex. It merged a number of practices that included camp but also *gufeo*, a verbal exchange where puns and linguistic dexterity often serve to make fun of the incongruous. This was not camp as defined by queer white men, but a related sensibility that many clearly saw as a cultural resource, without quite grasping the difference.

Specifically, I think that the wit of queer Puerto Ricans combined a sense of ethnic and sexual exteriority that was "intellectual," in the sense that it assessed the social as a comedy, but also "heartfelt," seeking connections to the audience. In fact, Jack Smith and Charles Ludlam (1992) particularly liked Mario Montez because he was successful in immediately eliciting the sympathy of the audience. This was also Woodlawn's strength and what she wanted to achieve as a performer. At the same time, the fact that queer audiences admired these performers did not reconfigure the shame of their social identities. For Smith and for Ludlam, Puerto Rican drag performers were still objects to be used and recycled as needed to enhance their own art. This was double-edged for Puerto Rican performers: they wanted to be "aesthetic outlaws," yet by remaining "objects" they never acquired the dignified status they so intensely sought.

RG: In *Boricua Pop*, you also critically assess the field of "shame studies." I am curious about your framing of shame as constitutive of social identities generated by conflict within asymmetrical power relations, not privatized pathologies. I think I might side with sociologist Jack Katz's formulation of shame as "personally and historically contingent."[4]

FNM: I think that both formulations are compatible in one sense. In the Puerto Rican case, the embodiment of and discourse on shame/pride as a constitutive part of a public identity emerge from specific and changing social, historical, and political conflicts in a colonial context. Shame is, then, historically contingent. Concerning the "personal" aspect of Katz's definition, I was definitely cautious in my wording because there is a substantial body of work about Puerto Ricans that basically suggests that the group's "failings" (poverty, colonialism) are the product of our individual lacks, a move that contributes to constituting Puerto Rican subjects in shame. Another consideration is that while in some queer writings shame is very personal and private, in the Puerto Rican case it has been played out in public, often aimed at the American gaze, at once construed as benevolent and loathsome.

Furthermore, although I agree that the shame of *boricua* identification is experienced at a "personal" level, shame is constitutive of Puerto Rican subjectivity to the extent that it is a collective identity. While modern Puerto Rican ethnonational identity is not a simple effect of colonialism, as a socially meaningful sign, *boricua*-ness has been constituted through and from these constraints. In other words, *boricuas* do not freely choose to affirm themselves as Puerto Rican, American, and/or Latino; they are, as sociologist Kelvin Santiago-Valles writes in his book *"Subject People" and Colonial Discourses*, "the effect of a subjection much more profound than themselves."[5] Santiago-Valles's book is, in fact, one of the few theoretical texts that challenge the otherwise popular notion that Puerto Rican national "identity" is a transhistorical social fact.

RG: Well, you do in fact go on in *Boricua Pop* to discuss shame as "bodied." Is there a way to deal with the complexity of shame's location both on the body itself and on the ethnonational body?

FNM: Shame lodges in bodies; in that sense it can only be narrated or staged through the subject. In honor of this, *Boricua Pop* includes a section in which I look at critically exposed body parts such as Jennifer López's butt and Ricky Martin's hips. But when shame is constitutive of an ethnic group, of the group's poetics of identification, we are faced with a different object than that of queer theory. For instance, it is individual queers, rather than the gay community, that are most frequently the subject of shame. In the Puerto Rican case, it is the *boricua* subject as part of a colonized group that is constituted in shame by symbolic, economic, and racist violence. The theoretical challenge is how to understand the relationship between Puerto Rican subjects—in their heterogeneity—and the process of subjection that makes us "all" Puerto Ricans.

RG: Going back a minute, what do you mean by a "poetics of identification"?

FNM: I am referring to the symbolic repertoire available to a specific group as it struggles to fashion and reproduce itself as such. This repertoire is neither arbitrary nor infinite, but quite vulnerable to power (dis)locations. For instance, over at least the last decade, new generations of upwardly mobile Puerto Ricans in the United States are increasingly representing themselves as Latinos or as Americans of Puerto Rican descent. These identifications demand a different poetics of identification.

RG: Is a *boricua* poetics present in *Brincando el charco* (1994), your first experimental film narrative?

FNM: Yes and no. Curiously, my own film work to date has been antipoetic in this sense. Most of my films resist the ways that majority Puerto Rican culture represents itself through mass media. My films, for example, do not represent cultural heroes, nor are they comforting to spectators seeking relief from "American" culture. As the protagonist of some of these films, I am also an "unrepresentative" subject on the axis of sexuality, gender, and migratory history. Yet to the extent that *Brincando el charco* was openly and ferociously engaged with hegemonic nationalist discourse, it is part of a nationalist debate and arguably did not transcend it. In addition, I feel this film is flawed in at least two other ways—first, it is too invested in "representing" multiplicity rather than allowing it to be particular, and second, it is too invested in fortifying the "I" of the triply subaltern subject instead of engaging with the flesh of shame itself.

RG: Speaking of "the flesh of shame," Puerto Rican literary scholar Lawrence La Fountain-Stokes recently wrote an open letter to Douglas Crimp critical of the invisibility of race and ethnicity (and colonialism) in Crimp's "Mario Montez, for Shame" (this volume). How do you envision your own historical/theoretical project in regard to both queer and feminist notions of shame?

FNM: You have hit somewhat of a sore spot. When I read Larry La Fountain-Stokes's letter, I could not help but respond. After doing some homework, including looking at the site that listed the Gay Shame conference's over-whelmingly white participants and reading Crimp's text, I wrote a letter to the organizers, in which I basically argue that it is impossible not to speak of ethnonational shame when assessing the shame of Mario Montez's per-formance. This was even evident to Montez's contemporaries, including Ludlam, who once commented that Mario was the first Puerto Rican per-former to know that he was Puerto Rican and use it.

Importantly, Montez performed for Andy Warhol at a time when Puerto Ricans were represented as, literally, the garbage of New York City. Let us not forget that the first community action that the Young Lords undertook in New York was to pick up the garbage from the streets because the author-ities basically refused to provide this service. Examples of the low symbolic capital attached to Puerto Ricans also abound in Andy Warhol's *Diaries*, ed-ited by Pat Hackett (1989). In fact, everything trashy, ugly, or "primitive" be-came Puerto Rican for Warhol in the 1977–85 period. Buildings were ugly be-cause they were painted in "Puerto Rican colors."[6] People were ugly because they looked "Puerto Rican and Cuban and South American."[7] Ultimately, Puerto Ricans stood in as a sign of absolute barbarity, as when Warhol com-ments on how angry he became when a Puerto Rican family just watched as the neighborhood garbage went up in flames. Given this context, how could one address the shame of Mario Montez without taking into consideration his subjection as a Puerto Rican? It seems impossible to me.

RG: Although Crimp attempts to follow Eve Sedgwick's axiom that "people are different from each other" (this volume, 63), or, in his words, claim the "ethical necessity of developing finer tools for encountering, upholding, and valuing others' differences" (63)—he seems to go on to formulate that all (queer) shame is the same.

FNM: Absolutely. Crimp's essay also has another quality that disturbs me— the repetition of "poor Mario" as a chorus that underscores that the writer is looking at Mario from a complicit white shaming gaze. The color blind-ness of so much queer theory is to a large degree what makes it thorny for my own work. And here I have to underscore a very different position than the one found in Crimp and other (white) theorists regarding shame.

As contradictory as shame can be, being socially constituted by shame is not desirable for most people who are so hailed. Yes, shame is cultur-ally "productive." But I find the narcissism that shame brings forth politi-cally problematic, especially if one becomes enamored of it. In this regard, I would never advocate a politics "for shame" that desires Mario Montez to be sacrificed to the aestheticization of white queer shame. It seems to me that only the privileged can advance this proposition, people who have not been able to pose a generative or transgressive politics from their "real" position of relative power. In other words, I would suggest that many of us are not as powerless as we like to think.

Also, I am critical of the nostalgia embedded in a "return to shame" strategy. It's like those who long for the days when most of the population in Puerto Rico had next to nothing to eat as a way to challenge today's "consumer" culture. Or like those who would prefer to see Jennifer López crushed under the weight of her behind for the rest of her life. López did a major cultural workout with the shame of her body that made possible an important cultural debate and arguably even had an impact on how certain bodies circulate in public culture. But I do not desire shame on anyone for my personal or political enjoyment. For if one's greatest political priority is to "resist" normalization rather than contest the "evil eyes" of shame, it probably means that one is pretty "normal" already and should take a better look at that new location. In this regard, I am closer to Nietzsche's observation that the most humane thing is to spare someone shame than to the idea that shame is now the response to the pride that was the response to shame.

RG: What intrigues me about the Warholian superstars that you discuss—and thank you for beginning what I hope will be an extended treatment of the contributions of Puerto Rican queer aesthetics to Warhol, Smith, Ludlam, and others—is the difference between Holly Woodlawn and Mario Montez. Holly Woodlawn's own complex *desgracia* [misfortune] and pride did in fact hinge on her ability to "pass" as a white woman. Montez's racialized and "manly" body did not allow him an easy transition. In his performances in *Harlot* (1964), *Lupe* (1965), *Normal Love* (1963), and *Chelsea Girls* (1966), among others, I'm always struck by his genuine defiance in the face of this "failure" to be white (and pretty).

FNM: Yet Woodlawn was not "pretty" either in any conventional sense, and her whiteness, I think, was made possible only through much effort.

RG: Certainly there was/is a lot of labor involved in Woodlawn's realness, but for Mario (not "poor" Mario), there were bodily markers (muscles, pigmentation) that could not be layered over. I think of his bodily excess and the way he stuffed his body into a Jean Harlow persona, or a platinum blonde harlot sitting on a divan, or a blanched mermaid. Montez did not seem to have the same racial hang-ups as Woodlawn.

FNM: That relates to the distinction I made earlier concerning modalities of shame. As early twentieth-century writer and tobacco worker Bernardo Vega put it in his critical pre-1950s migration text, *Memoirs of Bernardo Vega* (1984), better-off *boricuas*—who more often than not "looked" white— would try to "pass" as Spaniards in New York, while workers were not afraid of being called "spics." While not at all times, popular performances are more likely to ebb out in the enjoyment or display of the lacking self. In this sense, the option of passing was not available to Montez, and he opted for the "popular" rather than "privileged" staging of shame.

RG: In Latin America, much of the studies of national "character" have been written by a male league of national intellectuals. Here I am more familiar with Mexican intellectuals—from Samuel Ramos to Octavio Paz. Did you at any moment feel you were running the risk of replicating a patriarchal type of diagnosis of the national character? I think of the diagnosed "melancholy" of the Mexican, for example.

FNM: Of course—and I did—in response to a long line of male nationalist discourse and figures that includes José de Diego, "el Caballero de la Raza," with his appeal to Puerto Ricans that they must learn how to say a virile "no"; the key intellectual of the 1930s, Antonio S. Pedreira, with his melancholic prose about Puerto Rican conformism, an alleged product of our miscegenation; and, last but not least, the nationalist leader and icon Pedro Albizu Campos, with his call to young men that they stop being sissies and to women that they leave their "loose" morality behind and build the nation.

RG: Why use the term *queer* to describe Puerto Rican ethnonationality?

FNM: It disrupts macho nationalism. I guess that I found it irresistible. But more systematically, I am using the term in two ways, depending on location: as "weird" (nonnormative) and gender discordant. I am sure that some will misread this usage and argue that what I am saying is that all Puerto Ricans are gay. Yet, what I am proposing is that the way that Puerto Ricans have been imagined as national subjects and have negotiated with this location has had the result of generating a "queer" sense of nationhood that has largely rejected dominant (virile) definitions of nationhood as the product of an epic past supported by infinite wealth and military might.

RG: Can you also address this feminist/queer critique of the male guard of Puerto Rican intellectuals, particularly the points where you find the stakes of the ethnonational replicating some of the binarisms of past writing on national character? I think you were beginning to express this in another of our conversations—when you commented about how you were looking for ways to offset the notion of the "fucked" (feminine) state involved in articulating ethnonational shame.

FNM: This is a critical dilemma. In Western culture, the feminine (including "passive" male queers) are the "fucked" ones. Puerto Ricans have been historically represented as either effeminate Cubans or violent bimbos. At the same time, that Puerto Rican ethnonationality has been constituted as feminine does not mean that there is no "violence," "resistance" in nonnational terms, and junctures of macho performances. In *Boricua Pop*, I established that as ethnonational subjects, Puerto Ricans appear effeminate when measured against hegemonic definitions of nationhood, and this location has produced a set of cultural interventions and ways of representing ourselves in the world that are explainable in terms of how we have been socially constituted through these categories.

Yet the questions that come next are even more difficult. Is it more politically desirable to assume the "feminine" position? But, if so, which one? If history can easily provide examples of "masculine" and "feminine" performances of nationhood in any national context, are these gender categories useless? Also, if the Puerto Rican "national" experience is actually less exceptional than it appears, because most contemporary nations do not control their territory and are subject to more powerful interests beyond their borders, is the alternative to speak in multiple vernaculars that work through the nation as a problematic fantasy?

It was precisely this line of questioning that prompted me to edit the volume titled *None of the Above* (2007). Here, the volume invites the contributors and readers to stretch the imagination as it if were a neglected muscle. At one level, the gesture of refusal embedded in "none of the above" allowed some contributors to challenge the categories through which Puerto Rico and Puerto Ricans continue to be produced as racially, culturally, and politically deviant from national, racial, or linguistic norms. At another level, the term's ambiguity invited alternative ways of theorizing cultural and political practices that we may not yet fully understand. At its most radical, the perennial source of Puerto Rican shame—national ambiguity—becomes a resource to imagine alternatives to the master narratives of colonialism, nationalism, and masculinity.

RG: Are you in a "none of the above" moment?

FNM: One could say that. I have begun to work in a different direction, one that is increasingly interested in particularity not as an allegory of national identity or ethnic discourses, but in its own conflictive, terms—one that produces a practice that I call the politics of small problems. Importantly, I was not able to arrive at this point without first acknowledging and then working through shame. I believe that for shamed subjects, this process is a prerequisite to producing new ways of seeing ourselves and relating to others. Not surprisingly, my new films and book projects are not about Puerto Ricans as national subjects, but about characters literally reframing the ghosts that haunt them—right at home.

Notes

1. Juhasz, *Women of Vision*, 281.
2. Halberstam, "Shame and White Gay Masculinity," 226.
3. Schneider, *Shame, Exposure, and Privacy*, 20.
4. Katz, *How Emotions Work.*
5. Santiago-Valles, *"Subject People" and Colonial Discourses,"* 53.
6. Warhol, *Diaries*, 320.
7. Ibid., 241.

Works Cited

Biella, Peter, and Frances Negrón-Muntaner., dirs. *AIDS in the Barrio: Eso no me pasa a mí.* New York: Cinema Guild, 1989.

Crimp, Douglas. "Mario Montez, For Shame." This volume, 63–75.

Halberstam, Judith. "Shame and White Gay Masculinity." *Social Text* 23, nos. 3–4 (Fall–Winter 2005): 219–33.

Juhasz, Alexandra. *Women of Vision: Histories in Feminism Film and Video*. Minneapolis: University of Minnesota Press, 2001.

Katz, Jack. *How Emotions Work*. Chicago: University of Chicago Press, 1999.

Ludlam, Charles. *Ridiculous Theatre, Scourge of Human Folly: The Essays and Opinions of Charles Ludlam*, ed. Steven Samuels. New York: Theatre Communications Group, 1992.

Morrissey, Paul, dir. *Trash*. Produced by Andy Warhol. Chatsworth, CA: Image Entertainment, 1970.

Negrón-Muntaner, Frances. *Boricua Pop: Puerto Ricans and the Latinization of American Culture*. New York: New York University Press, 2004.

———. "Jennifer's Butt." *Aztlan: A Journal of Chicana Studies* 22, no. 2 (1997):181–94.

———, ed. *None of the Above: Contemporary Puerto Rican Cultures and Politics*. New York: Palgrave Macmillan, 2007.

———, dir. and prod. *Homeless Diaries*. 1996.

———, dir. and prod. *Puerto Rican ID*. 1995.

———, dir. and prod. *Regarding Vieques*. 2008.

———, and Peter Biella, dirs. and prods. *Brincando el charco: Portrait of a Puerto Rican*. 1994. United States video and film distribution: Women Make Movies.

Santiago-Valles, Kelvin A. *"Subject People" and Colonial Discourses: Economic Transformation and Social Disorder in Puerto Rico, 1898–1947*. Albany: State University of New York Press, 1994.

Schneider, Carl D. *Shame, Exposure, and Privacy*. Boston: Beacon, 1977.

Smith, Jack, dir. and prod. *Normal Love*. 1963.

Vega, Bernardo. 1984. *Memorias de Bernardo Vega: Contribución a la historia de la comunidad puertorriqueña en Nueva York* (The Memoirs of Bernardo Vega: A Contribution to the History of the Puerto Rican Community in New York), ed. César Andreu Iglesias. Rió Piedras, Puerto Rico: Ediciones Huracán, 1984.

Warhol, Andy. *The Andy Warhol Diaries*, ed. Pat Hackett. New York: Warner Books, 1989.

———, dir. and prod. *The Chelsea Girls*. 1966. United States video and DVD distribution: The Andy Warhol Foundation for the Visual Arts.

———, dir. and prod. *Harlot*. 1964.

———, dir. and prod. *Lupe*. 1965.

SPECTACLES
OF SHAME

[ELISABETH LADENSON]

Shame on Me

Introduction

When David Halperin originally contacted me, in July 2002, to invite me to participate in the Gay Shame conference that was to take place in Ann Arbor in April 2003, I was thrilled. When he explained that what he and Valerie Traub envisioned was less a conventional academic conference than a genuine forum for spontaneous debate, I was impressed, although also skeptical in general at the idea that academics could be induced not to give formal papers, as well as apprehensive in particular, because delivering formal conference papers is the one skill I have managed over the course of my career so far to master to some degree. Still, I was excited at the prospect of what they were trying to do—right up until the moment, that is, when David unveiled their plan for me. The conference would begin with a showing of Andy Warhol's film *Screen Test #2*, he explained, followed by a discussion of Douglas Crimp's essay on the film, "Mario Montez, For Shame." So far so good, I thought; sounds great. My queasiness set in when David added that what he and Valerie wanted me to do was to present the essay and lead the discussion.

My reaction at the time continues to surprise me now, and I hope it is more a testimony to the persuasive powers of the conference organizers than to my own reckless disregard for self-preservation: despite my misgivings I agreed immediately. My hesitation sprang from three pertinent facts: I had not seen the film, I had not read Crimp's essay, and I knew little about Warhol. I pointed all this out to David, even as I shamelessly accepted the invitation. I further asked him what it was that had made my name come up in this regard. After a pause he admitted that he didn't know; it had seemed like a good idea at the time. Well, I said, OK, but if you change your mind once you sober up I'll understand. For reasons I have made sure not to inquire into too closely, the proposal was never retracted. Between

July and April I read the article, saw the film, and made an attempt to learn something about Warhol, even if not much of this is evident from my remarks. What follows is, for better or worse, the largely unrevised text of my pseudo-introduction to Douglas Crimp's essay.

Shame on Me

As I was preparing to do no more than lead the discussion of Warhol's film and Crimp's essay I ended up feeling that I should somehow justify the fact that my airfare was being paid for, so whether I liked it or not I intended to make a few preparatory remarks on the place of shame in our culture, taking the pretext of three relatively recent events.

First: In the third episode of the second season of *The Sopranos*, there is a scene in which Janice (aka Parvati) Soprano goes to visit her mother in the hospital. Livia Soprano, the dreadful matriarch of this felonious clan, is suffering the aftermath of a stroke, or more precisely what appears to be a psychosomatically induced strokelike episode following her instigation of a hit on her own son. When Livia begins a litany of resentful complaint in front of another visitor, Janice tells her to stop her refrain, deploying a powerful familial weapon: "Don't you have any shame?" Livia imperturbably replies to this question, which was presumably meant to be rhetorical, telling her daughter: "Shame? Oh I've got plenty of shame. Believe me, you don't want to hear what I'm ashamed of." Janice, whose ability to wield shame and the lack thereof as an offensive and defensive weapon has clearly been honed by years of training by her interlocutor, comes back with an invitation worthy of Clint Eastwood: "Go ahead and shoot your best shot." Which Livia obligingly does: "Never you mind," she says ominously, adding, even more ominously: "Just remember what we talked about." The conversation, unsurprisingly, ends there.

This scene is interesting, I think, in a number of ways. For one thing, it foregrounds the extent to which the unsaid trumps the said every time. In the process, the dialogue makes it clear that Janice's question is ill-advised: although she thinks that the evocation of shame should be enough to stop her mother in her tracks, on the grounds that no one wants to be thought shameless, the latter, a formidable opponent in this game, is immediately able to turn the subject of shame to her own paradoxical advantage by suggesting that she has great shame—that she is in fact shamed by her daughter. In other words, the two accuse each other of lacking shame, each aggressively claiming shamefulness as the moral high ground by suggesting to the other that she should be ashamed of her lack of shame.

Second: another instance of some of the strange valences of shame in our culture, this one from daily e-life. My university-provided e-mail program, Eudora, contains a function called Moodwatch. This software is designed to tip one off to potentially offensive language, as I discovered not long ago to my mixed horror and delight. It has, among other things, allowed me to explore some of the many ways in which I routinely send messages that would, as the warning device puts it, offend the average reader. One of my countless formulations deemed offensive by Eudora was the following sentence I wrote—I am, yes, slightly (but only slightly) ashamed to admit—to a former student: "You should be ashamed of yourself." Disconcerted to find myself reprimanded by Eudora for this apparent transgression, I experimented a bit and found that while I could not with impunity suggest that my interlocutor should be ashamed of herself, the very same hortatory pronouncement passed without comment when self-directed. "I should be ashamed of myself" was a statement that my software program no doubt heartily agreed with; in any case it expressed no reprimand. Shame, it seems, is a good thing in our culture at large, but only when claimed in the first person; thus we are back to the moral of my first example. *The Sopranos* and the Eudora Moodwatch program would appear to be situated at ethically opposed poles of our society, the former representing a milieu steeped in retrograde notions of violence, vengeance, and face-saving, whereas the latter is the very epitome of politically correct attempts to preclude any possibility of offense and enforce verbal nonviolence to the point of generalized blandness of tone. It is truly remarkable what a range of communicative gambits Eudora finds offensive; certainly few lines from the script of any given *Sopranos* episode would pass muster with the Moodwatch function. Nonetheless, on this point Eudora and *The Sopranos* agree: shame is bad when assigned to another; a fine thing when claimed for oneself. Of course, it is also true that computer programs are notoriously tone-deaf, and the offensive overtones of "Oh, I've got plenty of shame," unlike those of the question "Don't you have any shame?," would pass undetected only because Moodwatch, despite its name, is incapable of discerning such subtle deployments of aggression as in Livia Soprano's masterful reply. But enough of that; the point is that both these examples suggest, in their very different ways, that our culture fosters shame as a good thing when claimed for the self, a bad thing when overtly assigned to others.

Third: one further non–Douglas Crimp–related example will, I think, bring us closer to the topic at hand, which is after all gay shame and not mafia shame or computer shame. I recently picked up a book entitled *Kick Me: Adventures in Adolescence* by one Paul Feig, the man responsible for the quickly canceled sitcom on the same subject called *Freaks and Geeks*. Having liked that show, and seduced by the book's cover, which features a circa-1972 family studio portrait of possibly unparalleled embarrassingness, I read the book, because tales of adolescent shame and humiliation exert a strange power, one that might well merit a conference to itself. In any case, *Kick Me* is cute, replete as promised with truly horrifying stories of growing up in the 1970s, but not really worthy of extended commentary were it not for one exceptional element. The book details the manifold shame of a boy growing up in the 1970s who is terrible at sports, cannot understand why he should care about sports teams, is constantly called fag (his name, remember, is Paul Feig, pronounced Feeg; not even the most virile of preadolescents could have warded this off), as well as homo, girl, and the rest of the litany of feminizing degradation still reserved for sports-eschewing male children in our culture.

What's more, young Feig prefers the company of girls to that of other boys. To top it all off, as a preadolescent he discovers a wig belonging to his mother and clandestinely explores a transient though keen taste for dressing up in her dresses and putting on her makeup. One day, of course, he is observed by three schoolmates as well as various passers-by doing the twist in front of a mirror while dressed in his mother's wig, makeup, dress, and white go-go boots. More shame and humiliation ensue. I need hardly go on; you all know the story. One sentence should suffice (the subject is our hero's horror at being required to show up at school with proper gym attire): "I guess the problem was that my best friends were mostly girls, and that while these guys were playing football and basketball, I had been sitting around the house with Mary, Sharon, and Stephanie playing Mystery Date and Art Linkletter's House Party" (123–24).

The only reason I bother to bring up this particular version of the all-too-familiar story is that the adolescent boy in question in this book is, and remains, heterosexual. As a result, the narrative trajectory of his shame is different. That is to say, his shame has nowhere to go, as it were, because it is not recuperable as pride. He has nothing to come out as, especially because the shame of his early unmasking as a young transvestite seems to have cured him of his most spectacular gender dysphoria. He thus cannot march in any parade; as far as I know there is no Geek Pride movement, Bill Gates and Steven Spielberg notwithstanding. Our culture loves transformation stories, though, and even though there may be no specific movement, there is certainly something resembling Geek Pride; we have *Revenge of the Nerds* films to prove it. We also have the fabulous success stories of Gates and Spielberg and their ilk. What is it, then, that sets someone like

Feig apart? I would suggest it is that he succeeds only to the extent that he fails. Where Gates and Spielberg represent the financial—and therefore, given our culture, social—revenge of the heterosexual nerds, resounding success crowning the tale of nerdly adolescent failure, Feig's story is one of failure transcendent. He never wins: this, paradoxically, is why we (OK, I) buy his book; but in his book he is not really successful, which is as it should be, in the end. He gets neither the girl (nor for that matter the boy, because he never wanted one in the first place), nor the huge fortune, nor even the viewing or reading public.

Despite its uncanny resemblance to coming-out stories, Paul Feig's book has nowhere to go beyond the fact that this former pseudo-fag became the creative voice behind a quickly canceled television show. Actual success would compromise the narrative. (Paul Feig himself may well feel differently, but this is my essay, not his.) The accolades on the back cover of the book bear inadvertent witness to this consummate failure, in various ways: for instance, Ira Glass, host of NPR's *This American Life*, says: "It's shocking that one person could have had so many humiliating experiences and even more shocking that he chose to remember them." However jocularly he may have meant this remark, it could not be more clear that Glass is a heterosexual nontransvestite, one, moreover, who has never read a coming-out novel (or, for that matter, any other coming-of-age story). Joel Hodgson, creator of *Mystery Science Theater 3000*, says on the back of Feig's book: "Paul Feig's *Kick Me* is an astute study of growing up in the seventies that thinks it's a happy-go-lucky humor book." In other words, Glass finds the book remarkable for its unashamed portrayal of what he takes to be unusually potent humiliation stories, while Hodgson lauds it for its historical testimony masquerading as humor. Unsurprisingly, neither recognizes what I take to be its most salient quality, which is that it is a coming-out story without the *as*, as it were: in this book Feig goes through all the familiar stages of alienation and self-recognition without there being anything clear for the narrator to come out *from*, or, more pertinently, *into*. Feig has neither sexual nor financial identity going for him. The back cover of his book, certainly, sports no laudatory comments from self-proclaimed homosexuals, because that would compromise the book's appeal to its targeted audience of heterosexual (former) geeks; it is also possible that the author's heterosexuality has prevented him from recognizing, or from wanting to recognize, his story's queer relationship to the coming-out genre. Feig's shame, as it is presented, because it is neither gay shame nor crowned by any sort of resplendent subsequent success, cannot *become* anything; in particular, it cannot become pride. Geek pride is pride at no longer being a social outcast. Gay pride, similarly, is pride not at sleeping with members of one's own sex, which would be absurd, but at not being ashamed of doing so.

Gay pride is pride at lack of shame, which is problematic, as in fact is all pride; yet let us not forget that pride is, for good reason, one of the deadly sins. Shame, "the dysphoric affect," as Sedgwick, cited by Crimp, puts it, "functions as a nexus of production: production, that is, of meaning, of personal presence, of politics, of performative and critical efficacy." Warhol—you see, I do in fact intend to come back to my actual subject—Warhol is in this context to be made into "an exemplary figure for understanding" how this happens.

How, then—let us take up the question from the beginning—how does shame function as a nexus of production? Before we turn, finally, to the ways in which Warhol and Mario Montez can be made to figure this, I want to resume my three little examples of the power of shame in our culture. According to the Soprano women, it seems, the only thing one has to be ashamed of is lack of shame itself. According to my e-mail program, I have a great deal to be ashamed of, in particular my shameful attempts to shame others. According to the back cover of *Kick Me*, Paul Feig's shameless account of his adolescent shame is laudable for its shock value—that is, for its very narrative shamelessness—or for its value as historical documentation. Shame for shame's sake, which is what Feig's book ends up looking like, doesn't quite fly. Shame is productive above all of first-person narrative, but that discursive productivity must observe certain rules. Livia Soprano's ominous reply to her daughter's relatively amateurish attempt to shame her implies that it is better to let shameful dogs lie, as it were. When she says, "Believe me, you don't want to know what I'm ashamed of," she suggests that once shame begins to speak it contaminates everyone within shaming distance. Livia is proud of her shame, it would seem, and proud especially of what she implies is its necessary reticence. Moodwatch, on the other hand—and I suspect it's also possible that the difference between *The Sopranos* and Moodwatch has much to do with the difference between shame and guilt cultures, but my sketchy memory of my anthropology class does not permit me to elaborate, you'll be relieved to know—is happy to have me prattle on endlessly about my own shame, as long as I don't try to impose it on others.

All this does, I think, have bearing on Crimp's essay, which I will now, with feelings of hope and relief, invite you to discuss, especially in terms of the idea that in showcasing Mario Montez's shame Warhol somehow escapes a murkily voyeuristic relationship to the shame of others—the idea, as Crimp puts it toward the end of the essay, that "Warhol found the means to make the people of his world visible to us without making them the objects of our knowledge." "Put on a wig before you judge," says Michael Warner in a remarkable passage cited by Crimp. With that in mind I feel justified in approaching this conference as an extended discursive drag show, and with metaphorical wig and white go-go boots I now turn over the floor to a discussion of "Mario Montez, For Shame."

Postscript

Although the above remarks seemed to be well received, to my disappointment no further mention was made of *The Sopranos* over the two days that followed. I am not sure why that was, beyond the conjecture that, at least so far, *The Sopranos* is too resolutely heterosexual to become an object of much interest in the gay-shame context. My attempts to interest the assembled company in traditional heterosexually tinged shame were perhaps doomed to failure from the start. I find it hard to believe that there were no *Sopranos* fans present, and can therefore only assume that it was heterophobic shame that kept this topic from the forefront of public discussion during the conference.

As for Crimp's assertion about Warhol's having found the means to make Mario Montez visible without by the same token making him the object of our knowledge, I suggested during the discussion, and would continue to maintain, that the audience response to *Screen Test #2* when it was shown on the first evening of the conference belied this overly optimistic (to my mind) interpretation. The audience was only too happy to identify, sometimes quite vocally, with the offscreen voice of Ronald Tavel in his deadpan mockery of Montez's desire to be cast as Esmeralda rather than Quasimodo in the fictional *Hunchback of Notre Dame* project. Manifestly, given the audience response at the showing in Ann Arbor, Montez does quite spectacularly become the object of what the audience believes, at least, to be its knowledge. The discrepancy between our presumed knowledge and its relative lack of foundation is precisely, I would hazard, where much of the interest of this exercise lies. What we take to be our "knowledge" participates in and results from our necessarily vacillating identification with, alternately, the tacitly masochistic Montez, the sadistic voice-off, and—perhaps above all—the implacably static Warholian lens.

The discussion of "Mario Montez, For Shame" was lively and productive, in any case, and it is to be hoped that some of the important issues raised by Crimp's essay and by conference participants will be followed up: in particular, I would cite the distinction between shame and humiliation in a gay context, and the questions of identification, complicity, and voyeurism in approaching a spectacle like that of Mario Montez in Warhol's film. And finally, I would like to thank the conference organizers for inviting me to participate in what turned out to be a strange and interesting adventure.

[N A D I N E   H U B B S]

On the Uses of Shame and Gifts of a Bloodmobile

MUSINGS FROM A MUSICAL QUEER APPRENTICESHIP

I want to be my own man, self-made. Naturally. In America, everybody does—and with good reason. After all, who wants to see themselves or their life as determined from outside, by other people? Worse yet should those others be your enemies—the last ones on earth you'd want controlling your destiny! Whether it turns out to be grand or modest, your own life story should be your greatest creation (I know this from soda and sneaker ads). Even the humblest life is noble in its fashion, if you can say at the end of it all, "I did it my way."

But I'll stop myself here—because I didn't mean to wax philosophical, or morbid. That's no way to begin. So I'll just leave that thread dangling for now and begin as I meant to: by telling a story. It's a story from my former life as a music student in northern Ohio, and it dates back to 1985—which was still "pre-Stonewall," as far as we knew. This new girl came to town, and I couldn't help but notice (discreetly, of course) her dazzling curves, or the bright unwavering eyes with which she seemed to be—was she?—checking me out. I finally figured out the answer, but only after overcoming the formidable mechanisms of studied cluelessness that had been instilled by my small-town Ohio upbringing, and by fears of humiliation in being called out as a freak, accused of coveting and salivating over That to Which I Was Not Entitled. I was, in that incarnation, a young working-class dyke from the cornfields, dark Catholic in a land of fair Lutherans, carrying

Thanks to David Halperin and Valerie Traub for providing the opportunity and incitement for this essay, even as they completely shielded my tenure-focused self from the heavy lifting of conference planning and organizing. I dedicate the essay to B, Barry, and Bob, in fond memory of cold Ohio evenings warmed by lasagna, Valpo, and ribaldry.

my motorcycle helmet with me to my fall orchestra audition (I couldn't afford to have it stolen). And I'd be damned if I was about to get caught in that predatory-dyke freak trap the world had laid for me. If I had to be lonely, at least I'd have my pride. With all the kinds of shame that seemed to lie in wait for me in those days, that pride was something I fed and watered, and guarded vigilantly.

Maybe I shouldn't say that I overcame my cultivated cluelessness, because it was more the case that she—let's call her B—that B got tired of waiting for me to solve the mystery definitively, once and for all. So, she just sort of tapped me on the shoulder: "Yeah, you!" That's all it took. I had a new lover, who became my girlfriend for the next six or seven months.

B had just moved from Rochester, New York, an obscure Rust Belt, Snow Belt city by standards of virtually everyone except for classical musicians, for whom Rochester was and is something of an international capital. As home of the legendary, excellent, and highly competitive Eastman School of Music, Rochester provided an address of considerable distinction in our world. I was naturally eager to take in B's dispatches from the Eastman School, from which she had graduated a few months before we met. She was an aspiring orchestral conductor hoping to start over in a town where no one knew the secrets of her past: for at Eastman, B had been a standout student in . . . the *voice* department. Worse yet, our would-be titan of the podium was a coloratura—and a good one! (She had tried valiantly to pass as a mezzo but was eventually found out.)

From B I gained some handsome new additions to my lexicon of classical-music camp, fresh coinages from the Rochester branch of our esoteric guild, a rich and lively underground society residing at the intersection of two rarefied subcultures: of classical music and homosexuality. I learned, for example, "dirty-whore white noise" as an apt designator for a certain sort of unfortunate singing tone; also "Betty Blackhead" as a moniker for the German diva Elisabeth Schwarzkopf (multilingual puns were an important subgenre here). B dished dirt on who was and who wasn't among the Eastman faculty and the many celebrated performers who were in residence there or stopped by to give master classes. But of all B's Rochester recountings, none made so lasting an impression or provided such a basis for familial bonding as the story she told about the Eastman School and the Bloodmobile.

As I mentioned, this was about 1985—still early days in the AIDS crisis, and not long after the Red Cross discovered the HIV virus in its own blood supply and thus added a new question to its screening survey: have you ever had sexual contact with a homosexual? The Eastman School was a big place, a community of nearly a thousand musicians, and it had long been a lucrative stopover for the Red Cross, who would send their Bloodmobile to campus the better to garner donations from students and faculty deeply absorbed in busy practice and performance schedules. But what happened when the new question appeared? Well, according to B, it sent the Bloodmobile right back to the depot. So numerous were the yeses in response to the query about homosexual involvements among these elite musicians that the Red Cross decided it wasn't worth the drive. Good luck visiting the Eastman School in search of queer-free body fluids—ha! Turns out you can't poke enough nonhomos there to justify gassing up the truck.

Now, I've never verified this account, nor would I try. It would be irrelevant to the point I'm after, which has to do with our response, B's and mine and our cohort's, to what we immediately perceived as the moral of the story: that American classical music was *ours*, up through the very highest levels. That the artistry we worshipped and to which we devoted our lives was—unlike so many other objects held up by mainstream culture—attainable for, and indeed (it appeared to us) predominated by, our people. The story flooded us with pride. It was a feeling, warm and full, that I can still recall. But it's not one I can replicate in the present, and certainly not in association with this story.

For what I'm calling our "pride" in that instance was in fact a more complex and manifold quantity. It was a feeling the fullness of which was supplied by the prior and ongoing abundance of another, ostensibly opposite feeling, a pride that arose only and directly in relation to shame. This shame was conditioned by our knowledge and continual confrontation with the fact that, according to our culture and society, we weren't supposed to exist, and that our insistence on existing nevertheless was an embarrassment to everyone. But we did exist, plentifully, at the Eastman School and in elite musical institutions throughout America and Europe: classical music, understood (by us) as a widely acknowledged locus of some of humanity's most profound achievements, was crawling with our kind. My cohort and I possessed a rare, secret, and vindicating item of knowledge about queers and their usefulness, their right—*our* right—to take up space and breathe air. And this knowledge was deeply satisfying, even though we didn't know then (most people still don't) about Eastman's shameful history of homosexual purges in the 1930s and 1940s.[1]

All this brings me back now to what I started to say at the very beginning, about being my own man. I think gay identity too has often wanted, understandably, to present itself as self-made, and not as something determined by others, nor, certainly, by the enemy. Proclaiming our pride, we taunt and defy that outsized social and ideological apparatus intent on shaming us. Thus, at last, we seize control of our lives and write our own scripts—right? Well, if so, I'm afraid I've missed the boat again. Actually, I've never seen the sorts of gay-pride declarations we've come to know in recent years as handles by which I might somehow grasp control over my own queer destiny. More often the rhetoric of gay pride has felt alien and alienating and has encouraged me to see myself as harboring (shamefully) a very individual and probably pathological condition in living and experiencing my queerness as I do. That is, in finding some self-identificatory resonance in places like this passage from Andrew Holleran's 1978 novel *Dancer from the Dance:*

> What can you say about a success? Nothing! But the failures—that tiny subspecies of homosexual, the doomed queen, who puts the car in gear and drives right off the cliff! That fascinates me. The fags who consider themselves worthless because they are queer, and who fall into degradation and sordidness! It was those Christ befriended, not the assholes in the ad agencies uptown who go to St. Kitts in February![2]

From a gay-pride standpoint, this paean doesn't make much sense, except maybe as evidence of old-school internalized homophobia, testimony to what can happen if you allow others, the enemy, to tell you who you are. But of course the passage is not only about homosexual *identity*; it's also, vividly and inextricably, about queer *identification*—and identification in shame. In fact, this passage maps some of the major routes for collective and individual queer identification in Anglo-American modernity: that is, in its sentimentalized transvaluation of success and failure, and in its Christic identification—both of which trace historically to our camp forebear Oscar Wilde, and to the aestheticized queer theology he instigated in *De Profundis.*[3]

But who among us, these days, can conjure a credible sense of realness around, or necessity for, the tragic homosexual abnegation and abjection that was still viable as recently as 1978? Within a postmodern, post-Stonewall cultural logic grounded in assumptions of identity's social constructedness (among other things), the bittersweet sensibilities of homosexual abjection and camp may inspire nostalgia, admiration, envy, or disgust. But neither old-style homosexual worldviews and feeling-tones nor their traditional symptoms and markers can be understood outside that now-discredited frame in which homosexuality constituted "an inborn, immutable stigma; a tragic accident of fate and nature; a damning originary wound that might, however, hold redemptive potential à la Wilde in *De Profundis.*"[4] And whence this queer redemption? Well, think of James Merrill's epic *Changing Light at Sandover*, or even of my erstwhile music-student cohort: In both, queer redemption, like queer stigma, attaches to what we *are*—which is understood in terms of innate exceptionality at once monstrous and exalted.[5]

Shame's attachment to what we are rather than what we do is emphasized in Michael Warner's queer analysis, and (implicitly) in Erving Goffman's 1963 study of stigmatized identity.[6] But what about what we do? As the Brooklyn and San Francisco Gay Shame organizers trenchantly suggest, what gay pride appears to do by now seems less about renouncing than about merging with those "assholes in the ad agencies uptown." Gay complicity with corporatization and with sex, race, class, and sero-status discrimination and domination gives us good reason to think about shame, and about whose interests are privileged in the identity rubrics we may find ourselves under.[7]

In the introduction to his essay collection *The Culture of Queers*, Richard Dyer notes that "it would . . . be perfectly possible to write the history of the age of queers as that of the slow birth of gay." He elaborates: "The negativity of queer was always resisted, contested, evaded, or flouted. . . . [But] queer always had an awareness of negativity, had always to bear the weight of it. 'Gay' sought to think and feel without a consciousness of negativity." Dyer underscores the centrality of shame, or "negativity," in his own queer consciousness and cultural productivity, claiming that the essays in his collection are "made possible by this: I remember being a queer and have never been entirely convinced that I ever became gay."[8]

The present *Gay Shame* collection can suggest a related proposition: that the "gay" that's been subsumed under "pride," and the "shame" so long relegated to the queer, can no longer pass as divergent or discrete from one another. Rather, gay pride must bear, has always borne, a weight of shame— even as shame's chafe has polished the objects of gay pride. And if we no longer subscribe to certain structures of identity that have sustained gay shame in the past, that doesn't mean we've eliminated such shame from our current identities or identifications, nor that we should be any less engaged with shame's rich and complex productive effects—those effects highlighted in the gay-shame analyses of Eve Kosofsky Sedgwick and Douglas Crimp.[9] Of course, if we as queer-engaged scholars, artists, and activists don't collectively take up the onus and offerings of gay shame to illuminate its intricate social and cultural dimensions, undoubtedly it will flourish nonetheless—in the realm of individual pathology. But there's nothing new, or proud, in that.

Notes

1. These purges are discussed in Ned Rorem, *Knowing When to Stop: A Memoir* (New York: Simon and Schuster, 1994), 335–36; K. Robert Schwarz, "Composers' Closets Open for All to See," *New York Times*, June 19, 1994; and in my book *The Queer Composition of America's Sound: Gay Modernists, American Music, and National Identity* (Berkeley: University of California Press, 2004), 127, 156, 168, 169. See the latter two sources regarding the extent to which queers were prevalent in twentieth-century American classical music, particularly in the middle third of the century.

2. Andrew Holleran, *Dancer from the Dance* (New York: William Morrow, 1978), 18.

3. *De Profundis* (1897) was Wilde's long letter "from the depths" (literally) of his imprisonment and abjection in Reading Gaol. Ellis Hanson has illuminated Wilde's role in creating here a modern queer spiritual sensibility, fusing a highly aestheticized Catholicism with potentially redemptive shame and suffering. See Hanson, *Decadence and Catholicism* (Cambridge, MA: Harvard University Press, 1997).

4. I have raised this point previously in very similar terms and here quote from my own language in *Queer Composition*, 92.

5. Merrill's famous epic posits a cosmological scheme (revealed to the gay poet by divine messengers) in which homosexuals occupy an exalted place in the advancement of humanity thanks to their singular contributions to intellectual and artistic culture; see James Merrill, *The Changing Light at Sandover: Including the Whole of the Book of Ephraim, Mirabell's Books of Number, Scripts for the Pageant, and a New Coda, the Higher Keys* (New York: Alfred A. Knopf, 1992). For a mention of the poem's construction of a sort of pre-Stonewall "pride" asserting gay white men's exalted exceptionality, see Christopher Nealon, *Foundlings: Lesbian and Gay Historical Emotion before Stonewall* (Durham, NC: Duke University Press, 2001), 179–80.

6. Michael Warner, "The Ethics of Sexual Shame," chapter 1 in *The Trouble with Normal: Sex, Politics, and the Ethics of Queer Life* (Cambridge, MA: Harvard University Press, 1999), especially 28; and Erving Goffman, *Stigma: Notes on the Management of Spoiled Identity* (1963; reprint, New York: Touchstone, 1986), e.g., 7, 14–15.

7. Relevant details of the Brooklyn and San Francisco Gay Shame events invoked here are given in David M. Halperin, "Why Gay Shame Now?," this volume, 41–42.

8. Richard Dyer, *The Culture of Queers* (New York: Routledge, 2002), 8, 13.

9. Eve Kosofsky Sedgwick envisages an "urgent" project "of understanding how the dysphoric affect *shame* functions as a nexus of production: production, that is, of meaning, of personal presence, of politics, of performative and critical efficacy" (135) in "Queer Performativity: Warhol's Shyness/Warhol's Whiteness," in *Pop Out: Queer Warhol*, ed. Jennifer Doyle, Jonathan Flatley, and José Esteban Muñoz (Durham, NC: Duke University Press, 1996), 134–43; Douglas Crimp, "Mario Montez, For Shame," this volume 63–75.

[DAVID CARON]

Shame on Me

OR THE NAKED TRUTH ABOUT
ME AND MARLENE DIETRICH

For Rufus Wainwright, whose shamelessness I often envy.

D.C.

I admit it took me completely by surprise although, in retrospect, I realize I should have seen it coming. I was in Paris, and a couple of friends had taken me to see a cabaret act in a small, intimate basement venue in Ménilmontant. The singer, named Michel Hermon, was performing songs from his new CD entitled *Dietrich Hotel* (fig. 4). Accompanied by a pianist, he sang numbers from Marlene Dietrich's film and stage repertoire, as well as other songs evocative of the decadent atmosphere of 1920s Berlin and Paris. The show was lovely and I enjoyed it very much. Hermon's entrance, however, was a different matter altogether. My friends and I were at a table near the back of the room, conveniently sitting a few feet away from the bar. The room went dark, Hermon's low, husky voice was heard singing Lou Reed's "Berlin"—this was going to be great. Slowly, he made his way down the stairs and appeared at the door wearing—what else?—a black swallowtail suit like the one Marlene dons in *Morocco*'s famous scene, the one where she kisses a woman on the lips (fig. 5). Hermon is now near the middle of the room, and "Berlin" seamlessly makes way for "Black Market," an original Friedrich Holländer song from Billy Wilder's *A Foreign Affair* and a camp masterpiece. I just love this song. Genuine Marlene *and* a pure gem of self-irony, it is, in other words, quintessential Dietrich. I'm in heaven. But instead of making his way to the little stage, the bald, middle-aged, made-up singer starts swishing toward the bar right behind me and soon lies down on top of it in an exaggeratedly lascivious pose. Naturally, the spotlight is now right on me, and so are the eyes of everyone in the audience. My friends are trying very hard not to laugh. I'm in hell.

Figure 4. Cover of Michel Hermon's CD *Dietrich Hotel*.

Most people would think of this merely as a slight embarrassment, like being called onto the stage by a magician or something. And what's there to be ashamed of since, after all, people were not really looking at me, right? Wrong. They *were* looking at me. You see, liking Marlene Dietrich is quite different from liking, say, macaroni and cheese. Nobody wants to *be* macaroni and cheese. But when you're a teenage gay boy you want to be Marlene Dietrich. At least I did, and identifying with a glamorous screen legend was at once a very empowering feeling and a feeling of self-denying shame. If queer kids are directly or indirectly pressured to be someone else, I'm not so sure it is Marlene Dietrich our censors have in mind. But I can't think of a more fabulous way for boys and girls alike (since Marlene's queer appeal crosses gender lines) to obey and disobey the injunction in one single move—to be someone else, all right, but the wrong person. This mode of identification represents, in a way, a failure to understand the injunction, as if instead of trying *to be* someone else, queer kids tried *being* someone else. The attempt to normalize, innocently transformed into an experiment with the abnormal, reveals, in the end, the founding failure that is self-realization as self-alienation and suggests that queer lives are a matter of troping. Back in my teenage years, the relationship between the fantasy of performing "Black Market" in a roomful of drunken sailors and that of being fucked up the ass was already clear to me. In fact, both fantasies alternately "took place" behind closed doors in my bedroom. Admitting to

Figure 5. Marlene on the set of *Morocco*, 1930: gender as image. (Photo: Don English; © Kobal Collection)

the former was, for whoever could read it, tantamount to admitting to the latter, and as a youth I often proclaimed my love for Marlene as a coded, that is, at once timid and provocative, form of coming out. As I said, it was both an empowering and a shameful gesture inasmuch as it simultaneously announced and silenced what it stood for. In other words, it needed to be read. And this is precisely what I felt was happening at the Hermon concert. The audience was looking through me and could see my adolescent fantasy of myself, my secret shame embodied—my very big faggotry wallowing on the bar like some cheap harlot and finally exposed for all to see. I'm overdoing it a little, of course, because I no longer feel so victimized by my shame, for better or for worse. Yet, this episode brought it back to my memory in an unexpectedly vivid way. Years later I remembered my shame, and what more spectacular way is there to remember shame than to feel it again, to reawaken a past you thought was safely behind you, to experience all of a sudden the shocking fragility of years of so-called progress? And can such a memory possibly be a good thing? I think it can.

The idea of reclaiming shame has recently become a topic of inquiry among queers, theorists and otherwise. In New York, San Francisco, and other American cities, gay-shame celebrations have been organized in opposition to the increasingly normative and commercialized gay-pride parades and against the emergence of a conservative gay agenda. An interdisciplinary Gay Shame conference was organized at the University of Michigan in March 2003. Following in the footsteps of Queer Nation, a short-lived group that attacked what they saw as the exclusionary bourgeois values of established urban gay communities in the early 1990s, Gay Shame activists and scholars are reclaiming practices and identities that have now been abjected not only by the dominant heterosexual culture but by many gay people as well. Public and anonymous sex, gender indeterminacy, promiscuity, class specificities, and other markers of nonconformity may be reclaimed as alternatives to more mainstream values such as marriage or the right to wear military uniforms for real. My purpose here is not to determine whether shame is better than pride or *queer* better than *gay*. I have my opinion on the matter, of course. It is fairly simple, and it goes something like this: Pride, because it is predicated on its dichotomous opposition to shame, always reasserts what it repudiates. Moreover, pride produces an additional level of shame—it makes us ashamed of our shame. No matter how you look at it, shame, it seems, just won't stay away. So what interests me more is to raise the question of what kind of community could be grounded in feelings of shame. And, yes, what role Marlene Dietrich plays in all that. This is where I'll start.

"I've Been Photographed to Death!"

There is perhaps one photo of Marlene that has always fascinated me more than the others, and it wasn't until my episode at Michel Hermon's concert that I fully understood why. It is a black-and-white photo by Nickolas Muray (fig. 6). I don't know its exact year, but judging by Marlene's face, hair, and dress, it probably dates from the early 1930s, shortly after she arrived

Figure 6. Marlene photographed by Nickolas Muray in the 1930s: layers of artifice. (Photo: Nickolas Muray; © International Museum of Photography, George Eastman House, Syracuse)

in Hollywood to become a contract player at Paramount. The setting is also a good indication of the context in which it was taken. Marlene is photographed from the hips up, wearing a severe white dress with wide shoulders and an upturned collar. It shows no flesh, and the only adornments are a stone-encrusted matching belt and bracelet. Her face is coldly beautiful as she stares blankly to her left, one hand on her hip and the other resting on some piece of furniture that is almost entirely outside the frame. She is the epitome of what American audiences of the time saw as exotic European sophistication. The way her expressionless face catches the light, with her hair emphasizing her forehead, betrays the fact that Dietrich, in those years, was marketed as Paramount's answer to Greta Garbo. But Paramount isn't MGM. Metro's image was one of class, gloss, and glamour; its biggest stars were Garbo and Norma Shearer. Paramount had Mae West and Marlene, and both of them almost always played whores. Sultry sex with a touch of irony was, in other words, what Paramount was all about, at least in the pre–Code era.[1] So although Muray's portrait of Marlene appears to duplicate Garbo's aloofness, it also undermines the divine Swede's image of ethereal beauty by having Marlene pose in front of a painting representing a bare-chested black woman in the same position. The message is simple enough and largely relies on intersecting clichés about race and the sexuality of women: remove the restraining veil of white sophistication and you'll find a wild, natural woman. Under all that veneer of propriety lies the promise of unrestrained sex.

This picture, revealing the naked truth behind Marlene Dietrich, her nature, is not all black and white, though. On the one hand, it reproduces in visual terms certain traditional notions about truth as being simultaneously behind (the clothes, the veil) and above (the contingencies and imperfections of the human). But by revealing the truth as a painting, it also suggests that truth is itself a representation, in this case a work of art. In that sense the photograph provides both a perfect definition of what Marlene Dietrich is all about and a complex and subversive model of queer identification.

Nearly all photos of Marlene emphasize artifice (see the ones I have selected for this essay, for example), and her screen persona was always one of distance—not existential distance, as with Garbo, but rather the more inviting kind of rhetorical distance effected by ambiguity and irony. Her image developed through her unique working relationship with the director Josef von Sternberg in the six pictures they made together at Paramount, following *The Blue Angel*, between 1930 and 1935, and it was a far cry, for example, from Bette Davis's image at Warner Brothers, a studio known for its social realism. Fan magazines always portrayed the private Marlene as no different from her public image. And the first glimpse the American moviegoing public got of her was the cross-dressing, same-sex kissing scene from *Morocco*, a picture whose advertising tag line was "The woman women want to see." In Hollywood she was refused entry to several clubs and restaurants for wearing male attire, and she was reported even to prefer male undergarments.[2]

But beyond gender ambiguity, which would have been enough to make her the ideal queer diva for both gay men and lesbians, Marlene's drag opens up a deeper, really bottomless, abyss of representation. The Muray picture shows how the removal of one layer of representation reveals not the real Marlene but yet another layer of representation, hinting at a perpetual de-

ferral of reality until eventually the referent vanishes altogether. Jean Coc-
teau once said of Marlene Dietrich, "You wear plumes and fur that seem to
belong to your body like fur on wild beasts and plumes on birds."[3] This description can be read in two ways. We may understand it as suggesting that
Marlene is an animal, a fabulous, mythical one having all at once the beauty
of a bird and the wildness of a beast. But more interesting perhaps is the reverse: Marlene is herself a fabulous (in the gay sense of the term, this time)
item of clothing with no actual being underneath. Implied in the latter interpretation is the notion that whether wearing male or female attire, Marlene is pure drag and, in a kind of pre-Butlerian move, that categories of sex
are only a matter of performance. Marlene herself was quite aware of that,
I think. After seeing Helmut Berger impersonate her in Luchino Visconti's
The Damned, she sent the young actor a photograph of herself in the same
costume, that of Lola-Lola, the character she played in von Sternberg's *The
Blue Angel*, with a note saying, "Which one of us is the prettier?" In so doing
she effectively separated Marlene Dietrich from the actual human being
who bears that name and made it something to be enacted by anyone, regardless of sex.

In the second half of her career, when she progressively abandoned the
screen for the stage, her show was often divided in two parts. In one she
would wear a male outfit and sing, as a man, songs about women; in the
other, she would wear her famous naked gown (fig. 7) and sing as a woman.
This so-called naked gown was so notorious back then, it deserves a few
words of explanation here. Designed by Jean Louis for Marlene's opening
night at the Sahara in Las Vegas in December 1953, it created quite a sensation, for it appeared to be completely transparent and scandalously revealing.[4] In reality, thanks to the trickery and genius of Jean Louis, it revealed absolutely nothing. Once again, Marlene's nakedness happened to
be an illusion—and an illusion she was intent on maintaining.[5] When anyone approached the stage a little too closely, she would gesture her admirer
to keep his or her distance and say, "Don't ruin the illusion!" One could be
cynical, of course, and think she did this because she didn't want her audience to realize she was completely plastered and that her face was pulled up
by safety pins tucked under her wig. Could the staunchest devotion survive
the ghastly spectacle of truth? Probably not. But, be that as it may, I want to
see Marlene's injunction as one more sign that there was in fact no real Marlene, and that she was quite earnest when she explained to the director Max-
imilian Schell why she didn't want him to film her for his 1984 documentary
about her. "I've been photographed to death!" she said, as if all the pictures
had annihilated and replaced her.

Figure 7. At the Olympia, Paris, in the 1950s: Jean Louis's notorious "naked gown."
(© Paris Match)

Compare Marlene's stage persona to that of another, and perhaps the grandest, gay diva, Judy Garland. If Marlene's self-conscious artificiality has the effect of removing nature from the (bourgeois) system of representation, thus depriving it of its transcendent legitimation, to see and hear Judy Garland, especially in concert, is to experience her disturbing sincerity as an excess of nature rather than the lack of it. She was so different from my Marlene it took me years to get her. I just found her embarrassing and emotionally inappropriate. But that, of course, is the whole point: there is an element of shame in Judy Garland, of shame and abjection. (The two are kin.) When she sings, Judy performs the dissolution of the boundary between the private and the public, the personal and the nonpersonal. Her insides are out, to use Juli Highfill's apt description.[6] Nowhere is this more evident than in a pose that became a trademark of Judy's live shows. After performing all alone for awhile, in a staging of the self that singularizes her and makes her the fabulous star that she was, she then motions forward and sits at the edge of the stage, typically to sing "Over the Rainbow," creating an impression of intimacy between her and the audience. By sitting at the very line separating the public's area from her own, she subverts the boundary that defines the individual and the collective, the self and the nonself, as pairs of mutually exclusionary terms. Instead, she becomes one with her public, and we may become her. No wonder Judy is so often impersonated by drag queens! And it's easy to see why my friends and I keep repeating a line from her biopic *Life with Judy Garland*: "You think it's hard working for Judy Garland? Try *being* Judy Garland!" I have no idea whether Judy ever said it or not. If she didn't, the line is truly a stroke of genius on the part of the writers, because it encapsulates her to perfection. It seems that all Judy ever told us was to try being her—desperately. But the self we identify with is a product of its staging and does not exist without performance and the communal experience of spectatorship. Rufus Wainwright's series of concerts in 2006 and 2007, in which he performed Judy's legendary 1961 show at Carnegie Hall, song for song and in the same arrangements, is thus a fitting tribute. Rufus essentially did in public what he used to do in private years ago, and in his stage banter he repeatedly emphasized the community formed by and with the audience thanks to his performance. During the last of these shows, at Los Angeles's Hollywood Bowl on September 23, 2007, he even established a connection with the large number of gay men who attended Judy's original concert. He honored them as brave trailblazers and reminded us that many of them couldn't attend his show because of the ravages of AIDS, making them a ghostly presence that haunted not only the Hollywood Bowl that night, but also the community at large. As he alternated between genuine emotion and ironic impersonation, or better yet seamlessly blended the two, Rufus functioned as a mirror for his audience and erased the gap between the present and the past, the living and the dead, the singular and the plural. Although they contrast in form or style, Judy's excessive sincerity and Marlene's distant artificiality achieve similar results. Star and audience seem to be saying to each other, "Without you, I'm nothing."[7] Borrowing from Flaubert, I could proclaim, "Marlene Dietrich, c'est moi!"

The ultimate erasure of the natural self, I want to suggest, is what can be appropriated by queers for purposes of community. Consider again the performance by Michel Hermon. Lying both behind and above me, he mirrored the position of the black woman's painting in relation to Marlene, a position I symbolically depicted as that of truth in relation to representation. The shame I remembered/experienced as a result signaled that I felt exposed, that my corporeal self was but a representation while my truest, most private self was being revealed by Herman's allegorical performance of it—and that it was worthy of shame. But that supposedly authentic self took the form of another man wearing what was in effect double drag—a man dressed as a woman dressed as a man. The true self I felt was exposed that night comes not so much from identification with a real but forbidden object—the other sex—as from a spiral of pure representation. Unlike gay pride's bourgeois discourse of authenticity, urging us to come out and be our true selves, this shameful mode of identification forsakes all claims to authenticity and reveals naturalness as yet another artifice. The system of norms and values that defined me as shameful in the name of truth and nature is thus deprived of the very terrain that grounds its legitimacy. The fact that my shame was experienced through, and because of, a collapse of the private and the public, of the self and the collective, is why it can be so politically powerful. Shame is located at the precise boundary defining the normal and the abnormal. Such feelings, of course, are supposed to be manifestations of internalized social policing, warning signs that give us a foretaste of what it would be like to be completely desocialized and, as a result, make us want to rush for safety to the side of the normal. But what if we don't? What if shame relived, the persistence of one's lonely past alongside the present, could be a factor in the formation of community?

The Power of Positive Shaming

In his essay "Mario Montez, For Shame," Douglas Crimp draws on the works of Eve Kosofsky Sedgwick and Michael Warner in order to study shame's "capacity for articulating collectivities of the shamed."[8] Starting with Sedgwick's observation that one can be flooded by someone else's shame,[9] Crimp writes:

In taking on the shame, I do not share in the other's identity. I simply adopt the other's vulnerability to being shamed. In this operation, most important, the other's difference is preserved; it is not claimed as my own. In taking on or taking up his or her shame, I am not attempting to vanquish his or her otherness. I put myself in the place of the other only insofar as I recognize that I too am prone to shame.[10]

And he goes on to quote Warner: "Queer scenes are the true *salons des refusés*, where the most heterogeneous people are brought into great intimacy by their common experience of being despised and rejected in a world of norms."[11] As Warner, Sedgwick, and Crimp all notice, heterogeneity, that is to say singularity, is at the core of any collectivity to be constituted by shame. Sedgwick describes "this sensation whose very suffusiveness seems to delineate my precise, individual outlines in the most isolating way imaginable"; and Crimp, referring to Mario Montez, the Puerto Rican drag queen whose interview in a film by Andy Warhol is the focus of his piece, concludes, "I am thus not 'like' Mario, but the distinctiveness that is revealed in Mario invades me—'floods me,' to use Sedgwick's word—and my own distinctiveness is revealed simultaneously. I, too, feel exposed."[12] Just as I felt exposed by the spotlight that shone on me at the concert. At that very moment, when shame, brutal and inarticulate, completely overwhelmed me, I felt no sense of community whatsoever with the two gay friends who were with me that night or the other queers who made up much of the audience, let alone with the singer who shamelessly embodied that rejected part of myself. I felt completely separated from everyone else, gay or straight. In other words, as Sedgwick points out, the moment of shame is one of isolation, not communion; it feels hyperindividualizing.

Yet, this extreme singularity also enables the collective. As I mentioned earlier, I am both over my shame and not over it at all, for to remember it is to relive it with exactly the same intensity and pain. Strictly speaking, it may not even be a matter of remembering because, by shining a spotlight on one's singularity, feelings of shame temporarily remove you from the social, and without the social there can be no memory. Shame, therefore, can never be a thing *of* the past in that it stubbornly refuses to stay *in* the past. Getting over one's shame is not a process to be completed. If I feel shame today, it isn't because I'm not completely over it yet. If that were the case I would probably feel less and less ashamed each time and, at worst, a bit nostalgic about that long-gone piece of my life. Instead, the very physicality of that intense emotion, its Proustian suddenness and sense of immediacy, suggests that I am in contact, in touch, with a self that I no longer am yet still am. As Gloria Gaynor famously put it in her 1970s gay disco anthem, "I Am What I Am." But I am also what I am no longer. If, as Michael Warner proposes, communities of the shamed are defined by intimacy between heterogeneous people, they are also constituted by people who, in a sense, are not even similar to themselves and who embrace that disconnectedness from an unknowable self. This is where queer (community) and gay (identity) overlap but diverge. In the gay rhetoric of pride, the speech act of coming out is akin to a birth; it inaugurates a new self. Think of ACT UP's slogan "I am out, therefore I am." In this view, the gap between our past and current selves is not one that may be bridged by a kind of developmental or evolutionary continuity. At least symbolically, it is supposed to be a radical repudiation, a personal Stonewall, as if the foundational, emancipatory moment of the modern gay movement were to be internalized by each gay individual in a move that would from now on attach the self to the collective. Much of this could be embraced by a queer analysis, but although the rhetoric of pride demands that our two selves be forever disconnected, queerness reconnects them without erasing their discrepancy. This is what remembering our shame is all about. It isn't nostalgia for the closet, which would amount to a simple reversal of pride's dichotomy and would lead to the same aporia. The recent development of scholarly interest in the pre-Stonewall era, for example, is less a matter of archaeology than a search for viable forms of queerness as alternatives to standardized, and standard-enforcing, gayness. Indeed, the gay rhetoric of pride has always depended on its ability to produce an archaic past against which to define itself, either by ignoring the fact that communities, whether urban or not, all-white or not, male, female, or mixed, did exist before Stonewall; or by denying these communities' usefulness in articulating current cultural modalities. As D. A. Miller suggests in *Place for Us [Essay on the Broadway Musical]*, the "gay identity to which we have entrusted our own politics, ethics, sex lives . . . stands in an essentially reductive relation to the desire on which it is based."[13] Reclaiming our shame today, then, may finally do justice to the elusiveness and complexity that homosexual desire had for us yesterday, before we even knew what it was, and before we could harness it to an identity. And this may indeed include a rethinking of the closet as culture, i.e., as a question of collective as well as individual experience.[14] From this perspective, reclaiming shame is not a rejection of all feelings of pride, but rather a critique of a rhetoric of progress that mirrors nineteenth-century bourgeois discourses—the same discourses that defined queers as essentially archaic. Think of psychoanalysis's construction of anality as belonging to the past and of the shame generated by all things anal in modern Western culture. Reclaiming our own archaism is a desire to touch our past, that is, the Otherness in us, in order to redefine our present. This, in turn or perhaps simultaneously, creates intimacy with Otherness in general. What produces community in shame, then, is not shame per se—an affect that, like trauma, cannot be articulated in language and therefore, cannot articulate social relations. What produces community in shame is its memory—always a collective process. Using the term "queer" in its old, negative, and singularizing sense rather than in its current theoretical sense, the film scholar Richard Dyer remarks, "I remember being a queer and have never been entirely convinced that I ever became gay."[15] And what shame tells us, with its overwhelming power to make us relive it at the most unexpected moments, is that our past isolation can never be safely rejected. I'll repeat it: to remember shame is to experience it anew, isolation and all. A community in shame is one that can be neither naturalized nor positioned as dominant because it is consciously defined by the active and persistent memory of its own negativity.

As opposed to the family-based models of community so popular in mainstream gay rhetoric these days, queer communities are thus predicated on the impossibility of stability and self-sameness. According to the philosopher Peter Sloterdijk, the myth of the expulsion from paradise anchors all human self-consciousness in shame: "From then on, shame, along with feelings of guilt and separation, would become the oldest and most powerful instance of self-referentiality through which the individual 'makes an image' of himself. The deepest traces of Being as an extant shortcoming are inscribed in this image."[16] My point here is that the first conscious image of oneself that young homosexuals "make" *as homosexuals* is one of guilt and separation from the family, a domestic fall from grace in which we realize that we were not exactly made in our parents' image. This "extant shortcoming" generates the first instance of gay shame and, from then on, posits identification as discontinuity and difference *from* the family rather than as continuity and sameness *with* the family.[17] The memory of our separation from the familial Eden and subsequent isolation reminds us that there hasn't always been community and that, therefore, there may not always be community. An identity thus defined by its own negation through an identification mediated by disconnectedness and difference cannot produce communities simply on the basis of a shared positive trait. It doesn't *ground* communities so much as disseminate them on a free-floating diasporic model of out-of-placeness and out-of-timeness, in which the self can only be comprehended through its contact with others and experience its selfness always as otherness. Indeed a queer community is a community of spatial discrepancy and asynchronicity, where past and present are concurrent and in which we enjoy the pleasures of the collective and relive our original isolation at the same time.

I may have felt completely out of place when Michel Hermon sang "Black Market"; I may have felt out of time too (I mean, come on, who worships Marlene Dietrich these days?), but in the end it made a pretty good story, didn't it? Its confessional mode, however, does not inscribe it so neatly in the logic of Foucault's *aveu*, according to which the confession of deviance produces the pathological species of the homosexual.[18] In fact, when you tell a story like this one, chances are someone in your audience will retort, "Oh, darling, you think *that's* bad? Well, listen to *this*." Then a third person may join in with an even more humiliating story. And so on, and so forth, until the story, which must retain its genuine confessional dimension in order to achieve the twofold status of parody, momentarily deactivates the disciplinary power of confession and turns isolation into something like a membership card. Sharing such stories makes a rather interesting community, slightly on the freakish side perhaps, but one where I feel right at home. So, as Marlene, and Michel Hermon, used to sing, "See what the boys in the backroom will have, and tell them I'm having the same!"

Notes

1. The pre-Code era refers to the years 1930-34, when the Hollywood Production Code of censorship was not enforced.

2. See Thomas Doherty, *Pre-Code Hollywood: Sex, Immorality, and Insurrection in American Cinema, 1930-1934* (New York: Columbia University Press, 1999), 175.

3. See Thierry de Navacelle, *Sublime Marlene* (Paris: Ramsay, 1982), 11; the translation is mine. The whole quote, in French, is: "Marlene Dietrich . . . Votre nom débute par une caresse et s'achève par un coup de cravache. Vous portez des plumes et des fourrures qui semblent appartenir à votre corps comme les fourrures des fauves et les plumes des oiseaux. Votre voix, votre regard, sont ceux de la Loreleï, mais la Loreleï était dangereuse; vous ne l'êtes pas parce que votre secret de beauté consiste à prendre soin de votre ligne de coeur."

4. See Alexander Walker, *Dietrich* (New York: Harper & Row, 1984), 174-76.

5. In *A Foreign Affair*, she also sang a song called "Illusions." Like "Black Market," it was originally written for her by Friedrich Holländer.

6. Personal communication, April 2003.

7. This phrase is the comedian Sandra Bernhard's, and she knows a thing or two about fabulousness.

8. See Douglas Crimp, "Mario Montez, For Shame," this volume, 72; Eve Kosofsky Sedgwick, "Queer Performativity: Henry James's *The Art of the Novel*," *GLQ* 1, no. 1 (1993): 1-16; Michael Warner, *The Trouble with Normal: Sex, Politics, and the Ethics of Queer Life* (New York: Free Press, 1999).

9. Here is the complete passage quoted by Crimp: "One of the strangest features of shame (but, I would argue, the most theoretically significant) is the way bad treatment of someone else, bad treatment *by* someone else, someone else's embarrassment, stigma, debility, blame or pain, seemingly having nothing to do with me, can so readily flood me—assuming that I'm a shame-prone person—with this sensation whose very suffusiveness seems to delineate my precise, individual outlines in the most isolating way imaginable" (Crimp, "Mario Montez," 70-71; Sedgwick, "Queer Performativity," 14).

10. Crimp, "Mario Montez," 71.

11. Ibid., 72; Warner, *The Trouble with Normal*, 35-36.

12. Crimp, "Mario Montez," 73.

13. D. A. Miller, *Place for Us: [Essay on the Broadway Musical]* (Cambridge, MA: Harvard University Press, 1998), 132. I thank David Halperin for suggesting that I look at Miller's essay. See also Halperin's reading of Miller in "Homosexuality's Closet," *Michigan*

Quarterly Review 41, no. 1 (Winter 2002): 21–54. There is much in Miller's and Halperin's analyses that intersects with mine, especially when they underscore the limitations of explicit gay identification in relation to desire.

14. A Web site called Closet Culture, developed on a nonprofit basis by graduate students from the University of Michigan's School of Information (but no longer in operation "due to security concerns and lack of volunteers"), defined its mission as follows: "Closet Culture (CC) is a unique online community that connects closeted and questioning individuals in an anonymous environment. At CC, you will find *community without being outed*" (http://www.closetculture.net; my emphasis).

15. See Richard Dyer, *The Culture of Queers* (New York: Routledge, 2002), 13. I thank Nadine Hubbs for this quote.

16. Peter Sloterdijk, *Weltfremdheit* (Frankfurt am Main: Suhrkamp, 1993), 25; quoted in Scott Spector, *Prague Territories: National Conflict and Cultural Invasion in Franz Kafka's Fin de Siècle* (Berkeley: University of California Press, 2000), 24.

17. If I posit queerness and family as incompatible, I do not imply that queer individuals cannot enjoy good relationships with their families. What I mean is that if a queer's queerness is not to be erased, the family has to be queered. See David Caron, "Intrusions: The Family in AIDS Films," *L'esprit créateur* 38, no. 3 (1998): 62–72.

18. See Michel Foucault, *La volonté de savoir* (Paris: Gallimard, 1976).

[E L L I S   H A N S O N]

Teaching Shame

The veil of modesty torn, the shameful parts shown, I know—with my cheeks aflame—
the need to hide myself or die, but I believe by facing and enduring this painful anxiety I shall, as a result of my shamelessness, come to know a strange beauty.

Jean Genet, *The Thief's Journal,* 1949

Is there a queer theory of pedagogy? What does it reveal? Or, in the veil-
ripping rhetoric of queer hermeneutics, what does it *expose*, what does it *interrogate*, what mystifications are shown in all their nakedness? It tells me, if
anything, I am a failure. Most discussions of teaching in the field of lesbian
and gay studies orbit around the politics of identity, or sometimes just its etiquette, especially in the confessional moments of sexual self-identification
and affirmation. Students come out, teachers come out, administrators
come out, and they try to be proud about it. This is revolutionary, but I am
not very good at it. "I like the kind of sex that's embarrassing," I said to my
students in my most recent failure to come out properly in a classroom. "If
you're not ashamed of the sex you're having, chances are you're not doing it
right" (they wrote this down for the quiz). In the spirit of Leo Bersani, I have
come to value sex, gay and otherwise, as a respite from pride, as a relatively
pleasurable and reliable source of degradation, its success often predicated
paradoxically on its failures. "Male homosexuality," he writes, "advertises
the risk of the sexual itself as the risk of self-dismissal, of *losing sight* of the
self, and in so doing it proposes and dangerously represents *jouissance* as a
mode of ascesis."[1] According to this logic, the focus on "male homosexuality" is somewhat arbitrary. It is not a different commodity from "the sexual itself," it just "advertises" better; like a centerfold, it makes everyone's
risk and shame more visible. Can one risk betraying the self of "male homosexuality" too? Can one come out in the classroom as just such a failure?

Whenever I stand accused in the witness box of gossip, which is happily quite often, I feel it my pedagogical duty to confess to every crime, especially crimes of identity, and most especially the ones I have not yet bothered to commit. Genet had the right attitude: "The mechanism was somewhat as follows (I have used it since): to every charge brought against me, unjust though it be, from the bottom of my heart I shall answer yes."[2] This is close to my ideal of coming out, but it smacks too much of pride. I have altered the mechanism somewhat as follows: to every confessional demand leveled at my person—"Are you this, are you that? Have you done this? But have you done *that*?!"—from the bottom of my heart I shall answer, "Yes. Oh, yes! *But I'm not very good at it.*" This confession has a greater probability of being true than the one Genet uses. A one-size-fits-all admission of guilt, it points up the inevitable failure inherent in identity itself. What Judith Butler has said of heterosexuality is, as she has often demonstrated, readily applicable to identity in general: it is "always in the process of imitating and approximating its own phantasmatic idealization of itself—*and failing.*"[3] Failure makes identity political. Failure can make it sexy. It shows the cracks in idealization and renders identity politics an inexhaustible resource for shame. Moreover, every conference, every seminar, every inquiry into the politics of identity is another pedagogical occasion for the exquisite lacerations of shame, whether turned inward in theatrical self-flagellation or outward in public displays of indignation or remonstration.

Can I be affirming about my shame? Can I find it beautiful? Can I teach it? Would I be good at it? Shame is at once elusive and ubiquitous. As in my epigraph, whenever one seeks to affirm one's own shame, it seems always to morph into its opposite: shamelessness, or even pride. One literally faces shame, or faces it down, since where but the face does one feel it more acutely—"cheeks aflame," Genet writes in hot dashes, disrupting the placid countenance of his sentence with a new syntax of averted eyes, bowed head, and halting speech. As Michael Warner has observed, the most popular strategy for outsmarting shame is to "pin it on someone else" as quickly as possible,[4] though one does not always succeed in convincing one's own conscience or banishing the residue of anxiety that even a false accusation can leave, that wagging finger we preserve in our imagination long after anyone else cares enough to remonstrate with us. Or one seeks to mitigate shame through penitence, reparations, or pity, thereby marking the triumph of that gaze. Or I can hide myself or die, as Genet says. But is shame to be valued only at the moment one no longer feels its inflammation?—as an affect to be transcended?—as a goad for the social discipline of others? Why is this strange beauty of which Genet speaks deemed to be a mystical enigma somewhere on the other side of shame, not properly within it? In his insistently Christian theology of queer shame, Genet demands a mortification no less trying than the Passion of Christ, and the beauty of its abjection shimmers in the distance, vaguely, mystically, like some New Jerusalem in which we will find ourselves, one day perhaps, redeemed. He found it embarrassing sometimes that his shame was always receding absurdly into pride, the self-betrayal of a self-betrayal that cancels itself out. In a 1964 interview, he said, "I like being an outcast just as, with all due respect, Lucifer likes being cast out by God. But it's out of pride, and that's not my good side. It's a bit stupid. It's a naïve romantic attitude."⁵ He always ends up wanting to show us his good side by showing us his bad side, which makes him immediately grow nostalgic for his "painful anxiety" and search for some fresh and more reliable embarrassment. It is shame, not shamelessness, that he finds most alluring and elusive: shame for its own sake, or for the sake of a seemingly unrequited love inherent in it.

By affirming shame, I am not merely indulging a decadent fascination with my own abjection, though that alone would be sufficient to recommend it to me. Its intensities are alluring, however painful, but they can also be reassuring in that they presume a powerful bond with other people, a civility far from serene or static, a mobility of affiliation with little respect for the conventional limits of identification or even rational judgment. Like aesthetic bliss, like desire, like love, shame affords its greatest pleasure in a violence to the ego that keeps the self in motion even while keeping it in check. Shame defies me, defines me, overwhelms me. Even the thrill of shame is elusive, tantalizing, the erotic intensity of degradation quickly devolving into banality with the repetition of any transgression, any obscene occasion, that might seek to reproduce it and command it, such that it seems at once an ever-retreating limit and an ever-surprising intrusion, the cheeks aflame cooling ever more to paleness with each failed attempt at mastery. Shame embraces me like a siege, a suffocation, but I cannot embrace it. I cannot address it at all. It rarely condescends to respond to my formal invitations, preferring to bide its time until it is most unwelcome and then make a dramatic entrance. I can at best make space for it, entertain it. I do not perform my shame so much as it performs me. It reorganizes my pleasures and my limits according to a logic in which I participate but cannot definitively assert my will. Shame is humiliating that way.

How does one make space for shame, rather than seeking transcendence through shamelessness or pride? The gesture is hardly conservative, nor is it particularly progressive. Shame may be, and often is, valued and deployed for political reasons, for its effectiveness in social management, and that

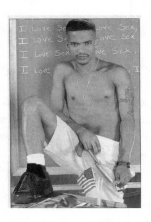

Figure 8. Shortly before I am tenured, a conservative talk-show host, "Dr. Laura," airs an opinion that my course on child sexuality "has crossed the threshold from the merely absurd to the potentially dangerous." The dean, the chair of my department, and the president of the university get angry letters from hundreds and hundreds of outraged people, including a minister in Maryland who claims I seek to "normalize criminal thought" and lead the university into "a quagmire of iniquity." Someone named "Pedo Hunter," evidently offended by the same course, writes to me to say, "All I can PROMISE you is I'll TRACK YOU DOWN FOR THE MANGY DOG YOU ARE!!!" Using his real name, an undergraduate circulates a fantasy on the Internet in which he takes me to a Brazilian leper colony and tortures me to death because I am teaching a course on lesbian fiction and am clearly a lesbian myself.

I have an unpleasant suspicion that these shaming tactics, not my views on Plato or Genet, make my teaching queer. With this improbable pornography of violence and moral panic, they expose me, they expose themselves, they expose teaching itself. Have they no shame?

includes the social management of progressive change. There is, however, an inevitable logic of failure built into this deployment of shame, and that failure poses a radical challenge to the shaming pieties of law and order, political unity, and even progressive activism. This failure gives shame its disruptive potential, its edge, though that edge is never easily appropriated for a particular political cause. Gay shame, for example, has rarely been attractive to gay politics, except as a villain. Gay pride can be deployed, and certainly has been, as a shaming technique, a conservative tool for assimilation by which gay people whose conduct is deemed relatively normal or acceptable acquire social benefits at the expense of gay people whose conduct is not. It is largely because of this conservative deployment of shame that Warner calls for a queer "ethics of shame," a connectedness to others in a queer context where all are fallen and all are shamed.

Warner is very eloquent and astute about the queer sort of generosity that comes from a mutual recognition of abjection. This generosity is immensely important to me as well, though I find it as difficult as he does to conceptualize. When Warner evokes it, he sounds like a more redemptive version of Genet. He writes, "Shame is bedrock. Queers can be abusive, insulting, and vile toward one another, but because abjection is understood to be the shared condition, they also know how to communicate through such camaraderie a moving and unexpected form of generosity. No one is beneath its reach, not because it prides itself on generosity, but because it prides itself on nothing."[6] Genet would have dwelt with greater delectation on the queers who are "abusive, insulting, and vile" to one another (I have been to *that* conference), but Warner awaits the bluebird of queer "generosity," where shame speaks through humility rather than aggression. Like Genet, however, Warner is drawn by shame to a queer utopia somewhere beyond shame, a *salon des refusés*, as he describes it, where everyone is equally shamed and so, paradoxically, no one has to feel bad. Genet never quite arrives there. Warner, on the other hand, all but gives us the address and wishes more lesbians and gay men would show up there instead of at A-list fund-raisers for gay marriage rights.

Warner's argument culminates with a carnivalesque evocation of his salon that makes it sound invitingly shameless and certainly more fun than anything in Genet: "The rule is: Get over yourself. Put a wig on before you judge. And the corollary is that you stand to learn most from the people you think are beneath you. At its best, this ethic cuts against every form of hierarchy you could bring into the room." Except, of course, for the inverse hierarchy of queerness itself, the game of feeling queerer-than-thou (I have been to *that* conference too). Warner points out approvingly that queer culture has its own way of "keeping people in line," and here things apparently start to get "abusive, insulting, and vile" again: "In queer circles, you are likely to be teased and abused until you grasp the idea."[7] With queers keeping one another in line this way, who needs homophobes? A queer "ethics of shame," like most ethical systems, can easily become yet another social discipline with good subjects and bad subjects, those who are shamed for failing to conduct their shame appropriately. Moreover, Warner's queer vision can sound like a Sunday-school ethics reconfigured as camp: judge not at the gay bar lest ye be judged at the gay bar. I think I would like that, but I would probably not be very good at it. What I find most difficult is the tall order of the golden rule, "Get over yourself," since I have quite enough trouble getting into myself. Is this a command to get "in line"? Is it even possible? One could easily deconstruct it by trying rigorously to obey the absurd and excruciating logic of its imperative. It would return us to Genet by aestheticizing shame as an ascesis for its own sake. What is the self that got over itself, and does it not itself deserve a good getting over? As Genet discovered, the negativity of shame, its downward spiral of abjection, easily becomes an absurdist *mise en abîme* of self-effacements and self-betrayals.

Pride, whether gay or not, is no less problematic. Pride and shame form a perilous dialectic in which they are ever in danger of trading places. However eagerly I might seek it, pride is embarrassing. I also find it inert. Shame is invariably assaultive, but pride is generally construed in gentler, more passive terms, a feeling one struggles for but not a feeling that stalks one. It is an achievement. It languishes on pedestals, waiting to be seized as a reward for an assault of one's own, a hopeless assault on the moving target of shame. One *takes* pride in one's work, one possesses this pride and makes it the condition of further work, such that its very celebration of success is always compromised by a sense of grasping desperation. Hence, in part, the unstable status of pride as both a virtue and a sin. However enviable it may seem when I do not have it, pride can easily appear arrogant, delusional, self-indulgent—in a word, shameful—when I do have it. As soon as I embrace my pride, I am assaulted again by a shame that strangles my enjoyment. I cannot be seen enjoying my pride, or I will be punished. I have to be modest about it, as if it were something to be ashamed of. I feel obliged to disguise pride however thinly as humility, to take pride only in others, especially in God, or in institutions, or in other people, never in myself.

I run the risk here of claiming that shame is an originary affect and pride merely one of its more desperate manifestations, but I am accustomed to hearing pride dubiously eulogized in just the opposite terms. In the popular, quintessentially American rhetoric extolling self-esteem and identity affirmation for absolutely everyone, pride is one's birthright, one's proper condition, a sign of one's full citizenship and self-realization, while shame is pathologized as an anomaly to be purged through self-assertion, a readjustment of one's values, a liberation of one's libido, a transcendence of adverse circumstances, a robust *no* spoken to power. One should feel pride, in other words, because one has something others do not. Either through their accomplishments or through their association with an accomplished group of people, the proud among us "put others to shame." Once everyone shares pride, no one has it. We may shift pride from one person to another, but far from banishing shame, we ensure its persistence, its irreducibility, in our own self-definition. Not surprisingly, despite the blandishments of self-help books, I feel besieged by shame no matter how many ways I put others to shame, even when, with an eye to some more or less definite principle of progress, I readjust my values, liberate my libido, transcend my traumas, or speak a thunderous *no* to power. As Eve Kosofsky Sedgwick writes, shame and pride are "different interlinings of the same glove."[8] Could I ever take the glove off? Could I touch anyone without its mediation?

Sedgwick writes that "the forms taken by shame are not distinct 'toxic' parts of a group or individual identity that can be excised; they are instead integral to and residual in the processes by which identity itself is formed. They are available for the work of metamorphosis, reframing, refiguration, *trans*figuration, of affective and symbolic loading and deformation, but perhaps all too potent for the work of purgation and deontological closure."[9] She sees in shame a powerful occasion for creativity—and she takes no less creative an example of aestheticism than Henry James to make her point. Furthermore, she valorizes shame as a key affect for queerness and a nodal point for queer theory: "'queer performativity' is the name of a strategy for the production of meaning and being, in relation to the affect shame and to the later and related fact of stigma."[10] Shame is not, in her view, simply good or bad, not something that one could banish for the sake of a politics of pride and self-affirmation, gay or otherwise. It is an organizing principle of identity, perhaps the key principle for queer identity in particular, and therefore a nexus for the communal connections, for the transformational political and artistic efforts, that have characterized that identity.

Shame is my curse and my oldest friend. It is a sign of my failure to connect with others and my urgent appetite for reparation. Without my shame, I could hardly recognize myself—indeed, I would not have a self to recognize—and so to banish shame would be absurd. Shame gives identity its peculiar serration. It cuts the flesh in a manner at once punishing and gratifying. What Genet hides in plain sight is not so much his self, nor even just his face, but his pleasure in the passivity of mortification, the unconsenting connection to other people, the strange and sudden apprehension of the self at its very limits, the reassuring rudeness, cruelty, and treachery of self-definition. Punishing, obviously, but gratifying too in that shame generates paradoxical forms of love, as revealed by his passionate attachment to the very thieves and sailors he betrays. I read Genet not for the quality of his transgressions, but for the quality of his love. Not for his shamelessness, but for his shame. With his cheeks aflame, he offers us—repeatedly, tirelessly—a love as primal as shame, love of oneself and other people, love even of objects and places, that is nevertheless predicated on the appreciation of error, vulnerability, unworthiness, disgust, abjection, and powerlessness—a shameful love, in other words, that can insist on nothing, claim nothing, but itself. Shame is an occasion for artistry without mastery, love without possession, connection without community, and desire without dignity.

In "Mario Montez, For Shame," an essay first published as a tribute to Sedgwick, Douglas Crimp draws on her work to explore the feelings of love that shame so often affords and the role it might play in queer politics. The essay, reprinted in this volume, was also a focus of the Gay Shame conference at the University of Michigan. I dutifully reread the essay for the conference, but the real thrill was to feel the essay in relation to the bodily presence of Crimp himself that weekend. He has a peculiar proneness to shame that I find alluring. During his presentation, he sat by himself at an absurdly large table in front of a large audience, and oddly far off to his right the appointed commentator heaped criticism on him. At breakfast before his presentation, he had said to me that he dreads this sort of academic performance and wished people would just discuss his essay without his having to answer for it in person. But there he was, dreading it in person at the front of the room and having to answer for various points he "failed" to discuss (*failed*, with all its shaming meanness, is now the accusatory word of choice in academic criticism). I am probably projecting here, but he looked sheepishly tactful to me, oddly lonely, painfully helpful, as if he were testifying at his own trial after having already pled guilty to a crime he was not sure he had committed. He was now proving the force of his argument about shame by enacting it, or inciting me to enact it. In speaking of his relationship to Mario Montez, he might just as well have been speaking of my relationship to him: "I feel alone with my shame, singular in my susceptibility to being shamed for this stigma that has now become mine and mine alone. Thus, my shame is taken on in lieu of the other's shame. In taking on the shame, I do not share in the other's identity. I simply adopt the other's vulnerability to being shamed."[11]

Citing Warner, Crimp argues for a politically valuable love that attends the shame of being queer, a certain generosity that seems to trump any meanness of one queer to another. He offers as an example his acute feeling of shame in watching Andy Warhol's "screen test" of Mario Montez. Crimp is distressed by the shaming of Montez, especially by his interlocutor, Ronald Tavel, whose offscreen voice prods the drag performer into various acts of degradation by way of an audition for a part in a film. Crimp writes that Montez is "clearly caught completely off guard" and it is "obvious he's still hoodwinked."[12] Yet Crimp offers no evidence for this clarity or obviousness apart from his own emotional intuition, which may be pure projection. I personally thought Mario Montez was playacting shame for the sake of a joke about casting couches and Hollywood vanity. His pupils were so dilated, despite the bright lights of the set, that I assumed he was too high to feel much of anything. In other words, what Crimp thought was shame I thought was irony. I often see irony in people whether they intend it or not, because it is one of my primary modes of being in the world, but sometimes irony finds shame seductive. Irony is hardly the opposite of shame, after all, though it may be the most effective defense against shame. This vulnerability in Crimp's argumentation—oh, let us call it his "failure"—is for me the most compelling dimension of his essay. Ultimately, what matters in this essay is that Crimp felt shame, and the reader might love him for it. Shame is so contagious, one can catch it from a person who may not even have it. I felt protective of him during his presentation, whether he wanted to make himself available for that protection or not. The medium was the message: the lesson is in the shame-prone erotics of the pedagogical relationship itself.

Shame teaches, but will not be taught, will not be lectured to: teaching shame, an affect as a discipline, a disciplinary gesture, but never in itself the thing to be disciplined, refigure it and reframe it as I might. Shame remains itself intractable, though it is pedagogical by its very nature. As a driving force in teaching, it inheres in every conception of pedagogy I know. Pedagogy without shame is like punishment without pain. Genet never writes much about his formal education, such as it was, and I will have very little more to say about him here, except that teaching his work, rereading it in the context of my teaching, I am tempted to claim that teachers and students are like his sailors and thieves. In their fallen world, their incommensurability, their betrayals, their inequalities, their sacrificial enthusiasms for each other, they reveal a certain love that militates against the affectations of dignity we call professionalism. Nowhere in my life do I feel the pinch of shame so bitingly, in such sensitive nether regions, as

Figure 9. Sudden twinge of shame, which sometimes takes the form of concern, amusement, or intellectual distraction, where a body or an affect, whether someone else's or my own, interrupts the smooth course of my lecture. Sleepiness, drunkenness, inordinate pulchritude, and hiccups, of course, in my own classes no less than in Plato's Symposium, where they pose a powerful challenge to the intellectualizing discourse on eros, but I have also witnessed helpless giggling, uncontainable enthusiasms, bursting into tears, bleeding, fainting, screaming, shouting, sneezing, spilling, stumbling, pencil-gnawing, gum-chewing, breast-feeding, wardrobe malfunctions, horniness, speechlessness, embarrassment, nausea, panic, and obstreperous bolting from the room for typically undisclosed forms of relief. I feel obliged to carry on with whatever train of thought still has tracks. Thinking is done with bodies, and as in Plato, they sometimes rewrite the pedagogical script.

in the mundane activities that have characterized my career as a student and a teacher. Teaching demands a harsh discipline of my body, a most excruciating etiquette, such that it feels at times like an alternative sexuality, an alternative criminality, where passions have more meaning and play for higher stakes. It is my livelihood, of course, but culture itself seems to be at stake, its symbolic investment in the body, the demands, the expectations, the responsibilities, mortifying the flesh with dignity and impersonality. I am the subject supposed to know, eminently exposed to the cultural symbolic, eminently answerable for it, and this role is shaming, eroticizing, scandalizing, precisely because I fail to disappear into it. I know with my cheeks aflame the need to hide myself and teach.

In a series of lecture notes published in English under the somewhat spooky title "Where a Teaching Body Begins and How It Ends," Jacques Derrida meditates on this symbolic overdetermination, this paradox of theatricality and disappearance, in the body of the teacher:

My body is glorious. It gathers all the light. First of all, that of the spot-light above me. Then it is radiant and attracts all eyes. But it is also glorious in that it is no longer simply a body. It is sublimated in the representation of at least one other body, the teaching body of which it should be at once a part and the whole, a member letting the gathering together of the body be seen, a body that in turn produces itself by erasing itself as the barely visible, entirely transparent, representation of both the philosophical and the sociopolitical corpus, the contract between these bodies never being brought to the foreground.[13]

He repeats the word *body* here as if, like a modern-day Frankenstein, he were hoping to zap to life the teaching body, his own teaching body, through sheer jolting repetition. In this passage, he entertains a pun that works equally well in French and in English, "the teaching body" as flesh, but also faculty and function in many senses of those words: the sexually overdetermined flesh of an individual person, but also the professional corporation of people who teach, their gathering for an event, their empowerment and purpose, and the sociopolitical abstraction of teaching as an institution that is defined by no mere individual. Teaching becomes an abstract function, a party of ghosts, figured paradoxically as the very "body" whose sensuous particularity it has ostensibly transcended, the "body" indeed that it has symbolically murdered. The "student body" would serve equally well here, especially because the pun already enjoys a history of ribald humor, by which a particularly fetching class president not only represents the student body, but is the student body, the one who defies the symbolic role of ascetic studiousness by recalling our attention to the scandal of alluring flesh. The distinction between the intellect and the flesh, however, is not as simple as the joke would have us believe, neither for the fetching student nor for the fetching professor. We can never absent ourselves, even if we wanted to, from the erotic allure of the whole mise-en-scène of classrooms, podiums, office hours, conferences, and books through which the improbable romance of teaching is enacted. In more recent high-profile narratives of pedagogical eros, from David Mamet's *Oleanna* to J. M. Coetzee's *Disgrace* (not to mention the feminist version by Jane Gallop, which I will discuss in a moment), the focus shifted to dubious accusations of sexual harassment, but the sense of the pedagogical body being a scandal to any rigid academic system has become only more embattled. As Elaine Showalter writes, "To many authors looking at the university around 2000, it seemed that the risks and the joys of the erotics of teaching had succumbed to an increasingly bureaucratic and soulless institutionalization."[14] For Derrida, this self-erasure of the pedagogical body is not some recent function of sexual harassment codes, but rather a result of the institutionalization of thinking itself.

Derrida is certainly no stranger to the gloriousness of the teaching body, its glamour, its charisma: his flash of white hair, his flash of radical ideas, his flash of gnomic style, and its gloriousness is never fully discernible from the corporate "teaching body" that he represents and that erases him. This glamour does not inhere in his flesh, nor is he its author: rather, he participates in it, advertises it, from an eccentric position even as he most appears to be the center of attention:

More than a center: a center, a body in the center of a space, is exposed on all sides. On the one hand, it bares its back, lets itself be seen by what it does not see. On the other hand, the excentricity of the teaching body, in traditional topology, permits at once the synoptic surveillance that with its glance covers the field of the body taught— every part of which is indistinguishable and always surrounded—and the withdrawal, the reserve of the body that does not surrender, offering itself from only one side to the glance that it nonetheless mobilizes with its entire surface.[15]

The teaching body is as diffuse as the discourse, the desire, the pedagogical gaze that it promotes and that inheres in neither a student nor a teacher, but possesses both, fetching them from obscurity. This pedagogical gaze is panoptical not because the professor is omniscient, but because professor and student are both vulnerable, seen by what they do not see. This dynamic, as Derrida describes it, is rich with shame, and through the exposed behind he alludes to that rear window of anality that queer theorists such as Lee Edelman have analyzed as the seat of a desire that defies mastery, even the mastery of that preeminent subject supposed to know, the university professor.[16] In this conception of university life, academic discourse is rigid with a relentlessly sadistic sodomitical power of penetration from behind. To err is to be caught with one's pants down, as if truths and their professors had no behind. The more rigid the professionalization, the canonization of ideas, the disciplining of the intellectual body, the more apt the metaphor. And, one might argue, the sexier the classroom.

Hailed by these academic discourses of the utmost rigidity, but never wholly taken up by them, never quite justified by them, both the teacher and the student enjoy endless occasions for shame. Failure approaches, often unexpectedly, from behind, to dwell on Derrida's figure, which is not necessarily literal, though it might feel that way sometimes. A face distracts, an obsession looms, a fact is forgotten, a text eludes, an eyelid droops, a paper goes astray—a behind, in brief, is shamefully exposed. A professor's behind, a student's, perhaps even a text's. Derrida valorizes this contingency and mobility of the flesh over the rigidification of discourse. He pits flesh against discourse in sexual terms that nevertheless militate against his point: "This capturing by erasure, this fascinating neutralization, always takes the form of a cadaverization of my body. My body only fascinates while playing dead, the moment when, playing dead, it is erected in the rigidity of the cadaver: stiff but without strength proper. Having no life of its own but only a delegation of life."[17] The teaching body is stiff, but in all the wrong places—stiff like a corpse, not like a sexual organ. In this passage Derrida valorizes most polemically his resistance to the stagnation of philosophy as a discourse and the institutionalization of teaching that professionalizes philosophy into professorial repetition. Through discourse I expose the phallus, but it is not exactly mine; furthermore, I am ever in danger of revealing my behind.

Derrida enacts this very problem in the course of this passage, in which he is at great pains not just to produce a sexy metaphor, but also to subdue it. His argument seeks to validate the fleshly and the mobile, but it has the contradictory effect of making even the most patriarchal, the most unimaginative of pedants seem oddly perverse and naughty. This pedant waves his erection even as he waives it. He becomes a full-frontal flasher, a necrophile, a vampire, but also a pedagogical eunuch. The cadaverous professor is a hard-on with spectacles, as stiff as his lectern, and hence his fascination for us. He is also a failure, a phallic joke. But what is not to like? To evoke the erect penis is always to risk applause. Derrida must then somehow render the erection flaccid, fetching from thin air the phrase "stiff but without strength proper," whatever that means. Setting aside the dubious distinction here between stiff dead and stiff sexy, one might ask should we become more phallic? Should we present our behinds? Are there other erogenous zones we should explore in the classroom? He returns us to what is often deemed the very primal scene of shame, the exposure of those parts we call private, as if teaching, even in its most conservative mode, were a more or less unconscious pretense of striptease.

It is a paradox readily evident in Plato's *Symposium*, which remains for me the great touchstone of queer theory on pedagogy, though its author would have found my honorific mystifying. The text begins with an anxious erotics of pride, culminating in the invincibly sublimating figure of Socrates himself; however, with the belated appearance of the drunk and amorous Alcibiades, a more poignant and paradoxical queer shame enjoys the last word, even though Socrates talks all the others under the table before heading home to bed, alone of course, at dawn. Until Socrates speaks, *The Symposium* can easily strike a modern ear as an exercise in gay pride. I am not surprised to see the enthusiasm with which queer students in my courses still glimpse that flicker of pride about halfway through the speech by Pausanias. My reference to my own students is not gratuitous here, for the scene of my own teaching, the pedagogy of the queer theorist, inevitably invites comparisons to the long tradition of what David Halperin calls "deviant teaching," the anxiety of the male teacher as pederast or sodomite initiating young male pupils. As Halperin demonstrates, scandals over the emergence of gay studies in the academy may be seen as the latest development in a long and anxious tradition of turning pedagogical eros into tragedy or farce, and the scandal always turns on the professorial body, which might at any moment dangerously enact the illicit desire it studies. "Both feminist studies and lesbian/gay studies promote forms of knowledge that are not limited to the application of a disembodied understanding to a body of material but that include the researcher within the field of research," he writes, having already noted parenthetically the unease this embodiment has generated: "all those initiatory procedures still represent something of an embarrassment to the formal definition of academic training, which is why they are coming to be ever more strictly routinized and policed."[18] As Joseph Litvak has pointed out, gay teachers are peculiarly susceptible to a toxic and shame-laden double bind: "I found myself stereotyped at the same time as the bearer of a sexuality popularly conceived either as a surrender of power or as an abuse of it."[19] Under the homophobic accusation of sexual pathology or sexual recruitment, the queer professor of queer studies might negotiate that shaming tactic through anger, disavowal, sublimation, or confession and expiation—or through that queer generosity of which I have been speaking. What do I enjoy most about teaching *The*

Figure 10. When Ham sees Noah, his father, drunk and naked, he goes outside and blabs about it. But Shem and Japheth, also Noah's sons, approach their father with their faces turned away and lay a garment over his shoulders. Shame here is an act of judgment, but also a theatrical practice of love. I imagine Noah, one eye open, secretly enjoying this performance, which is arguably more absurd than his own.

Idiotic essence of professorial shame: wrong = naked. Truths can be naked, but it seems their professors cannot.

At MLA, Jane Gallop introduces me to her son, who is sitting with her. I remember a nude portrait she published in Living with His Camera: *herself posed like Manet's Olympia on a sofa with her son, also nude. She had been concerned about what her colleagues might think. Cat's out of the bag, I guess.*

Refreshing departure from biblical precedent.

Symposium? That anxious, delicious, endearing, shameful moment when the students realize that we are not just analyzing the text, but reenacting it, or trying very hard not to reenact it, which amounts to the same thing.

Pausanias and Aristophanes whet our hopes for what appears at first blush to be gay pride *avant la lettre*. Nevertheless, for all their celebration of what is most noble, generous, and intellectual in the erotic love of one man for another, these speeches bristle with an anxious defensiveness. Pausanias is especially eager to put a respectable spin on this desire, which he and Agathon are seen by other speakers to embody. He offers an apologia disparaging the tyrants of Persia and even the citizens of Athens for their failure to appreciate such "strong friendships and personal bonds,"[20] which come to figure a Greek ideal of democracy in the course of his argument. Nevertheless, like a great many modern pronouncements on gay pride, through which one seeks to redeem one's fellow homosexuals as good spouses, good soldiers, good teachers, good television stars, or good members of Congress (curious phrase), this sublimation is haunted by sexual shame, the bad queer who allows desire to undermine conventional discipline and dignity. Pausanias says, "I said earlier that the lover's willingness to undergo every kind of slavery isn't humiliating or reprehensible. Similarly, according to our rules, there's only one remaining type of voluntary slavery that isn't reprehensible: the type which aims to produce virtue."[21] There is slavery and then there is slavery, so it seems, and it is the sheer fineness of that distinction and its unbearably high stakes that give his argument its emotional suspense. Ironically, pederasty, the disciplined pedagogical erotics of man and boy, rescues him from humiliation, and at times rescues him from sex altogether. Aristophanes too offers a eulogy for eros between men, and he is similarly defensive: "They are the best of their generation, both as boys and young men, because they are naturally the bravest. Some people say that they are shameless, but that isn't true. It's not out of shamelessness that they do this but because they are bold, brave and masculine, and welcome the same qualities in others."[22] Not even in the defense of gays in the military does anyone reach for this sort of argument any more. As soon as he makes this claim, however, he feels certain, and with good reason, that Eryximachus is going to make fun of him. Like Pausanias, Aristophanes argues against shame in a manner that promotes it.

As if coaxed into existence by this sexual paradox, Socrates enters the debate not just to refine this idealization of desire between men, but to embody it in all its contradiction. He is the impossible pedagogical ideal, desire in the service of truth alone. He rivets our attention to his body precisely to erase his own corporeality. He speaks of eros all the better to make it vanish into its figuration of a desexualized pedagogy. His flirtations are an exercise in ascesis. He seduces with a passionate chastity. He gives a certain play, though not a very free play, to pedagogical eros. Socrates, the irresistible old goat, sidles up to Agathon, the really cute boy, but then expresses his love only through edifying sarcasm about the boy's intellectual shortcomings. In the punishing erotic spirit of this dialogue, this shaming sarcasm proves irresistible to cute boys and readers alike. Socrates has already made the same move on Alcibiades, slipping between the sheets with him and then neglecting to do anything but insult his intelligence—it is the most famous fuck that never happens. "I swear to you by the gods, and by the goddesses," Alcibiades says with polite inclusiveness, "that when I got up next morning I had no more slept with Socrates than if I'd been sleeping with my father or elder brother."[23] If this is not a reference to incest, then we can assume he is ashamed by the slight. The body is foresworn for intellectual abstraction, and sex is subsumed into philosophy.

Nevertheless, Alcibiades understands the beauty of the gesture, perhaps better than Socrates himself and with a sharper sense of irony. When Alcibiades arrives drunk at the symposium, Plato becomes queer theory. Straight away, Alcibiades makes a spectacle of his own shame. He ought to be ashamed of his shame, he says, but he talks about it with so much enthusiasm that I feel envious and want to get down there with him to wallow in it. He says of his teacher, "He's the only person in whose company I've had an experience you might think me incapable of—feeling shame with someone; I only feel shame in his company."[24] Like a Greek Genet, Alcibiades seduces with shame. The other speakers do the same, after their fashion; however, Alcibiades does it not by banishing his shame or hiding from it, but by making a spectacle of it. In this way, he participates in the same ethics as Socrates, the same discipline, and yet exposes what is most excruciatingly absent from Socratic thought: the beauty and humanity of lust, error, and weakness. As Martha Nussbaum once remarked, he endears himself to us by showing us his "cracks and his holes," and she is well aware of the anatomical fantasy, the invitation to homosexual panic, in her metaphor.[25] She admires Alcibiades for his outrageous expressions of love. "The Symposium," she observes, "is a work about passionate erotic love—a fact that would be hard to infer from some of the criticism written about it."[26] Alcibiades does not simply illustrate the truth of Socrates' speech about Diotima and his chillingly abstract conception of desire as the pursuit of knowledge; rather, he leaves us with a dialectical tension between the rational and the irrational, good love and shameful love, that The Symposium leaves unresolved. With great irony and wit, he performs for us all that we might find most disappointing in Socrates' speech. Nussbaum finds in Socrates an ascetic refusal to live in the world, and his clever appropriation of the intensely physical language of eros seems more like a pretense than a genuine insight. She writes elegantly on the erotic wisdom of Alcibiades:

I can follow Socrates only if, like Socrates, I am persuaded of the truth of Diotima's account; and Alcibiades robs me of this conviction. He makes me feel that in embarking on the ascent I am sacrificing a beauty; so I can no longer view the ascent as embracing the whole of beauty. The minute I think 'sacrifice' and 'denial,' the ascent is no longer what it seemed, nor am I, in it, self-sufficient. I can, on the other hand, follow Alcibiades, making my soul a body. I can live in erôs, devoted to its violence and its sudden light. . . . And then, if I am a rational being, with a rational being's deep need for order and for understanding, I feel that I must be false to erôs, for the world's sake.[27]

By delivering himself up to the embrace of shame in eros, to what Nussbaum calls his fragility, Alcibiades reveals a pathos of embodiment that Socrates' admirable abstractions disavow.

Alcibiades draws on the same figure of enslavement and servility that gives Pausanias's speech both its stigma and its romance, but instead of banishing shame to the bad sort of slavery, he locates it firmly in the good slavery of a sublime pedagogical encounter. Pedagogy is erotic dominance and submission at its most refined. As Gilles Deleuze has written, and every teacher and student soon learns, "The masochistic contract implies not only the necessity of the victim's consent, but his ability to persuade, and his pedagogical and judicial efforts to train his torturer."[28] Alcibiades repeatedly and explicitly describes how Socrates has made him feel like a slave. At a party where very real slaves silently fill the drinking cup of a philosopher even as he speaks of democracy, this metaphor of slavery is perilously fraught with irony and class anxiety. Contemporary debates on consensual erotic relationships between student and teacher often gravitate to the same hyperbolic arguments about power, lending a pornographic, melodramatic, masochistic edge to the discussion, as the innocent student is ensnared by a corrupt superior, made a slave by the professor's desire, intellect, or social influence. Alcibiades says, "So I act like a runaway slave and escape from him; and whenever I see him, I'm ashamed because of what he's made me agree to. Often I've felt I'd be glad to see him removed from the human race; but if this did happen, I know well I'd be much more upset."[29] I think I have been to this club, but are they speaking of teaching or sex? He later adds, "Although I felt I'd been humiliated, I admired his character, his self-control and courage. . . . I was baffled; and I went around more completely enslaved to this person than anyone else has ever been to anyone."[30] Humiliation becomes romance.

As in many relationships called for better or worse "masochistic" or "pedagogical," it is not always clear who is the top and who the bottom, and Alcibiades remarks on the irony of not knowing whether he is *erastes* or *eromenos*. Is he lover or beloved? Is he teacher or student? Is he praising Socrates or abusing him? With this extravagant performance of vulnerability, is he making love to his mentor or assaulting him? Is he using his own shame to put Socrates to shame, to claim him for shame? When the student praises the teacher for his restraint, his virtue, his superhuman ability to withstand the cold and to drink without getting drunk, Socrates becomes in my eyes a phallic parody of himself. The more glorious the teaching body in this praise, the more inhuman it appears, the more cadaverous, numb, sexless, absurd. Socrates is aware that Alcibiades' praise may be ironic, and that it will make Agathon, the really cute boy, think that this pedagogical eros is nothing but an intellectual scam and look elsewhere. Beyond this joke, however, Alcibiades points up the irony that Socrates has disavowed the very sexual pleasures upon which the pursuit of knowledge depends for its metaphors, for its very articulation. His disavowal ironically constitutes his sexual appeal, an aggravation of the sexual desire that he devalorizes. Alcibiades resexualizes shame not as a goad to sublimation, not as an escape from the slavery of the flesh, but as an admission of sensual ravishment incited by the stimulation of the mind with ideas, personalities, and bodies. He reverses the figural movement of Socrates by which sex is merely an allegory for intellectual endeavor: philosophy really is sexy, he really is drunk, he really is in love in the unsublimated sense of the word. The entire party share in what he calls "the madness and Bacchic frenzy of philosophy." Philosophy is noble only because it is excruciatingly shameful. The vulgar and uninitiated should stop their ears at such "shocking things,"[31] for philosophy in The Symposium is not *like* a Bacchic frenzy, it *is* one.

For Socrates, sex has vanished into its purely figural function, and for no good reason, since it is by no means clear what Alcibiades would fail to learn if he and Socrates did indeed fuck, as smart people often do. Does Socrates suppose that truth is pursued through a discipline of sex rather than an exertion of intellect? Socrates is all symbol and no flesh, all symbolic phallus and no penis. Like the "teaching body" in Derrida's essay, he is stiff, but not in all the right places. He is the teaching body as stiff, as glorious corpse, and perhaps no less alluring for that dubious displacement. Bersani puts the paradox most succinctly when he writes that through Socrates "homosexuality can be ethically articulated only by being erased."[32] Alcibiades tears the veil from this modesty. If shame is indeed bedrock for queerness, then Alcibiades, as both teacher and student, *erastes* and *eromenos*, might serve as a fine queer theorist of pedagogy. Through a cross-cultural comparison, I find in him an occasion to question the erotics of modern university life, where teaching has been professionalized and wine and flirtation have been all but legislated out of the classroom. Socrates is no specialized academic, Alcibiades no fee-for-service undergraduate, and their symposium no corporate-style institution for credentialing a professional elite. But Plato is still the philosopher I turn to for a queer theory of pedagogy, though more for the tensions *The Symposium* leaves intact than any doctrine it explicitly espouses.

Shame organizes a whole range of affects that leave me and my students feeling vulnerable, even sexually exposed: ravishment, submission, confusion, helplessness, fear, anger, aggression, tenderness, love, and of course pride. In her highly anecdotal writing on sexual harassment and pedagogical eros, Jane Gallop is especially adept at exploring this range of affects in pedagogical relationships, even as they inhere in the dynamics of shame, and for this reason she is to my mind the most important queer theorist of pedagogy since Plato. Her books *Feminist Accused of Sexual Harassment* and *Anecdotal Theory* are discussions of pedagogical eros cleverly disguised as discussions of sexual harassment, even though she never engages in what she or I would call harassment. Student-teacher sex is only one of many forms of pedagogical shame, but it is a potent one. When one tries to talk about it, the theme of harassment and its attendant shame looms so ominously that it often takes up all the oxygen in the room, as if there were no other paradigm for discussing the issue. Gallop, however, is unique in that she is a dedicated feminist speaking from a position of shame in this debate, the shame of a sensational accusation, albeit evidently a groundless one, to restore a sense of ethical nuance to a discussion that has at times lapsed into a moral panic over consensual sex. Both she and I find sexual harassment reprehensible: it's bad, it's a problem, one shouldn't do it. Once we admit, however, that most of us never actually do sexually harass our students, that we are generally protective of them, we are left to puzzle all by ourselves over that vast range of affects, those loves and desires and shames that are not particularly interesting in an analysis of harassment and power inequities, but which nevertheless occupy us far more often. Pedagogical eros is everywhere suppressed yet everywhere discussed, scrutinized, worried over, gossiped about, fantasized about, giggled over, and otherwise launched into discourse so that we might come to know it through a paranoid language of shame, transgression, and retribution.

Figure 11. I am lecturing to undergraduates on erotic domination and submission in the work of Genet, Reik, and Foucault. I am wearing leather fetish gear, and it feels more embarrassing than the usual jacket and tie, though not unpleasantly so. Some students ask if they can handle my whip. One of them, who likes my boots, sends me a very formal letter to ask if he can be my slave. The letter is oddly de-sexualized and businesslike, as if he were requesting that I be his academic advisor, and the gesture seems appropriate to me, even endearing. He writes of his shame in asking, and his rhetoric is impeccably pedagogical: he wants me to "train" him, he wants to read more on the subject. What to tell the registrar, I wonder. Independent study, perhaps? Or field work?

The teacher's body is always already pornographic. We need to keep it under wraps, all the better to reveal its charm and preserve its power of scandal. Academic discipline is a seductive contradiction that has become increasingly anxious about itself. We police one another almost as mercilessly as we police ourselves. Our weapons are adjectives, and their characteristic style is hyperbole. The most cutting adjectives have a patina of psychiatric rigor that fails to disguise their cold metal of sexual discipline: words like *exhibitionistic*, *delusional*, and *narcissistic*. These can be hurled without a trace of irony by university faculty and administrators who have read Foucault and ought to know better. Can we do without these epithets, which in their scientific and polysyllabic elegance disguise prejudice as sophistication? Perhaps the most delicious term of abuse in this debate is *lecherous*. This epithet wields an archaic moralizing authority that is positively biblical. Gallop zeroes in on its lurid appeal in her review of a feminist critique, *The Lecherous Professor*, that she finds phobic about sex, gay sex in particular. As she points out, the word *lecherous* invites a volatile sensationalism whose shaming techniques are typically undermined by their own sexiness. She rearticulates the shaming tactic to exploit its erotic underpinnings: "I must confess," she writes of this book, "that what really moved me to read it was the novelistic title, whose sensationalism I wanted to transmit by putting it in the title of my essay."[33] She makes me want to confess too. I am a *lecherous* professor, but I am not very good at it. I have been well schooled in making a very particular spectacle of my own disappearance, fetishizing my body as that which is, above all, of no importance in itself. When I teach, I cannot help but play the role of an anxious grotesque, and my desire, insofar as it is apparent at all, is readable only as shame. My desire can be only a tragedy or a farce. Sublimation is my sanctuary and dumpiness, my disguise. Nevertheless, if my teaching is any good, I eroticize both in a paradox of fetishism by which, however improbably, a shabby tweed makes me as glorious as a centerfold and reveals as much as it seeks to hide.

What I find most brilliant about Gallop's essay on *The Lecherous Professor* is her articulation (long after the fact, in a separate introduction) of her shame in writing it. She is ashamed that she was ashamed, embarrassed about her own essay about embarrassment:

This is not the anecdotal theory I am proud of; it is the anecdotal theory that embarrasses me. I see myself in this essay struggling to theorize there where I feel so embattled. The writing and the thought are marred by the strident tone of my desperation. This may be anecdotal theory more as acting out than as working through.

If in the present context of proclaiming anecdotal theory this essay embarrasses me, it seems worth noting that the essay displays its own embarrassment as the anecdotal nature of its theory.[34]

She is embarrassed by her claim that the book is homophobic, and she is right to point out that her argument is strained. Like the rest of us, she knows how to pin her shame on someone else, even a feminist writer on sexual harassment who is a singularly unlikely target. Nevertheless, Gallop reveals herself here as a critic exceptionally well attuned to her own shame and to the sometimes unconscious shame dynamics of academic inquiry. By foregrounding her own shame, she is also disarming the reader, whose eagerness to say "Shame on you!" will be reduced to redundancy. She beats the reader to it by announcing her narcissism in advance, thereby proving, sneakily, that she is not narcissistic after all. She is covering her behind, of course, but more important, she also invites an analysis of shame's productive, transformative energy. She catches herself trying to run from her own teaching body in the text, "to rise above the mire,"[35] as she puts it, of a debate in which she is deeply, personally, sexually implicated. Ironically, she reveals her shame most poignantly at the moment she feels she has most energetically defended herself from it. She feels her prose is therefore marred, yet she publishes it, presumably because the scar is riveting for the reader as a sign of both the psychic damage and the erotic investment she describes.

I call Gallop's work queer theory, though she is hesitant to apply the term to herself. She has increasingly found the word *queer* useful in her writing, and she is refreshingly frank about the queerness of her own sexuality. In a chapter in *Anecdotal Theory* on the problem of regulations against "consensual amorous relations" between teacher and student, she writes, "With this essay, I'm trying to theorize pedagogy in a way that resists the norm and that bases itself in my own particular preference, a way of theorizing I might want to call queer—if that word didn't already have another meaning in the present contexts. Rather than queer theorizing, then, let me call it exorbitant, or maybe romantic."[36] Queer theory might justly be described as both. The conceptual flexibility of the word *queer*, which defines not so much an identity as an antinormative political stance and a certain dynamic of shame, allows her to characterize her own teaching practices as queer even when they have little to do with gayness. Her teaching is a scandal, an illicit romance, an exorbitant supplement to the discourse of reason that universities traditionally represent. On the distinction between thought and passion in contemporary pedagogy, she sounds queerly Platonic: "Do we want an ethics based upon that sad norm? Do we want policies to enforce that norm? To punish those queer enough to pursue the ideal?"[37]

Gallop is what Alcibiades would look like if he were a modern queer feminist writing about teaching and its attendant dynamics of shame. In *Feminist Accused of Sexual Harassment*, she seems to recognize this affinity with *The Symposium*, though only implicitly. She mentions a conference she wanted to organize where philosophers "would take us back to Plato where we could study Socrates's erotic relations with his students,"[38] but the spirit of *The Symposium* is even closer to her heart than that: "bacchanalian frenzy" is the phrase she lifts from Alcibiades to describe her initiation into the women's movement in 1971 when she attended a women-only dance where students and teachers bared their breasts for one another, "intoxicated with the joy and energy of our young feminism."[39] I too have used the phrase "bacchanalian frenzy" to describe my own initiation into queer theory. Yet her idealism is challenged when she is accused of sexual harassment and finally reprimanded for engaging in what was officially deemed "consensual amorous relations" with a student. She says, "Since being accused of harassment, I feel like my life has fallen into sensationalism. I've become a spectacle. Despite the urge to hide in shame, I've decided to speak from this sensational location. I'd like to make spectacle speak."[40] Sensationalism, spectacle, shame, speak, sensational, spectacle, speak, the alliteration of *s*'s and the repetition of words enact through her style the very sensation it describes, the persistent and repetitive hiss of public shaming that punishes the desiring body as if it were a pearl effervescing in a glass of acid.

I love Jane Gallop. I love her with that exorbitance of affection I reserve almost exclusively for people I hardly know. I first presented a version of this essay at an MLA panel called Critic Love. The panel was for the division on literary criticism, and it was a lineup of queer theorists in particular. We were asked by Lee Edelman, the organizer, to discuss our love for a particular critic, and what it meant to love a critic at all. Not envy, not aggression, not ambivalence, just love. Because Gallop was scheduled to speak, I chose her. This MLA symposium on love seemed to me the ideal occasion to consider not only Plato's *Symposium* as queer theory, but also the queer role of eros in Gallop's criticism and her teaching. After all, it was she who wrote, "A good conference is likely to be an eroticized workplace,"[41] and so what better place to consider the inevitably shame-prone erotics of critiquing someone else's work in person and in public? And to consider also the role of the pedagogical body in her work, since here we were, critical *erastes* and *eromenos*, bodies on display, dignity at risk. "Are you dreading what I'm going to say?" I asked her. "Of course I am," she replied. The shame she most dreaded never quite materialized, for I was speaking in a more than usually gallant mode, but her body, my body, the shame dynamics of academic performance, as with any performance, riveted ideas to flesh and gave the words a greater sensuousness and suspense than they have for me on the page.

How else could I enter such a symposium on love but with vine leaves in my hair? I have always eschewed the usual bottled spring water with its vaunted purity, its chaste plastic seal, its neat and soldierly stance of attention in front of each speaker. I favor a variety of more challenging spirits in my own glass, some wine, some champagne, a martini, a beer. Not red wine for this symposium, I thought, but a manhattan, because the MLA was in New York that year, and besides, I had only twenty minutes, and a manhattan is quicker than wine. It is with good reason even a modern academic gathering is often called a symposium and why alcohol has been thought in certain historical periods, not necessarily our own, to lubricate the intellect and loosen the petrifying effects of discipline. In Plato, wine is like eros in that it ironically excites and sustains the very alembic of discourse that would further distill it into a mere metaphor for the pursuit of wisdom.

I sometimes find this essay embarrassing, especially while I am presenting it in person. Giving a lecture is always embarrassing for me, and in this one in particular I sought to thematize that embarrassment and ironize my experience of shame even as it was happening. I found myself once again in the position of enacting what I am analyzing. A few months after the MLA, I gave this paper again in a very different form at the Gay Shame conference, and I focused more on Plato than Gallop. I also included a series of photographs of Kiko, five of which are reproduced here. There is never an Alcibiades on hand when I need one, and so I turned to Kiko to help me make my point. The body of a graduate student scandalized the teaching body of Jane Gallop; my body was scandalized, rather, by a porn star. Kiko is playing an academic role (in his pictures, in my lectures), and the dialectical tension between his body and mine, especially their apparent racial and class differences, served to destabilize my own performance of an academic role. The tensions between teacher and student, mind and flesh, voyeur and object, Anglo and Latino, bourgeois and working class—or, more to the point, a set of assumptions about those tensions and how they might play out on our bodies—are already rendered ironically in the photo spread, which was first published in the premier issue of *Latin Inches*. The classroom, a classic mise-en-scène of that tension at its most sublimated, becomes a porn shoot and striptease, a classic mise-en-scène for the collapse of sublimation. One scene cannot sustain itself without the other; one becomes the other turned inside out, revealing its interlining structure of erotic shame.

Kiko—the only name I have been able to locate for him—is plugging his new films, punningly entitled *Learning Latin* and *Learning Latin 2: Crammin'*. The puns are particularly suggestive, for it is not altogether clear who, Kiko or the viewer, is doing the learning in these photographs and who is doing the teaching, nor is it clear what exactly is getting crammed and which version of Latin, that of ancient Rome or that of contemporary Puerto Rico, is on the syllabus. Here, Kiko dresses in a preppy collegiate style—shorts, polo shirt, book bag—and poses at, on, and around a school desk and chalkboard in a trompe-l'oeil classroom decorated like a Ralph Lauren fantasy of tony academic decor that seems to make a comedy of its own fakeness. In the course of several pages, Kiko acts out a pedagogical drama of seduction that makes him seem oddly like an illustration for the disruptive appearance of Alcibiades in Plato's *Symposium*. He reads a porn magazine, thereby making himself an allegory for the mode of his own presentation, for voyeurism, for reading as seduction. Perhaps he is a teacher reading a gay porn magazine with what appear to be white male models, sometimes men in S/M gear, and we the student voyeurs are taking notes behind the camera. Perhaps he is a student who is being punished for reading that porn magazine, who is ordered in S/M fashion to write "I love sex" over and over again on the chalkboard by us, the invisible teachers who ogle him from the camera's point of view. His Latin inches, this instantiation of the almost mythic cock of color that is the organizing principle of the magazine in which he appears, indeed the all-too-reliable point of reference for most critiques of racial fetishism since Frantz Fanón, emerges like the ultimate truth from behind its veil of boxer shorts, only to invite ironic speculation. Why does such a cock require the crutch of a cock ring? Why does it find its visual analogue in the perky American flag with which he so suggestively poses? What is the relationship between the penis and the phallus, flesh and symbol, in this scene of pedagogy and seduction? By seducing the onlooker, by addressing the camera or the page with his various looks—a look of absorption, of invitation, of challenge, of contempt?—I find he renders scandalously visible a shame dynamic by now so naturalized by my professional training that I am sometimes oblivious to its encryption on my body and its fascination for the participants in queer conferences. His image exploits the phantasmatic scene of pedagogical eros, rendering explicitly pornographic what is already implicitly pornographic, thereby exposing not only his own body but also mine, the pedagogical body that is erotically, racially, nationally, historically marked as an emblem of knowledge, discipline, professional identity, and their attendant dynamics of shame. He often excites shame, especially among academics. On whom would you pin this shame, if pin you must? On Kiko for posing, the producers for producing, fetishists for fetishizing, the "system" for systematizing, yourself for looking, me for presenting? I have watched someone do each of the above.

By introducing Kiko into my lectures on *The Symposium*, I invite that disruption into the scene of my own pedagogy. I have lectured on this topic in the drag of doctoral robes I have worn to look like a fantasy of an academic, I have lectured wearing the shorts and polo shirt that he wears, and I have played the same game of trompe l'oeil to ironize the apparent lines of contention, but also of identification and desiring, between our bodies, to let the text of the body say one thing while the text of the lecture says—as it so often does—something different. The very fakeness of the scene points up its status as fantasy construction, while touching also upon a great many material realities, among them the history of exclusion of Latinos from the very educational tradition it cites and satirizes. The shameful, shameless racial fetishism of the images—the raison d'être of the magazine and Kiko's films—further raises the question of racialized and sexualized spectatorship (at conferences, in classrooms), though it fails to offer any easy answers: who is looking at these images, what do these viewers see, why do they see it, why does the magazine boast a Latino staff and address itself to a Latino audience and then slip into the language of Latin exoticism? What, in short, is exposed, either in the poser or in the viewer? Kiko points up for me the differences that contemporary racial politics can make in our conception of the erotics and shame dynamics of the teaching body. Like Alcibiades, like Gallop, like me, Kiko represents a certain articulation of the body that disrupts an idealizing Socratic discipline of the classroom.

Kiko—or perhaps Kiko and I in juxtaposition—proved a pungent instigator of gay shame at this conference, and probably not because of sex. No one at a queer conference gets excited about sex; our real fetish is power, and we are embarrassed to be seen too near it. We are the prudes of power. As it happened, I was largely upstaged by my own illustrations and greeted afterward with an odd mixture of bafflement, silence, sarcasm, and delight, almost none of it in reference to Plato. The most sustained criticism came the next day from Hiram Perez (many others chimed in), who angrily expressed his contempt for poststructuralism, invoked Jeffrey Dahmer, and claimed that I had traumatized him with my illustrations and caused him to lose sleep the night before. Like *lecherous*, the word *traumatized* is another one of those terms of abjection whose tendency to hyperbole in academic

contexts is sadly resistant to critique. Despite my disagreement with virtually everything Perez said, I felt shame for enjoying Kiko, shame for looking
and talking the way I do, shame for angering someone I do not want to anger, shame for the spectacle he was making of himself, shame for the spectacle he was making of me, shame for the spectacle I was about to make of
myself by responding to him, and shame for feeling shame for no very good
reason. In short, I found the comment interesting in spite of itself.

Conferences such as Gay Shame are usually ripe with ritual theater of
this sort: identity politics is the memorized script, shame is the ruling affect, and the plenary session is the modus operandi of choice. Calling the
conference "Gay Shame" was just begging for it. I felt a certain surprising
smidgen of reparative generosity, a desire to connect, that was a function
of the otherwise unfortunate shaming power of such exchanges and their
frequent tendency to failure. I am reminded of Sedgwick's theorization of
shame as a "form of communication" that has to do more with failure than
with anything so sexy as transgression or prohibition. Citing Silvan Tomkins and Michael Franz Basch, she speaks of shame as an "uncontrollable relationality"[42] that seeks to repair the feeling of isolation when the expected
smile of jubilant recognition from the other fails, for whatever reason, to
materialize. Shame is an involuntary act of love, and it is sometimes pursued with the unlikeliest of partners—a severe critic, an enemy, a stranger,
a fool, a photograph, a faceless object, a deserted room, an abstraction.

At conferences, I find race works at least as well as sex to lead everyone
into a really shame-inducing discussion of power where the antagonisms
get excruciatingly personal. Ideally, one brings race and sex together with
gender on these occasions, and then the question of racial fetishism is especially volatile. The most sensitive and nuanced essay I have read about the
shame dynamics of what is called, for better or worse, racial fetishism—
and certainly the essay I have used most often in my own teaching on the
subject—is still Kobena Mercer's "Looking for Trouble," a reconsideration
of Robert Mapplethorpe's nude or seminude portraits of black men. He describes his first response to these images in much the same language that
Hiram Perez used to characterize his response to Kiko's sudden appearance
in my lecture: "I was so shocked by what I saw!" But later he describes his
ambivalence:

*We were fascinated by the beautiful bodies and drawn in by the pleasure of looking
as we went over the repertoire of images again and again. We wanted to look, but we
didn't always find what we wanted to see. We were, of course, disturbed by the racial dimension of the imagery and, above all, angered by the aesthetic objectification that re-*

duced these black male bodies to abstract visual "things," silenced in their own right as subjects and serving only to enhance the name of the white gay male artist in the privileged world of art photography. In other words, we were stuck in an intransitive "structure of feeling"; caught out in a liminal experience of textual ambivalence.[43]

One name for this ambivalence might be shame. I have certainly shared that sense of shock when I have identified with imagery I deemed abject. One feels urgently, mysteriously, the need for damage control on one's own ego even though it is not oneself in the picture. One then demands the most excruciating etiquette of shame from everyone else in the world.

In queer culture, this sort of etiquette is, much to everyone's relief, difficult to sustain for long. In the course of his essay, Mercer questions its value as well. One is "of course" disturbed by the racial dimension, though mostly because one perceives it through one's own fantasy of the ogling, contemptuous Other, the pinch of whose authority one feels acutely. One feels "of course" a political duty to be disturbed, to acknowledge the usual academic critique into which such imagery can slide with surprisingly little theoretical lubrication. Mercer writes, "Such fetishism not only eroticizes the most visible aspect of racial difference—skin color—but also lubricates the ideological reproduction of 'colonial fantasy' based on the desire for mastery and power over the racialized Other."[44] I buy that. Nevertheless, depending on the context, that ideological reproduction might need considerable lubrication to work at all, especially for the sort of person likely to read Mercer's essay or attend queer conferences. When I reread the essay to see who actually has this colonial fantasy, I find Jesse Helms and his wife are virtually the only culprits named. A problem arises for me. Certainly, one can do a variety of harmless things with one's colonial fantasies, but I failed to have any. Once I admit that I have looked at Mapplethorpe's *Black Book* and even the far less arty images of Kiko but failed to entertain the requisite fantasies about colonial domination or to identify with Jesse Helms (or his wife), I am left with the question of why these photographs might be giving me pleasure anyway.

Mercer notices right away that his earlier condemnation of Mapplethorpe theorizes his own desire out of existence, and he spends the rest of the essay in a remarkable attempt to recover it. I wonder if he recovers my pleasure as well. He concludes that Mapplethorpe's "images can elicit a homophobic reading as easily as a homoerotic one, can confirm a racist reading as much as produce an antiracist one,"[45] an indeterminacy indicative of the projective dynamics of shame in interpretation. In modifying his earlier argument, he makes a powerfully reparative move toward articulating his

Figure 12. I use these images of Kiko as a digital chalkboard for my lecture notes on Plato. Undergraduates tell me they are "so into him," and sometimes they mean Plato too. Certain people at the Gay Shame conference also told me, though always in private, that they enjoyed these images. Judith Halberstam explained to me that only white gay men would say such a thing (shame on them!). Her formula certainly simplifies matters, but these people were not all white, they were not all gay, and they were not all men. She seemed to think I must be up to no good anyway. She said angrily that she hoped I liked being shamed in public and she was going to make sure it happened. Performative speech act, somewhat infelicitous.

Gay Shame meets Lesbian Piety. But have we accounted for the pleasure yet?

own pleasure and offering a political argument that would make that pleasure available to others. Thus he is well attuned to the rich range of affects
he experiences that were obscured by rage when he was in a more polemical
mode. He speaks, for example, of ambivalence, arousal, admiration, jeal-
ousy, envy, and intellectual interest. He shifts elegantly from the articulation of shame through outrage, to the articulation of shame through reparation, which has a greater affective range and nuance. He offers a difficult
and candid discussion of his vulnerability to pleasure, a discussion that
seems urgent to me though it is not exhausted nor even necessarily defined
by a critique of oppression.

There is a very familiar argument about sexual and racial fetishism:
it objectifies people, it can exploit the disempowered, and you should be
ashamed of yourself for participating in it. There is also a very familiar argument about pedagogical eros: it objectifies students, it can exploit the
disempowered, and you should be ashamed of yourself for participating in
it. They are interesting arguments, but they raise more questions than they
resolve. Is there a pedagogy without eros, and is its expression in intense
sexual relationships necessarily traumatic? Is there someone who is never a
sexual and racial fetishist? Is it somehow worse than being a gender fetishist (which is to say, a homosexual or a heterosexual)? What better purpose
than fetishism has sexual and racial difference ever served? In the spirit
of Sedgwick's work, I am hoping this shame and this pleasure over bodies
and their exposure can be made more available for political redeployment,
critical rethinking, and aesthetic refiguration, especially in those contexts
where identity politics is most embattled. What do you see, what might
you see, when you look at these photographs, when you look at a teaching
body, at a student body? Is it well served by an epithet? I am indeed a sexual and racial fetishist, I am indeed a lecherous professor, though perhaps I
am not very good at it. I can point up the incommensurability between my
body and that rigid, defensive thing, that curious fetish object, the "teaching body" we might call it, the "student body," behind which I feel obliged
to hide myself or die. The veil of modesty torn, the shameful parts shown,
this strange beauty I discover may be a victimless crime of love.

Notes

1. Leo Bersani, "Is the Rectum a Grave?" (1987), reprinted in *AIDS: Cultural Analysis/
Cultural Activism*, ed. Douglas Crimp (Boston: MIT Press, 1988), 222. For a fuller treatment
of this thesis, especially with regard to Genet, see Bersani, *Homos* (Cambridge, MA: Harvard University Press, 1995).

2. Jean Genet, *The Thief's Journal*, trans. Bernard Frechtman (New York: Grove Press, 1964), 175–76.

3. Judith Butler, "Imitation and Gender Insubordination," in *Inside/Out: Lesbian Theories, Gay Theories*, ed. Diana Fuss (New York: Routledge, 1991), 21.

4. Michael Warner, *The Trouble with Normal: Sex, Politics, and the Ethics of Queer Life* (Cambridge, MA: Harvard University Press, 1999), 3. All further references are quoted from this edition.

5. Jean Genet, interview, *Playboy*, April 1964, 50.

6. Warner, *The Trouble with Normal*, 35.

7. Ibid.

8. Eve Kosofsky Sedgwick, "Shame, Theatricality, and Queer Performativity: Henry James's *The Art of the Novel*," this volume, 51.

9. Ibid., 59–60.

10. Ibid., 58.

11. Douglas Crimp, "Mario Montez, For Shame," this volume, 71.

12. Ibid., 67.

13. Jacques Derrida, "Where a Teaching Body Begins and How It Ends," in *Who's Afraid of Philosophy: Right to Philosophy I*, trans. Jan Plug (Stanford, CA: Stanford University Press, 2002), 90.

14. Elaine Showalter, *Faculty Towers: The Academic Novel and Its Discontents* (Philadelphia: University of Pennsylvania Press, 2005), 99.

15. Derrida, "Where a Teaching Body Begins," 90.

16. See Lee Edelman, *"Rear Window's Glasshole,"* in *Out Takes: Essays on Queer Theory and Film*, ed. Ellis Hanson (Durham, NC: Duke University Press, 1999), 72–96. Edelman speaks of "this question of what stands behind the Symbolic order by taking us back to the anal compulsion that gives birth, paradoxically, to Symbolic meaning through the narrative of sexual difference" (72).

17. Derrida, "Where a Teaching Body Begins," 91.

18. David M. Halperin, "Deviant Teaching," *Michigan Feminist Studies* 16 (2002): 10–11.

19. Joseph Litvak, "Pedagogy and Sexuality," in *Professions of Desire*, ed. George E. Haggerty and Bonnie Zimmerman (New York: MLA, 1995), 29.

20. Plato, *The Symposium*, trans. Christopher Gill (London: Penguin, 1999), 14.

21. Ibid., 16.

22. Ibid., 25.

23. Ibid., 59.

24. Ibid., 55.

25. Martha C. Nussbaum, *The Fragility of Goodness: Luck and Ethics in Greek Tragedy and Philosophy* (Cambridge: Cambridge University Press, 1986), 194.

26. Ibid., 167.

27. Ibid., 198.

28. Gilles Deleuze, "Coldness and Cruelty" (1967), reprinted in *Masochism*, trans. Jean McNeil (New York: Zone, 1989), 75.

29. Plato, *The Symposium*, 55.

30. Ibid., 59.

31. Ibid., 57.

32. Leo Bersani, "Pedagogy and Pederasty," *Raritan* 5, no.1 (1985): 16.

33. Jane Gallop, *Anecdotal Theory* (Durham, NC: Duke University Press, 2002), 36.

34. Ibid., 17.

35. Ibid.

36. Ibid., 78.

37. Ibid., 73.

38. Jane Gallop, *Feminist Accused of Sexual Harassment* (Durham, NC: Duke University Press, 1997), 59. See also her discussion of Sade's use of the verb *socratiser*, "The Immoral Teachers," *Yale French Studies* 63 (1982): 119.

39. Ibid., 13.

40. Ibid., 6.

41. Ibid., 83.

42. Sedgwick, 51.

43. Kobena Mercer, "Looking for Trouble" (1991), reprinted in *The Lesbian and Gay Studies Reader*, ed. Henry Abelove, Michèle Aina Barale, and David M. Halperin (New York: Routledge, 1993), 351.

44. Ibid., 352.

45. Ibid., 359.

[A M A L I A   Z I V]

Shameful Fantasies

CROSS-GENDER QUEER SEX
IN LESBIAN EROTIC FICTION

I don't know how long I went on. I get lost in cocksucking sometimes; it's like a ritual that disconnects me from my head, all the more so when it's anonymous. I hadn't even seen this cock I was sucking, and that made me feel I could be anyone, even an adventurous gay boy in a South of Market alley, sucking Daddy's big, hard dick. Any second now he could realize that I was no ordinary boy, and that gave me a great rush of adrenaline, a lust to have it down my throat. Until he discovered me I could believe this illusion myself, and with most men this was all I could expect to be, a cock-sucker until they turned the lights on.

Carol Queen, *The Leather Daddy and the Femme*, 1998

The epigraph is an excerpt from an erotic novel that tells the adventures of Randy, "a bisexual cross-dressing femme switch with a taste for leather daddies,"[1] who finds at last a leatherman willing to play with her and has all kinds of sexual adventures with him. The topos of cross-gender queer sex, that is, of lesbians making it with gay men, is at the center of several texts of lesbian erotica, most of them published in the 1990s. A representative though not comprehensive list of texts that treat this topos includes Pat Califia's "The Surprise Party" (1988), Lady Sara's "The Triangle" (1993), and Carol Queen's *The Leather Daddy and the Femme* (1998).[2] I'd like to examine this body of work through the focalizing lens of shame. Another novel with this topos is Helen Sandler's *Big Deal* (1999), which I will merely allude to here without discussing it in detail.

The question of shame bears on these texts in a number of ways. First and most obvious, the very fantasy of cross-gender sex is a shameful or at least an embarrassing one for a lesbian to entertain. Sex with men, or even the desire for it, undermines one's lesbian identity and troubles one's rela-tionship with the lesbian community that affirms and sustains this identity (remember the fantasized group-trial scene in *Go Fish* when one of the protagonists is revealed to have had sex with a man). Or at least that is how it *used* to be before the advent of "queer." Indeed, cross-gender queer sex could be regarded as the logical—if most radical—manifestation of the very definition of "queer" as a shared unisex identity, which organizes sexual attraction around a deviant erotic community. It is precisely in such a way that Pat Califia formulated the erotic logic of cross-gender queer sex in her 1983 article "Gay Men, Lesbians, and Sex: Doing It Together," which predates both the queer era and the literary manifestations of this theme. Califia writes: "I have eroticized queerness, gayness, homosexuality—in men and women. The leatherman and the drag queen are sexy to me, along with the diesel dyke with greased-back hair, and the femme stalking across the bar in her miniskirt and high-heeled shoes. I'm a fag hag. . . . In a funny way, when two gay people of opposite sexes make it, it's still gay sex."[3] Similarly, nearly a decade later, in 1991, Doug Sadownick, in an essay whose very title ("The Birth of Queer Nation and the Death of 'Gay' and 'Lesbian'") heralds the queer era, advocated sex between gay men and lesbians as a queer and queering practice.[4] In the context of queerdom, sex between lesbians and gay men is no longer taboo and has even become de rigueur at certain moments and in certain circles. Thus I need to qualify my initial claim concerning the shamefulness for lesbians of the fantasy of sex with gay men. As Eve Sedgwick has astutely pointed out, "shame and pride . . . are different interlinings of the same glove,"[5] and cross-gender queer sex, precisely *because* of its transgressive aspect, has been claimed (like so many other transgressive identities and desires) as a source of pride.

In fact, we can see the process of gradual legitimation reflected in the trajectory traced by the texts themselves when examined chronologically. In Pat Califia's "The Surprise Party" (1988), the protagonist's ambivalence about her attraction to men and her concern over its implications for her lesbian identity are major preoccupations of the story. Not only that, but the status of the whole encounter is one of a forbidden fantasy coming true, and it does so, significantly, in the context of dramatized violence. The story depicts an S/M scene on the theme of police arrest between a butch S/M dyke and three gay leathermen who, masquerading as cops, "abduct" and "rape" her. Participating in the scene only as an unwilling victim, the protagonist is given a role that is distanced as much as possible from any exercise of free will, especially because the consensual frame is revealed only toward the end of the story. By contrast, in *The Leather Daddy and the Femme* (the first two chapters of which were published in 1994), Randy actively cruises gay men, and her problem is not one of self-legitimation but of being accepted by her male objects of desire. And in Lady Sara's "The Triangle" (1993), Kris's daddy-boy relationship with her own leather daddy is not problematized in any way. Her problem is gaining recognition for her cross-gendered status and cross-gendered object choice from her surrounding environment. Apparently, the five- to six-year span that separates "The Surprise Party" from its successors—a period marked by the emergence of queer identity and the increasing acceptance of bisexuality in the gay world—made it possible to imagine a lesbian (or queer) identity that could accommodate cross-gender sex.

But shame comes into play in these texts not only in relation to the core fantasy of sex with gay men, but in other ways as well. To address those aspects, I need first to make a general comment concerning the ontology of pornographic texts. It is customary (and in the context of the feminist debates on pornography, it has been politically strategic) to refer to pornographic texts as "fantasies."[6] However, although discussions of pornography in terms of fantasy tend to emphasize the clear demarcation between sexual fantasy and sexual behavior, writers such as Elizabeth Cowie and Teresa de Lauretis, who draw on the psychoanalytic theory of fantasy to discuss both porn and mainstream media, also stress the distinction between individual fantasy scenarios and public forms of fantasy (which nevertheless nourish and structure one another).[7] Cowie, following Freud, remarks on the process of secondary revision involved in turning a fantasy into a work for public consumption.[8] In a similar vein, it is worth noting that many pornographic works, including the ones I discuss, are actually not pure fantasy, but rather straddle the gap between fantasy and everyday reality. That is, these are phantasmatic scripts that already make concessions to reality, that meet reality halfway, as it were. Such texts are concerned precisely with the problem of translating fantasy into realistic terms. (Not all pornographic works are like that, of course. In the Marquis de Sade's work, for example, there is a complete overlap between the fantasy and the fictional world, in the sense that the fiction represents a utopian realm whose laws are those of the author's desire. But the majority of pornographic fiction is not entirely utopian but involves more complex negotiations with external constraints and personal inhibitions.)

Hence, the works in my corpus accommodate and come to terms with feelings of ambivalence and embarrassment, fears of rejection or ridicule— all of course with the ultimate aim of overcoming and sublating them in a teleology of erotic redemption. Thus, Randy in *Leather Daddy* fears being rejected by Jack at several moments during their first date. First she fears he'll kick her out when he finds out she's not a real boy; later, when she switches to her femme persona, she risks rejection once more; and the next morning, when she straps on her dildo and surprises him in the shower, she's anxious that her nonrealistic dick will turn him off or that he'll refuse being flipped by a girl. None of this happens, of course, because we are in the ideal realm of porn, but the anxieties that attend the fantasy do gain admittance to the fantasy itself. In fact, fear of rejection seems to be endemic to the lesbian fantasy of sex with gay men. For a lesbian to want sex with a gay man means flirting with the possibility of being found unlovable, of being shamed by someone one desires and perhaps identifies with. This risk of rejection is also the flip side of the pleasure of transgression. One of the recurrent motifs in these texts is the thrill of trespassing into gay male territory, whether it is Randy, whom Jack takes to a private play party with a select group of top men disguised as a boy, or Lane from *Big Deal*, who, also passing as a boy, ventures into the darkroom of a gay male club, risking exposure.

But the pleasure of transgression alone does not seem to constitute a sufficient motivation for the lesbian fantasy of sex with gay men. It is possible of course to attribute this fantasy to residual bisexuality, but such an explanation does not account for the emphatic preference for gay men over straight ones—despite the former's likely reluctance to play with lesbians (whereas the latter would be only too willing). In my view, the turning toward gay men as objects of desire forms the logical sequel to the adoption of the gay male model of sexual subjectivity in lesbian pornography and in lesbian sex culture in general. Lesbian sex culture since the 1980s is in many ways modeled after the gay male one: categories of erotic identity, erotic styles, sexual attitudes, sexual etiquette, ideals, and fantasies are largely derived from gay male sex culture and the gay male cultural imaginary. This tendency is even more pronounced in the realm of fiction, where fantasy is unimpeded. Such extensive borrowing from gay male sexual culture should be seen, I believe, as part of an attempt to articulate female sexual subjectivity.[9]

Gay male pornography since the 1970s has at least partly unraveled the cultural knot linking sexual receptivity and nonsubjecthood. It reconceives receptivity as manly endurance—an ability to "take it like a man"—and as an assimilation of the phallus, which is to say an assimilation of the agency of the penetrating partner. The symbolic system of gay male S/M, in particular, reinscribes the subject/object binarism in strictly positional terms—top and bottom—thus highlighting the potential instability or fluidity of these roles and their performative, rather than essential, character. Also, because S/M is *about* the possession and domination of one individual by another, penetration is dislodged from its privileged status as the ultimate symbol of possession and domination and becomes merely one practice among others. Striving to articulate female sexual subjectivity, lesbians have adopted these cultural forms, attitudes, and symbolisms and profited from the symbolic realignments they afford. Mediating desires traditionally coded "feminine" through a (gay) male subject position enables lesbians and feminists not only to sever them from biological determinism but also to reinscribe them as transgressive and hence compatible with sexual subjectivity.

Yet, as the texts in my corpus demonstrate, the adoption of the gay male model of sexual subjectivity seems ultimately to call for male ratification, and it is this need for ratification that lies at the heart of the fantasy of cross-gender queer sex. Paradoxically, the project of articulating female sexual subjectivity ends up recapitulating the traditional gesture of seeking male endorsement. This need for approval not only finds expression in the core fantasy of sex with gay men, but also figures recurrently in the texts in the form of various challenges and the performance anxiety those challenges evoke. To give head as proficiently as a gay man, to endure as much as a gay man, to satisfy with a dildo a gay man who can have "the real thing," and, finally, to be able to "pass" as a gay man—all these are challenges that betray the same need for ratification of one's sexual subjectivity, and since gay men provide the model for this sexual subjectivity, it is from them that ratification is sought within the sexual arena itself.[10]

It is interesting and telling that all these texts are couched in S/M eroticism. This is so, I believe, for two reasons. First, S/M functions as a common language, a shared system of signs and norms that provides the symbolic terrain on which gay men and lesbians can meet sexually. Second, S/M is concerned with humiliation, and humiliation is intimately linked to the fears of rejection, ridicule, and failure that the lesbian fantasy of sex with gay men gives rise to. Here we come up against an interesting paradox, because shame itself can in no way be considered an erotic affect. Shame is rather an affect that blights all erotic potential—inasmuch as it leads to withdrawal, it runs counter to sexual arousal. Humiliation, however, does have clear ties to the erotic and forms one of the mainstays of S/M eroticism. I would therefore like to suggest a tentative distinction between shame and humiliation. Michael Franz Basch, quoted by Sedgwick, speaks of a "shame-humiliation response," treating these two affects as indistinguishable;[11] trying to pry them apart analytically is a tricky business indeed, for they both partly overlap and occasionally metamorphose into each other. Nevertheless, I would like to propose some tentative and patently nonscientific criteria for distinguishing between the two. Shame can be a solely intrasubjective affect, while humiliation always involves a relationship—coming from the Latin *humilis*, meaning "low," it assumes hierarchy, hence a relationship. Shame can function as an ethical affect, whereas humiliation has no such ethical dimension; this is because shame involves internalizing an external negative judgment against oneself, while humiliation can be strictly situational. One can be shamed without being humiliated (for example, by being made to feel guilty) and humiliated without feeling shame, as in the case of erotic humiliation. And although it's possible to shame someone unintentionally, humiliating another person usually involves not only purposive action but also a certain ceremonial dimension.

This aspect of ceremony or ritual brings us back to S/M eroticism and to the role of humiliation in it. To account for the erotics of humiliation, one can opt for various types of explanations; we can, in the spirit of Catherine MacKinnon and Andrea Dworkin, invoke our patriarchal conditioning to respond sexually to hierarchy,[12] or we can, in a more psychoanalytic vein, trace our response back to the infant's experience of helplessness or to childhood conflicts over dependency and recognition.[13] But the explanation I would like to offer here is one that derives from George Bataille's notion of eroticism as the desire "to bring into a world founded on discontinuity all the continuity such a world can sustain."[14] For Bataille, eroticism always entails violation of individual boundaries and loss of self-possession. Humiliation, like other forms of violence, violates—if only temporarily—our sense of self. Hence, by dissolving our boundaries and divesting us of our discontinuous self, humiliation can inaugurate us into the erotic. In the protective context of erotic ritual, this violent wrenching from subjectivity is also redemption from subjectivity—that is the way it is figured in S/M sexuality. In stories such as "The Surprise Party," we can see how, through S/M ritual, shame is transformed into humiliation—and humiliation into redemption. The protagonist's history of identity-forming and deforming shame—as a woman, a lesbian, a gender deviant, and a pervert—is performatively invoked through the misogynist and homophobic abuse she suffers from the mock "cops": their leader harasses her about carrying a wallet, suggests finding another "female pervert" so that the two would "put on a show" for them, and promises to do her "a big favor" before they're through.[15] Yet, the history of shame invoked in this ritual humiliation is also *transfigured* (to use Sedgwick's term) by it.[16] By converting shame to erotic humiliation and erotic humiliation to self-shattering jouissance, Califia's heroine is able to go, at least momentarily, beyond the "shame-delineated place of identity."[17]

Finally, and so as not to conclude on this redemptive note, I'd like to address briefly another way in which shame bears upon these texts. So far, I have discussed both the shameful nature of the very fantasy of sex with gay men and the ways in which shame comes up and is refigured within the textual elaborations of this fantasy. Earlier I referred to the multilayered structure of fantasy and the pornographic text as a modified version of a more original fantasy. I would now like to suggest that the fantasy of cross-gender queer sex, as embarrassing and controversial as it is, is in fact a moderately acceptable version of much more disturbing and identity-threatening wishes. In making this claim, I come to the part of my argument with which I am least comfortable, both because it is the most speculative and because it seems politically risky.

The claim that I'm ashamed to make, but that I nevertheless believe to be true, is that in all the texts that share my topos, the fantasy of sex with gay men—besides being rooted in the quest to articulate female sexual subjectivity—is a modified version of a more original unconscious wish, a wish that is both formative of lesbian identity and necessarily disavowed by it. To explain what I mean, let's turn again to "The Surprise Party." Abstracted of all specifics and reduced to its bare bones, the story as a phantasmatic script represents masochistic desire aimed at men—in other words, traditional female masochism. The protagonist's identity as S/M dyke both accommodates and redeems female masochism by directing it toward a female—not a male—object; it does not, however, give scope to masochistic desires aimed at men. Yet such desires are an almost inevitable component of female subjectivity in a male-dominated society—not because of any biological determination, but because masochism is a common psychic strategy that women (like other subordinated groups) employ to negotiate their subordinate status.[18] Thus, masochism is already a product of subjective negotiation rather than a simple internalization of dominant ideology.[19]

In "The Surprise Party," the S/M scene with the gay male "cops" affords the utmost possible approximation of the original (shameful) fantasy without wholly undermining lesbian identity. In this story, the process of gradual displacement of the original fantasy is even made manifest by the slippage in the ontological status of the fictional reality: what appears at first to be rape by straight cops turns out to be rape by gay cops and is finally revealed to be a consensual S/M scene with gay friends. This triple layering of the fantasy is reminiscent of Freud's analysis of the beating fantasy in "A Child Is Being Beaten,"[20] where from the conscious content of the male beating fantasy, "I am being beaten by my mother," he reconstructs a more primary unconscious fantasy "I am being beaten by my father," which itself stands for the original fantasy "I am being loved by my father." But while Freud needs to work back from the third, most disguised phase of the fantasy to reconstruct the previous two, in "The Surprise Party" all three phases of the fantasy are given—the third and most acceptable one (S/M scene with gay male friends) corresponds to the fictional reality, yet the first phase too (rape by straight men) maintains a spectral presence within the fiction, lending it its erotic force.

Similarly, we can read *Leather Daddy* as representing disguised Oedipal wishes. Oedipal desire, transformed into identification, may provide one of the trajectories of lesbian identity formation. For Freud, famously, female homosexuality is an extreme manifestation of what he terms the "masculinity complex," which forms one of the possible resolutions of the female Oedipus complex. But residual Oedipal investments are incommensurable with the lesbian identity to which they give rise and disavowed by it. Both *Leather Daddy* and "The Triangle" give expression, albeit in revised form, to the doubly forbidden Oedipal fantasy—originally forbidden as incestuous, and subsequently forbidden as threatening to lesbian identity. And in both fictions the threat to lesbian identity is reduced, thanks to the all-queer context. Additionally, in "The Triangle," Kris's daddy–boy relationship with her gay male daddy can be read as fulfilling her original wish to be a boy. This wish is accommodated to some extent by lesbian identity, through the range of legitimate and recognizable masculinities that lesbian culture opens up for women (for example, "butch" as an alternative gender category). But lesbian identity provides recognition of one's masculinity only by other women and cannot satisfy the wish to be recognized as a boy by men—precisely the wish that comes into play in the story.

In all these cases, we can see that lesbian identity is founded on wishes that it both defends against and gives indirect expression to through displacement, reaction formation, and other conversion mechanisms. These wishes nevertheless continue to haunt lesbian identity and press for more direct expression, and the fantasy of sex with gay men provides a closer approximation to them that is, however, not entirely incompatible with lesbian identity.

Saying that lesbian identity is partly constituted by wishes that, in order to be what it is, it needs to disavow does not amount to saying that these original wishes are somehow truer than or ontologically superior to the identity they give rise to, or that lesbian identity is reducible to these wishes.[21] It does, however, entail giving up on the supposed "purity" of lesbian identity, though without collapsing it back into heterosexuality. Similarly, reading the fantasy of cross-gender queer sex as a modified version of more primary masochistic or Oedipal fantasies does not amount to saying that this fantasy and its textual elaborations are reducible to female masochism and Oedipality. On the contrary, they are complex cultural products, specific to lesbian culture—and to a particular moment in it—and should be valued for their creativity, as well as for their implicit politics of lesbian–gay solidarity.

Notes

1. "Ganged," in *Best Gay Erotica 1996*, ed. Michael Ford (Pittsburgh, PA: Cleis Press, 1996), 38.

2. Pat Califia, "The Surprise Party," in *Macho Sluts* (Boston: Alyson, 1988); Lady Sara, "The Triangle," in *Leather Women*, ed. Laura Antoniou (New York: Rosebud, 1993); Carol Queen, *The Leather Daddy and the Femme* (San Francisco, Cleis, 1998); Helen Sandler, *Big Deal* (London: Sapphire, 1999). I am employing the adjective "lesbian" here in a rather loose sense. Of the three authors I discuss, one, Pat Califia, identified until several years ago as a dyke and currently identifies as transgendered; the second, Lady Sara, is anonymous; and the third, Carol Queen, is a self-identified bisexual. Califia's protagonist is unquestionably lesbian, while the protagonists of both Queen's and Lady Sara's texts seem to be lodged in a lesbian social context even as they stray out of it; Califia's and Queen's books came out with lesbian presses, and Lady Sara's story appeared in a collection, *Leather Women*, that for all its stated, ideologically motivated inclusiveness, comprises mostly lesbian fiction. If we take the identity of the author, the identity of the characters, and the publication context as three parameters for deciding a work's "lesbian" status, none of the three texts fully satisfies all three criteria, but all satisfy at least one. I therefore feel justified in regarding these texts as forming part of the field of lesbian erotica, while admitting that they challenge its very definitional boundaries.

3. Pat Califia, "Gay Men, Lesbians, and Sex: Doing It Together," in *Public Sex: The Culture of Radical Sex* (Pittsburgh, PA: Cleis Press, 1996), 185. It is worth noting that the "gender-blind" queer erotic sensibility articulated by Califia emerges out of a particular milieu—the San Francisco leather culture of the late 1970s and early 1980s—in which lesbians and gay men shared some sexual spaces and institutions. See Califia, "Gay Men"; Califia, "Identity Sedition and Pornography," in *Pomosexuals: Challenging Assumptions about Gender and Sexuality*, ed. Carol Queen and Lawrence Schimel (San Francisco: Cleis, 1997), 87–106; Gayle Rubin, "The Catacombs: A Temple of the Butthole," in *Leatherfolk*, ed. Mark Thompson (Boston: Alyson, 1991), 119–141.

4. "The Birth of Queer Nation and the Death of 'Gay' and 'Lesbian,'" *LA Weekly*, May 17–23, 1991. I'm indebted to David Halperin for bringing this article to my attention.

5. Eve Kosofsky Sedgwick, "Queer Performativity: Henry James's *The Art of the Novel*," *GLQ* 1, no. 1 (1993): 5.

6. For example, Judith Butler rejects MacKinnon's claim that porn turns itself into reality by suggesting instead an understanding of porn as depicting "compensatory fantasies" (*Excitable Speech* [New York: Routledge, 1997], 68). For an elaborate discussion of pornography as fantasy, see Elizabeth Cowie, "Pornography and Fantasy: Psychoana-

lytic Perspectives," in *Sex Exposed*, ed. Lynne Segal and Mary McIntosh (London: Virago, 1992).

7. Cowie, "Pornography and Fantasy." A broader discussion of the different modes of fantasy is found in Cowie, "Fantasia," in *The Woman in Question*, ed. Parveen Adams and Elizabeth Cowie (Cambridge, MA: MIT Press, 1990); Teresa de Lauretis, "Popular Culture, Public and Private Fantasies: Femininity and Fetishism in David Cronenberg's *M. Butterfly*," *Signs* 24, no. 2 (1999): 303-34; de Lauretis, "On the Subject of Fantasy," in *Feminisms in the Cinema*, ed. Laura Pietropaulo and Ada Testaferri (Bloomington: Indiana University Press, 1995).

8. Cowie, "Fantasia," 166.

9. My argument in no way contradicts or excludes an understanding of this process of cross-cultural borrowing as an effect of the greater cultural contact between lesbians and gay men following the AIDS crisis and the activism it spawned, and as a reaction to the sexual restrictiveness of 1970s lesbian-feminism. Rather, I am attempting to underline the active dimension of a process that is often conceived as simply reactive, and the feminist logic behind what might seem as a move away from feminism.

10. For a broader discussion of how the project of articulating female sexual subjectivity motivates borrowing from gay male culture, and the paradoxical outcomes of this borrowing, see Amalia Ziv, "The Construction of the Female Subject in Pornographic Fiction," Ph.D. diss., Tel Aviv University, 2005.

11. Sedgwick, "Queer Performativity," 5.

12. See, e.g., Catharine MacKinnon, *Toward a Feminist Theory of the State* (Cambridge, MA: Harvard University Press, 1989), especially the chapters on sexuality and pornography.

13. For the first explanation see Leo Bersani, *The Freudian Body: Psychoanalysis and Art* (New York: Columbia University Press, 1986); for the second, see Jessica Benjamin, *The Bonds of Love* (New York: Pantheon, 1988).

14. Georges Bataille, *Erotism: Death and Sensuality* (San Francisco: City Lights, 1986), 19.

15. Califia, "The Surprise Party," 212, 214, 215. What gets acted out or dramatized in the story is mostly various aspects of butch abjection—the shame of gender deviance and, concurrently, the shame of being a woman, the shame of being faced through sexual humiliation with the "truth" of being a woman—a shame that is exacerbated by a context in which the standard is the male body.

16. "The forms taken by shame . . . are available for the work of metamorphosis, reframing, refiguration, *trans*figuration, affective and symbolic loading and deformation" (Sedgwick, "Queer Performativity," 13).

17. Ibid.

18. Cf. Kaja Silverman, who notes that masochism "is an accepted—indeed a requisite—element of 'normal' female subjectivity providing a crucial mechanism for eroticizing lack and subordination." ("Masochism and Male Subjectivity," *Camera Obscura* 17 [1988]: 36). To avoid misunderstanding, I'd like clearly to distance my discussion of female masochism from Freud's notion of "feminine masochism." Since Freud regards femininity as synonymous with passivity, masochism (whether in men or women) is for him es-

sentially feminine. Further, he sees masochism as natural to women due to constitutional factors (such as their role in intercourse and reproduction): see especially the lecture on femininity in Sigmund Freud, "New Introductory Lectures on Psychoanalysis (1933), Lecture 33: Femininity," in *The Standard Edition of the Complete Psychological Works*, trans. and ed. James Strachey, vol. 22 (London: Hogarth, 1964), 112–35.

19. See Amalia Ziv, "The Pervert's Progress," *Feminist Review* 46 (Spring 1994): 73.

20. Sigmund Freud, "A Child Is Being Beaten," in *Standard Edition*, vol. 17 (1919), 179–204.

21. Cf. Judith Butler's comment that "if gay identities are implicated in heterosexuality, that is not the same as claiming that they are determined or derived from heterosexuality" ("Imitation and Gender Insubordination," in *The Lesbian and Gay Studies Reader*, ed. Henry Abelove, Michèle Aina Barale, and David M. Halperin [New York: Routledge, 1993], 313).

Excluding Shame

In less than twenty-four hours, the emphasis of this conference has changed in a significant and, for me, disheartening way. In Warhol's film, and in Douglas Crimp's enlightening comments on the film, we were being asked, at least implicitly, to consider shame in its psychic dimensions. To do so would, I think, have led us to some valuable and disturbing questions, such as: What is the role of the individual unconscious in both the production and the experience of shame? In what sense is shame an isolating factor that blocks the thinking and the formation of politically viable communities? Such inquiries have been virtually excluded from the conference by today's emphasis on gay shame as something imposed on gays by a homophobic society. In this perspective, the problem raised by shame becomes how it can be transformed into a new kind of pride, one that resists both the homophobic stigma of shame and the temptation, among gays and lesbians, to adapt to "normalizing" imperatives that support the apparatus of homophobic blame. Thus a conference on gay shame risks becoming yet another occasion for gay self-congratulation: the shamed are the proud victims of evil heterosexism. There is obviously truth in, and moral justification for, this last claim, but it involves eliminating other, painfully unflatteringly truths. To avoid looking at these truths is, to me, intellectually dishonest and politically counterproductive. The rigor with which any such self-examination has, for the most part, been avoided can be measured by the topics that appear to have been excluded from serious analysis. With, as I recollect, a single exception, you would never have known from the combination of political correctness and infighting that has largely characterized today's events that psychoanalysis exists.

This and the correlative exclusion of any reference to the unconscious (with one exception in Amalia Ziv's essay) in the course of a serious consideration of a psychic phenomenon are, to say the least, astonishing. I am also struck—and depressed—by the silence on the topic of AIDS, and the various forms of shame inseparable from it (shame nurtured from both outside and within the gay community). Connected to this, not a word about barebacking except for a casual dismissal of the media for attributing any importance to it. Instead, we have had the self-righteous ranting of the representatives from Gay Shame directed at evil, smart-ass academics, and the simmering, ethnically correct rage at the use of a Latino male with a shamefully divine endowment as a filmic background to a scholarly presentation on Plato's *Symposium*.

DISABLED
SHAME

[ROBERT McRUER]

Shameful Sites

LOCATING QUEERNESS AND DISABILITY

The rapid convergence of queer theory and disability studies over the past few years has been nothing short of extraordinary. The convergence has produced texts, events, communities, and institutions that many of us are very proud of: not only a special issue of *GLQ: A Journal of Lesbian and Gay Studies*,[1] but also Eli Clare's *Exile and Pride*,[2] the first international queer disability conference at San Francisco State University in June 2002; the Queer Bodies working group out of the Center for Lesbian and Gay Studies (CLAGS), whose central focus is disability; visual art by Dylan Scholinski and others; performance art by Terry Galloway, Greg Walloch, and others; the Queer Disability online Listserv; and the panel on disability and queerness at the Gay Shame conference at the University of Michigan in March 2003. The list could go on. Queer theory and LGBT studies have arguably come together with disability studies more than many other "identity"-based fields, not surprisingly given the oft-remarked areas of overlap: socialization for queers and for people with disabilities often occurs in heterosexual and able-bodied families isolated from queer community or disability community; the rhetoric of coming out that now permeates the disability movement has clear antecedents in the gay liberation movement and at its best does not signify discovery of some deep essential truth but rather coming out to a vibrant movement intent on collectively and often quite literally rebuilding the world around us; some of the identities shaped in both fields come with some of the same limitations, especially when those identities are used to understand non-Western locations (that is, the extent to which models of disability identity are adequate for describing other times and places is currently an open question); and both communities have faced medicalization or pathologization and face similar new dangers, normalization perhaps at the forefront (and I'd say the disability movement seems primed to enter some of the same normalizing territory that structured the gay 1990s). Teasing out these linkages, seeing them come together and apart, has been incredibly generative for me and for many of us committed to both fields.

If, however, that generativity is easily readable within the recognizable and historical framework of both gay and disability pride, that pride is always inevitably haunted by shame. And as queer theorists have begun to recognize, we have been perhaps too quick to dismiss the complex ways in which shame functions. Douglas Crimp's contribution to this volume, "Mario Montez, For Shame," opens with a quotation from Eve Kosofsky Sedgwick on Andy Warhol that emphasizes shame as a nexus of production: "From shame to shyness to shining—and, inevitably, back, and back again: the candor and cultural incisiveness of this itinerary seem to make Warhol an exemplary figure for a new project, an urgent one I think, of understanding how the dysphoric affect shame functions as a nexus of production: production, that is, of meaning, of personal presence, of politics, of performative and critical efficacy."[3] Crimp himself, however, complicates this emphasis on production, or creativity: "Just as shame is both productive and corrosive of queer identity. . . . so too is it simultaneously productive and corrosive of queer revaluations of dignity and worth."[4] Building on Sedgwick's assertion, in other words, Crimp considers the ways in which production and corrosion are linked, suggesting that if in fact queer shame has produced or allowed for the queer revaluation of dignity and worth, it also clearly has the ongoing capacity to corrode that revaluation.

In my own case, shame had an uncanny capacity to rewrite the queer/disabled success story of the past few years, in ways I avoided thinking about prior to the Gay Shame conference at the University of Michigan. For months, the question of *what* about queerness and disability produces or causes shame was completely overshadowed by the question of *where* shame about queerness and disability is produced and sustained. And the answer was quite literally there, in southeast Michigan. Shame blossoms for me in that impossible space where it's very difficult to take refuge in abstract theorizing. I told the organizers when they invited me to present on queerness and disability that they were holding the conference in the original site of gay shame, for I grew up about thirty miles from the university, in what David Wojnarowicz would label "the tiny version of hell called the suburbs"[5]—and the Oakland County, Michigan, suburbs, with their often-complete detachment from the city of Detroit (the place my mother at times referred to as "that wicked city"), have always struck me as quintessentially suburban. And as should be clear from my mother's investment in "wickedness," I grew up in an extremely religious, fundamentalist Baptist church—a mega-church, in fact, of several thousand members (where I was president of Southfield Christian School's class of 1984). The ingredients for a tremendous amount of shame, then, were all right there, even though I was at the same time a bit ashamed to talk about them—not just because I didn't want to be read as simplistically confessional or because I had never written autobiographically, but because these facets of my past were on some level so banal: just another white, middle-class gay boy from Christian and suburban roots alienated from the place he came from, alienated from his religious, disapproving, shaming family. It may be outrageous that my parents asked me, the last time I broke up with a lover, "Do you think the Lord is moving you away from a same-sex relationship?" but it's not particularly remarkable.

But gay shame and disabled shame were thoroughly intertwined for me there as well. A few months before the Gay Shame conference, my mother asked me, "Do you do disability studies because of Dad?"—one of the most jarring questions she had ever posed, because the answer was so decisively "no." My trajectory to disability studies was quite clearly, in my mind, from earlier work on and around HIV/AIDS. What my mother was referring to with her question, however, was the fact that my seventy-five-year-old father has lived with Parkinson's for about fifteen years and is by most measures, at this point, significantly disabled. His mobility is extremely limited. He moves very slowly and cannot drive; he takes an extensive regimen of drugs, some of which at times cause serious hallucinations; he uses bars in the shower and protective clothing at night; his speech is difficult to understand. I'm ashamed to say, in fact, that most telephone conversations have to be, to some degree, translated for me by my mother—in other words, I don't talk to him enough to understand on my own. In an abstract academic sense, I can watch something like the Shakespeare Theater's production of *King Lear* in Washington, D.C. (where I now live and work, and where—in contrast to suburban Detroit—I generally feel very much at home), and think that it's brilliant that Cordelia is cast as Deaf, with her signed lines translated by the fool; the idea that Lear never bothered to learn Cordelia's language seems like a smart new disability-inflected interpretation.⁶ Offstage, however, in Farmington Hills, Michigan, the question of not bothering to learn a child's language, or a parent's, is more complicated.

I'm the only disability studies scholar in the family, and certainly that makes a difference: I was the one who installed those bars, I have no doubt that I use the word "disability" more and perhaps differently from other members of the family, and I detest and (I hope) consistently refuse the ways in which others around my father patronize him. But when it comes right down to it, I don't interact with him much, and caregiving responsibilities (to my shame) fall almost entirely on the women in my family—my mother and my fundamentalist Christian sister, who still lives in the area. In my professional life, the study of sexuality and disability, I'm proud to say, are thoroughly enmeshed in very satisfying ways, but bring it all home, to the specific location where I grew up, and sexuality and disability clash and diverge in incredibly complex and painful ways, and what is enmeshed for me there is usually alienation and shame.

I suspect that at times the dazzling answers many of us attempt to put forward in essays and conference presentations consciously or unconsciously serve to displace such shame, so in the spirit of an ongoing, open-ended inquiry into shame's productive and corrosive effects, I mostly defer answers here in favor of questions that remain about queerness, disability, and shame. Returning once again to southeast Michigan, however, I conclude by tentatively tracing some of the limits of queer/disabled identification.

Where in fact is shame located? Sedgwick locates it in "that childhood scene of shame," but if that scene occurred in an actual place, then the people in that place change, and inevitably disability enters it if it wasn't there from the beginning. So if for Sedgwick that childhood scene of shame is an "inexhaustible source of transformational energy,"[7] it's also, to riff on the phrase from a disability perspective, ultimately a transformed scene where, for some, energy and ability are exhausted.

In what ways is subjectivity within LGBT communities (or perhaps all subjectivity) currently forged between a cult of ability and multiple cultures of disability? And by referring to "cults of ability," I do not necessarily mean gay gym culture; given the ways in which some people with HIV use the gym, it may at times in fact mark one of those "cultures of disability." Is the marriage movement perhaps in some ways our most problematic cult of ability?

How does queer/disabled shame lead to mutual recoil? One of the founding moments of contemporary gay liberation, the removal of homosexuality from the third edition of the American Psychiatric Association's *Diagnostic and Statistical Manual*, after all, can be interpreted as a distancing from disability. To what degree do able-bodied queers, still perceived in the straight mind as somehow disabled, and heterosexual people with disabilities, often understood as a little queer (as ongoing stereotypes of asexuality or hypersexuality attest), react to that cultural shaming by disclaiming any connection to the other group? And what are the ramifications for those who in fact, of necessity or for any other reasons, claim both disability and queerness?

How are issues of queer/disabled shame gendered? If queerness is at times gendered male (given the militancy of AIDS activists, the marginalization some women felt within queer movements in the late 1980s and early 1990s, and the overrepresentation of men in the projects of both queer activism and queer theory) and disability female (given the historical association of women and caregiving or the ways disability is perceived as compromising dominant and compulsory forms of masculinity), how can that historical and contingent gendered binary be acknowledged, critiqued, and surpassed? How have queer men and women learned (or resisted learning) from the unique cultures of disability that each have shaped, from lesbian feminist spaces where a wide variety of bodies are valued to Free Sharon Kowalski groups, from buddy systems for people living with HIV/AIDS to support groups for drug and alcohol dependency?

How have AIDS activists responded to disabled shame? What are the multiple ways in which the rhetoric of "living positively" has functioned? What identifications has the rhetoric facilitated or precluded? How, in turn, have disability activists responded over the past two decades to the stigmas associated with HIV/AIDS? Much of the shame connected to HIV/AIDS historically may be tied more to location than are other forms of queer/disabled shame, as some gay men with AIDS returned, for the final months or years of their lives, to Ohio, or Arkansas, or other locations far from the urban centers where they had shaped most of their adult lives. Is disabled shame somehow compounded in these spaces not generally understood or experienced as gay or gay-friendly?

Crimp writes of the need to articulate "collectivities of the shamed."[8] What forces have precluded realizing that need? How have current dominant rhetorics of neoliberalism, for instance, kept us from articulating collectivities of the shamed? Neoliberalism globally privatizes out of existence accessible public cultures and rights such as health care, and these global shifts have disproportionately impacted people with disability and people with HIV. If activism resisting corporate and neoliberal globalization has been the most vibrant activism globally over the past decade, has such activism articulated collectivities of the shamed? How have these movements been connected to queerness and disability, or indebted to earlier queer and disabled movements?

Finally, if from one perspective shame does look back so decisively to childhood, to what degree does our avoidance of talking about the other direction, aging issues (our own aging and the aging of those close to us), have to do with disabled shame? To echo Sedgwick once more, this inevitably brings me back, and back again, to southeast Michigan. As a scholar well versed in disability studies, I have for a long time seen my own relationship to disability as very complex: perceived as able-bodied (however temporary or tenuous that may be, and however consistently I critique or resist the disciplines of compulsory able-bodiedness), I have at times been partnered with men with HIV or other disabilities, I claim solidarity with movements for disability rights, and I teach, write, and think about disability more than any other topic. My own return to southeast Michigan, however, inescapably stages a very different relationship to aging and disability: even if I can no longer see myself in the place where my father lives, I nonetheless cannot help but see myself in his face and movements; even when I fail to understand him, I cannot help but hear myself in his speech. Identification is not so easy to claim or refuse in such a location, as the connection, or love, I feel according to my bond (to my father and to disability communities) is always tempered by ambivalence about my past and, perhaps, my future.

In general, LGBT and disability movements have been about claiming identity and, from that moment of first-person identification, discovering or constructing new communities, new locations. I wonder, however, whether we will ultimately learn more about shame and its effects from inversions of that trajectory from identity to new locations; I wonder, in other words, whether the return to *old* locations, to shameful sites, tests the limits of queer and disabled identification and what the results of that testing might be. Although it is by no means guaranteed, such an itinerary might lay the groundwork for revaluing that which is old rather than only reaching, again and again, for that which is new. What is guaranteed is that such an itinerary will displace the queerness and disability with which we're most comfortable. And yet, in the end, how can queer and disabled projects be shaped otherwise?

In memoriam, A. G. McRuer, 1928–2006

Notes

1. Robert McRuer and Abby L. Wilkerson, eds., "Desiring Disability: Queer Theory Meets Disability Studies," special issue, *GLQ: A Journal of Lesbian and Gay Studies* 9, nos. 1–2 (2003).

2. Eli Clare, *Exile and Pride: Queerness, Disability, and Liberation* (Boston: South End Press, 1999).

3. Quoted in Douglas Crimp, "Mario Montez, For Shame," this volume, 63.

4. Ibid., 71.

5. David Wojnarowicz, *Close to the Knives: A Memoir of Disintegration* (New York: Vintage, 1991), 151.

6. In Deaf and disability activist communities, "Deaf" is capitalized to mark cultural and linguistic identity (most prominently in the use of American Sign Language [ASL]); the lowercase "deaf" is used to mark an auditory condition.

7. Quoted in Crimp, "Mario Montez," 71.

8. Ibid., 72.

[ABBY WILKERSON]

Slipping

Somehow I managed to believe I would be fine until I was sitting in the stylist's chair and the pain was so intense I thought I would vomit. No, this is not a bad-haircut story (although it could have been the worst cut of my life for all I remember), but a slipping-on-the-ice-on-the-way-to-the-salon story. I was intent on continuing with my errands, so with teeth gritted I hobbled in. But as the poet Mary McAnally said, "Pain teaches us to take our fingers OUT the fucking fire,"[1] or in my case not to keep putting my weight on what turned out to be four broken bones in my foot. This time, not only the external world but even my own foot was refusing to operate as an instrument of my will.

But I knew what to do. I was ready. I had read my disability studies, and I knew, or at least managed to admit soon enough, that the trick was not to pretend. Not to try to fit in, approximate my previous way of moving and acting, but to go with what my body was telling me. And didn't I know from queer theory and coming out as bisexual in multiple worlds, each with its own distinct brand of bi-phobia, that again, the answer was not to pretend or try to approximate someone else's version of what I was supposed to be?

Living with this new (temporary) disability was overwhelming in a lot of ways. Shortly before my mishap, my sister had been injured in a car wreck, my brother was thrown from a horse and crushed three vertebrae, and my mother was killed in an accident. The world was not seeming too safe. But I knew from people with disabilities and a thousand critiques of medicine that I didn't have to be a passive victim. I could take pride in my creativity, my ability to find new ways of doing things like making a cup of tea and carrying it into another room while balancing on crutches, my right foot never touching the floor.

Then I got the idea of using a wheelchair, at least at school and on oc-

casional outings to the movies, if not in my small apartment. This idea,
I should note, came not from my doctor or any health-care provider, but
from a shopping trip to Target, where two kinds of wheelchairs were
thoughtfully provided for my shopping convenience. In the week or so I'd
been using crutches, even after one of my classes had been moved to the
same building as my office and my other classes, walking down the suddenly very long hallways to get to class was extremely painful and drained
me of energy. Once I got the wheelchair, getting around was awkward, due
partly to my own ineptitude and partly to the poorly planned physical environment, but far less painful and draining. I felt a little strange in the chair,
but as I had learned first from the novelist Jean Stewart and then from other
disability activists, wheelchair users have reason to see themselves as enabled rather than confined by their chairs.[2] Mine, I reasoned, would just be
a tool for me to get around until my foot healed.

But I was not prepared for everything. When someone I knew saw me
for the first time on crutches, they usually expressed sympathy and tried
to make some gesture of help. When I switched to the wheelchair, reactions were magnified to something not far short of what I would expect
had I waved a bloody stump in their faces. One morning I was trying to get
the chair into my classroom doorway when a colleague (who already knew
about the injury) saw me and swooped down upon me. She threw her arms
around me (in front of the class) and cried, "Oh, Abby, how I grieve for you!"
(Don't feel bad, some of us actually *like* to teach composition, I should have
said.)

Another day, rolling through an open area outside my building on campus, I got to the doorway where one of my former students had come running from her classroom where she had seen me through the window. "Oh
my God," she said, her face filled with horror, "what happened to you?"
Later I got the same stricken response from an administrator in the hallway. When I saw her the next week she had a cast on her arm and a brace on
her neck.

When people I knew, able-bodied people, saw me in a wheelchair, they
seemed to feel I was gone, leaving some pitiful husk of myself behind, and
I wasn't coming back. I had crossed over. And if it could happen to me . . .
well, it wasn't going to happen to them! Ann, a kind and maternal presence,
said, "Abby, next winter I am watching you on the ice like a hawk!" Watch
yourself too, Ann, I said.

My recovery didn't go exactly as I hoped. I had complications, knee and
shoulder problems that still haven't cleared up. But I could expect this disability to be temporary. Still, somehow it gradually began to affect my sense

of reality in subtle but far-reaching ways. I had undergone a conversion experience, after all. For years I'd tried to integrate disability into social analysis along with other vectors of oppression. I had tried to raise awareness of disability-related needs, attend to the perspectives of people with disabilities, highlight able-bodied privilege, explore what it would mean to create a more accessible society. But that first sunny spring day when I couldn't go to the park because I simply couldn't figure out a way to get my wheelchair out my door and to the street, I felt I had understood nothing at all about disability and access until that moment. I was shamed. All at once everything I had written about disability seemed unspeakably weak and ineffectual, utterly lacking in . . . *robustness?* Even my metaphors were horrifyingly ableist! That summer at the Society for Disability Studies conference I was introduced to a disability studies scholar (herself disabled) whose work I admired. She mentioned some of my work and spoke well of it. I recoiled in shame: she had read the pre-conversion experience work, written eons before Long Branch Parkway, my inaccessible street, became the Road to Damascus. Clearly she was just being polite, when she should have had the conference organizers just print IMPOSTOR on my name tag.

Hmm. This feeling was all too familiar, from feminist spaces where lesbian separatism was influential. I'd spent years in those places as the feminist sleeping with the enemy while dreaming of the girls, telling everyone, in the hypothetical, that were I not with him, who knows, maybe I'd be with a woman. After all, wouldn't *any* feminist say the same if she only had the guts to admit that she'd been brainwashed into compulsory heterosexuality? But I didn't identify as bi, because I obviously wasn't queer enough to count if I was with a man. And even after some rather eventful forays into girl-girl territory, and being with a man again, or still, had I really earned my queer stripes if I could be seen, as I sometimes was, as HeteroGirl (HetMom even!) masquerading as Miss Queer Enough in the lesbian underworld? I'd been around the block enough times not to try to crash the lesbian caucus at the feminist philosophy conference, no matter how hot the dykes taking their bagels and coffee into the inner sanctum.

And something else began to happen as I made the rounds from orthopedist to physical therapist to acupuncturist to the co-op, to pick up yet another homeopathic salve, supplement for joint health, lemons for detox, beets and greens to build up my blood. Those periods of depression that had come and gone for as long as I could remember began a kind of ontological shift before my eyes, the dots connecting unmistakably into a whole. I was living with depression all the time, even when the world seemed bearable. Maybe I was part of the disability club after all. Maybe I would now know what to say when someone asked me, as another disability scholar had at a conference, "What *is* your disability status, anyhow?"

Depression is difficult to claim for many reasons. It is not visible in the way that many physical disabilities are, and the stigma of mental illness only reinforces the felt need to keep it that way. It affects the body as much as the mind, so it confounds both the conceptual binary of physical and mental disability and divisions within disability communities. And it is particularly hard to claim as the basis for a defiant, anti-assimilationist sensibility such as the QueerCrip position demonstrated, for example, in the work of Carrie Sandahl and Naomi Finkelstein.[3] What's the depression equivalent—Mope Pride? Who are our flag bearers—Eeyore? Walter Matthau in *Grumpy Old Men?* Better to cast my lot with the Mad Liberation folks, taking Dylan Scholinski's signature "Don't Worry Be Crazy" as our motto. So maybe the zombie lethargy of depression is a little less dynamic than "madness" suggests. We have to work what we've got.

And what I've got, well, the shame's still attached. I couldn't escape the shame of being where I could never be sure I'd earned my place, maybe still haven't, even as I recognize that the shame belongs to a world of binaries where we are expected to be completely disabled or not at all, permanently/ incurably or with a finite, entirely predictable, and *brief* duration; completely and stably gay or completely straight; completely, hence predictably, man or woman, girl or boy. Physically disabled, or mentally disabled, or not at all. Visibly, reliably, identifiably disabled, or not at all. Slipping may be dangerous, but it's not always a bad way to move in the world.

Notes

1. Quoted in Audre Lorde, *Sister Outsider* (Freedom, CA: Crossing Press, 1984), 64.

2. Jean Stewart, *The Body's Memory* (New York: St. Martin's, 1989).

3. See Carrie Sandahl, "Queering the Crip or Cripping the Queer?," and Naomi Finkelstein, "The Only Thing You Have to Do Is Live," along with other examples of Queer-Crip sensibility, in "Desiring Disability: Queer Theory Meets Disability Studies," ed. Robert McRuer and Abby L. Wilkerson, special issue, *GLQ* 9, nos. 1-2 (2003).

[DYLAN SCHOLINSKI]

Where Is the Truth in Painting Today?

I paint for my survival and myself. Time and again, I have realized that without my art, I would likely be dead.

At the age of fifteen, primarily because I lacked signs of being a "heterosexual female," I was labeled "mentally ill" and confined to a psychiatric ward. I lost over three years of my youth. I consider all of my art to be autobiographical. I tell stories about my life: what I am thinking, feeling, experiencing, creating a sort of map of living and breathing emotions. I rarely hold my breath in a painting—unlike in real life, where the simple process of breath, the literal proof of my own existence, poses a daily challenge. The content of my paintings deals with the experiences I had leading up to and during my years in the hospital and continues to reflect the struggles I face being transgendered, gay, human, as well as an ex–mental patient.

My purpose in my work is to encourage the sympathetic indulgence of emotions to which most are ashamed to give way in their own lives, to try to get people to feel things, and to help to reacquaint them with themselves. As much as it is personal, my art is also a social commentary: as a society, we view the emotional world as an oversimplified dichotomy, seeing emotions as either "good" or "bad." We all spend outrageous amounts of time and energy trying to rid ourselves of the "bad." So long as we do this we will never truly experience the "good." It is only once we learn to embrace the entire spectrum of emotions that we will fully experience our lives, ourselves, and each other. We often find it hard to tolerate those with full emotion because it reminds us of all we don't feel ourselves. It holds up a mirror that we see as ugly, self-indulgent, and pitiful. What we rarely admit is that it is ourselves that we see, a side that many of us have fought very hard to leave behind. In my work I am attempting to be this mirror by showing myself. It is my hope that once you get in touch with these emotions in your-self you will be able to identify them in others, and as a result we will have better understanding, compassion, and tolerance of each other and all of our differences.

I don't think in terms of gay/straight, male/female, or who is more this way or that way. I believe that if we just came to terms with the fact that we are all everything, it wouldn't matter, and we would begin to see ourselves in everyone.

I have painted for most of my life, but it is only in the last ten years that I have realized my place as an artist. I have been to school, read books, and looked at art; and just as when I was thirteen and looking for myself in mag-azines, I have found it hard to see myself here. Where are the individual's passion, life, and emotion? Where is the truth in painting today? If it is true that art saves lives, as it has mine, then the truth must be shown; and my in-dividual goal is to be as honest as I can be.

These three works are from a series created while I was writing my memoir The Last Time I Wore a Dress *(Penguin/Putnam, 1997). In the process of writing I was*

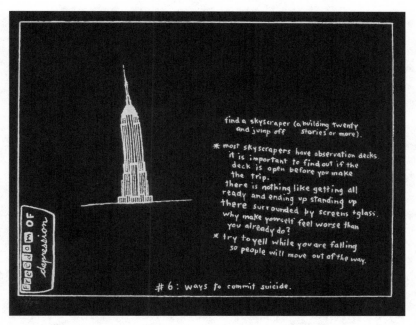

Figure 13. Dylan Scholinski, *#6 / Freedom of Depression: 9 Ways to Commit Suicide.* Screenprint, 11 × 14 inches. (© 1997 Dylan Scholinski)

Figure 14. Dylan Scholinski, *#8 / Freedom of Depression: 9 Ways to Commit Suicide.*
Screenprint, 11 × 14 inches. (© 1997 Dylan Scholinski)

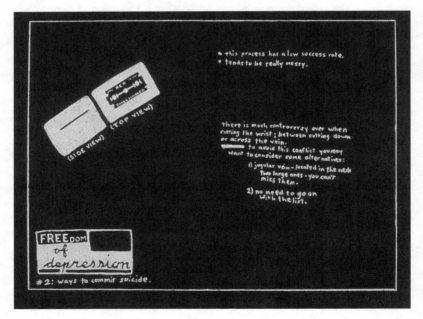

Figure 15. Dylan Scholinski, *#2 / Freedom of Depression: 9 Ways to Commit Suicide.*
Screenprint, 11 × 14 inches. (© 1997 Dylan Scholinski)

forced to think of all the friends I had lost to suicide as well as all the times I had tried to kill myself. I believe my sense of humor is what has saved my life, and with this I hope to add to yours. What I have come to appreciate most about this series is the conversations they start. Frequently viewers begin, sometimes for the first time, to talk out loud about themselves and/or the people they love.

[TERRY GALLOWAY]

Tough

Because my mother was given an experimental antibiotic when she was six months pregnant with me, I grew up hallucinatory and deaf (deaf then being the catchall word for any kind of severe hearing impairment).

I was a tomboy, but my Coke-bottle glasses and the Walkman-sized hearing aid that banged like a third breast between the two budding on my body seemed like beacons, signals to whatever wider world that deigned to notice that I was a girl—and not only was I a girl, I was a little crippled one.

As a little crippled girl I was expected to act that part. But what part was that? Patty Duke as Helen Keller in *The Miracle Worker*? I wouldn't have minded that in the least. She got to run around like crazy and break and shatter things in her furies, and there was nothing more appealing than her homoerotic attachment to Ann Bancroft. So boy, I was willing to try that role.

But no one else was willing to buy me in it. I could see three feet in front of my face so I could read lips. So if I kept my mouth shut (while undergoing the therapy to keep my speech from sounding "lak thsis"), I could pass. I just didn't have enough cripple capital to get away with the furthest extremes of uncivil behavior. I was expected to behave. No, more than that, I was expected to somehow be a little angel—as in half dead before my time. Like the crippled girl in *Heidi*—inert in that wheelchair, sickly, listless, and wan, missing something she'd never have, never know the joys of, perpetually wasting away from her envy of the put-together human being she should have been, that is, Shirley Temple, that perfect gold mine of child talent and cute who was always there at her elbow nagging her to get up, lazybones, and walk.

Even as a child it amazed me that Shirley Temple (and by implication, all perfect, cute, precocious children everywhere) could be so prescient, so intuitive, so right in her every impulse. Especially toward children who were more like me—the sad sacks with defective parts and no discernible reason for being. If only we could be passive and just listen to reason, listen to Shirley. We'd be able to get right up out of that chair and be cured. So said Shirley to her little crippled friend, whose name of course eludes me, but wasn't I impressed when after all those urgings she finally did stand up, did take those miraculous tottering steps forward. It was all just a matter of will. Of wanting. Of belief. So said my grandmother's pastor when he laid his hand on my head and commanded me to be made whole again.

I wanted to be whole. I willed myself to hear again, to be normal. I knew that unless I was whole I could never hope to play a role as heroic as Shirley Special Fucking Temple. My role would always be the victim, the poor hapless sap who was constantly being saved from the consequences of her own frowny disposition.

You'd think the hallucinations, with their whispering voices and sudden liftings through the air, would have put me on a little more equal footing, made me seem like a seer, something really special to be heeded and feared. And it's true that for a little while there my family (coming from a long history of quasi-lunatic psychics) thought maybe something more powerful was afoot when I told them I could leave my body and fly. But modern medicine stripped that illusion away. The truth was something I'd known all along—I was just a kid who couldn't hear and could barely see; and the mysteries visited upon me weren't profound revelations at all, just simple terrors.

I was such a mass of fear and imperfection I could hardly bear to lift my head up to the sky.

Is it any wonder I started to cross-dress?

I'd wake up from a nightmare, a vision, my own troubled mind. Everyone else in the house would be asleep. I'd put on my hearing aids and glasses, my jeans and the army shirt of my dad's I'd filched from the laundry room; I'd take the tie of his that I'd stolen long ago out from under the mattress where I kept it hidden, slip it around my neck, then steal through the living room and, grabbing my mother's lighter and cigarettes, open the side door that led to the carport.

Somewhere out there was danger and romance. And I was going to find it.

As a man I could do that, see—open the door to the uncertain dark, go out in it and stand under a starry sky, stare down my destiny, my terrible fate.

And yeah, I knew the truth of that too: that I was just a little girl playing dress-up late at night. But so what? I was being released from my body into a kind of fiction. And isn't that in essence what it meant to be a man? To be released from your body into a kind of fiction? And if that were true, why couldn't those stars be mine as much as anyone's? Why couldn't I become the hero of my own story?

As a skinny kid I played that role of man seriously, privately. As an adult woman suddenly that role became imaginatively impossible for me to play.

Part of playing the male role for me was playing tough. Not the kind of tough that had anything to do with real, unpretty survival with which I was familiar. But the kind of tough predicated on being slick, distanced, cool. Tough as just another fashion tool reserved for the perfect. The handsome James Dean-y–looking boys who were allowed to look wounded because there's nothing more fuckable than a tough-looking boy with a soft, swollen mouth.

But that kind of tough couldn't work for me. No matter how I strapped myself down, I'd become too round, too soft, too hippy, too womanly. It was impossible for me to make that leap from plumply pillowy to achingly angular, even in my own shameless imagination.

Besides, I'd been doing some thinking. And I didn't know if I much admired my own tough-boy stance anymore. It began to strike me as just another way of hating who I really was. Why was I so afraid of needing? Why was I so afraid of being vulnerable? I mean, besides the very real fear of being whacked on the head and robbed blind because I couldn't hear a mugger swaggering up behind me.

I began to examine the implications of my own ability to cross-dress. And when I did I started playing the role for laughs.

This is how I'd frame it:

I've always wanted to be or at least look a lot tougher than I really am. Because it's still a vicious world out there. And I'm deaf. And I'm queer. And I'm a woman. Iieeee! What is your only defense in a case like that? Eyeliner. I love eyeliner. It lets me change my look. (*I start marking out a beard on my face with the eyeliner.*) See, I'm one of these people, I wake up in the morning, the sun is shining, the birds are all a-tweet, and all I can think is, "Please, great nature, don't eat me up today." Part of my problem is that I'm a woman who smiles a lot. And there are people out there who think that when I smile and say hello I'm really smiling and saying, "Hello, there. Why don't you beat me black and blue and rape me sixty times?" So it's no wonder I want to tough-guy things up. (*I use mascara to fill in the outline of the five o'clock stubble.*) Grrrr. But I'd rather look a friendly kind of tough. This is kind of gross. (*I shove tissue paper up my nose.*) A little blush. (*I dust my nose with pink blush.*) What else? Oh something to hide the voluptuous curves of my body, because, whatever else they may be, boobs are not tough. (*I put on a trench-coat.*) A little spit to dull the sheen of my hair. Nah, something to hide it altogether. (*I put on a slouch hat.*) Now, to take up a disgusting habit that will turn some people who are still on off. (*I take out a cigarette.*) And voila. You've crossed over a line. And on this side of the line it is an entirely different dark night of the soul. On this side of the line it's always . . .

(*I whip around and then turn back around in the persona of a tough-guy detective.*)

4:25 A.M. The city they call "The City" is sleeping like a baby. A baby shark. And sharks don't sleep. Neither do I. Me, call me Jake. Call me the next time you're in trouble. Trouble's my business. I'm Jake Ratchett, Short Detective. Yeah, you heard me, sweetheart. A gumshoe. A private eye. A hard-bitten dick. Crooks don't like me. Cops don't like me. But hookers let me ride half fare. It's a dirty, lousy, rotten, nasty, filthy, stinking job, but I'm just the dirty, lousy, nasty, filthy, stinking guy to do it. 'Cause in this cesspool they call a city, I'm the guy they call Tough Shit. How tough? Tough enough to take it like a man. This tough. (*I put the cigarette to the palm of my hand and then say in a rather more high-pitched voice:*) And when you're this tough (*catch myself and lower my pitch*) you can look death in the eye and laugh. (*Hold up the cigarette and laugh forcefully, take several deep, defiant puffs.*) Nothing scares me. There ain't a woman alive who can resist me. There ain't a man alive who can match me. And there ain't no bullet made that can kill me.

(*Shots ring out; I'm blown on my ass. Several long beats. Then I rise up still in Jake costume, but in my own voice:*)

The trouble with tough talk is that it works. You feel six feet tall, then blam! Six feet under. (*Blow Kleenex out of nose.*) Oh, god. Please forgive me. It's the makeup, it makes me do crude and vulgar things. (*Pick up the used snotwad.*) Souvenir? I'm sorry, I'm sorry. Let me just get this stuff off. (*Grind out cigarette on the floor. Rip off hat and throw it down; rip off coat and throw it down. Look at the mess; do a double-take.*) Men are such pigs!

(*The rest of the talk is delivered while I remove the tough-guy makeup.*)

Framing the tough male role comically like that made me realize that if I—the inappropriate, the imperfect, unvalued female—can embody the male (that perfect and valued essence) so absolutely, if so amusingly, then some joke has been turned upon itself.

And the implications of that turnabout are both humbling and freeing. All those absolutes that intimidated me as a woman and a child, all those typical rationales for being, the grand undertakings—conquering nature, bringing the other to its knees, repopulating it all in your own likeness—all those ambitious posturings for power that one seems to take on when one takes on male garb, becomes the dick—suddenly all of that is reduced to a kind of ridiculousness.

And when that happens, those realities that so often bully us into keeping our traps shut and our heads down are exposed as just another lot of shameful fictions. And they are ours for the rewriting.

[TOBIN SIEBERS]

Sex, Shame, and Disability Identity

WITH REFERENCE TO MARK O'BRIEN

Introduction

We watched a movie about disability and sexuality. The movie consisted of four or five able-bodied men joking and laughing about how they once lugged their crippled friend up a flight of stairs to a whorehouse. . . . After the movie, a doctor talked about disability and sexuality. . . . I will always remember his closing line: "You may think you'll never have sex again, but remember . . . some people do become people again."

Mark O'Brien, *How I Became a Human Being,* 1997

My goal in this essay is to use the discourse of gay shame as a jumping-off point to provide some details about the sexual existence of people with disabilities. My strategy and pleasure are to pursue this goal with constant reference to the writings of Mark O'Brien, the Berkeley poet, now deceased, who spent all but six years of his life in an iron lung due to polio and whose poetry and journalism represent a vivid testimony to the fusion between the three key terms of this essay: sex, shame, and disability identity. Eve Kosofsky Sedgwick, of course, argues that shame has ethical leverage because it manages the threshold between identity construction and erasure.[1] Shame promotes a kind of queer identity—an identity in which difference may metamorphose into shared dignity with and ethical sympathy for victimized people. Nevertheless, Sedgwick does not illustrate the capacity of shame to create a new ethics with examples from the gay community. Rather, she uses disability to exemplify shame, whether representing the shared humiliation felt before the "toothless face" of New York's post–September 11 cityscape or her own identification with Judith Scott, the fiber artist with Down syndrome portrayed on the cover of *Touching Feeling.*[2] In fact, Sedgwick's principal technique for illustrating the ethical power of shame is to ask her presumptively nondisabled audience to visualize an "unwashed, half-insane man" who might wander "into the lecture hall mumbling loudly, his speech increasingly accusatory and disjointed, and publicly urinate in the front of the room, then wander out again." The example of this man, she explains, calls the members of her audience into burning awareness of their own "individual skin," while being unable at the same time "to stanch the hemorrhage of painful identification with the misbehaving man."[3] The audience members feel alone with their shame, singular in their susceptibility to being ashamed for a stigma that has now become their own.[4] For Sedgwick, shame is the queer emotion by which we put ourselves in the place of others. It is ethically useful because it legitimates the question of identity without giving identity the status of an essence. And yet Sedgwick interrogates neither the shame nor the identity of the disabled man.[5]

While I share Sedgwick's interest in ethics, the example of the "unwashed, half-insane man" compels me to ask a basic political question about shame. Who gets to feel shame? The question may seem strange. Aren't all human beings ashamed of something? Isn't the human condition—social creatures that we are, living under the gaze of others and subject to their judgments and scrutiny—predicated on the possibility of feeling ashamed? What would it mean to deny the feeling of shame to a class of human beings? Would they become less human? Three categories dear to the cultural criticism of the last thirty years will shape my interrogation of shame and the sexual existence of people with disabilities: agency, the split between the private and public spheres, and the sex/gender system. My emphasis throughout is on how these categories rely on the ideology of ability—the belief that the able body defines the baseline of humanness.

Agency

There is so much of it to wash,
"It" being me, a former person.

Mark O'Brien, "The Morning Routine"

Shame confers agency, according to Sedgwick. It floods the self, its heat pervading our physical and mental existence with a burning awareness of our own individual skin. The identity or being into which shame calls us, however, is not necessarily the one we desire. One of Sedgwick's formulations of shameful identity captures the problem succinctly: "one *is something* in experiencing shame."[6] Shame creates a form of identity in which one risks being some thing rather than some person. Shame is painful and isolating for this reason. Nevertheless, shame is so appealing because being something is better than being nothing. So what about nothingness? Do people to whom we ascribe no agency feel ashamed? Can one feel shame if one has no agency?

Disabled people are not often allowed to have agency, sexual or otherwise. Rather, they are pictured as abject beings, close to nothing, empty husks. To be disabled in the cultural imaginary is to cease to function. Our highways are scattered with "disabled" vehicles—sad, static things of no use or importance. Lack of movement and autonomy equals lack of ability to act and to will. The lone girl in the power chair, failing to part the sea of human beings in a crowded hallway, comes to a halt, displaying infinite patience with the people in front of her, but she has little chance of being recognized as a person, of being addressed as a human being by those around her. "How many people," Nancy Mairs asks, "do you know who would willingly take home a television set that displayed only snow or a loaf of bread that had fallen from a shelf under the wheels of a shopping cart?"[7] Broken or discarded objects are rejected as belongings; the disabled do not belong, and rare is the human being who finds them appealing. People with disabilities are cast as objects of mourning. The feeling of grief directed at them exposes the idea that they have somehow disappeared—that they have become nothing, that they are dead—even though they may insist that they are not dead yet.

Mark O'Brien caught polio in 1955 at age six. He had the use of one muscle in his right foot, one muscle in his neck, and one in his jaw. He spent the rest of his life in an iron lung—a wind machine, replacing his lungs, drowning out the sound of human breathing with the rush of air propelled by the external contraption of shifting atmospheres. He knew that other people thought of him as nothing—a piece of "dried out bubble gum stuck on the underneath of existence," he called himself (5).[8] What could he offer to them that would make them think otherwise? A poem, perhaps, one that speaks to the absence of shame in parts of his life, suggesting that this absence has to do with the fact that people with disabilities are not allowed human agency. The poem is called "Questions I Feared the Journalist Would Ask":

When was your most recent orgasm?
Were you by yourself?
What did you fantasize?
In this fantasy,
while you were wearing the wig,
the bra, the makeup,

did you imagine what kind of person
was pushing the vibrator up your ass?
Why do you have this thing for Black men?
But isn't that racist in itself?
And why did you leave the curtain open?

But she never asked me these,
damn her to hell.[9]

The prying questions of journalists, no matter how shameless, reveal a dependence on a culture that targets those people—celebrities and politicians—thought to have the most power, allure, and agency. If Mark O'Brien's speaker is not worth a prying question, it is because he is thought to have no worth. Having nothing to be ashamed of, then, is not a sign of either moral integrity or moral failure. It is a sign of social worthlessness. Any human being will display shame if only his or her social value is sufficient to merit being asked a prying question.

The problem of social value is urgent in the case of people with disabilities and their sexual existence. Because they are thought to have no social value, they are not allowed to feel shame or do not feel it, and they are handled in an entirely different way from the nondisabled. A classic example pertains to the masturbation training sometimes used on people with disabilities who have been institutionalized. It has a variety of goals and entails specific exercises designed to teach a person how to attain the bodily sensations of arousal.[10] Its uses in the institutional setting are multiple, some for the benefit of better institutional control, some for the benefit of individual patients: (1) to help patients with mental disabilities understand that sexual acts should be private, allowing authorities to eliminate offensive behavior from public spaces; (2) to provide patients with a means of releasing tension and controlling frustration, creating a more passive and manageable population for caregivers; (3) to teach safer methods of masturbation to patients who are injuring themselves in the pursuit of sexual pleasure; and (4) to introduce the pleasures of sexuality as part of typical human existence to people for whom these pleasures are unknown. Because masturbation training is used most prominently on the mentally disabled, the issue of agency is paramount. It is usually not possible to obtain the consent of the patient. It is not always feasible to provide verbal instruction, and a hands-on approach may be the only possible method to teach an individual how to masturbate successfully.[11] The potential for sexual abuse is high, and institutions make attempts to curb it by having a committee decide whether a patient requires masturbation training.[12]

Thomas Laqueur has argued that masturbation defines the dirty little secret of liberal autonomy and its reliance on privatized subjectivity, and if he is right, masturbation training is not a neutral activity.[13] It provides instruction in political agency in addition to helping the patient achieve sexual agency, declaring victory when the patient manages to achieve orgasm unassisted on a regular basis. For example, among the principal benefits claimed for successful masturbation training are a sense of greater agency in daily life and an understanding of cause-and-effect logic. "The person begins to learn," as Kaeser puts it, "how to regulate his own sexual responses and consequently, may come to understand that he is capable of effectuating changes in his life. It may be possible for him to learn that he can purposely alter the way he feels simply by touching and manipulating his genitals. This should assist him in learning the broader concept that if he creates some action an associated and reciprocal reaction will occur."[14] To fail in masturbation training is to fail to become an autonomous agent, but this failure has everything to do with prejudices against disability, because achieving both political and sexual agency relies on the presupposition that the body and mind are nondisabled and will function properly if trained.

The Private and Public Spheres

These people wear their bodies in downtown crowds
without embarrassment.

Mark O'Brien, "Sonnet #3"

A recurring motif in the literature on shame touches on the public confession of shameful emotion. Shame is terrifying because it relies on public exposure: the etymology of "shame" derives from a pre-Teutonic word that means "to cover oneself," covering being a natural expression of shame. But shame is also a sumptuous emotion. To stand out in public has its own delights. The feeling of shame, then, turns on the movement between the private and public realms, and this fact has a number of implications for people with disabilities. It implies access to the public sphere. It implies the possibility of privacy. The closet is the place of shame in gay culture, but it is not always obvious that coming out is about movement from one place to another.[15] This movement is not always metaphorical. It also depends on access and mobility.

What happens if one is always in the public eye? What if one has no privacy? What if the access between the private and public spheres is obstructed or blocked? What if one is not sufficiently mobile to move between them?

Mark O'Brien's writings attack these questions in a variety of ways, providing examples of how the collapsing of the boundary between the private and public spheres affects the emotion of shame and practices of disabled sexuality. "Marlene," a poem about sex with a nurse under the all-too-public conditions of the institution, is emblematic of the extremes imposed by the split between the private and public spheres experienced by people with disabilities who want to express sexual feelings. It is difficult to tell whether the poem recounts an episode of sexual abuse or sexual generosity—a riddle made unfathomable, I suggest, by the fact of institutionalization itself:

My balls knew what was coming
when that washrag touched my hardening dick.
Seared by shame and lust,
I restrained myself until she turned me. . . .
The old black janitor stepped through the curtains,
wiped the come off the linoleum, not saying a thing.
Letting me down on my back,
she spanked my crotch,
her face stony with boredom.

My greatest fuck.
First of many, I assumed.
Wrong.
Last one ever. (14)

The sponge bath as sexual adventure animates cultural fantasies associated with the hospital stay. But the speaker in "Marlene" is not in the hospital, and his stay is neither short nor voluntary. O'Brien makes clear the difference between the fantasies associated with what one might call hospital pornography and the sexual imaginary created by institutionalization. If the first is utopian in its preservation of sexual privacy and excitement, the second pictures a dystopian world where privacy does not exist and no one cares—not because lack of privacy increases the excitement of sex, but because sex in the institutional context is both an effect and a cause of boredom. Sex only makes the floor dirtier, though it is nothing that a wet mop cannot fix.

The sexual existence of people with disabilities, then, casts a different light on the boundary between the private and public spheres. A few more examples of the effect of institutionalization on sexual practices and values: the enlightened institutional position holds that masturbation is "normal" but should take place in private. However, the question arises whether there are opportunities for privacy available to people in institutions, especially people with cognitive disabilities. On homosexuality, the enlightened institutional position takes the form of making sure that homosexual acts are not the only sexual option.[16] A certain amount of experimentation is said to be "normal," but the institutional setting should not determine sexual orientation or behavior. Nevertheless, for people who have spent most of their life in a single-sex institution, discussion of options is irrelevant because the choice of sexual partners is predetermined. In an enlightened institution, an interest in pornographic materials is seen as a typical part of growing up. However, it is illegal to use pornographic materials in a public place such as an institution, where their appearance may sexually harass staff and other patients.[17]

The dependence of people with disabilities on personal attendants further complicates the relationship between sexual behavior and the public sphere.[18] What are the sexual limits affecting the use of personal attendants? Does my attendant help me dress in sexy lingerie, arrange my partner and me in sexual positions, fetch the vibrator, take us to the bathroom afterward? We have trained professionals willing to spend their life helping people eat, go to the toilet, move from place to place, and bake cookies. Professionals are not trained to help someone masturbate or have sex. Irving Zola suggests how overwhelming is the sexual frustration of some people with disabilities and how few their opportunities for satisfaction. Here he transcribes remarks by a paralyzed man named Johan: "I can't do anything myself. I can't even masturbate. What can I do? How do you ask someone? If you ask it once, how do you ask again? What about them? What will they think of you? What will they say to others? And if they leave, what then? You will have to start all over again with someone else."[19]

Johan's frustration is not any less poignant for being a familiar feature of the sexual life of some people with disabilities. It reveals that the distinction between the private and public spheres is a function of the able body and that people with disabled bodies are often forced to suppress feelings of shame caused by the erosion of privacy in their everyday life if they want to have a sexual existence.

Sex/Gender

Tracy called herself a fag hag
saying she liked pictures of gay men fucking
"Will you be my fag hag?" I asked, desperate.

Mark O'Brien, "Tracy Would've Been a Pretty Girl"

Jacques Lacan's famous parable of gender attribution imagines gender as a train destination. Owing to the necessity of satisfying natural needs away from home, restrooms are provided in public places. Lacan posits this convenience as a way of thinking about the assignment of gender. A train arrives at a station, and a little girl and little boy, sister and brother, look out the train window and see two different signs—"Ladies" and "Gentlemen." Each child believes that the sign names the train's destination, but the sign also reflects a gender destination. "For these children," Lacan concludes, "Ladies and Gentleman will be henceforth two countries towards which each of their souls will strive on divergent wings."[20] Lacan's parable provides a rich conception of the signifying practices of gender, although it does not require too much thought to realize that some behavior may go on behind these two doors that does not match the binary opposition of Ladies and Gentlemen.[21]

Had Lacan visualized an accessible restroom at the train station, he would have had to tell a different story. More often than not, accessible toilets are unisex. There are no Ladies and Gentlemen among the disabled because the ideology of ability conceives of people with disabilities as ungendered and asexual. Ladies and Gentlemen with disabilities see the sign on the door, but they cannot enter. The practice of using unisex accessible toilets exposes the fact that able-bodiedness overdetermines the assignment of gender. It also reflects the mainstream belief that people with disabilities must relinquish feelings of embarrassment or shame normally associated with being displayed to the so-called opposite sex.[22] In the game of signifying practices, the difference between ability and disability trumps the difference between Ladies and Gentlemen every time.[23]

The example of Lacan suggests that the presence of disability nullifies gender assignment, but it is equally critical to understand that able-bodiedness is itself a diacritical marker of sex/gender. The stereotypical idea of castration promoted by psychoanalysis gives the disabled body a unique role in gender differentiation. Psychoanalysis defines castration as the social wound that any one person must overcome to achieve psychological maturation and social integration, but because this social wound summons necessarily the imagination of physical wounding, castration also presents as the problem to which variation in gender identity is the answer. Whether any given variation is the right choice depends on value judgments driven by gender stereotypes, and part of the quandary of gender identity involves navigating with and against these stereotypes. Able-bodiedness usually connotes masculinity. It may be, in Terry Galloway's words, a "fictive able-bodiedness," but able-bodiedness it remains. Femininity supposedly represents lack, defect, and disability. These gender stereotypes obtain for both gay and straight orientations, but individual embodiments of them may vary from emotions of pride to shame to angry rebellion. That lesbian and straight women are often unashamed of their masculinity, while gay and straight men may be humiliated by their femininity, probably derives from the unequal social mobility and cultural access produced by the equation between femininity and disability.[24]

After living independently for twelve years, Mark O'Brien began to experiment in the early 1990s with the sex/gender system through the practice of cross-dressing.[25] He began to wear lipstick, eyeliner, powder, rouge, eye shadow, a skirt, a blouse, and a wig of long, black hair, as often as he dared and could arrange it with his attendants. He wrote about discovering a new sense of happiness and freedom in his dream of becoming a beautiful woman. In the same period, he finished a cycle of poems about womanliness in which he struggled against the stereotypical connections between sex/gender and disability. "Femininity," perhaps the key poem in the cycle, elicits several interpretations whose logic is made difficult, I want to assert, by the ideology of ability and its effect on gender identity and sexual practices:

Naked on the gurney
in the hospital corridor,
surrounded by nurses,
tall, young, proud of their beauty,
admiring my skinny cripple body.
"You're so thin,
you should've been a girl."
"I wish my eyelashes
were as long as yours."
Such pretty eyes."
I thought
or think I thought
or wish I'd said,

"But your bodies work,
Get scissors,
cut my cock and balls off.
Make me a girl,
without anaesthesia,
make me a girl,
make me a girl." (39)

Part of the challenge of "Femininity" is to unpack the contradictions that it is compelled to embrace because of the way that sex/gender stereotypes map onto disability. For the same reason, various interpretations of the poem demonstrate not only contradictions with one another but internal contradictions as well. My strategy of interpretation, although somewhat artificial, is to offer a series of readings as numerical steps in an attempt to show where O'Brien's representation of disability collapses gender stereotypes based on the able body. My conclusion here is that research on the sexual existence of people with disabilities requires that more work be done on the sex/gender system.

According to a first reading, the poem represents disability identity as acceptance of lack. The male speaker, already symbolically castrated because he is disabled, invites real castration where most able-bodied, heterosexual men would balk. For the speaker, castration is the lesser of two evils because it is worse to be a disabled male than a nondisabled female: "But your bodies work, / Get scissors." The poem views femininity, then, as a device to restore the disabled, male body to able-bodiedness, but this device is possible only because of the disabled man's willingness to pay the physical price for the symbolic gain. His acceptance of lack helps him trade the physical disability of quadriplegia for the symbolic disability of womanliness—a net gain. A second reading of the poem understands disability as symbolic of femininity. The nurses hovering around the disabled speaker's body misunderstand disability as femininity, most obviously because they confuse the effects of paralysis with the characteristics of female beauty: "You're so thin, / you should've been a girl." Because the disabled man is already a symbolic woman, it is only a small step to embody the symbolism: "make me a girl, / make me a girl." Gender stereotypes admit of no such thing as disabled masculinity. Apparently, in the society described by the poem, all disabled people are women.

There is only one problem with these two readings. A castrated man, no matter how insistent the stereotype, is not a woman, and a third reading of the poem would claim that there is, in point of fact, little room in

"Femininity" for women. They are merely bystanders, part of the audience to which the disabled man makes his pitch, and although the pitch makes a mockery of gender stereotypes, its end result is not an embrace of femininity. I note immediately that the absence of femininity is not necessarily the effect of a chauvinistic choice made by O'Brien. The ideology of ability produces the effect. Indeed, it produces the same effect on masculinity because there is, in second point of fact, little room in "Femininity" for men. Men are merely bystanders—or, better, "Walkers"—part of the audience to which the disabled man is making his pitch. O'Brien describes the pitch to "Walkers," in the poem of this title, as "telling them the lies they need, / like disability's no big deal" and "Licking ass most skillfully" to win "all kinds of goodies . . . / chess sets, books, TVs, / maybe even our very own lives" (36). If the able body is one of the diacritical markers of gender, once the choice to embrace disability erases the marker, both femininity and masculinity as we know them disappear, and O'Brien stops representing gender as typically understood.

"Femininity," in this third reading, gives a place to neither femininity nor masculinity. Rather, the poem triangulates the able-bodied concepts of woman and man with disability to represent the speaker's identity as either castrated macho or virile female. The only sex/gender category close to these identities appears to be the classical concept of "effeminacy," a "category unto itself," according to David Halperin, who explains that it was for a long time "a symptom of an excess of what we would now call heterosexual as well as homosexual desire."[26] On the one hand, O'Brien exploits the ties of effeminacy to male sexual excess to represent virility, allowing the speaker of the poem to assert his male macho: "Get scissors, / cut my cock and balls off. / Make me a girl, / without anaesthesia." On the other hand, O'Brien uses effeminacy to represent womanliness, supporting the speaker's desire to become an attractive sexual object: "make me a girl, / make me a girl." My first two readings of the poem therefore require revision. First, the poem represents disability identity as acceptance of lack, but only insofar as lack appears as a marker of sexual power. The speaker's command that the nurses castrate him, "without anaesthesia," represents an excess that demands to be read as male sexual desire. Second, the poem understands femininity as symbolic of lack, but only insofar as lack appears specifically as the enactment of sexual attractiveness. The speaker's intention to mimic the nurses' sexual beauty reads as female desire. In both cases, O'Brien uses disability to confuse gender categories with sexual ones for the purpose of rejecting the stereotypical asexuality of disabled people and asserting that they desire to be both sexually active and attractive.

The sex/gender system as conceived by early feminists defined sex as the biological material on which the social construction of gender is based, and although the distinction has driven powerful and important critiques of women's oppression, it has been difficult to maintain in the face of new developments in gender and sexuality studies. Radical feminists claim that the oppression of women will never end until they control their own biologically distinctive capacity for reproduction, while LGBT theorists view sex as an enormously complex, cultural array of sexual practices and orientations. For example, in *Gender Trouble* Judith Butler argues that a heterosexual matrix has always already gendered sex.[27] The inclusion of disability, I want to suggest, further complicates the sex/gender system by putting its terms into even greater motion. Disability studies makes clear that both terms of the sex/gender system rely on the more fundamental opposition between ability and disability. One of the critical stakes of the sex/gender theory is, if we believe Sedgwick's argument in *The Epistemology of the Closet*, to maintain as its crucial pivot point the simultaneous impossibility of separating sex and gender and the analytic necessity of making the attempt.[28] I agree with this argument, but the inclusion of disability requires an adjustment. The simultaneous impossibility of separating sex and gender and the analytic necessity of attempting it constitute not merely a pivot point in the sex/gender system. Rather, the emergence of contradiction in this system relies on a variety of pivot points, one of the most significant being that the reciprocal economy between sex and gender depends on their reference to the able body.

Disability represents a significant pivot point where the difference between sex and gender becomes problematic. Gender in the presence of the disabled body does not overlay sex in the typical way because the difference between ability and disability trumps the difference between Ladies and Gentleman, suppresses the assignment of gender, and denies the presence of sexuality. In the case of the nondisabled body, the sex/gender system usually dictates, for better or worse, that the presence of sexual activity mandate the construction of gender identity; but in the case of the disabled body, sexual behavior does not necessarily lead to a perception of gender. For example, the repeated attempts by O'Brien to assert his sexuality fail to make other people imagine him as either man or woman. Instead, he remains only "a bad, filthy thing that belonged to the nurses" (*How I Became a Human Being*, 23), and yet when he begins to experiment with crossdressing, he manages to assert his sexuality, and so do the speakers of his poems.

Disability changes the analytic distinction between sex and gender because it not only reverses the causal polarity of the system, but also shows that each pole is rooted in the ideology of ability. If an able-bodied man succumbs to cross-dressing, it indicates that he has a "mental disease" that makes him oversexed. His effeminacy is an offense against gender because it calls his masculinity into question.[29] If a disabled man tries cross-dressing, the result is different. It indicates the presence of sexual desire where none was perceived to exist previously. It is only by appearing oversexed that the disabled man appears to be sexed at all. His effeminacy is not an offense against gender because he has no gender identity to offend. Rather, his effeminacy is an offense against the ideology of ability and its imperative that disabled people have no sexual existence. O'Brien's gender play marks out the presence of sexual desire on the otherwise desexualized landscape of the disabled body by attacking the distinctions among sex, gender, and sexuality and by exposing their mutual dependence on stereotypes of the able body.

Conclusion

Whooshing all day, all night
In its repetitive dumb mechanical rhythm,
Rudely, it inserts itself in the map of my body. . . .

Mark O'Brien, "The Man in the Iron Lung"

The ideology of ability shapes not only the sexual existence of disabled people and their susceptibility to shame, but also whether a person becomes a person at all. It controls the capacity of disabled people to live independently and to act, and whether they have agency, sexual or other, in their own life. It defines the spheres of existence in which they dwell, determining how they have sex and when they pass between the private and public spheres. It exerts enormous pressure on the assignment of gender and on whether a body is viewed as having sexual properties. Able-bodiedness represents an ideological horizon beyond which it is difficult to think or move. Perhaps this is why disability cannot escape its association with shame, why we are tempted to use disability to illustrate the individualizing effects of shame, and why people with disabilities never know when and where they will be permitted to feel ashamed. We all share, it seems, Mark O'Brien's bed in the iron lung, our head poked outside, trying to think beyond the "pulsing cylinder" (2), our body held inside, stored in "metal hard reluctance" (2), obedient to a narrow map of assumptions about what a body is and can be.

Notes

1. Eve Kosofsky Sedgwick, "Shame, Theatricality, and Queer Performativity: Henry James's *The Art of the Novel*," this volume; originally published as "Queer Performativity: Henry James's *The Art of the Novel*," *GLQ* 1, no. 1 (1993): 1–16.

2. Michael Warner's ethics of gay shame in *The Trouble with Normal: Sex, Politics, and the Ethics of Queer Life* (New York: Free Press, 1999) also bears on disability. He draws a direct connection between disease transmission and gay shame, arguing that shame salts sex with the thrill of death (198). Gay people have a hard time reflecting on the risk of HIV/AIDS, he concludes, because their desires are clouded by shame (215). For Warner, the only solution is to embrace an actively funded and fully committed campaign of HIV prevention that combats shame rather than sex (218).

3. Sedgwick, "Shame, Theatricality, and Queer Performativity," this volume, 50–51.

4. See also the interpretation of Sedgwick's theory of shame by Douglas Crimp, "Mario Montez, For Shame," this volume, esp. 70 and 71, who defines shame specifically as a positive emotion by which we feel sympathy for the oppressed.

5. Sedgwick adds the reference to the disabled man in the revision of the essay in this volume, where it follows an autobiographical account of her struggles as a "person living with a grave disease" in *Touching Feeling: Affect, Pedagogy, Performativity* (Durham, NC: Duke University Press, 2003), 34. It is difficult to understand Sedgwick's rhetorical usage of the "half-insane man" in the context of her own disability identity as a cancer survivor and its transformative effect on her teaching and scholarship.

6. Sedgwick, "Shame, Theatricality, and Queer Performativity," 51.

7. Nancy Mairs, "Sex and the Gimpy Girl," *River Teeth* 1, no. 1 (1999): 44–51, esp. 47.

8. Unless otherwise noted, all references to poetry are to Mark O'Brien, *The Man in the Iron Lung* (Berkeley, CA: Lemonade Factory, 1997).

9. "Questions I Feared the Journalist Would Ask," Mark O'Brien Papers, BANC MSS 99/247 c, Bancroft Library, University of California, Berkeley. Copyright 1999, Lemonade Factory, Berkeley, CA. Used by permission. My thanks to Susan Schweik for obtaining materials from this archive for me and to Susan Fernback for giving me permission to use them.

10. References are to Frederick Kaeser, "Developing a Philosophy of Masturbation Training for Persons with Severe or Profound Mental Retardation," *Sexuality and Disability* 14, no. 1 (1996): 295–308, esp. 298. It is worth remarking that masturbation training is usually a same-sex activity, except for the rare situation when the patient has declared a same-sex orientation, in which case a trainer of the opposite sex is assigned (302, 305).

11. Ibid., 302.

12. Ibid., 304. See also Simon B. N. Thompson, "Sexuality Training in Occupational Therapy for People with a Learning Disability, Four Years On: Policy Guidelines," *British Journal of Occupational Therapy* 57, no. 7 (1994): 255–58, esp. 256.

13. Thomas W. Laqueur, *Solitary Sex: A Cultural History of Masturbation* (New York: Zone Books, 2003).

14. Ibid., 302.

15. I explore disability passing and coming out in "Disability as Masquerade," *Liter-*

ature and Medicine 23, no. 1 (2004): 1–22. See also Brenda Jo Brueggemann, "'It's So Hard to Believe That You Pass': A Hearing-Impaired Student Writing on the Borders of Language," and "On (Almost) Passing," in *Lend Me Your Ear: Rhetorical Constructions of Deafness* (Washington, DC: Gallaudet University Press, 1999), 50–80, 81–99; Brenda Jo Brueggemann and Georgina Keege, "Gently Down the Stream: Reflections on Mainstreaming," *Rhetoric Review* 22, no. 2 (2003): 174–84; Georgina Kleege, "Disabled Students Come Out: Questions without Answers," in *Disability Studies: Enabling the Humanities*, ed. Sharon L. Snyder, Brenda Jo Brueggemann, and Rosemarie Garland-Thomson (New York: MLA, 2002), 308–16; Rod Michalko, *The Mystery of the Eye and the Shadow of Blindness* (Toronto: University of Toronto Press, 1998); and Mitchell Tepper, "Coming Out as a Person with a Disability," *Disability Studies Quarterly* 19, no. 2 (1999): 105–6. On the limits of coming-out discourse, see Ellen Samuels, "My Body, My Closet: Invisible Disability and the Limits of Coming-Out Discourse," in "Desiring Disability: Queer Theory Meets Disability Studies," ed. Robert McRuer and Abby L. Wilkerson, special issue, *GLQ* 9, nos. 1–2 (2003): 233–55.

16. For example: "it is necessary to be satisfied that a situation has not been created in which homosexuality is the only option" (Thompson, "Sexuality Training," 257).

17. Thompson, "Sexuality Training," 257.

18. For a good introduction to the issues, see Kyle Stoner, "Sex and Disability: Whose Job Should It Be to Help Disabled People Make Love?," *Eye*, August 12 1999, at www.eye.net/eye/issue/issue_08.12.99/news/sex.html (accessed April 30, 2005).

19. Irving Zola, *Missing Pieces: A Chronicle of Living with a Disability* (Philadelphia, PA: Temple University Press, 1982), 150.

20. Jacques Lacan, "The Agency of the Letter in the Unconscious or Reason since Freud," in *Ecrits: A Selection*, trans. and ed. Alan Sheridan (New York: W. W. Norton, 1977), 146–78, esp. 152.

21. See the adaptation of Lacan by Lee Edelman, "Tearooms and Sympathy; or, The Epistemology of the Water Closet," in *Homographesis: Essays in Gay Literary and Cultural Theory* (New York: Routledge, 1994), 148–70.

22. It is also the case, however, that some people experience the genderless zone of the unisex toilet as a safe space apart from the scrutiny and requirements of able-bodied, normative society.

23. The ideology of ability also exercises its power on gender identity beyond the heterosexual world of "Ladies" and "Gentlemen." The lesbian community accepted lesbians with disabilities early in its history, while disabled gay males have a hard time joining the gay community to this day, although the AIDS crisis has had enormous influence on the ethical relation of the gay community to disability. See Victoria A. Brownworth and Susan Raffo, *Restricted Access: Lesbians on Disability* (Seattle, WA: Seal Press, 1999), for a sense of the rich history of lesbians with disabilities. Kenny Fries, *Body, Remember: A Memoir* (New York: Plume, 1997), provides examples of the difficulties facing gay men with disabilities, esp. 101, 110–15, 123.

24. On drag kinging, see Judith Halberstam, *Female Masculinity* (Durham, NC: Duke University Press, 1998); on drag queening, see Esther Newton, *Mother Camp: Female Impersonators in America* (Englewood Cliffs, NJ: Prentice-Hall, 1972).

25. The Mark O'Brien Web page traces this development, including both accounts by him and photographs of his cross-dressing: http://www.pacificnews.org/marko/shriek,html (accessed April 29, 2005).

26. See David Halperin's discussion of effeminate masculinity in *How to Do the History of Homosexuality* (Chicago: University of Chicago Press, 2002), 110–17, 122–23, esp. 111.

27. Judith Butler, *Gender Trouble: Feminism and the Subversion of Identity* (New York: Routledge, 1999).

28. Eve Kosofsky Sedgwick, *Epistemology of the Closet* (Berkeley: University of California Press, 1990), 29. I have relied in this section on Sedgwick's account of the history of the sex/gender system (27–30).

29. I take inspiration and language for this discussion from Halperin's analysis of the effeminate male in *How to Do the History*, 34, 36–37.

HISTORIES
OF SHAME

In Ghana, with his cook (left) and chauffeur

Anyway... I did a lot of fieldwork with my students. I began to collect African art, and some of my students took me to visit their homes. There I learned how formalized and ritualized Ghanaian life is: the student stood behind his father's chair and behaved towards him almost like a servant. The old type of family authority is still very much in force in Ghana.

I also remember how I drove with my chauffeur through the jungle, until – deep in the jungle – we came to a village. There I saw for the first time what it means not to have any electric current; instead, there were hundreds of little flames from lamps that everyone carried. The people were still on the street, many things were happening in the street. 'A white man has come' – and then they surrounded me and asked me where I came from and where my wife was. That was always one of the first questions: 'Where have you left your wife? Where are your children?' That I did not have a wife they found incomprehensible, unimaginable.

I had one of my most memorable experiences in connection with the planning for a new power station on the Volta. The government had to prepare the inhabitants of a number of

Figure 16. Norbert Elias in Ghana, with his cook (left) and his chauffeur.

[H E L M U T P U F F]

The Shame of Queer History/Queer Histories of Shame

Historically speaking—and "Histories of Shame" is the title of this section—shame gives birth to modernity. This is at least what the German Jewish sociologist Norbert Elias argues in his monumental two-volume study, *On the Civilizing Process*, of 1939.[1] For Elias, shame is a tool of discipline. Shame helps to move history from external forces of control to the internal (and ultimately more effective) colonization of the self that is characteristic of modernity.

Elias himself provides a brilliant example of how central shame is to the workings of modernity. No word from him about his close bonds to a stream of male secretaries and companions who supported him emotionally and in a flurry of endeavors. Equipped with Eve Sedgwick's remarks about shame's theatricality, however, we may arrive at a different reading, a differently shamed Elias so to speak—a shame that is a tool of self-fashioning as much as of discipline. The Elias, for instance, who on page 69 of his *Reflections on a Life* included a suggestive photograph of himself between two unnamed Ghanaian men, both young: "his cook (left) and chauffeur."[2]

Notes

1. Norbert Elias, *Über den Prozess der Zivilisation* (Basel: Haus zum Falker, 1939); translated as *The Civilizing Process*, trans. Edmund Jephcott (Oxford: Blackwell, 1994).

2. Norbert Elias, *Reflections on a Life*, trans. Edmund Jephcott (Cambridge: Polity Press, 1994).

[D E B O R A H   B.   G O U L D]

The Shame of Gay Pride in Early AIDS Activism

The subject of this essay, lesbians' and gay men's organized political responses to the AIDS crisis in its early years (1981–86), provides us with empirical material for thinking about gay shame: the way it masks itself through articulations of gay pride, its capacity to discourage and invalidate certain actions as well as to encourage and authorize others, and the effects it can have on lesbian and gay politics. Michael Warner has argued persuasively that gay shame—specifically shame about gay sexual difference—has encouraged the mainstream lesbian and gay movement to repudiate gay sexual difference, and indeed sex itself, and to embrace a "normalizing" political agenda that elevates campaigns such as the current one about gay marriage, eclipsing all struggles that require an acknowledgment of gay sexuality.[1] This essay builds on Warner's argument, using Eve Sedgwick's conceptualization of shame as deriving from nonrecognition to posit a direct relationship between gay shame, on the one hand, and a powerful and pervasive anxiety in the contemporary mainstream lesbian and gay movement, on the other hand, about what has been variously construed as confrontational, militant, or radical political activism. That is to say, gay shame has not only influenced the place of sex in lesbian and gay politics and has not only swayed the agenda in a normalizing direction, but has also played a decisive role in the character of lesbian and gay protest, encouraging relatively non-confrontational and nonthreatening activism.[2]

Thank you to David Halperin for his consistent support and for his specific editorial suggestions on this article, to Ann Cvetkovich whose comments on an earlier version pushed me to situate my argument better, and to members of my two writing groups in Pittsburgh who offered thoughtful criticism. Laurie Palmer, as always, has been an insightful reader as well as a constant source of inspiration and encouragement.

That might sound unremarkable. Indeed, many observers of lesbian and gay politics, queer theorists included, seem to take for granted that within the mainstream lesbian and gay movement, anxiety about sexual difference and about political "extremism"—which is how more confrontational forms of activism are often coded—frequently go hand in hand. To be sure, that assumption is borne out in much of the historical evidence.[3] But we nevertheless need to explore *why* the two anxieties tend to accompany one another. The reason is not simply that lesbian and gay sex radicals historically have engaged in militant activism, spurring anxious criticism of political militancy. Although the two are related, gay anxiety about political militancy, it seems to me, cannot be reduced to anxiety about gay sexual difference. We gain better leverage for thinking about the frequent linkage between these two anxieties if we consider the possibility that both derive from gay shame, understood here not simply as sexual shame, but as a psychosocial phenomenon that revolves around the pain of nonrecognition and thwarted desire for human communication and connection.[4]

Nonrecognition and Gay Shame

Drawing on the work of Silvan Tomkins and on more recent work by the psychologist Michael Franz Basch, Sedgwick argues that early experiences of shame do not derive from prohibition—from a parental injunction against what one is doing or wants to do, for example.[5] Instead, shame "floods" one when a desired circuit of communication with another is disrupted by nonrecognition on the part of either person.[6] When a revealed wish for communion is met with nonrecognition, when one's attempt at identification through communication fails to be taken up, one might feel, in Tomkins's words, "naked, defeated, alienated, lacking in dignity or worth."[7] Feelings of social isolation take hold, as does a desire to "reconstitute the interpersonal bridge."[8]

As writers such as Simone de Beauvoir (in *The Second Sex*, 1952), W. E. B. Du Bois (in *The Souls of Black Folk*, 1903), and Frantz Fanon (in *Black Skin, White Masks*, 1952) reveal, this sense of not being acknowledged, or even seen, this experience of social nonrecognition by an audience that is at least to some degree a desired audience, is common for members of socially marginalized and subordinated groups who are part of society but also exiled from it owing to their perceived difference. Individuals navigate the experience of nonrecognition in different ways, of course, but by virtue of living in a society that marks them as different, they tend to be familiar with the experience of refused "identificatory communication," to use Sedgwick's phrase.[9] In this specific case, those who identify as lesbian or gay tend to be subjected to occasions of nonrecognition in their ongoing relations with heterosexual parents, siblings, friends, co-workers, neighbors, and others with whom they desire interaction. In a heteronormative society that marks them as irredeemably and ineluctably different, lesbians' and gay men's revealed wishes for the sort of interpersonal communication that constitutes and simultaneously validates their identities are always at risk of being spurned (even if their wishes also are sometimes, even oftentimes, met). When such wishes are spurned, gay shame is one possible result.

Gay shame, then, derives from the stigma of gay sexual difference. But its effects encompass more than anxiety about displays of that sexual difference. The experience of a severed or never-established connection, of nonrecognition resulting from one's sexual difference, generates anxiety about continued nonrecognition and social isolation, as well as a felt need for "relief from that condition."[10] The search for relief might encourage a disavowal of gay sexual difference, but given the wide variety of sites where recognition or its refusal might occur, the search for relief also might urge restraint in other activities that put recognition at risk. For reasons that I explore below, the mainstream lesbian and gay movement frequently has seen militant, confrontational political activism as one such activity. Although scholars have demonstrated that gay shame encourages attempts by the mainstream lesbian and gay movement to hide gay sexual difference by normalizing lesbians and gay men, they have not explored the role of gay shame in shaping the degree of contentiousness—in form and substance—that lesbian and gay activism takes. Lesbian and gay AIDS activism in the early years of the epidemic provides an opportunity to explore that relationship between gay shame and lesbian and gay politics.

Gay Shame, Gay Ambivalence, Gay Politics

Before turning to my account of early AIDS activism, let me situate my work in the recent scholarly discussions about gay shame. Discussions within queer theory have begun to explore the politically productive possibilities of queer shame. Sedgwick, Crimp, and Warner, for example, have all considered the capacity of shame for forming collectivities without squashing difference.[11] A collectivity of the shamed need not be premised on sameness or identity; indeed, due to its "peculiarly contagious and peculiarly individuating" capacity,[12] shame can generate connection through a shared experience while leaving difference and singularity intact.[13]

Although I am intrigued by Crimp's suggestion that "for shame" perhaps could become a new slogan for queer politics,[14] this essay is spurred by a sense that we have more to plumb in analyzing shame's negative effects on lesbian and gay politics. Specifically, I want to consider how a desire for relief from the painful condition of nonrecognition owing to sexual difference can create a pull toward social conformity, and specifically toward adoption of mainstream political norms. In noting that individuals want to be proximate "to the sacred center of the common values of the society" in which they live, Erving Goffman suggests that conformity exerts a formidable pull on most individuals under any circumstances.[15] How much stronger might be the pull toward that sacred center—toward everything that society sanctifies, hallows, consecrates, deems good and valuable—for those who have been cast out to the margins of society?[16] In a country such as the United States, where voting, lobbying, and an occasional march or rally are the acceptable and routine avenues for expressing grievances and trying to effect change, engagement in militant collective action and protest politics not only violates this country's political norms, it also suggests a too-severe, and possibly even subversive, critique of what is at the sacred center of the United States—an image of the United States as a flourishing democracy and the land of freedom and equality. To question the sacred, the inviolable, is to bring suspicion on oneself.

I am arguing that the pull toward conformity is forceful, not that individuals and groups inevitably accede to it and thus steer clear of confrontational politics. There are often counter-pulls as well, of course. Indeed, one's experience on the margins might spur one to reject society altogether, or at least to hold an ambivalent attitude toward it. Just this sort of ambivalence seems prevalent among lesbians and gay men. Warner notes that "identity ambivalence"—contradictory feelings about self and about one's identity group—among lesbians and gay men is widespread.[17] But so is ambivalence about mainstream society, contradictory feelings that derive from identity ambivalence. In 1972 the early gay liberationist Martha Shelley suggested a connection between the two types of ambivalence:

You [heterosexuals] have managed . . . to drive us down and out into the gutter of self-contempt. We, ever since we became aware of being gay, have each day been forced to internalize the labels: "I am a pervert, a dyke, a fag, etc." And the days pass, until we look at you out of our homosexual bodies. . . . Sometimes we wish we were like you, sometimes we wonder how you can stand yourselves.[18]

The other side of identity ambivalence is both attraction toward, and hatred of, a society that makes one hate oneself. Or, put another way, nonrecognition may become reciprocal.

For lesbians and gay men, then, experiences of nonrecognition and attendant ambivalence about self and society exert psychic pulls toward both social conformity and confrontation. Those contradictory pulls may explain why lesbian and gay politics historically have oscillated between activism that is variously termed moderate, assimilationist, and accommodationist, on the one hand, and militant, liberationist, radical, and confrontational, on the other. That is, although internal lesbian and gay community debates about the merits of so-called moderate and so-called militant activism often seem to derive from strategic, tactical, or ideological conflicts, we should consider the role that ambivalence about self and society plays in generating and structuring such conflicts. Freud suggests that ambivalence is discomfiting and that efforts to "resolve" it in one direction or the other—by repressing one of the contradictory feelings, for example—can be intense. But any resolution to it is necessarily temporary and unstable insofar as any ostracized feelings are never entirely vanquished. Those characteristics of ambivalence not only help to explain the oscillations in lesbian and gay activism; they also suggest that we cannot assume a given relationship between ambivalence and politics, but rather need to explore more precisely how lesbians and gay men navigate such contradictory sentiments and what the political effects of those navigations might be.

The divergent psychic pulls and the instability of any resolution to ambivalence might also explain why lesbian and gay political discourse—as evidenced in lesbian and gay newspapers, organizational newsletters, and activists' speeches, for example—is saturated with emotional language that seems designed, not necessarily in a conscious manner, to navigate ambivalence by bolstering one side of the ambivalent feeling and suppressing the other. That is certainly the case with regard to early AIDS activism, as we will see. To make the argument in more general terms first, the experience of nonrecognition and consequent ambivalence exert a strong, if indeterminate, influence on lesbian and gay politics. The pull toward social conformity and political quiescence is powerful, and any defiant actions, including confrontational activism, therefore require an effort of persuasion. But given the way ambivalence is structured, there is a simultaneous affective pull in the direction of challenging dominant, heteronormative society; under conditions of nonrecognition and ambivalence, that pull toward confrontation and oppositionality raises anxiety about further nonrecognition, thus generating efforts to quell lesbians' and gay men's anger.

The Seduction of Moderation

Both efforts—one that encourages political confrontation and another that discourages it—are evident in lesbian and gay political discourse, but during the period of early AIDS activism that I explore in this essay, prior to the emergence of ACT UP, the pull toward political moderation prevailed.[19]

What I've said thus far provides some insight into why activism that is in line with mainstream political norms often dominates lesbian and gay politics. The experienced pain of nonrecognition and attempts to find relief from that condition by reestablishing identificatory communication with those who have refused it encourage lesbians and gay men to align themselves with dominant social values so as to avoid further rejection. That is to say, in a context of thwarted desire for recognition, the pull exerted by the "sacred center"—with its political norms—is strong.

I think there is an additional psychic phenomenon—also deriving in part from the stigma of gay sexual difference—that helps to explain the tendency toward political moderation. For reasons that I'll discuss below, gay militants pose a dual threat to dominant society—to both its reigning sexual order and to the more general social order—and I think lesbians, gay men, and other sexual outlaws know as much, if only on an unconscious level. I propose that the consequent anxiety—about both the disruptive potential of gay militancy as well as the possible nonrecognition and rejection by straight society that might follow in its wake—encourages a widespread embrace of relatively moderate political activism and initiates efforts to discourage behavior that might be perceived as too threatening to dominant society.

When sexual outlaws openly engage in oppositional and disruptive protest politics, their actions potentially provoke anxiety—among observers, gay and straight, and among the participants themselves—for two distinct but related reasons. First, their visibility as sexual outsiders who, as such, are making demands on state and society raises the specter of sexual disorder. Their very existence, in public, suggests the unraveling of the prevailing sex/gender/sexuality system and of a system of compulsory heterosexuality that privileges heterosexual monogamy over all other forms of intimacy; even more, the actions of sexual outlaws create a sense of the world put at risk by the potential triumph of hedonistic and irresponsible pleasure seeking over practical, rational, tempered living.[20]

The second reason gay militants potentially provoke anxiety is that militancy itself tends to provoke anxiety in the United States. Given a widespread view that humans are naturally aggressive and that social institutions—in the form of laws, moral codes, and norms, for example—are needed to rein in human aggression, social conflict is potentially unsettling, especially if it is particularly heated and suggests or portends the failure of such institutions. Mild concern about social conflict can readily transform into powerful anxiety about utter social disintegration.[21] Contentious, disruptive, confrontational activism by sexual minorities, therefore, raises more than the specter of sexual disorder. It also raises the specter of general social disorder, of broken social bonds and consequent social conflict, of unleashed aggression between different groups of citizens, of the breakdown of law and order, even of civilization as we know it.[22]

It may even be the case that lesbian and gay political activism of *any* sort, including fairly routine types of action, raises fear of social disorder insofar as even mild forms of lesbian and gay activism challenge the heteronormative sexual order that stabilizes the social order through the institutions of gender, monogamy, and the family. That is, anything that raises the specter of an unordering of the prevailing sex/gender/sexuality system and of dominant norms about when, where, how, and with whom to have sex raises the specter of larger social disorder as well. (In this sense, sexual minorities stir anxiety simply by existing; hence the futility of efforts to convince others that queers should be granted rights because they are "just like straights.")

As members of society, lesbians, gay men, and other sexual minorities are themselves not immune to anxiety about sexual and social disorder. If and when experienced, such anxiety might temper any pull toward confrontational activism. And gay shame is a factor here as well insofar as the experience of nonrecognition and thwarted desire, and the inclination to avoid the pain associated with it, might similarly discourage any embrace of confrontational, disruptive political activism because of its association with social disorder.

Emotion and Politics

All of the above suggests the urgency of looking more closely at the relationship between emotion and politics. Because emotionality is often cast in opposition to reason and equated with irrationality, a standard view, especially among those charged with the study of politics—political scientists—is that feelings undermine politics, which should, it is argued, be ruled by reason. Work across the disciplines—in the social sciences, humanities, and natural sciences—disputes this view, instead arguing that emotion is an inextricable component of reason. Our feelings help us to come to know, to understand, to make sense of things. As such, emotion plays a role in all aspects of politics and thus cannot and should not be relegated to the role of "problem." Moreover, the centrality of nonrational processes in human sense-making means that we cannot ignore them. We need, then, to explore the relationship between emotion and politics. Important questions include: How are feelings produced? How are power relationships exercised through and reproduced in our feelings? How do a society's or social group's prevalent feelings and its largely unspoken, unconscious, taken-for-granted understandings and norms about what and how to feel—what might be called its emotional habitus[23]—constitute and discipline its members? How does such an emotional habitus come into being and get reproduced, and how might it shape both our attitudes about and our engagements in distinctive forms of activism?

With such questions in mind, the remainder of this essay analyzes the relationship between emotion and politics in lesbian and gay communities during the first years of the AIDS epidemic, paying particular attention to the role of gay shame. I explore the ways in which repeated expressions and evocations of specific feelings established, reinforced, enlarged, and also circumscribed lesbians' and gay men's collective political horizon—what they saw as politically possible, desirable, and necessary—and helped to shape their activist responses at this moment in the fight against AIDS.

Why Study Early AIDS Activism?

In 1990 Cindy Patton wrote that an amnesia regarding the early history of AIDS activism had set in. She saw the origins of this amnesia in the growing professionalization of the AIDS service industry but argued that the loss of this history was reinforced by progressives who "[had] begun to locate the beginning of AIDS activism in 1987 or 1988, with the emergence of ACT UP."[24] Early AIDS activism history has been eclipsed even further since 1990, part and parcel of the erasure from national consciousness of AIDS as a crisis. Even the history of ACT UP has disappeared, in a manner similar to the erasure from official history of other defiant social movements and practices of resistance in the United States.

What we lose if the history of AIDS activism in this country is forgotten is the memory of a government of a wealthy, ostensibly democratic country unmoved by the deaths of hundreds, thousands, and finally tens of thousands of its own inhabitants, in large part because the overwhelming majority of them were gay and bisexual men.[25] Like other horrific events and processes that have helped to structure U.S. society, this one too has been obscured by a subsequent sanitizing of U.S. history. People who have come of age since the Reagan/Bush years likely have no idea about the early years of the AIDS crisis, no concept of the depths of homophobia that shaped early AIDS policy. Indeed, when the gay scholar and activist Michael Bronski taught a course on AIDS at Dartmouth College in the fall of 2003, only three of his thirty-four students "had any idea that AIDS was once widely regarded as a gay-male disease."[26] People have forgotten, or never knew, that President Ronald Reagan publicly mentioned the word "AIDS" for the *first* time in 1985, four years and 10,000 deaths into the epidemic, and only in response to a reporter's question; he did not give a policy speech on AIDS until 1987, and then it was only to call for mandatory testing of certain populations. We are at risk of losing as well the history of lesbian and gay collective political resistance in the face of the government's negligence and punitive policies regarding AIDS.

There is another reason it is important to study early lesbian and gay AIDS activism. As I will argue, the form and content of that activism was shaped by lesbians' and gay men's painful experiences of nonrecognition by heteronormative society and the consequent desire for relief from that condition, for some form of recognition and social acceptance. Investigating this period of AIDS activism, then, allows us to explore some of the political effects of gay shame, with thoughts to the past, but also to the present and future.

The Heroic Narrative

I begin here with what I think is the dominant, and rather heroic, narrative of lesbian and gay AIDS activism between 1981 and 1986: from the earliest days of what since has become known as the AIDS epidemic, amid the incredibly hostile and budget-cutting climate of the Reagan years and in the face of almost no governmental or other outside help, lesbians and gay men—friends and lovers of people with AIDS (PWAs), community activists, sympathetic medical professionals, and PWAs themselves—worked together to provide services and care to people who were ill and dying. Facing government inaction, and out of gay pride, self-respect, and love for their sick brothers and for their beleaguered communities, they formed the earliest AIDS service organizations. They assembled vital information and disseminated it to their communities and to the public. Even before an infectious agent had been identified and isolated, they invented safe sex. They also lobbied for government funding and held the government accountable for its negligent and punitive responses to the crisis.

Much in this narrative is accurate, and, most important, it challenges the common perception that AIDS activism began in 1987 with the founding of ACT UP/NY. Still, it has three problems, each of which will become clearer in the course of this article. First, it overlooks the contradictory sentiments about self and society that historically have existed among lesbians and gay men and that AIDS reinforced; as a result, the heroic narrative obscures the ways in which unmentioned feelings such as shame about gay sexual difference and a corollary fear of ongoing social nonrecognition and rejection, along with the love, self-respect, and pride that are included in the narrative, shaped early lesbian and gay political responses to AIDS. Second, the narrative disregards the tensions that existed within lesbian and gay communities about how to respond to the epidemic. And third, in light of the emotional valence that attached to this narrative during the period in which it was unfolding, as well as the emotional charge that still attaches to it today, we might better understand it as a quasi-accurate historical depiction that itself manifests both a promise of, as well as a bid for, gay respectability.

This essay complicates the heroic narrative by illustrating how gay shame and its companion sentiments—all of which are absent from as well as masked by the standard narrative—influenced the form and content of lesbian and gay political responses to AIDS during the early years of the epidemic. My analysis starts with an acknowledgement of the painful nonrecognition that lesbians and gay men experience in a heteronormative society and our concomitant ambivalence about both self and society. We can well imagine how the experience of nonrecognition and of contradictory sentiments about self and society might affect lesbian and gay politics. How do you confront a society when you feel unrecognized and desire relief from that painful condition, when you want to be part of society but you simultaneously reject it, in part because it has rejected you? How do you make demands of state and society when you simultaneously feel proud *and* ashamed of your homosexual identity and practices? To explore this question of the relationship between, on the one hand, gay shame and ambivalence, and, on the other hand, lesbian and gay politics, I turn now to an investigation of lesbians' and gay men's collective political responses to AIDS during the early and mid-1980s.

Revisiting the Heroic Narrative

Given our current vantage point, from which some have (prematurely) declared "the end of AIDS," it might be easy to forget the bafflement, terror, and panic that surrounded the first years of the AIDS epidemic. The magnitude of the health crisis was unclear, but the forecasts were dire. Dozens and then hundreds of previously healthy gay men were suddenly being diagnosed with mysterious and rare diseases that indicated a breakdown in their immune systems; the mortality rate was unknown, but some thought it might be close to 100 percent, and the deaths often followed a long illness marked by multiple debilitating and painful diseases. Equally troubling, the diseases seemed to be striking gay men in particular, suddenly reinforcing implausible antigay rhetoric that linked disease to gay identity itself.[27] From the very first reports, understandings of the epidemic have almost never focused solely on its medical aspects; as others have noted, discourses about AIDS have consistently overflowed with moralizing stories.[28] Initial medical and mainstream media reports were premised on a heavy dose of homophobic sensationalism about gay male sexual practices, foregrounding social taboos such as anal sex, anonymous sex, and frequent sex with multiple partners. The media in particular focused on the most stunning and dramatic cases of gay men with histories of over one thousand sexual partners while ignoring those whose sexual histories were more conventional.[29] Their hysteria reflected and reinforced dominant discourses that equated homosexuality and homosexuals with disease and perversion. Meanwhile, the Reagan administration was aggressively ignoring the epidemic, refusing to provide adequate funding for research, services, and prevention efforts. Most local and state governments were similarly failing to respond to the crisis; indeed, by the mid-1980s, government seemed less concerned with addressing the needs of people who were sick than on proposing and enacting repressive laws, including quarantine measures. The mysteries, ambiguities, horrors, and devastation of the epidemic alarmed and terrified lesbians and (more directly) gay men, particularly those living in the urban centers most affected by AIDS.

In this terrifying and politically hostile context, as the heroic narrative suggests, the mobilization in lesbian and gay communities to deal with the crisis on its many fronts was extraordinary and utterly indispensable in the fight against AIDS. Drawing from existing community resources, the earliest AIDS activists provided support for people with AIDS, educated doctors on how to diagnose symptoms, created and disseminated safe-sex information, raised consciousness as well as money, formed AIDS service organizations, and created numerous ways for lesbians and gay men to donate their time and resources to fight the health crisis.[30] The efforts of these early AIDS activists were heroic indeed, and the movement of dozens, hundreds, and soon thousands of volunteers into AIDS service organizations in these early years should be understood as a successful mass political mobilization.

The huge need to respond in the face of government inaction was important in animating this mobilization, and the community's resources enabled it. Nonetheless, this political response was never inevitable. Lesbians and gay men might have tried to distance themselves as far from AIDS as possible. The frequent mobilization of feelings such as gay pride and love for one's sick brothers and for the community at large was crucial to the effort, both because such expressions countered the shame and fear surrounding AIDS, and because they enlisted massive numbers of lesbian and gay volunteers, as well as tremendous amounts of community resources, to address the health crisis. The following invocation of pride in the community's efforts against AIDS, articulated in a report to the lesbian and gay community from the San Francisco AIDS/KS Foundation in December 1983, was typical:

We as an entire community can be proud . . . of the co-operation within all segments of the gay and lesbian community. . . . Alone, this community has educated, lobbied, demonstrated and fought for government action. The only services that have been delivered are those which have been demanded or those which have been provided by the community itself.[31]

In gay politics, and likely in other movements of socially marginalized people, public discussion about the movement's political actions, even a mere description, usually exceeds itself—by which I mean it is usually about more than it purports to be. Such discussions in gay politics, for example, often additionally express, or gesture toward, lesbian and gay ambivalence: they contain implicit or explicit judgments about how gay people should or should not present themselves and act in the public realm. For example, when the *Advocate* reporter Larry Bush asserted in a 1983 news article how unique the gay community spirit was in motivating individuals to come together in order to provide services for people with AIDS, and when in the same article the executive director of the National Gay Task Force, Virginia Apuzzo, was quoted as saying that "the community has responded, with its heart, with its pocketbook, with its political savvy,"[32] both Bush and Apuzzo were speaking in a specific emotional register, one that evoked gay pride about gay efforts to fight AIDS. Whether intending to do so or not, the many expressions of pride in this moment—by lesbian and gay leaders, by AIDS service providers, by gay and lesbian newspaper reporters and editors, by individuals writing to editors of gay newspapers—offered lesbians and gay men a way to feel: rather than feel ashamed, as mainstream discourses suggested, lesbians and gay men should feel proud of the community's extraordinary efforts in the face of immense adversity.

As well, in offering a template for what to do with gay pride, those expressions of pride effectively, and affectively, encouraged lesbians and gay men to volunteer and to donate money rather than to disidentify from the mobilization around AIDS.

Although it was one of the most pervasive and motivating of sentiments at the time, pride wasn't the only feeling evoked in these early public discussions. Pride—rhetorically linked to activist endeavors such as service provision, volunteer caretaking, and lobbying—helped to establish those responses as the political horizon, as the forms of AIDS activism that were thinkable and desirable. But other feelings that are largely absent from the heroic narrative—gay shame and a corollary fear of recurring social rejection, for example—also contributed to establishing and limiting that horizon. As I will show, pride was in fact often articulated or elicited in a manner that implied more than itself, in ways that evoked, generated, and reinforced gay shame and fear of social rejection as well. Although unacknowledged in the heroic narrative, gay shame, as well as lesbians' and gay men's ambivalence and their conscious and less than fully conscious efforts to navigate those contradictory feelings, significantly influenced their collective political responses to AIDS.[33]

We can get a sense of the important role that gay shame and ambivalence played by looking at public, largely internal discussions in lesbian and gay communities about AIDS as recorded in the gay media and in AIDS service organization literature. These discussions were saturated with language revealing numerous contradictory feelings. Articulations and elicitations of shame about gay sexuality and anxiety about social nonrecognition and rejection were widespread; gay pride was also frequently expressed when noting and encouraging the community's responsible efforts to fight AIDS; articulations of anger sometimes occurred, but they often were suppressed or defused. Repeated articulations and evocations of some feelings along with the suppression of others formed a prevailing constellation of sentiments as well as a set of largely taken-for-granted understandings and norms about feelings and their expression; this emotional habitus—with its implicit pedagogy about what to feel and how to express one's feelings about self and society—influenced lesbians' and gay men's self-understandings as well as their attitudes about homosexuality, AIDS, dominant society, and political activism. As will become evident through the examples given below, in crystallizing lesbian and gay ambivalence this emotional habitus offered a resolution of sorts to the political dilemmas posed by the experience of such contradictory sentiments about self and society. That is, this repeatedly expressed and evoked constellation of feelings helped to establish a political horizon that authorized some forms of activism while de-legitimizing others—that, for example, encouraged lesbians and gay men to equivocate about gay male sexuality, to focus on the vital work of caretaking and service provision, to embrace routine interest-group tactics such as lobbying, and to suppress more confrontational rhetoric and activism that might compromise their social acceptability.

The Trope of Responsibility

With this background in mind, we can better capture the emotional resonances of the pride-infused trope of responsibility that figured prominently in gay newspapers' and AIDS organizations' rhetoric about the gay community's efforts to fight AIDS in the early and mid-1980s. For example, in 1982, at one of Gay Men's Health Crisis's earliest fundraisers, the president of GMHC, Paul Popham, gave a speech in which he noted that the community, by coming together in a spirit of cooperation during this health crisis, had shown that "we *can* get things done, that we *can* act responsibly, and that we *do* care about each other."[34] Similarly, a GMHC advertisement proudly asserted that GMHC and its volunteers were "showing the world that the gay community is as cohesive, strong, determined, and responsible as any other."[35] Ed Power, of the Kaposi's Sarcoma Research and Education Foundation, wrote a column for the San Francisco *Sentinel* in 1983 that presented the AIDS crisis as an occasion both to convince gay people of their own worth and to prove something to the straight world: "This crisis presents us with the opportunity to show ourselves—and the world—the depth and strength of our caring."[36] A letter to a gay paper in Los Angeles that was reprinted in San Francisco's *Bay Area Reporter* echoed GMHC's and the KS Foundation's tone almost precisely. Urging lesbians and gay men to volunteer their skills, time, and money to the cause, it offered the following behavioral pedagogy: "The world is watching us. . . . Let's show them how we *can* take care of our own."[37]

What was this rhetoric of responsibility about, and what kinds of effects did it have? Its recurrence certainly should be understood as a rebuttal of dominant society's homophobic rhetoric about AIDS that constructed gay male sexual practices, gay culture, and the gay community as a whole as irresponsible: excessive, hedonistic, immature, and dangerous. Lesbians and gay men understandably wanted to bolster lesbian and gay self-esteem and to fight the greater stigma attached to homosexuality in the context of the AIDS epidemic. Gay articulations of the community's responsible efforts against AIDS also might be understood as an attempt at salvaging gay respectability by those gays who themselves blamed AIDS on the "fast gay lifestyle" and the "irresponsible promiscuity" of the 1970s, as well as by those who simply suspected or feared such a link. The rhetoric of responsibility shifted the lens from scrutiny of the shameful sexual gay past to approbation for the respectable (i.e., desexualized) gay present.[38] In his 1982 speech, before extolling the gay community's responsible efforts against AIDS, Paul Popham indicated his anxiety about gay sexuality when he stated: "Something we have done to our bodies, and we still don't know what it is, has brought us all, in a sense, closer to death."[39] By foregrounding the active and caring responses of lesbians and gay men to the threat of AIDS, community spokespeople were trying to counter fears that gay men had "done something" to their bodies that brought AIDS on themselves. Popham was not alone in articulating a vision of the epidemic that placed the blame for it on those affected by it. The cover of the March 18, 1982, issue of the national gay magazine the *Advocate*, for example, similarly pointed the finger when it asked, "Is the Urban Gay Male Lifestyle Hazardous to Your Health?" Its answer to that largely rhetorical question was, plainly, "yes." More vitriolic in its blaming and shaming was a contemporaneous statement by an anonymous gay doctor: "Perhaps we've needed a situation like this to demonstrate what we've known all along: Depravity kills!"[40] Given the pervasiveness of such sentiments in lesbian and gay communities, not to mention the homophobic hysteria of mainstream rhetoric, it is likely that the promotion of an ethic of responsible behavior was a retort to prevalent straight and gay discourses that, by placing lesbians and gay men far outside of "respectable" and "normal" personhood, heightened gay shame and an already pervasive fear of social rejection. Proud assertions that gay communities were responsibly addressing the crisis offered an antidote to gay shame, likely eliciting pride while also spurring lesbian and gay involvement in AIDS organizations (presumably another, more practical, goal of the rhetoric of responsibility).

The rhetoric of gay responsibility had other effects as well, however, something that we might expect in a context where lesbians and gay men have contradictory feelings about gay sexuality and dominant society. In emphasizing that the community's efforts were "showing the world" how responsible the gay community was, this rhetoric expressed concern about social acceptance, which it held out as a prospect, but only if the community continued to act in such a responsible, and thus respectable, manner. The rhetoric thereby raised hopes about social acceptance but simultaneously elicited shame about gay difference and fear that continual social nonrecognition and rejection would follow if that difference were not counterbalanced by gay respectability.[41]

A column in the *New York Native* about volunteer AIDS work being done by gay men and lesbians in San Francisco indicates how articulations of gay pride about the community's responsible efforts to fight AIDS often simultaneously enlisted gay shame and fear that the painful state of social nonrecognition would continue. The columnist wrote: "Not surprisingly, the AIDS struggle has given [gay] San Franciscans new cause for civic pride, pride of a deeper sort than the pride we felt when we were the gay party capital of the world." The writer then approvingly quoted a friend: "'We have a chance to prove something now, to show the world that we aren't the giddy, irresponsible queens it often takes us to be. Sure, AIDS has changed things here, but not necessarily for the worse.'"[42] He encouraged lesbians and gay men to see the silver lining of AIDS, indeed, perhaps even to be grateful for the AIDS epidemic, because they could now feel proud that their responsible efforts to address it had earned them respect and recognition from a society that previously had misunderstood them, or perhaps had understood them only too well.

To be sure, such articulations of pride revolved around the community's tremendous and indispensable response to AIDS. Also, in a context where dominant discourses about AIDS blamed and shamed gay men, discourses of gay responsibility helped to restore a sense of dignity to the gay community, and, as I suggested earlier, they likely inspired gay pride. But these articulations of pride encompassed more than just the feeling of pride: they conveyed an unspoken but palpable sense of relief that gays could now be construed by others as virtually normal; they indicated a widespread hope that that appearance of normalcy would erase or override gay difference and thereby invite social acceptance. As such, they evoked and magnified shame about gay sexual practices and the ostensibly "irresponsible" gay past, as well as a corollary fear of ongoing social rejection if gays failed to act in a respectable manner.

In other words, these articulations and elicitations of gay pride drew from, were implicated within, and reinforced dominant heteronormative value systems. Such expressions of pride often dealt with shame about gay difference by burying it, at least those components of difference that were most despised, most abject. This gay pride instead pointed toward gay similarities with dominant society—gays as responsible, mature caretakers. In that sense, it was a pride that was largely premised on an agreement with dominant views about what is shameful, about what is beyond the pale and thus unrecognizable, and deservedly so, by "normal" society. An article in the *New York Native* that discussed a shift in gay pride's object suggested that a new, improved version of gay pride required the suppression of gay sexuality. Recalling early gay liberationist declarations of "pride in their gay-ness" and public displays of same-sex kissing as its expression, the reporter wrote of a transformation in the meaning of gay pride that he thought was evidenced in a somber memorial AIDS march held the night before the 1985 Gay Pride Parade in New York: "This year, with sadness, fear, and anger, and with pride, gay men and women acknowledged Stonewall with the first an-nual Candle Light AIDS March. . . . This year, gay pride meant honoring the thousands of gay New Yorkers who have already died of AIDS, their lovers, friends, and families."[43] Following the implications of the reporter's seem-ingly approving account of this shift in the meaning of gay pride, it seems that part of the perhaps unconscious impulse behind the repeated articu-lations and elicitations of pride about the community's responsible efforts against AIDS was to address the widespread ambivalence about gay sexu-ality and about dominant society by disavowing that which separates gays from straights (nonnormative sexuality as revealed in such activities as same-sex kissing) and highlighting those things that show their common humanity (grieving, mourning, and responsible caretaking).

Gay Pride and the Establishment of a Political Horizon

How did the frequently articulated, proud rhetoric of gay responsibility in the fight against AIDS help to establish ideas about what was politically pos-sible, desirable, and necessary? As I suggested earlier, the rhetoric of gay re-sponsibility exceeded its ostensible topic. On the one hand, it rebutted anti-gay stereotypes; on the other hand, by evoking a variety of feelings—pride, shame, fear of nonrecognition, and desire for social acceptance—asser-tions of gay responsibility also traversed questions of, and offered opinions about, gay selves in relation to dominant society. Through the rhetoric of gay responsibility, pride and respectability became tightly linked: a proud gay identity now derived from gay respectability and required it as well. The proud articulations of gay responsibility inspired hope that recogni-tion and social acceptance would be forthcoming, provided the commu-nity continued to show the world how responsible it was. Holding out such a conditional hope raised fears that the condition would not be met and that gays would face social rejection rather than acceptance. The trope of responsibility, then, played into the shame-saturated idea that gays, some-how undeserving, had to be "good" in order to get a proper response to the AIDS crisis from state and society. In effect, the rhetoric of responsibility articulated and enlisted feelings that established and bolstered, while also circumscribing, the political horizon. It authorized and validated reputable activism such as provision of services, caretaking, candlelight vigils, and tactics oriented toward the electoral realm such as lobbying, while delegitimizing and thereby discouraging political actions that might jeopardize gay respectability.[44]

Before further developing this analysis of the relationship between emotional dynamics and the establishment of a political horizon, let me pause to say that, as the concept of emotional habitus suggests, I am not arguing that lesbians and gay men intentionally mobilized certain feelings and downplayed others in order to direct lesbian and gay politics toward service provision and lobbying and away from confrontation. Some may have been so strategic and deliberate, but most were in all likelihood simply drawing from and repeating existing, familiar, highly charged discourses. For lesbians and gay men, gay shame and fear of social rejection were nothing new; rather, they had figured prominently in lesbian and gay experience for decades and were then heavily reinforced by dominant society's responses to AIDS. Those feelings, in short, were recognizable; we might even say they "made sense." They could be readily articulated all the more persuasively in the context of a health crisis in which lesbian and gay communities had significant reason to be concerned about societal perceptions and acceptance. In other words, regardless of intent, such expressions of feelings were available and resonant, and their articulation or elicitation required little if any reflection. My contention is that the effects of these repeated articulations, more important than the intentions that lay beneath them, bolstered such feelings among lesbians and gay men. The power of an emotional habitus comes from its operating beneath conscious awareness; indeed, the social derives much of its forceful influence from being written into individuals' bodily sensations and thereby naturalized.

The Consolidation of the Existing Political Horizon: Dealing with Growing Anger

By the spring of 1983, a growing anger about the slow pace of scientific research and the low level of government funding to tackle the AIDS epidemic threatened to destabilize the prevailing emotional habitus in lesbian and gay communities and to shift the political horizon.[45] Some, such as Larry Kramer, cofounder of GMHC and later of ACT UP/NY, and Virginia Apuzzo, executive director of the National Gay Task Force, proposed an expanded political horizon inclusive of more confrontational activism. In his widely published article "1,112 and Counting," for example, Kramer angrily called on lesbians and gays to fight back, to take to the streets, to commit civil disobedience in order to save gay men's lives. Similarly, Apuzzo concluded a speech at a New York candlelight vigil in 1983 by vowing: "If something isn't done soon, we will not be here in Federal Plaza at night in this quiet, we will be on Wall Street at noon! . . . No politician will be immune to a community who will not take no for an answer."[46]

Responses to Kramer's article in particular are interesting for what they reveal about lesbian and gay anxieties that angry activism might rock the boat and jeopardize social acceptance.[47] Lesbian and gay leaders responded in an emotional register that seemed designed to dampen the grumbles of discontent and defuse the growing anger, to distance the mass of lesbians and gay men from "any commitment to the event," in Stuart Hall's words;[48] whether they intended to do so or not, their efforts helped to reaffirm and delimit the political horizon, encouraging socially acceptable activism while discouraging the sorts of unconventional, disruptive activism that Apuzzo and Kramer were advocating.

Consider, for example, a *Native* editorial that was published a few weeks after Kramer's article. It acknowledged that Kramer's piece had generated controversy and stated that the *Native* had published it to raise awareness of the threat of AIDS, "in spite of some reservations about [Kramer's] attacks on public officials." The editorial called on everyone to "cool the rhetoric" and concluded by commending New York's mayor, Ed Koch, for appearing at an AIDS symposium and for having recently appointed a gay man to direct a new city office that would focus on AIDS.[49] The *Native*'s editorial, revealing discomfort with Kramer's angry, confrontational rhetoric and discrediting his denunciation of Koch by strongly praising the mayor's (notably minor) recent actions on the AIDS front, represents an attempt to generate faith in the government and to quell anger and any militant activism that might follow in the wake of Kramer's call to action. The *Native*'s praise for Koch is particularly striking considering that San Francisco's Mayor Dianne Feinstein had by then committed $1 million to AIDS research and patient care, while Koch had released a scant $25,000, despite the fact that New York City had the highest caseload in the country.[50]

The editors of Chicago's *Gay Life* similarly downplayed and marked as extreme Kramer's angry, oppositional, militant rhetoric. They did place Kramer's article on the front page, suggesting a degree of sympathy with his indictment and call to action.[51] However, the editorial in the same issue—encouraging people to call the White House to demand increased AIDS funds—could easily be read as an attempt to counter Kramer's interpretation of the crisis and his confrontational rhetoric and propositions for action. In the editorial, *Gay Life* lauded Chicago's Mayor Jane Byrne and the city's Department of Health for their response to the AIDS crisis, despite the fact that the city of Chicago had yet to allocate even one dollar of city funding specifically to AIDS. Further dampening any local anger that might be directed at the city government, the editorial asserted that the idea for the national phone drive to the White House "arose out of anger and dissatisfaction in *other* parts of the country . . . where AIDS and AIDS-related fatalities have been reported in high numbers, and where the city governments have been slow in acting with the community to attack the problem." It continued, "Chicago has been more fortunate than others. . . . Mayor Byrne's administration has responded effectively."[52] Anger, perhaps legitimate in other cities, was unnecessary in Chicago, despite the fact that there were by then dozens of diagnosed cases but no city AIDS office or city AIDS funding.[53] *Gay Life*'s editorial seemed intent on curbing any anger and impetus toward confrontational activism that Kramer's call to action might have inspired. In its effects, by evoking feelings of gratitude toward the City of Chicago and satisfaction with its efforts to address AIDS, the editorial discredited Kramer's outrage and propositions for action, potentially lessening any anger that Kramer's article might have generated and validating the existing political horizon. Whether intended or not, the editorial evoked feelings that bolstered attraction toward, rather than opposition to, the powers that be, and thereby encouraged the existing, comparatively staid political course of action rather than the stepped-up, more confrontational efforts that Kramer had advocated.[54]

Street activism of the sort contemplated by Kramer and Apuzzo was rarely mentioned in the gay papers during this period, but the few times it was broached, it was often immediately qualified or even discounted. For example, in an article in the San Francisco *Sentinel*, the Stonewall Gay Democratic Club political vice president, Ralph Payne, mentioned his disgust that the Democrats were scapegoating gays for losing the 1984 presidential election. He was quoted as saying, "It's time to take to the streets," but he then immediately clarified that he "wasn't necessarily advocating civil disobedience, but rather the tactics of mass organizing—demonstrations, picketing, petitions."[55] The article concluded with information about how to get involved in AIDS lobbying and fundraising. Oppositional activism such as civil disobedience was not part of the political horizon at this point. Indeed, even mentioning street activism seemed to require a disavowal of any tactic so confrontational as civil disobedience.

Cleve Jones, a San Francisco gay activist, gave a speech in November 1985 that helps to explain why more confrontational action was largely unthinkable at this time. Although it may not have been Jones's intent, his speech appears to be an attempt to defuse anger and militant action, and such a rerouting could understandably have been its effect. The occasion was a somber candlelight vigil to commemorate the 1978 assassinations of Harvey Milk, a gay city supervisor, and George Moscone, San Francisco's mayor. Jones, the only speaker at the vigil, recalled the White Night Riots that occurred in San Francisco when the killer, Dan White, was convicted of manslaughter rather than murder and sentenced to only five years in prison:

That night we did not march in silence and the light that filled this plaza came not from candles but from burning barricades and exploding police cars. All that is history now. . . . The candlelight march is an annual opportunity for us to face our community's loss together in a spirit of strength, love, and hope. Above all else, this march is a symbol of hope.[56]

Jones named friends of his who had died from AIDS and then vociferously criticized state and federal government for letting PWAs die. Rather than using his indictment as an opportunity to make demands or to call for community action targeting the government, Jones then simply concluded:

We send this message to America: we are the lesbians and gay men of San Francisco, and though we are again surrounded by uncertainty and death, we are survivors, we shall survive again, and we shall be the strongest and most gentle people on this earth.[57]

Jones invoked the 1979 riots, but only to push them into the recesses of history, where, presumably, they belonged. After all, proud and gentle people, with an eye to the American public, do not riot, no matter how angry they are about government negligence in the face of thousands and thousands of deaths. Jones named only two courses of action, street riots and gentle, dignified, candlelight marches, and only the latter was actually thinkable. Notably, in a 1995 interview, Jones said that he led such marches in a manner that would defuse lesbians' and gay men's anger.[58] His political universe, and seemingly the gay political universe more generally, allowed for no other options.

Others in the community also seemed to encourage the channeling of a growing anger among lesbians and gay men away from confrontational activism and into more reputable political work such as care for PWAs. At an AIDS memorial candlelight procession in Chicago in 1985, anger was articulated and elicited but then quickly defused and directed toward compassion rather than confrontational activism: One speaker asked the crowd, "Are you mad? Are you angry?" He continued by saying that he was "pissed" because no one outside the lesbian and gay community was doing anything about AIDS. The crowd loudly agreed with him. He then concluded by advising: "Take your anger and turn it into love for your brothers." Perhaps following his suggestion, the procession concluded with marchers singing the refrain "We are a gentle, angry people" from Holly Near's "Singing for Our Lives."[59] A similar emotional dynamic occurred at an AIDS memorial candlelight vigil and march in San Francisco in 1985. The 5,000 marchers somberly proceeded with "an almost painful slowness" from the Castro neighborhood to the Civic Center. When Dean Sandmire, the co-chair of the PWA Caucus of Mobilization against AIDS, announced that Governor George Deukmejian would not be attending the march, "there were loud catcalls and hisses" from the crowd. The press report noted that Sandmire "rose to the occasion quickly" and yelled to the crowd: "This is not why we're here. We're here to honor the dead and those who are still living."[60] Anger, and whatever actions anger might prompt when expressed in a mass of people, was pitted against the more appropriate feelings—love and respect for one's brothers—and thereby affectively defused.

In those instances when public expressions of anger were not defused or rechanneled, they still tended to confirm, rather than alter, the existing political horizon during this period. Consider the following remarks by Charles Ortleb, publisher and editor-in-chief of the *New York Native*, made in an editorial about press reports that Robert Gallo of the National Cancer Institute had "stolen" a sample of HIV from its French discoverers and had thereby set treatment and research back "immeasurably." Ortleb concluded with the following exhortation to action:

Get angry, as angry as you'd be if someone had just killed your lover. Then call up every Senator, every Congressman you can get on the phone and demand an immediate investigation of Robert Gallo . . . before this fraud and this scientific standstill in fact does kill you, your lover, and millions of other Americans.[61]

The political horizon stopped at the electoral realm. Anger, even in the face of the death, indeed even in the face of *murder*, of one's lover and perhaps oneself, should be channeled toward phoning one's elected representatives.

Anger and Respectability

The words of Nathan Fain, a gay man who worked at GMHC, offer some insight into gay anxiety about anger and confrontational politics and the resulting political horizon that excluded militancy. Speaking about gay anger and AIDS politics, Fain revealed unease with anger, an unease that seemed to derive in part from his own ambivalence about gay difference and gays' relationship to dominant society. Darrell Yates Rist reported on Fain's speech at an AIDS conference and included excerpts from a conversation he had had with Fain a few days before:

Fain told me that gay men's anger over AIDS had begun, he knew, to seethe. . . . He was perturbed: "factions" in the gay community had out of hand condemned the government and its scientists—"offended many of our friends"—when they didn't have an inkling of how much the government had been doing and was, he was convinced, about to do. Today his speech concedes that some of us have reason to be angry. But, he says . . . we must grow up, "assume the responsibilities of adulthood." . . . We must turn our backs on the politics of our "collective childhood," and not permit ourselves to be rebellious—like a bunch of "drag queens throwing bricks at cops." If we don't behave, the "real world" won't respect us.[62]

If lesbians and gay men wanted to be accepted and respected, they should assume the proper emotional demeanor and engage in activism that was sanctioned by mainstream American political norms.

Although Virginia Apuzzo's comments at a meeting of elected and appointed lesbian and gay officials came from a perspective opposite to Fain's, they reveal that Fain was not alone in the view that anger and militancy were immature, irresponsible, and disreputable, and, if expressed, would understandably affront those in straight society who otherwise were allegedly poised to help in this time of crisis:

For those of us who have earned—for whatever silly, transient, cheap reason—the respect and regard of [the political] system, we must be willing to spend it on this [AIDS] issue. We must be willing to mount a multiple offensive on what is coming down on us. Yes, we must negotiate. Yes, we must lobby. Yes, we must litigate. . . . But we must also remember where we come from, and return to allowing that rage to be expressed and not think for a minute that there is something not respectable about that.[63]

Here again Apuzzo was attempting to broaden the political horizon, and she did so by directly challenging the logic that pitted gay expressions of rage against respectability. The comments at the same meeting by Massachusetts Congressman Barney Frank sounded the more typical cautionary note:

The political system has responded better to [the AIDS crisis] at this point than I would have hoped. . . . [That means] in my judgment, that the political course of action that has been chosen [by the lesbian and gay community] is correct.[64]

Feelings like faith in the government's goodwill, love for one's brothers, pride in the community's responsible efforts to fight AIDS, gay shame, fear of continual nonrecognition and social rejection, and desire for acceptance were often mobilized in a manner that either suppressed militant anger or rechanneled it toward more acceptable and standard political actions such as service provision and electoral politics. As was the case with the rhetoric of gay responsibility, the emotional dynamics that were set in motion by the growing anger—dynamics that revolved around the imperative of respectability—excluded confrontational activism from the political horizon, from the repertoire of tactics that were seen as politically possible, desirable, and necessary.

While it is surely true that lesbians and gay men were swamped with caretaking work that made engaging in other forms of activism difficult, that does not sufficiently explain the absence of confrontational activism in this period, particularly because a few people *were* calling for more oppositional activism. What the evidence shows is that leaders and others in the lesbian and gay community actively discouraged more confrontational AIDS activism during this period. Their efforts, whether intentional or not, dampened sentiments toward militancy.

In the early to mid-1980s gay shame and a corollary fear of ongoing social rejection were important components of the reigning emotional habitus in lesbian and gay communities. I have argued that a social group's emotional habitus is a decisive factor in the generation of a political horizon, in part because it provides an affectively charged pedagogy of political behavior. In this case, gay shame and its companion sentiments, repeatedly elicited in lesbian and gay public discourse, made some forms of activism thinkable while others, confrontational street activism in particular, became wholly unimaginable.

This emotional habitus, like all, was historically contingent, the product of various practices among lesbians and gay men that helped to reproduce a constellation of feelings as well as axiomatic norms regarding feelings and their expression. Elsewhere I have shown how this reigning emotional habitus was upended in the middle of 1986 in the wake of the U.S. Supreme Court's *Bowers v. Hardwick* antisodomy ruling.[65] Rather than provoking alarm, as they previously had, growing anger and indignation now gained traction in lesbian and gay communities, effectively and affectively submerging gay shame. This emergent new emotional habitus toppled the inducements toward social conformity and created a space for the kind of defiant and oppositional activism visibly manifested in ACT UP's direct action street AIDS activism.

Shame on You? Shame on Me?

I'd like to conclude with some comments about my own shame about sham-ing. I worry that the very concept of lesbian and gay ambivalence, by claim-ing the existence of residual gay shame in spite of the gay movement's proc-lamation of gay pride, is itself shaming. In noting gay self-loathing and self-doubt, in arguing that we ourselves sometimes buy the right wing's antigay rhetoric, in claiming that the painful experience of social nonrecog-nition can inspire attempts to procure social acceptance even at the cost of suppressing gay difference and buying into mainstream oppressive values, in portraying these undersides of gay pride, have I exposed too much, and in that glare of exposure elicited even greater shame? A few lesbians and gay men who read earlier versions of the larger work from which this es-say is drawn have suggested as much. They expressed ambivalence about my emphasis on ambivalence and disputed my claim of widespread shame. Sometimes they acknowledged that their difficulties with my terms might stem from their own ambivalence and shame; even so, do I really want to provoke more shame? Just as shaming, perhaps, is my challenge to the heroic narrative of lesbian and gay responses to AIDS in the early to mid-1980s. I worry that my argument that some discourses of gay pride in this period elicited and reinforced gay shame could be interpreted as a kind of finger wagging, a shaming of lesbian, gay, and AIDS activists who engaged in this early vital work.

My goal is to offer critical appraisal, not to shame, but in this case the line between the two may be quite fine. If I have crossed it, perhaps a dis-cussion of my intent and of my analysis will allow me to cross back. My investigation of these emotional dynamics is primarily at the level of so-cial structure and social relations, not at the level of the individual; it is de-signed to explore how social dynamics functioned in this period, in the hopes that we can thereby strategize about how to understand and poten-tially disrupt them in the present and future. Structural conditions—for example, mainstream homophobic discourses about AIDS, heteronorma-tivity, and an emotional habitus in lesbian and gay communities that in-cludes ambivalent sentiments about self and society—roused lesbian, gay, and AIDS activists to try to counter the pervasive shaming of gay men with proud arguments of gay righteousness. The same conditions encouraged those activists to alleviate the painful condition of social nonrecognition in part by countering the rhetoric of gay irresponsibility with articulations of gay responsibility, and to do so, perhaps inadvertently, in a manner that let stand the implication that "gay irresponsibility" was to blame for AIDS. In invoking gay responsibility in a manner that suggested that social acceptance of gays was, and perhaps should be, contingent on gays' respectable behavior, activists were responding to their social ostracism and attending to their felt need to be addressed, to have communication with and be recognized by those who were refusing any such acknowledgment. The structural conditions, in other words, provide an explanation for the eliciting of shame during this period. Gay shame understandably encourages a disavowal of gay difference, and any such disavowal is bound to shame in its bid for respectability.

As powerful and influential as these structural conditions may have been, however, they were not determining. Indeed, some lesbians and gay men explicitly countered the shaming and blaming that was widespread in gay and straight discourses about AIDS. Most forcefully in debates about closing gay bathhouses, they articulated a gay liberation–inspired pride that celebrated gay sexual difference and challenged dominant heteronormative values. Rather than countering shame by disavowing that which the mainstream deems shameful and unworthy of recognition, they challenged society's understandings of what is shameful.

It appears, then, that articulations of pride were cacophonous in this period, drawing from gay liberation discourses as well as from well-worn, deeply grooved mainstream understandings of gay sexuality and from mainstream values more generally. It is likely that people were experiencing both types of pride. Still, my sense, from looking at hundreds of articles from gay newspapers and documents from AIDS organizations, is that pride about gay responsibility was more frequently mobilized and had a more prominent place in the community's emotional habitus during this period than did pride in gay difference—likely because AIDS vastly heightened shame about gay sexuality and about gay difference, effectively suppressing sentiments of pride about gay sexuality that many may have previously felt. In any case, those who articulated a pride that did challenge the shaming and blaming indicate that some lesbians and gay men defied structural conditions, even if most did not.

That raises another concern. I've indicated my worry that my discussion of gay shame goes too far, but there is also the possibility that I've pulled my punches and haven't gone far enough. When a previous critic who had taken issue with my argument about gay shame read a revision and said he was now convinced, I was in the same moment relieved and self-questioning: had I watered down my argument and made it more palatable? Was it possible that I had blunted my critical edge, and did I instead want to argue in a more normative vein that articulations and elicitations of gay shame, fear of social rejection, and desire for social acceptance actually hampered, rather than simply shaped, lesbian and gay responses to AIDS in this period? Did a fear of betraying "my people," and the shame I might suffer as a result, push me to tone down my conclusions? I can't say for sure, but I don't think so. My goal has been to show how gay shame affects lesbian and gay politics, not to advocate for confrontational activism per se. Feelings such as gay shame and fear of social rejection did temper early lesbian and gay AIDS activism, as I argue, but they did not disable activist efforts. In fact, it is undeniable that those early efforts were vital to the fight against AIDS. And no one can know for sure whether more confrontational AIDS activism in this period would have saved more lives. In any event, that's not the point. Instead, by presenting this analysis I hope to spur us to think about how an emotional habitus is made and how it can establish a particular political horizon while foreclosing others.[66] There may be tactical reasons to embrace relatively moderate activism in a given moment, but I do not think that lesbian and gay rights and liberation are advanced when the embrace of such politics, and a rejection of anything more confrontational, is motivated by gay shame and fear of ongoing social nonrecognition. In *The Trouble with Normal*, Warner challenges the idea that a repudiation of sex will lead to the redemption of gay identity. The evidence here suggests that a similarly false promise of redemption motivated the embrace in this period of nonconfrontational AIDS activism and the discouragement of anything more militant; that promise too needs to be challenged.

This is why I believe that we need to consider how gay shame shapes lesbian and gay politics. The story of lesbian and gay responses to AIDS in the early to mid-1980s provides a telling illustration. The stakes are high, for gay shame is not confined to the past. At the start of the twenty-first century, we need to consider more thoroughly how the very real psychic effects of marginalization and oppression shape lesbian/gay/queer activism today. Even more, we need to think about the ways in which lesbian/gay/queer activism sometimes undermines, and at other times bolsters, gay shame.

Notes

1. Warner, *The Trouble with Normal*.
2. Naming the members of a social group is always an exclusionary process. In this article I use the exclusionary nomenclature "lesbian and gay"–rather than LGBT, for ex-

ample—because during the period I am discussing, the movement identified itself as the lesbian and gay movement and early AIDS activists tended to identify themselves as lesbian or gay. I am ambivalent about the phrase "lesbian and gay," but alternatives like "LGBT" and "queer" are unsatisfactory as well in that they are anachronistic.

3. See, for example, D'Emilio, *Sexual Politics, Sexual Communities*.

4. I use the word "psychosocial," awkward as it is, to convey a linkage between the psychic and the social, and, in this case specifically, to suggest that the shame gay men, lesbians, and other sexual minorities experience should be understood as one very real psychic effect of living as a sexual "other" in a heteronormative society.

5. Sedgwick, "Shame, Theatricality, and Queer Performativity," 50.

6. I agree with Sedgwick that shame flows from the experience of nonrecognition, but it is not the only feeling that can be stirred by nonreciprocated interest in connection. Along with shame, the experience of nonrecognition might generate other feelings such as anger, contempt, disbelief, sadness, frustration, resignation, and despair. A conversation with Lauren Berlant helped to clarify this point.

7. Tomkins, in Sedgwick and Frank, *Shame and Its Sisters*, 133.

8. Sedgwick, "Shame, Theatricality, and Queer Performativity," 50.

9. Ibid., 50.

10. Basch, quoted in Sedgwick, "Shame, Theatricality, and Queer Performativity," 50.

11. Sedgwick, "Shame, Theatricality, and Queer Performativity"; Crimp, "Mario Montez, For Shame"; Warner, *The Trouble with Normal*.

12. Sedgwick, "Shame, Theatricality, and Queer Performativity," 50.

13. Crimp, "Mario Montez," 71–72; Warner, *The Trouble with Normal*, quoted in Crimp, "Mario Montez," 72.

14. Crimp, "Mario Montez," 74.

15. Goffman, *Presentation of Self*, 36.

16. In *Stigma: Notes on the Management of Spoiled Identity*, Goffman explores the efforts deployed by stigmatized individuals to manage their "spoiled" identities, elaborating on this idea of the pull toward conformity, especially among the socially marginalized.

17. Warner, *The Trouble with Normal*, 31–32; see also Gould, "Sex, Death, and the Politics of Anger" and "Rock the Boat."

18. Shelley, "Gay Is Good," 33–34.

19. A thank you to Mary Patten for the turn of phrase used for the heading of this section.

20. See Bronski, *Pleasure Principle*, especially chapter 2. See also antigay rhetoric of politicians from both major political parties, as well as the rhetoric of the religious right; to be sure, there is a strategic component to their antigay rhetoric, but that does not preclude their believing it as well.

21. The exaggerated media reports in August and September 2005 about looting, shootings, murders, and rapes in New Orleans on the heels of Hurricane Katrina and the catastrophic flooding of the city—and the fact that many people believed the media reports even though they were unsubstantiated rumors that by and large turned

out to be false, and the fact that issues of "criminality" were prominent in public discussions even as people were stranded and dying, having gone without food and water for days—suggest the power and widespread nature of anxieties about the breakdown of law and social order. The racial and sexual components of such anxieties are clear in this example.

22. Any group that engages in confrontational protest politics raises the specter of social disorder, but the particular characteristics of the protesting group may amplify or mute that anxiety. For example, the Black Power movement—angry and militant, armed and defiant—raised immense anxiety among whites about outraged and organized black people seeking revenge for centuries of racist oppression, about the possible decline of state-sanctioned white supremacy and its system of rewards and punishments, and about the disintegration of the society that they knew and benefited from.

23. As far as I know, the phrase is Anne Kane's, drawn from the work of Norbert Elias, Pierre Bourdieu, and Thomas Scheff. See Kane, "Finding Emotion," especially 253-54.

24. Patton, *Inventing AIDS*, 19-20.

25. The other social groups who have been most severely affected by HIV/AIDS are similarly viewed as expendable—injection drug users as well as poor men and women, a disproportionate number of whom are black and Latino/a.

26. Bronski, "O Brave New World."

27. Medical and media reports stated that the men were "gay." It would have been more accurate to say that they were men who had sex with other men, thus recognizing that some of them may have identified as bisexual or heterosexual. By categorizing those affected in terms of sexual identity rather than sexual practices, the initial reports created the impression that the diseases were affecting gay men specifically, and because of their identity rather than because of specific practices. The policy ramifications were significant: government and other institutions' responses to this ostensibly "gay" epidemic—including the dissemination of effective and targeted safe-sex information—were slowed immeasurably.

28. See, e.g., Treichler, "AIDS, Homophobia, and Biomedical Discourse"; Ross, "Ethics of Compassion"; Watney, *Policing Desire*; Loughery, *Other Side of Silence*.

29. Men with modest sexual histories were among the first reported cases of what later became AIDS. Of four of the first patients seen by clinicians in Los Angeles, "one had been monogamous for four years, two had several regular partners, and only one 'was highly sexually active'" (Michael S. Gottlieb et al., *"Pneumocystis carinii* Pneumonia and Mucosal Candidiasis Found in Previously Healthy Homosexual Men," *New England Journal of Medicine* 305 [December 10, 1981]: 1425-31), quoted in Epstein, *Impure Science*, 380 n. 15.

30. See Román, *Acts of Intervention*, for an eloquent analysis that foregrounds the importance of early lesbian and gay interventions in the AIDS crisis for gathering people "into the space of performance, wherever that may be, in order to raise funds, promote consciousness, initiate discussions, and to strategize and coordinate plans of support for those affected," always with the overriding goal of stopping the epidemic (8-9).

31. San Francisco AIDS/KS Foundation, "Report to the Community," 1, 3. Originally the

Kaposi's Sarcoma Research and Educational Foundation, the group changed its name to the San Francisco AIDS/KS Foundation and ultimately became the San Francisco AIDS Foundation.

32. Bush, "Coping with a Crisis," 19.

33. Randy Shilts's *And the Band Played On* can be read as a challenge to the heroic narrative of early AIDS activism, but he and I proceed from very different standpoints. Whereas he castigates activists for being "in denial" about AIDS and for caring more about gay liberation–inspired sexual politics than gay lives (thereby setting himself up as the lone voice of reason in the gay community), I am more interested in explaining how anxiety about the possible further withdrawal of social recognition as a result of gay sexual difference—an anxiety that, incidentally, pervades Shilts's writings—shaped the early massive mobilization of lesbians and gay men to fight AIDS. For a trenchant critique of Shilts's writing, see Crimp, "How to Have Promiscuity in an Epidemic" and *Melancholia and Moralism*.

34. Popham, "We've Got Heart"; emphases in original.

35. Gay Men's Health Crisis, "Together This Is What We're Doing," 22.

36. Power, "Time for Action Not Panic," 4.

37. Rogers and Selby, letter to the editor; emphasis in original.

38. The rhetoric of gay responsibility in the early 1980s helps to explain why by the late 1980s, as Seidman has noted, AIDS was seen by many gays as marking "the beginnings of a new maturity and social responsibility among homosexuals" ("Transfiguring Sexual Identity," 189). Warner notes the continuation of such sentiments almost twenty years into the epidemic, arguing that AIDS had come to be understood by many gays as "a much-needed sobering lesson" that "shut down gay liberation . . . not a moment too soon" and brought "a new maturity, the coming of age of the gay movement after AIDS, after AIDS activism, and after sex" (*The Trouble with Normal*, 95, 51). Warner also examines the role that concerns about respectability more generally play in the contemporary lesbian and gay movement. For an analysis of the role that concerns about respectability have played in black political responses to AIDS, see Cohen, "Contested Membership" and *Boundaries of Blackness*. See Crimp, *Melancholia and Moralism*, for an incisive analysis that sees moralizing gay narratives about AIDS as a psychosocial response to the ongoing AIDS crisis.

39. Popham, "We've Got Heart," 13.

40. Quoted in Bronski, "AIDing Our Guilt," 9.

41. As the concept of emotional habitus suggests, the mobilizations of this rhetoric of responsibility were not necessarily conscious or intentional efforts to counter gay shame and encourage support for AIDS organizations, or to elicit desire for social acceptance and thereby encourage respectable behavior, or to convince society of gay respectability. Some of the articulations seem to have been made with such aims in mind, but we cannot know that with certainty. In any case, the *effects* of such articulations, which we can analyze, are perhaps more relevant to the question at hand about the ways in which feelings shape politics.

42. Hippler, "Year to Celebrate," 31.

43. France, "AIDS Demonstrations and Gay Pride Week," 14.

44. The concern about demonstrating gay respectability also had a longer history, drawing on an anxiety about rocking the boat that had taken root by the second half of the 1970s, when activists turned from the rhetoric and goals of gay liberation toward gay rights. Once gay activists gained some access to dominant institutions and resources, they embraced tactics that would ensure congenial straight–gay relations and continued gay access and shied away from activism that might jeopardize that progress. Lesbian, gay, and AIDS activists of the early to mid-1980s inherited and buttressed this political horizon, while also expanding it to include service provision and caretaking.

45. For evidence of a growing anger in some quarters, see, in Chicago's *Gay Life*, Kramer, "AIDS Crisis"; "Apuzzo, Enlow Testify"; and Streips, "NGTF's Apuzzo Blasts U.S. Government." In the *Native*, see Ortleb, editorial (1982); Kramer, "1,112 and Counting"; Pierson, "Federal Government's Cold Shoulder"; D'Eramo, "Not a Bureaucrat"; and Bush, "Reagan Response Blasted." In the *Bay Area Reporter*, see Berlandt, "New York Marches" and "Apuzzo Testifies for AIDS." In the *Sentinel*, see Martz, "Government's Effort to Fight AIDS Slammed."

46. Berlandt, "New York Marches." Apuzzo's comment was remarkably prescient: four years later, ACT UP/NY held its first action, shutting down Wall Street.

47. Reactions to Kramer's article are in part attributable to the fact that his writings often echoed mainstream society's homophobic characterizations of gay men and of gay male sexual culture. Still, anxiety about his anger and militancy played a role as well. I discuss in greater detail the complex reactions to Kramer's article in Gould, "Moving Politics."

48. Hall, "Deviance, Politics, and the Media," 286. Hall uses the phrase when speaking about elites' efforts at symbolic delegitimation of protesters, but his analysis is useful as well for thinking about power dynamics within social groups.

49. Editorial, *New York Native*.

50. Berlandt, "New York Marches."

51. Kramer, "AIDS Crisis."

52. "Call 1-(202) 456-7639"; emphasis mine.

53. For reports on the lack of any Chicago city funding allocated to AIDS, see "City, State Should Press"; "Pros and Cons"; and Robles, "Eight Years into Epidemic." For Chicago AIDS statistics from the period, see City of Chicago Department of Health, "AIDS Chicago."

54. In the version of Kramer's article that was printed in *Gay Life*, Kramer's call for volunteers to engage in civil disobedience was edited out. It may be the case that Kramer himself edited that part out, perhaps because he was looking for volunteers in New York City. But it's also possible that the editors of *Gay Life*, anxious about confrontational activism, did the editing, perhaps in an effort to suppress the affective and activist surge some readers might have felt.

55. Hass, "Becoming an AIDS Volunteer," 6.

56. Jones, "Text of Speech," 10–11.

57. Ibid., 11.

58. Shepard, *White Nights*, 39.

59. Cotton, "Marchers Remember Losses." Near's song, in various versions, was

popular at lesbian and gay candlelight vigils during this period. De la Vega remembers singing "We are a gentle, *loving* people, singing for our lives" after the New York City Council passed a gay rights bill in March 1986 ("Solitary Vigil"; emphasis added). Other versions of the refrain similarly excise anger from lesbians' and gay men's affective experiences: "We are gay and lesbian people;" "We are a loving, healing people;" "We are a justice-seeking people;" and "We are a peaceful, loving people." I recall AIDS activists during the late 1980s and early 1990s spoofing the song, singing: "We are gentle, angry people, and we are *whining, whining* for our lives."

60. Linebarger, "Spark Lives," 3.

61. Ortleb, editorial (1985).

62. Rist, "Going to Paris," 77; emphasis in original.

63. Walter, "Openly Gay Elected and Appointed Officials," 11.

64. Ibid., 13.

65. Gould, "Sex, Death, and the Politics of Anger" and "Rock the Boat."

66. For an analysis of the role that the unmaking of one emotional habitus and the construction of another played in ushering in more confrontational street AIDS activism, see Gould, "Moving Politics."

Works Cited

"Apuzzo, Enlow Testify for AIDS Research." *Gay Life*, May 19, 1983, p. 3.

"Apuzzo Testifies for AIDS in Congress; Requests $100 Million for Research." *Bay Area Reporter*, May 19, 1983, p. 4.

Berlandt, Konstantin. "New York Marches and Rallies for AIDS." *Bay Area Reporter*, May 12, 1983, p. 4.

Bronski, Michael. "AIDing Our Guilt and Fear." *Gay Community News*, October 9, 1982, pp. 8-10.

———. *The Pleasure Principle: Sex, Backlash, and the Struggle for Gay Freedom*. New York: St. Martin's Press, 1998.

———."O Brave New World: AIDS and Historical Memory." *Boston Phoenix*, January 9–15, 2004.

Bush, Larry. "Coping with a Crisis: Action and Reaction; The Community Responds to a Serious Health Problem." *Advocate*, February 17, 1983, pp. 19-21, 55.

———. "Reagan Response Blasted in AIDS Hearings." *New York Native*, August 15-28, 1983, pp. 14-15.

"Call 1-(202) 456-7639" [editorial]. *Gay Life*, April 28, 1983, p. 4.

City of Chicago Department of Health. "AIDS Chicago: AIDS Surveillance Report, 1981-1991." Chicago: The Department, 1991.

"City, State Should Press for AIDS Funding" [editorial]. *Gay Life*, July 21, 1983, p. 4.

Cohen, Cathy J. "Contested Membership: Black Gay Identities and the Politics of AIDS." In *Queer Theory/Sociology*, ed. Steven Seidman. Cambridge, MA: Blackwell, 1996.

———. *The Boundaries of Blackness: AIDS and the Breakdown of Black Politics*. Chicago: University of Chicago Press, 1999.

Cotton, Paul. "Marchers Remember Losses to AIDS." *Gay Life*, May 30, 1985, pp. 1, 5.

Crimp, Douglas. "How to Have Promiscuity in an Epidemic." *October* 43 (1987): 237–71.

———. *Melancholia and Moralism: Essays on AIDS and Queer Politics*. Cambridge, MA: MIT Press, 2002.

———. "Mario Montez, For Shame." This volume 63–75.

De Beauvoir, Simone. *The Second Sex*. New York: Vintage, 1989.

De la Vega, Ernesto. "A Solitary Vigil for Human Rights." *New York Native*, April 7, 1986, p. 17.

D'Emilio, John. *Sexual Politics, Sexual Communities: The Making of a Homosexual Minority in the United States, 1940–1970*. Chicago: University of Chicago Press, 1983.

D'Eramo, James. "Not a Bureaucrat." *New York Native*, May 9–22, 1983, pp. 13, 65.

Du Bois, W. E. B. *The Souls of Black Folk*. New York: Bantam, 1989.

Editorial. *New York Native*, April 25–May 8, 1983, p. 3.

Epstein, Steven. *Impure Science: AIDS, Activism, and the Politics of Knowledge*. Berkeley: University of California Press, 1996.

Fanon, Frantz. *Black Skin, White Masks*. New York: Grove Press, 1967.

France, David. "AIDS Demonstrations and Gay Pride Week: Has the Movement Redefined Pride?" *New York Native*, July 15–28, 1985, pp. 14–15.

Gay Men's Health Crisis. "Together This Is What We're Doing" [public service announcement]. *New York Native*, November 7–20, 1983, p. 22.

Goffman, Erving. *The Presentation of Self in Everyday Life*. New York: Anchor Books, 1959.

———. *Stigma: Notes on the Management of Spoiled Identity*. New York: Simon & Schuster, 1963.

Gould, Deborah B. "Sex, Death, and the Politics of Anger: Emotions and Reason in ACT UP's Fight against AIDS." Ph.D. diss., University of Chicago, 2000.

———. "Rock the Boat, Don't Rock the Boat, Baby: Ambivalence and the Emergence of Militant AIDS Activism." In *Passionate Politics: Emotions and Social Movements*, ed. Jeff Goodwin, James Jasper, and Francesca Polletta. Chicago: University of Chicago Press, 2001.

———. *Moving Politics: Emotion and ACT UP's Fight against AIDS*. Chicago: University of Chicago Press, 2009.

Hall, Stuart. "Deviance, Politics, and the Media." In *Deviance and Social Control*, ed. Paul Rock and Mary McIntosh. London: Tavistock, 1974.

Hass, Robert. "Becoming an AIDS Volunteer." *Sentinel USA*, June 20, 1985, p. 6.

Hippler, Mike. "A Year to Celebrate: Coming Up with New Strategies for Surviving in the Age of AIDS." *New York Native*, November 18–24, 1985, pp. 30–31.

Jones, Cleve. "Text of Speech, City Hall Steps, November 27, 1985." Reprinted in *Sentinel USA*, December 5, 1985, pp. 10–11.

Kane, Anne. "Finding Emotion in Social Movement Processes: Irish Land Movement Metaphors and Narratives." In *Passionate Politics: Emotions and Social Movements*, ed. Jeff Goodwin, James Jasper, and Francesca Polletta. Chicago: University of Chicago Press, 2001.

Kramer, Larry. "1,112 and Counting." *New York Native*, March 14–27, 1983, pp. 1, 18–19, 21–23.

————. "AIDS Crisis: Your Life Is On the Line." *Gay Life*, April 28, 1983, pp. 1, 5, 8.

————. *Reports from the Holocaust: The Making of an AIDS Activist*. New York: Penguin Books, 1989.

Linebarger, Charles. "The Spark Lives at Memorial Vigil." *Bay Area Reporter*, May 30, 1985, pp. 3-4.

Loughery, John. *The Other Side of Silence: Men's Lives and Gay Identities; A Twentieth-Century History*. New York: Henry Holt, 1999.

Martz, Steve. "Government's Effort to Fight AIDS Slammed as 'Too Little, Too Late.'" *Sentinel*, August 4, 1983, pp. 1-2.

Ortleb, Charles L. Editorial. *New York Native*, August 16-29, 1982, p. 3.

————. Editorial. "AIDSGATE." *New York Native*, June 3-16, 1985, p. 4.

Patton, Cindy. *Inventing AIDS*. New York: Routledge, 1990.

Pierson, Ransdell. "The Federal Government's Cold Shoulder." *New York Native*, April 25-May 8, 1983, pp. 15-16.

Popham, Paul. "We've Got Heart." *New York Native*, April 26-May 9, 1982, p. 13.

Power, Ed. "Time for Action Not Panic." *S.F. Sentinel*, March 31, 1983, p. 4.

"The Pros and Cons of AIDS Funding Bill." Editorial. *Gay Life*, September 22, 1983, p. 4.

Rist, Darrell Yates. "Going to Paris to Live: The Hope of HPA-23." *New York Native*, July 1-14, 1985, pp. 26-33, 77.

Robles, Jennifer Juarez. "Eight Years into Epidemic, City AIDS Office Only Now Gets Underway." *Chicago Reporter*, March 1988, pp. 1, 7-11.

Rogers, Buck, and Alan Selby. Letter to the editor. *Bay Area Reporter*, July 26, 1984, p. 7.

Román, David. *Acts of Intervention: Performance, Gay Culture, and AIDS*. Bloomington: Indiana University Press, 1998.

Ross, Judith Wilson. "An Ethics of Compassion, a Language of Division: Working out the AIDS Metaphors." In *AIDS: Principles, Practices, and Politics*, ed. Inge Corless and Mary Pittman-Lindeman. New York: Harper & Row, 1988.

San Francisco AIDS/KS Foundation. "A Report to the Community from the San Francisco AIDS/KS Foundation." December 1983. Document in author's ACT UP archive.

Sedgwick, Eve Kosofsky, and Adam Frank, eds. *Shame and Its Sisters: A Silvan Tomkins Reader*. Durham, NC: Duke University Press, 1995.

Sedgwick, Eve Kosofsky. "Shame, Theatricality, and Queer Performativity: Henry James's *The Art of the Novel*." This volume 49-62.

Seidman, Steven. "Transfiguring Sexual Identity: AIDS and the Contemporary Construction of Homosexuality." *Social Text* 19-20 (1988): 187-205.

Shelley, Martha. "Gay Is Good." In *Out of the Closets: Voices of Gay Liberation*, ed. Karla Jay and Allen Young. New York: New York University Press, 1992.

Shepard, Benjamin Heim. *White Nights and Ascending Shadows: An Oral History of the San Francisco AIDS Epidemic*. London and Washington: Cassell, 1997.

Shilts, Randy. *And the Band Played On: Politics, People and the AIDS Epidemic*. New York: St. Martin's Press, 1987.

Streips, Karlis. "NGTF's Apuzzo Blasts U.S. Government on Response." *Gay Life*, August 18, 1983, pp. 1, 14.

Treichler, Paula A. "AIDS, Homophobia, and Biomedical Discourse: An Epidemic of Signification." *October* 43 (1987): 31-70.

Walter, Dave. "Openly Gay Elected and Appointed Officials Hold 'Historic' Meeting." *Advo-cate*, December 24, 1985, pp. 10–13.

Warner, Michael. *The Trouble with Normal: Sex, Politics, and the Ethics of Queer Life*. New York: Free Press, 1999.

Watney, Simon. *Policing Desire: Pornography, AIDS, and the Media*. 2nd ed. Minneapolis: University of Minnesota Press, 1989.

[HEATHER K. LOVE]

Emotional Rescue

It used to be that I talked about my gay shame with only my friends—and then, really, only with my close friends. This shame took many forms, but it came out most often as ambivalence about myself and "others like me." I have heard such feelings described as "internalized homophobia," but I think this is an ugly phrase: I strongly prefer "ambivalence." The thing about ambivalence is that it isn't just bad: it's both bad and good. This is how it was with my gay shame. I felt bad things about myself and others: contempt and self-contempt; pity and self-pity; and a range of boomeranging feelings, including disappointment, anger, alienation, and embarrassment. But I also felt good things—and, what is strangest, perhaps, many of these good feelings came directly out of the bad feelings. A lot of the pleasure I felt in being gay was bound up with the thrill of talking bad about it. "Auntie, don't you ever wish that you weren't what we are?"[1] To me, there was profound joy in just thinking about a sentence like this one: it exploded the pieties of gay identity, raining down a shower of longing, complicity, and bile. For a long time this deliciously pungent mixture of feelings *was* my gay identity. Despite the indulgence of my friends and the evidence of a deep, rich vein of camp shame running through gay culture, I never really thought my way of feeling was widely shared. Well versed in the official discourse of gay pride, I knew enough to be ashamed of my gay shame.

Recently, however, the shame of feeling gay shame has subsided. No longer seen as just an embarrassing by-product of social oppression, shame these days is getting a lot more play among queer activists and academics. (I realized how much shame's fortunes had changed when I mentioned to a few students that I was attending the Gay Shame Conference. "Oh, right," they responded, "gay shame," apparently unsurprised that hip queer academics would choose to style themselves in this impeccably downbeat manner.) In the general move to question the politics of identity and of pride, many have begun to rethink shame, and to consider its potential, as Douglas Crimp writes, to "articulate[e] collectivities of the shamed."[2]

Despite shame's new cachet, plenty of doubts still swirl around this volatile affect. While over the last twenty years activists have successfully turned shame against seemingly shameproof institutions such as the health care industry, we are often reminded how easily shame can be turned back and used *against* the shame prone. In addition to concerns about shame's ability to do damage, many wonder how an inwardizing affect such as shame might serve as the basis for collective action. Eve Kosofsky Sedgwick, who has been crucial in drawing attention to the transformative potential of this feeling, describes the "double movement shame makes: toward painful individuation, toward uncontrollable relationality."[3] Although the capacity of shame to isolate is well documented, its ability to bring together shamed individuals into meaningful community is more tenuous. It's still not clear whether the uncontrollable relationality of shame should count as "good enough" relationality.

In thinking through the political potential of shame, it seems important to consider the possibility that some aspects of queer experience and queer culture may not be useful or productive.[4] Equally important, though, is recognizing that whatever is good about shame is bound up irrevocably with what is bad about it—that is to say, with its potential to hurt and to silence.[5] Just now, when so many queers are seizing the opportunity to "kiss shame goodbye," it's important to hold on to what is most difficult in the experience of shame. Given the recent history of gay acceptability—and the ongoing unacceptability of the social world—I think that those of us interested in profound social transformation need to be on the lookout for affects resistant to affirmation. Such resistance to affirmation is what I understand as the appeal of the concept of betrayal for Leo Bersani. In *Homos*, Bersani considers betrayal in the work of Jean Genet as an "ethical necessity."[6] Betrayal is hard to swallow. While it may not be useless for thinking about community, it takes us a while to get there. Bersani suggests that Genet's account of betrayal offers a possibility for remaking the world, not because it contains an image of a better world, but because if forces us to rethink relationality altogether: "Nothing *can* change in this world—or rather (and this, it must be acknowledged, is an uncertain bet), between oppression now and freedom later there may have to be a radical break with the social itself."[7]

Shame, like betrayal, is important because it resists the kind of idealist affirmation that is so attractive to a marginalized and despised social group. (I am talking about us.) Queers are hated; we wish we weren't, but wishing does not make it so. The main problem with the discourse of gay pride is that it turns attention away from the real problems that face gay, lesbian, and transgender people. Proponents of gay pride talk as if the main problem we face is shame, but shame isn't the problem: homophobia is. Shame, rather than being a last lingering burden we need to throw off, is more like a stubborn material imprint—a mark. This feeling is a psychic and corporeal reminder of what would need to change in order to render shame actually obsolete. What we have now is a situation of forced obsolescence: shame's shelf life is up; get over it.

In addition to shame, I think it would be productive to think seriously about a range of negative affects produced by the experience of social exclusion: self-loathing, anger, sadness, fear, the sense of failure, envy, despair, longing, loneliness—or a resistance to community altogether. Such feelings are like Xs marking the spot where the social is at work on us. They create in us both a desire to change our social context and an awareness of how difficult such change is. Feeling bad about being queer can serve as a reminder that the magical solution of affirmation is inadequate and push us toward different kinds of responses. It helps to remind us that looking on the bright side is only effective up to a point: it can't replace the work of making sure that there is, in fact, a brighter side to look on.

You Could Be Mine

In *A Lover's Discourse*, Roland Barthes writes, "The discourse of Absence is a text with two ideograms: there are the raised arms of Desire, and there are the wide-open arms of Need. I oscillate, I vacillate between the phallic image of the raised arms, and the babyish image of the wide-open arms."[8] Barthes construes the relationship between Desire and Need as consecutive: the lover vacillates between two different responses to Absence. It is striking to note, however, how often these images converge. Desire in its most infantile, its most reduced state is difficult to distinguish from Need; Need in its most tyrannical form nearly approaches the phallic image of desire. Barthes offers an image of such convergence in the photograph of himself as a boy in his mother's arms reproduced at the beginning of *Barthes by Barthes*. The caption reads: "The demand for love."[9] For Barthes, the notion of Demand captures the close link between Need and Desire.[10] In the photograph, the young Barthes offers an image of the demanding child, that slumped, pathetic figure who nonetheless manages to press his needs home with real force.[11]

If this photograph reveals the adult force of childish Need, we can call to mind many examples that reveal the babyish element in adult Desire. Think, for instance, of the sneering, sulking pout of that consummate erotic bully Mick Jagger. In almost any song by the Rolling Stones, the call to "just come upstairs" gets its heat not only from the authority of the de-siring father, but also from the hunger of the prodigal son. In "Emotional Rescue," for instance, macho posturing shades into schoolboy whining as Jagger intersperses deep-voiced promises to be your "knight in shining ar-mor," to "come to your emotional rescue," with half-mumbled assertions that last night he was "crying like a child, like a child." In the chorus, Jagger gives us the cry itself: "You will be mine, mine, mine, mine, mine, all mine / You could be mine, could be mine, / Be mine, all mine." In the infantile rep-etition of the possessive, one hears the pathetic cry of the child who isn't in a position to own anything.

You will be mine; you could be mine—but you probably won't be mine. This combination of demand and desperation, I want to argue, character-izes the relationship to the gay past. But queer critics tend to disavow their need for the past, focusing instead on the heroic aspect of their designs on the past. Like many demanding lovers, queer critics promise to rescue the past when in fact they dream of being rescued themselves.

In imagining historical rescue as a one-way street, we fail to acknowl-edge the dependence of the present on the past. Contemporary critics tend to frame the past as the unique site of need. But we might understand the work of historical affirmation not as a lifeline thrown to those figures drowning in the bad gay past, as it is often presented, but rather as a means of securing a more stable and positive identity in the present. At the same time, it allows us to ignore the resistance of queer historical figures to our own advances toward them.

In order to better describe how this fantasy works, I consider an exchange between Sappho and one of her most rapt modern readers. In her recent translation, Anne Carson offers the following version of one of Sappho's lyrics: "Someone will remember us / I say / even in another time."[12] Sappho's poem offers to its audience what sounds like foreknowledge: "Someone will remember us." The prediction seems to have the simple status of truth, but the "I say" at the center of this lyric attests to the longing and uncertainty that is the poem's motive and its subject. In making the prediction more emphatic, "I say" tips the hand of the speaker, shows this prophecy to be a matter of wishful thinking. The speaker protects her audience from the un-predictability of the future by means of a personal guarantee; the "I" of the poem offers its auditors a shelter from oblivion. (One of the uncanny aspects of the poem is its ability to offer this consolation—in person, as it were—not only to its immediate audience, but also to its future readers.)

The sheer density of longing in this short poem is striking. Crack the shell of its confident assertion of immortality and questions emerge: Can one be remembered in one's absence? When I leave the room, will you still think about me? Will we be remembered after death? The poem answers "yes": "Someone will remember us / I say / even in another time." The speaker promises her audience that they will be thought of not only tomorrow, or the day after, but "in another time," and by strangers. Sappho's lyric promises memory across death: once we and everyone we know and everyone who knows us is dead, someone is still going to think about us. We will be "in history."

This fragment of Sappho's offers a nearly irresistible version of what queer subjects want to hear from their imagined ancestors. The early twentieth-century lesbian poet Renée Vivien heeded this echo from the past and learned Greek in order to read Sappho's work; throughout her short life, she obsessively translated and rewrote her poems and even traveled to the island of Lesbos with her lover Natalie Clifford Barney to recreate the atmosphere of Sappho's school for girls. In her 1903 volume *Sapho*, Vivien offers translations and expansions of Sappho's fragmentary lyrics that take up themes of tormented desire, isolation, and lost love in the originals and amplify the historical resonances in them.

Vivien's attention to the vulnerability of cross-historical contacts is legible in her version of "Someone will remember us."

Quelqu'un, je crois, se souviendra dans
l'avenir de nous.

Dans les lendemains que le sort file et tresse,
Les êtres futurs ne nous oublieront pas . . .
Nous ne craignons point, Atthis, ô ma Maîtresse!
    L'ombre du trépas.

Car ceux qui naîtront après nous dans ce monde
Où râlent les chants jetteront leur soupir
Vers moi, qui t'aimais d'une angoisse profonde,
    Vers toi, mon Désir.

Les jours ondoyants que la clarté nuance,
Les nuits de parfums viendront éterniser
Nos frémissements, notre ardente souffrance
    Et notre baiser.

Someone, I believe, will remember us
in the future.

In the tomorrows that fate spins and weaves,
Those who come after us will not forget us . . .
We have no fear, O, Atthis my Mistress!
Of the shadow of death.

Because those who are born after us in this world
Filled with death-cries will cast their sighs
Toward me, who loved you with deep anguish,
Toward you, my Desire.

The wavering days that the clear light limns
And the perfumed night will render eternal
Our tremblings, our ardent suffering,
And our kiss.

While "making the moment last" is a commonplace of the Western lyric tradition, this trope takes on a tremendous weight in Vivien's rewritings of Sappho's lyrics. The promise of immortality that is associated with the aesthetic is put to work here as a bulwark against historical isolation and social exclusion. How can connections across time be forged out of fear and erotic torments? Vivien compares the transformation of fleeting moments into tradition to the way that "les jours ondoyants" make up an eternity even though they are made of nothing more substantial than light and shade. In this comparison, a love that is fleeting and filled with anguish becomes eternal simply by aging—by being continually exposed to the light of day and the perfumed shades of night. She also invokes a specifically erotic mystery: how the experience of shared erotic suffering, obsession, and anxiety can add up to eternal devotion.

Of course, it is never assured that such torments do lead to eternal devotion, but that is the conceit of the poem and it represents the deepest wish of Sappho's lonely historical correspondent. Vivien makes true love the model for cross-historical fidelity, and, speaking in Sappho's voice, promises recognition. Taking up the role of adoring lover, Vivien answers Sappho's call, leaving no doubt that someone in another time would in fact think of the speaker. Through such a response, Vivien seems to rescue Sappho—to repair the torn fragments of her text, and to stitch up the gap in the temporal fabric that her lyric address opens. But it is clear that by translating Sappho Vivien was working against the profound sense of alienation and historical isolation that she herself felt. By coming to Sappho's rescue, Vivien manages to rescue herself. She herself enters history by becoming Sappho's imagined and desired "someone."[13]

Although many cast queer historical subjects in the role of Sappho—as lonely, isolated subjects in search of communion with future readers—I want to suggest that it makes sense to see ourselves in the role of Vivien. That is to say, contemporary queer subjects are also isolated, lonely subjects—looking for other lonely people, just like them. Vivien finds in Sappho an almost perfect interlocutor; the echo chamber in which she replayed Sappho's fragments afforded profound satisfactions. But few encounters with the queer past run so smoothly. Historical texts rarely express such a perfect longing for rescue and are often characterized by a resistance to future readers and to the very idea of community. We do encounter some texts that say, "Someone will remember us / I say / even in another time." But some of these lost figures don't want to be found. What then?

Noli me tangere

Recently, long-standing debates about gay and lesbian history have shifted from discussions of the stability of sexual categories over time to explorations of the relationships between queer historians and the subjects they study. The turn from a focus on "effective history" to a focus on "affective history" has meant that critics have stopped asking, "Were there gay people in the past?" and have instead focused on questions such as "Why do we care so much if there were gay people in the past or not?" or even, perhaps, "What relations with these figures do we hope to cultivate?" Critics such as Scott Bravmann, Ann Cvetkovich, Carolyn Dinshaw, L. O. A. Fradenburg, Carla Freccero, Elizabeth Freeman, David Halperin, Christopher Nealon, and Valerie Traub have shifted the focus away from epistemological questions in the approach to the queer past; rather, they make central "the desires that propel such engagements, the affects that drive relationality . . . across time."[14] Exploring the vagaries of cross-historical desire and the queer impulse to forge communities between the living and the dead, this work has made explicit the affective stakes of long-standing debates on method and knowledge. Mixing psychoanalytic approaches with more wide-ranging treatments of affect, these critics have traced the identifications, the desires, the longings, and the love that structure the encounter with the queer past.[15]

My approach to queer history is profoundly indebted to this new field of inquiry. My focus is on the negative affects—the need, the aversion, and the longing—that characterize the relationship between past and present. This decision to "look on the dark side" comes out of my sense that contemporary critics tend to describe the encounter with the past in idealizing terms. In particular, the models that these critics have used to describe queer cross-historical relations—friendship, love, desire, and community—seem strangely free of the wounds, the switchbacks, and the false starts that give these structures their specific appeal, their binding power. Friendship and love have served as the most significant models for thinking about how contemporary critics reach out to the ones they study. I would like to suggest that more capacious and de-idealized accounts of love, friendship, desire, and community would serve to account for the ambivalence and violence of the relationship to the past—to what is most queer in that relationship.

Today, many critics attest that after Stonewall, the worst difficulties of queer life are behind us. Yet the discomfort that contemporary queer subjects continue to feel in response to the most harrowing representations from the past attests to their continuing relevance. The experience of queer historical subjects is not safely distant from contemporary experience: rather, their social marginality and abjection too closely mirror our own. The relationship to the queer past is suffused not only by feelings of regret, despair, and loss, but also by the shame of identification.

In attempting to construct a positive genealogy of gay identity, queer critics and historians have often found themselves at a loss about what to do with the sad old queens and long-suffering dykes who haunt the historical record. Some have disavowed the difficulties of the queer past, arguing that our true history has not been written and focusing on the more heroic episodes in queer history and representation. If critics do admit the difficulties of the queer past, it is most often in order to save it. By including queer figures from the past in a positive genealogy of gay identity, we redeem their suffering, transforming their shame into pride after the fact. I understand this impulse not only as a widespread but also as a structural feature of the field, a way of counteracting the shame of having a dark past.

Carolyn Dinshaw's book *Getting Medieval: Sexualities and Communities, Pre- and Postmodern* is a fascinating investigation into the affective dynamics of queer history. Dinshaw focuses on the metaphorics of touch in the relationship of contemporary critics to the medieval past; she explores the "strange fellowships" and the "partial connections" that link queer subjects across time. Dinshaw argues that the kinds of queer connections she is describing are made "not via shared identities but rather [through] shared isolation." Dinshaw specifically contrasts this fellowship of the "isolated, the abject, [and] the shamed" with a more idealized version of community: "I want to stress that the community across time formed of such vibrations, such touches, is not necessarily a feel-good collectivity of happy homos."[16]

Despite Dinshaw's interest in exploring shared isolation, the emphasis in *Getting Medieval* often falls on community at the expense of isolation. Roland Barthes constitutes an important example for Dinshaw in her elaboration of this kind of embodied, loving historical practice. She cites Barthes on Michelet: "For Michelet the historical mass is not a puzzle to reconstitute, it is a body to embrace. The historian exists only to recognize a warmth."[17] Barthes lovingly describes such relations throughout his work, and his identification with Michelet is undoubtedly grounded in his tendency to form similar attachments. But he also considers Michelet's physical repulsions at length. In another passage cited by Dinshaw, Barthes writes: "Fits of nausea, dizziness, oppression do not come only from the seasons, from the weather; it is the very horror of narrated history which provokes them: Michelet has 'historical' migraines."[18] Barthes's relationship to Michelet is put forth here as a model of the tenderness that is possible between contemporary queer critics and the subjects they study. Dinshaw writes that Barthes "created his own queer relation to Michelet by 'living with' him."[19] Do we need to be reminded that such an arrangement tends to be a source of pain as well as pleasure? That the darkened bedroom is a site not only of caresses but also of migraines?

Dinshaw focuses on the queer impulse to "touch the past" through a meditation on Christ's words to Mary Magdalene after his resurrection: "Noli me tangere" (Don't touch me). Dinshaw's chapter on Margery Kempe's "too heavy, queer touch" begins with an epigraph from Leslie Feinberg's *Stone Butch Blues*: "Touch is something I could never take for granted."[20] By attending to the history of queer abjection, Dinshaw constructs a genealogy of untouched and untouchable figures, subjects constituted through refusal. However, these subjects are portrayed as yielding, even warming to the touch of the queer historian. It is striking that in her extended meditation on the phrase "Noli me tangere" Dinshaw does not consider the potential resistance of such figures to the touch of contemporary queer historians. At stake in this omission from Dinshaw's extended and brilliant meditation on "Noli me tangere" may be not only the desire of the queer historian for a response from the past, but also a tendency to read the queerness of queer desire as an excess rather than a lack. Queer desire is often figured as "loving too much," as in Dinshaw's reading of Margery Kempe's excessive, dissonant desire. But it would also make sense to understand queerness as an absence of or aversion to sex.

Untouchability runs deep in queer experience. Willa Cather, thinking about the "sweetness and anguish" that characterize family life in Katherine Mansfield's stories wrote: "One realizes that human relations are the tragic necessity of human life; that they can never be wholly satisfactory, that every ego is half the time greedily seeking them, and half the time pulling away from them." And Cherríe Moraga remarked: "My recurring sense of myself outside the normal life and touch of human beings was again, in part, a kind of revelation." "Noli me tangere" is, in this sense, an apt motto for queer historical experience, but its effects are unpredictable. While it serves as protection against the blows of normal life, the family, and homophobic violence, it also works against other forms of community and affiliation, including, of course, queer community.

Contemporary critics approach these figures from the past with a sense of the inevitability of their progress toward us—of their place in the history of modern homosexuality. Their relationship to this future remains utterly tenuous, however. If their trajectory to a queer future appears inevitable, this appearance is perhaps best explained by the fact that *we are that future*. Our existence in the present depends on being able to imagine these figures reaching out to us. One is reminded constantly of the fragility of these connections in Dinshaw's text. Still, it remains difficult to hear these subjects when they say to us: "Don't touch me."

Against Identification

In *The Renaissance of Lesbianism in Early Modern England*, Valerie Traub takes a step backward from the intimacies that Dinshaw explores. More circumspect in its attachments than *Getting Medieval*, Traub's book offers a reflection on the ascendancy of the identificatory impulse in lesbian and gay historiography. Traub explicitly compares her own project to Dinshaw's: "Whereas Dinshaw's impulse is to foster queer community by 'touching' the medieval past, to make 'new relations, new identifications, new communities with past figures' . . . my impulse is to analyze the desires that propel such identifications" across time.[21] Rather than making alliances with the dead through taking up and extending such impulses, Traub offers a genealogy of identification, considering why it is that "looking at ourselves in the mirror" has become the dominant methodology in gay and especially in lesbian studies.

In Dinshaw's work, pleasure is figured as a resource for queer studies; in *The Renaissance of Lesbianism*, pleasure—insofar as it is bound up with identification—is a problem. Though Traub suggests that it would be impossible to completely rid historical or political practice of the impulse to identification, she links the pleasures of identification to cognitive failure. In the final pages of her book, Traub effects a turn away from identification and toward desire, suggesting that we might approach the figures from the past "not as subject *to* our identifications, but as objects *of* our desire."[22] In this way, Traub hopes to borrow some of the pleasure of psychic and historical identification and reinvest it in desire, figured here as an authentic encounter with an other who is different from and external to the self.

Eroticizing historical alterity is only part of the story here, though. Traub's more pressing concern is with the melancholic nature of lesbian studies. She argues that the "discovery" of early modern lesbians is a way of "compensating for the fact that, despite the categories we inhabit, our knowledge of ourselves as individuals as well as within group identities is vexed, uncertain, in continual and oft-times painful negotiation. Quite simply, we do not know who and what 'we' are, or how we might go about defining ourselves beyond the reaction formations conceived under the influence of heterosexism and homophobia."[23] According to Traub, lesbian critics have not come to terms with the pain of historical isolation and instead reenact that trauma through repeated searches for other lesbians "just like them" in the past: "The effort to identify early modern *lesbians* is not so much a case of individual misrecognition as a collective melancholic response to the trauma of historical elision. Despite the common invocation of how homosexuals have been 'hidden from history,' there has been little investigation into the effects on the collective *lesbian* psyche of the systematic denial of historicity."[24]

Traub's attention to the pain that is at the heart of lesbian and gay historiography is welcome, as is her call for an investigation of the psychic costs of repeated encounters with the "empty archive." One may certainly see both pain and the disavowal of pain in Renée Vivien's textual approaches to Sappho. Traub's "solution" to this problem is to move lesbian historiography beyond the impasse of melancholic disavowal by mourning those losses and by giving up on the dream of identification. In doing so, she draws a distinction between personal and collective responses to loss, suggesting that "the desire to view oneself in the mirror, however enabling personally, need not be the procedural ground of lesbian history":[25]

Rather than mourning our disconnection from women of the past and allowing them to exist autonomously through their textual traces, we have disavowed our mourning and encrypted the pain of that disavowal within our own critical procedures . . . Such a response is understandable and, at the level of the individual psyche, potentially productive. On a cultural and methodological level, however, it ensures a continued mel-

ancholic identification with, and dependence upon, the terms of erotic similitude, in a paralyzing enactment of queer trauma.[26]

Drawing on Wendy Brown's concept of "wounded attachments" as the basis of identity politics as well as work on mourning and melancholy by Judith Butler and Abraham and Torok, Traub suggests that contemporary critics work through psychic impasses in order to get over paralyzing and debilitating engagements with the historical past. What is troubling about such a suggestion is that some aspects of lesbian history live on in the present only through such wounded attachments, and severing them will mean putting important—if traumatic—parts of the past to rest. There is a real sense in which queer history is nothing but wounded attachments; a "debilitating engagement with the past"[27] might just be another name for the practice of history. Confronted with the unresolved grief of lesbian historical feeling, Traub suggests cutting the knot, in an act of methodological triage. However, there is something to be said for living with those bad attachments, identifying through loss, and allowing ourselves to be haunted.

Against Consolation

The historiographic method of Michel Foucault is regularly invoked in contemporary queer contexts as exemplary in its resistance to the temptations of identification and mirroring. In his work on genealogy, Foucault argues for the need to develop a historical method that does not rely on the past to secure the stability of the present. In his much-cited essay "Nietzsche, Genealogy, History," he writes:

"Effective" history differs from the history of historians in being without constants. Nothing in man—not even his body—is sufficiently stable to serve as the basis for self-recognition or for understanding other men. The traditional devices for constructing a comprehensive view of history and for retracing the past as a patient and continuous development must be systematically dismantled. Necessarily, we must dismiss those tendencies which encourage the consoling play of recognitions. Knowledge [savoir], even under the banner of history, does not depend on "rediscovery," and it emphatically excludes the "rediscovery of ourselves." History becomes "effective" to the degree that it introduces discontinuity into our very being—as it divides our emotions, dramatizes our instincts, multiplies our body and sets it against itself.[28]

Rather than moving forward from a determinate origin and proceeding according to a smooth logic of progression, history through the lens of genealogy begins accidentally and proceeds by fits and starts. Such a history, while useless for the "consoling play of recognitions" that is the mode of history favored by historians, serves to disrupt the seeming inevitability of the present. Divisive and incendiary, genealogy points out the otherness of the past and shows us our own image in the present as multiple, subject to an internal alienation.

Elsewhere in this essay, Foucault writes: "The purpose of history, guided by genealogy, is not to discover the roots of our identity, but to commit itself to its dissipation. It does not seek to define our unique threshold of emergence, the homeland to which metaphysicians promise a return; it seeks to make visible all those discontinuities that cross us."[29] In his descriptions of the unpredictable and accidental nature of events, Foucault argues against the idea that history's movement is continuous or marked by progress. As a result, he suggests that we can find no solid epistemological basis in the present for identifications in the past. Resemblances across time are not dependable, for over time the very terms of inquiry shift.

Contemporary queer critics have consistently attacked the concept of identity as both politically and philosophically bankrupt. Although such critiques of identity have fostered crucial changes in gay and lesbian politics and theory, it seems that the queer stance against identity has short-circuited important critical work on the history of identity. Identity is, as many of these critics have attested, a deeply problematic and contradictory concept; nonetheless, it remains a powerful organizing concept in contemporary experience and is a crucial category in the history of sexuality. But we need an account of identity that allows us to think through its contradictions and trace its effects. Such a history can offer a critique of identity without dispensing with it as a category of historical experience.

The commitment to the "dissipation of identity" among queer critics has often blinded them to the tenacity of this concept in both history and in individual subjectivity. Identity accounts not only for the shape of the past, but also for the feelings we continue to have about that past. It is in large part because we recognize these figures, emotions, and images from the past as like ourselves that we feel their effects so powerfully.

Rather than attempt to overcome identity, I want to suggest a mode of historiography that recognizes the inevitability of a "play of recognitions," yet sees these recognitions not as consoling but as shattering. What has been most problematic about gay and lesbian historiography to date is not, I want to argue, its attachment to identity, but rather its consistently affirmative bias. Critics imagine that no one would search out the roots of his or her identity if that history were not positive. But we are condemned to the search for roots and resemblances; we cannot help searching the past for images of ourselves. I want to suggest that we explore more extensively the negative or ambivalent identifications that we have with the past. Such a gutting "play of recognitions" can serve as a form of effective history. It does not attempt either to distance us from identity or to make it disappear; rather, it shows up the difficulties, contradictions, and impossibilities of "our" history.

At Night

The strange and difficult combination of identification and desire that informs Foucault's historiographic method is legible in another passage from the genealogy essay. This passage begins coolly enough with methodological injunctions and slowly builds toward a fantasy of historical encounter:

> A genealogy of values, morality, asceticism, and knowledge will never confuse itself with a quest for their "origins," will never neglect as inaccessible all the episodes of history. On the contrary, it will cultivate the details and accidents that accompany every beginning; it will be scrupulously attentive to their petty malice; it will await their emergence, once unmasked, as the face of the other.[30]

The genealogist appears here as an inexhaustible lover, attentive to every detail and waiting for the other's appearance as for the break of day. Foucault's approach to history is indelibly though often invisibly marked by desire, and, I would suggest, by specifically queer experiences, rhetorics, and longings. Foucault's own account of his famously ascetic historical practice appears to be anything but devoid of desire. Rather, it is grounded in an anxious, restless desire—a desire for a recognition that could hardly be called consoling.

In an essay that Dinshaw discusses at length, "The Lives of Infamous Men," Foucault describes his own experience in the prison archives of the Hôpital Général and the Bastille. Foucault attends to the difficulties of studying the lives of obscure men whose only trace is a criminal record and who reach contemporary readers through improbable and unnecessary paths:

> Having been nothing in history, having played no appreciable role in events or among important people, having left no identifiable trace around them, they don't have and never will have any existence outside the precarious domicile of these words.... This purely verbal existence, which makes these forlorn or villainous individuals into quasi-fictional beings, is due to their nearly complete disappearance, and to that luck or mischance which resulted in the survival, through the peradventure of rediscovered documents, of a scarce few words that speak of them or that are pronounced by them. A dark but, above all, a dry legend.... By nature, it is bereft of any tradition; discontinuities,

effacement, oblivion, convergences, reappearances: this is the only way it can reach us. Chance carries it from the beginning. . . . So that between these people of no importance and us who have no more importance than they, there is no necessary connection. Nothing made it likely for them to emerge from the shadows, they instead of others, with their lives and their sorrows.[31]

Foucault's wan description of the belated emergence from the archive of these obscure figures is at some distance from the heroic plots of historical discovery. Underlining the chance nature of the encounter between historians and the subjects they study, Foucault attempts to drain away the affect that surrounds the historical encounter: the legend of Foucault's "infamous men" is dark, but "above all, dry."

Foucault's de-cathexis of the historical encounter is also linked to a critique of the specular logic of historical discovery. Between these figures and "us" there is "no necessary connection": there is no reason that their traces should have reached us, and furthermore no reason why they should resemble us. Yet it is at the moment that Foucault emphasizes the purely contingent and unmotivated relationship between these infamous men and contemporary readers that he draws an explicit comparison between us and them: "So that between these people of no importance and us who have no more importance than they, there is no necessary connection." Although there may be no necessary connection here, there is in fact a sufficient connection; we share with these figures a lack of importance. We might even say that this lack of importance is the only important thing about us.

In a moment that is crucial to Dinshaw's theory of queer touches across time, Foucault describes being "physically affected" in the archive: he feels a vibration "still today" from these texts. He avows his affective investment in these stories, describing the book to follow as "a mood-based and purely subjective book," a "little obsession that found its system." The community of "abject others" that Dinshaw locates in Foucault's essay is grounded in a logic of the improbable, the contingent, and the insignificant. In this sense, the lack of importance of these figures is their most important trait—it is what draws Foucault, as another unimportant figure, to them. The world of the shadows that Foucault traces in this passage looks, on the one hand, like the dust heap from which all historical figures must be rescued; on the other hand, it looks like a kind of demimonde or queer underworld where men of no importance can meet for chance encounters.[32]

Foucault's attachment to these figures resonates perhaps most strongly in his descriptions of their encounters with power. He suggests that these subjects reach us only because of the violence that touched them:

What snatched these subjects from the darkness in which they could, perhaps should, have remained was the encounter with power; without that collision, it's very unlikely that any word would be there to recall their fleeting trajectory. The power that watched these lives, that pursued them, that lent its attention, if only for a moment, to their complaints and their little racket, and marked them with its claw was what gave rise to the few words about them that remain for us.[33]

Defending his methodology, and answering an imaginary critic who would argue that he imagines historical subjects not in themselves ("from below") but only in relation to power, Foucault responds with a question: "Would anything at all remain of what [these figures] were in their violence or in their singular misfortune had they not, at a given moment, met up with power and provoked its forces?"[34] One hears the catch in his voice when he describes the obscurity and violence that marked these lives—had they not met up with power, would *anything at all* remain? A bit later in the essay, Foucault amplifies this point, arguing that these figures are constituted by the violence they experienced. They are "infamous in the strict sense: they no longer exist except through the terrible words that were destined to render them forever unworthy of the memory of men. . . . Useless to look for another face for them, or to suspect a different greatness in them; they are no longer anything but that which was meant to crush them—no more nor less."[35] Hunted down by power, here figured as a lion rampant—or is it a clumsy bear?—these figures are legible only in their misery: it is in the cut, as it were, that we can locate Foucault's attachment. In this sense, we might say that his investment is not so much in these infamous men themselves as "in the darkness in which they could, perhaps should, have remained."

In drawing attention to this moment in the essay, I want to suggest that the sensation—the cross-historical touch—that Foucault feels in the archive may be as much a mauling as a caress. What he quickens to here is not only the caress of a queer or marginal figure in the past, but also the more brutal touch of the law. What happens in the archive is an encounter with historical violence, which includes both physical injury and the violence of obscurity, or annihilation from memory. Is it possible that Foucault wants his historical encounter *that way*?

Consider a related moment in a 1967 interview when, discussing his methodology, Foucault narrates a bad dream:

A nightmare has haunted me since my childhood: I am looking at a text that I can't read, or only a tiny part of it is decipherable. I pretend to read it, aware that I'm inventing; then suddenly the text is completely scrambled, I can no longer read anything or even invent it, my throat tightens up and I wake up.

I'm not blind to the personal investment there may be in this obsession with language that exists everywhere and escapes us in its very survival. It survives by turning its looks away from us, its face inclined toward a darkness we know nothing about.[36]

Here it appears that the "personal investment" that drives Foucault's approach to history is not an attachment to precursors, but rather an "obsession with language . . . that escapes us in its very survival." The "tightening of the throat" that he feels in the dream seems to be a response to historical loss, ignorance, and an expression of shame about pretending to read what he cannot. Despite the trauma of this loss, however, Foucault does not end by expressing a desire for the intact document. He does not, it seems, want to look history in the face; rather, his fascination is with the face that turns away and, perhaps even more, with the darkness toward which it turns.

This moment recalls Foucault's discussion of Eurydice and the sirens in his 1966 essay on Maurice Blanchot, "The Thought of the Outside." Foucault compares the heroic narrative of Ulysses' encounter with the sirens to the story of Orpheus's failed journey to bring back Eurydice from the underworld, suggesting that there is not much to distinguish the triumphant narrative from the tragic one.

Each of their voices is then freed: Ulysses' with his salvation and the possibility of telling the tale of his marvelous adventure; Orpheus's with his absolute loss and never-ending lament. But it is possible that behind Ulysses' triumphant narrative prevails the inaudible lament of not having listened better and longer, of not having ventured as close as possible to the wondrous voice that might have finished the song. And that behind Orpheus's lament shines the glory of having seen, however fleetingly, the unattainable face at the very instant it turned away and returned to darkness—a nameless, placeless hymn to light.[37]

Although Foucault does not read these figures explicitly in relation to the work of the historian, they are legible in terms of a contrast between history as a tale of heroic rescue and a "marvelous adventure" and history as a narrative that breaks off midway and that fails to bring the beloved back from the underworld. Clearly, Foucault throws in his lot with Orpheus, who offers an apt emblem of the practice of queer history. The failed attempt to rescue Eurydice is a sign of the impossibility of the historical project per se: the dead do not come back from beyond the grave, and this fact constitutes the pathos of the historical project. But we might also read the Orphic lament as an effect of the particular losses suffered by queer historical subjects. We can trace the aftereffects of that history in the characteristically minor key in which Foucault's desire for the past is played.

To explain what I mean, I want to turn to Blanchot's staging of this moment in the "The Gaze of Orpheus," the essay on which Foucault's discussion is based. Blanchot describes the way that the work of art must be wrested from the "heart of night":

By turning toward Eurydice, Orpheus ruins the work, which is immediately undone, and Eurydice returns among the shades. When he looks back, the essence of night is revealed as the inessential. Thus he betrays the work, and Eurydice, and the night. But not to turn toward Eurydice would be no less untrue. Not to look would be infidelity to the measureless, imprudent force of his movement, which does not want Eurydice in her daytime truth and in her everyday appeal, but wants her in her nocturnal obscurity, in her distance, with her closed body and sealed face—wants to see her not when she is visible, but when she is invisible, and not as the intimacy of familiar life, but as the foreignness of what excludes all intimacy, and wants, not to make her live, but to have living in her the plenitude of death.[38]

Blanchot casts Orpheus's relationship to Eurydice as an impossible one: by turning back he betrays her, losing her forever in the lower depths; but the refusal to turn back would count as a betrayal as well. Such is the relationship of the queer historian to the past: although we can't help wanting to save the figures from the past, the mission is doomed to fail. In part, this is because the dead are gone for good; in part, it is because the queer past is even more remote, more deeply marked by power's claw; and in part, it is because this rescue is an emotional rescue, and in that sense, we are sure to botch it. But, according to Blanchot, not to botch it would be a betrayal. Such a rescue effort can take place only under the shadow of loss and in the name of loss; success would constitute its failure.

Blanchot's reflections on Orpheus and Eurydice recall the moment when, in a 1983 interview, Foucault speculated that the "best moment" in the life of the homosexual is "likely to be when the lover leaves in the taxi." Foucault links this feeling to the availability of homosexual contacts; he suggests that because there is no contest to get someone into bed, the erotic is more bound up with retrospect than anticipation. But at the moment he invokes this explanation, Foucault also gestures toward a history of queer feeling grounded in the social impossibility of homosexual love. Foucault's desire for the boy has a queer specificity; he would not easily give up the dreamy and rueful retrospect he inspires. He wants the love of *that* boy, already receding into the distance—not the daytime love, the easy intimacies, of a domestic partner. He wants him in the taxi, just as Orpheus wants Eurydice in the night, in the underworld.

This structure of feeling is not a pathology, nor does it describe the essential nature of the homosexual. Neither would I call it an effect of the "dark pulsions" of the unconscious, though I suppose they play their part in this scene. Anyone, I want to insist, might be seduced by the figure of Eurydice: she is radiant in her withdrawal. But her specific attraction for queer subjects is an effect of a historical experience of love as bound up with loss. To recognize Eurydice as desirable is a way of identifying through that loss. Such an approach would be consistent with an important aspect of contemporary queer politics, which has tended to define community not as constituted by a shared set of identity traits, but rather as emerging from a shared experience of social violence. In this sense, following the trace of violence and marginalization—studying not only obscure men, but obscurity itself—would allow us to deflect questions of identity and to acknowledge the losses of both the past and the present.

I hear the trace of such losses in my own fantasized relationship to Foucault. I do dream about being with Foucault, but I imagine joining him in the underworld, just after he has turned away. I want him in that darkness, and bearing the marks of power's claw. How to explain such perverse, such intransigent desires? Queer history has been an education in absence: the experience of social refusal and of the denigration of homosexual love has taught us the lessons of solitude and of heartbreak. What I want to suggest, though, is that it has also, in its way, taught us "how to do the history of homosexuality": and this because, in the words of Neil Bartlett, "history can be a dark night too."[39]

Notes

1. A line from the film *Bell, Book, and Candle* cited in Bruce La Bruce and Glenn Belverio, "A Case for the Closet," in *Anti-Gay*, ed. Mark Simpson (London: Cassell Group, 1996), 143.

2. Douglas Crimp, "Mario Montez, For Shame," this volume, 72.

3. Eve Kosofsky Sedgwick, "Shame, Theatricality, Queer Performativity: Henry James's *The Art of the Novel*," this volume, 51.

4. Leo Bersani raised this possibility in his comments at the roundtable on the first day of the Gay Shame conference.

5. Sedgwick makes this point in a passage in which she considers the pitfalls of embracing "queer" as a name for a political movement that begins with shame. She writes that "there's no way that any amount of affirmative reclamation is going to succeed in detaching the word [queer] from its associations with shame and with the terrifying powerlessness of gender-dissonant or otherwise stigmatized childhood." Sedgwick, "Queer Performativity: Henry James's *The Art of the Novel*," *GLQ* 1, no. 1 (1993): 4. For a critique of the use of queer children as the exemplary figures for a consideration of the dan-

gers of "queer," see Angus Gordon, "Turning Back: Adolescence, Narrative, and Queer Theory," *GLQ* 5, no. 1 (1999): 1-24, esp. 15-21. For a consideration of Sedgwick's desire to free "queer" from the stigma of childhood shame in spite of her claim that it cannot be done, see my reading of this passage in Love, *Feeling Backward: Loss and the Politics of Queer History* (Cambridge, MA: Harvard University Press, 2007), 105-7.

6. Leo Bersani, *Homos* (Cambridge, MA: Harvard University Press, 1995), 151.

7. Ibid., 176.

8. Roland Barthes, *A Lover's Discourse: Fragments*, trans. Richard Howard (New York: Noonday Press, 1978), 16-17.

9. Barthes, *Roland Barthes by Roland Barthes*, trans. Richard Howard (Berkeley: University of California Press, 1977), n.p.

10. In this caption, Barthes is citing Jacques Lacan, who defines the concept of demand as the "demand for love." For Lacan too, Demand constitutes a kind of hinge between Desire and Need. Before the moment of the Mirror Stage, the infant's Need is still attached to objects and capable of satisfaction; but once the child enters the realm of the Symbolic, he becomes the subject of Desire. Desire exists under the law of the signifier; it is radically detached from objects and for this reason can never be satisfied. Demand for Lacan is linked to the Imaginary; it represents a moment when the subject is no longer a subject of Need but is not yet a subject of Desire.

11. The equivocal nature of this image is perhaps best evoked with reference to a linguistic slippage between the definitions of "demand"–"to ask for with authority; to claim as a right"–and "demanding"–"claiming more than is generally felt by others to be due." *The Random House College Dictionary*, revised ed.

12. Sappho, *If Not, Winter: Fragments of Sappho*, trans. Anne Carson (New York: Knopf, 2002), 297.

13. In this sense, we can understand Vivien's project of reclamation as evidence of Joan DeJean's claim in *Fictions of Sappho* that the indeterminacy of Sappho's textual corpus allowed her to be all things to all people. "A final meaning of translation is close to transference in the psychoanalytic sense. Fictions of Sappho are, at least in part, a projection of the critic's/writer's desires onto the corpus, the fictive body, of the original woman writer." Joan DeJean, *Fictions of Sappho, 1546-1937* (Chicago: University of Chicago Press, 1989), 3.

14. Carolyn Dinshaw, *Getting Medieval: Sexualities and Communities, Pre- and Postmodern* (Durham, NC: Duke University Press, 1999), 35.

15. See Scott Bravmann, *Queer Fictions of the Past: History, Culture, and Difference* (Cambridge: Cambridge University Press, 1997); Ann Cvetkovich, *An Archive of Feeling: Trauma, Sexuality, and Lesbian Public Cultures* (Durham, NC: Duke University Press, 2003); Dinshaw, *Getting Medieval*; L. O. Aranye Fradenburg, *Sacrifice Your Love: Psychoanalysis, Historicism, Chaucer* (Minneapolis: University of Minnesota Press, 2002); Carla Freccero, *Queer/Early/Modern* (Durham, NC: Duke University Press, 2005); Elizabeth Freeman, "Packing History, Count(er)ing Generations" *New Literary History* 31, no. 4 (2000): 727-44; David M. Halperin, *How To Do The History of Homosexuality* (Chicago: University of Chicago Press, 2002); Christopher Nealon, *Foundlings: Gay and Lesbian Historical Emotion before Stonewall* (Durham, NC: Duke University Press, 2001); and Valerie Traub, *The Renaissance of Lesbianism in Early Modern England* (Cambridge: Cambridge University Press, 2002).

16. Dinshaw made these comments in a forum responding to *Getting Medieval*: Dinshaw, "Got Medieval?," *Journal of the History of Sexuality* 10, no. 2 (2001): 203.

17. Dinshaw, *Getting Medieval*, 46.

18. Ibid., 47.

19. Ibid., 48.

20. Ibid., 143.

21. Traub, *The Renaissance of Lesbianism*, 334.

22. Ibid., 354.

23. Ibid., 352.

24. Ibid., 350. Throughout the book, Traub italicizes the word "lesbian" in order to indicate the anachronistic and unstable nature of the term when applied in the early modern context.

25. Ibid., 334.

26. Ibid., 350.

27. Ibid., 351.

28. Foucault, "Nietzsche, Genealogy, History," in *Essential Works of Foucault, 1954–1984*, vol. 2, *Aesthetics, Method, and Epistemology*, ed. James D. Faubion (New York: New Press, 1998), 380.

29. Ibid., 386–87.

30. Ibid., 373.

31. Foucault, "The Lives of Infamous Men," in *Essential Works of Foucault, 1954–1984*, vol. 3, *Power*, ed. James D. Faubion (New York: New Press, 2000), 162–63.

32. For other invocations of historical activity as cruising, see Neil Bartlett, *Who Was That Man? A Present for Mr. Oscar Wilde* (London: Serpent's Tail, 1988), as well as Isaac Julien's 1989 film *Looking for Langston*, in which he repeatedly figures the search for an obscure historical subject as "cruising the graveyard."

33. Foucault, "Lives of Infamous Men," 161.

34. Ibid.

35. Ibid., 164.

36. Foucault, "On the Ways of Writing History," in *Essential Works*, 2:290.

37. Foucault, "The Thought of the Outside," in *Essential Works*, 2:162.

38. Blanchot, *The Space of Literature*, 172.

39. Bartlett, *Who Was That Man?*, 216. I take the phrase "how to do the history of homosexuality" from David Halperin's book by that name.

[G E O R G E   C H A U N C E Y]

The Trouble with Shame

Half a century ago, in the summer of 1954, a gay New Yorker and longtime customer of the hustlers who gathered on Forty-second Street reflected on a sudden spate of newspaper articles that had portrayed his Times Square demimonde in the most lurid terms possible. The articles reminded him once again that "the righteous feel, doubtless, that . . . I am a monster, a changeling, a pervert—and they [straight hustlers] renegades, degraded and vicious." He found it more striking, though, that according to the articles, gay habitués of the Square such as he were "supposed to be furtive and ashamed" and their relationships with the hustlers to be characterized by mutual "loathing and contempt, shame and fear." As he mused in his diary:

The righteous doubtless wish it were that way—a fitting punishment for us, to live in fear, shame and contempt so long as our crime and sin is not found out and we are not put in prison or asylums. . . . But thank God, or something, that this is not so—wholly anyway. Society does its best to cause us fear and humiliation (and, occasionally, . . . tragedy) but mostly, in this great city, it fails. And it is the degree of that failure which is the so remarkable thing to which I draw attention.

It won't be hard for most readers to accept the diarist's first point: that in the 1950s, self-righteous heterosexuals wanted to believe that the homosexuals they loathed suffered from self-loathing and shame. What is more curious, and troubling, is that post-Stonewall lesbians, gay men, and queer scholars seem equally eager to believe that the queers of the 1950s generation lived in such abjection. The diarist's second point, that the humiliation rituals to which homosexuals were subjected in the 1950s did not always succeed—but, in his words, could and often did "fail"—is foreign to every side in the debate between gay pride and gay shame. Even the announcement for the Gay Shame conference explained that although it was designed "to confront the shame that lesbians, gay men, and 'queers' of all sorts still experience in society," these were "residual experiences of shame now that not all gay people are condemned to live in shame," as presumably they once were.

Historians and social theorists used to make a similar claim about enslaved people of African descent: that, cut off from their home cultures and subject to a powerful disciplinary regime, they absorbed their degradation and participated in it. A generation of scholarship has demonstrated that, on the contrary, slaves created a powerful alternative culture that resisted their masters' designs by sustaining alternative visions of themselves and the quest for freedom. We still haven't managed to grasp that this might be true for homosexuals as well.

I want in this short essay to challenge the assumption that all pre-Stonewall gay men lived in shame and to argue instead, along with the diarist, that the truly remarkable thing about 1950s queers was their refusal to play the role assigned them by the hostility of their own time and the condescension of history. Although the brevity of this essay makes it impossible to demonstrate my counterclaim here, I will draw on some of the research for my forthcoming book on postwar gay male culture to outline an alternative account of the 1950s. My purpose in doing so is to indicate my reservations about some of the ways we are beginning to theorize and deploy the concept of gay shame.

The Michigan conference on gay shame was an exemplary event. By simply posing a problem and inviting activists and scholars from a variety of disciplines to comment on it, the organizers encouraged participants to think through that problem collectively and creatively in ways conferences rarely allow. Two days of lively discussion persuaded me that the problem of shame can provoke new questions and insights into subjectivity, identity, ethics, and politics, and that shame might serve for a while as a problem that is good to think with. I remain unpersuaded, though, that shame can bear the burden of becoming a master term of queer theory, for its interpretive and explanatory powers remain limited, and its imprecision risks obscuring as much as it illuminates.

Just what do we mean by shame? Surely it is crucial at the outset to acknowledge that shame is no more natural or universal than race, sexuality, or any of the other phenomena we've spent the last generation denaturalizing, historicizing, and contextualizing. But at the conference we tended to invoke shame as if it were a natural and universal state: we all experience shame; we were all shamed as children; we are all ashamed of our bodies, our sexual desires, our sexual practices. Probably most of us can consent to at least some of those generalizations. But all of them? And all of us, whoever "we" are? And in the same way? Are sexual shame, racial shame, national shame, and bodily shame the same thing? Shame about failure to be a proper man, or woman, or normative sexual subject?

To the extent that we can talk about shame as a unitary phenomenon at all, surely we need to attend to its historicity and cultural specificity in any particular context and to recall that its production has always been uneven and its modalities varied. In my own research, I've found, not surprisingly, that sexual practices, shaming rituals, and objects of shame were organized differently in the racially segregated, class-stratified, and gender-differentiated black, white, and Latino neighborhoods of postwar New York, and they changed over time. Any theory of shame that fails to acknowledge these differences—by decontextualizing and universalizing the subject as most psychoanalytic theories do, for instance—is unlikely to help us understand the complex processes of social differentiation or historical change.

As Norbert Elias pointed out long ago, shame has a history, and it takes a lot of work to produce. Producing shame in the master class, let alone the lower classes and colonial subjects—shame about the body, its functions, and its difference from the colonizer's; shame about one's culture and one's place in a translocal social hierarchy—was a critical, but difficult and never entirely successful, part of the civilizing (and colonizing) project. Producing shame in homosexual subjects was just as critical, and just as vexed, an operation of power. Our usage of the term "shame" (which can be both a verb and a noun) tends to elide critical differences between the operations of power and the effects of those operations, between efforts to shame others and their success in producing a state of shame. If all queers of the past were condemned to live in shame, does that mean they were all, in fact, ashamed? Not all shaming operations succeed.

Let's go back to Times Square in 1954. More than half a century later, it is hard to comprehend the magnitude and pervasiveness of the shaming rituals to which queers were subjected then. Like most gay men and lesbians, the Times Square diarist regularly saw himself portrayed as a vicious degenerate in the press and heard himself denounced as a sinner from the pulpit. As a youth he was sent to a psychiatrist by his parents, and as a young man he was forced out of the ministry when his seminary learned he was homosexual. Years later he was forced out of his second career as a social worker for the same reason. His training and experiences meant that he was acutely aware of the problem of shame, and he thought deeply about the operations of shame in himself and the men he knew. It would be presumptuous of us to dismiss too easily his conclusion that although "society does its best to cause us fear and humiliation . . . mostly, in this great city, it fails." But what could that mean?

There's no doubt that pre-Stonewall gay culture was affected by the problem of shame. We can see its effects in the simple fact that it was widely pondered and discussed, in the way some men tried to cope with their shame by claiming their cultural superiority over heterosexuals, and in the way shame intensified the sharp divisions of race, class, gender, and sexual style that bitterly divided gay men. (This is nowhere clearer than in the fury some gender-normative queer men felt toward the effeminate queens, drag queens, and other gender-transgressive men who they thought brought shame to all homosexuals by so publicly renouncing their masculinity— and thus confirming the heterosexual charge and queer suspicion that all queer men were failed men.) But neither should we deny that post-Stonewall gay culture is affected by the problem of shame. How else could we explain how the determined profession of "Gay Pride" became its central slogan, even though those professing pride often deny it themselves?

My first point is simply that then, as now, there were variations in men's susceptibility and responses to shame, and no monochromatic portrait of their generation's relationship to shame will do them justice. Like the diarist, most gay men knew full well they were supposed to feel ashamed of their homosexuality, and they all knew men who were. Although they were not preoccupied with the problem of shame, they acknowledged, discussed, and reflected on it, often in ways that were more complex and subtle than those developed by the pride generation. Many men developed ideological resources to counteract the dominant culture's insistence that they should be ashamed, some of them tried to help troubled men overcome their shame, and most of them commented on men who had succumbed to shame. After meeting several men whose sexual repertoire was constrained by their shame, a gay serviceman from Ohio was pleased to write a friend in 1942 that the interesting man he had met the night before "has no feeling of shame about his or our indulgence of a natural desire." (The argument that homosexual desires were "natural" or "God-given" circulated widely among gay men in the early twentieth century, one example of the ways they used the logic of the dominant discourse against that discourse. This tactic infuriated those who wished to condemn them to shame. In 1917, to take just one example, an incensed medical man reported to his colleagues that a man whom he regarded as a "loquacious, foul-mouthed and foul-minded 'fairy'" was "lost to every sense of shame; believing himself designed by nature to play the very part he is playing in life.") Another serviceman stationed in San Diego wrote his friends in 1944 that he had decided not to pursue an attractive young minister he had just met because "the clergy are pretty sure to have strong blocks and conflicts about homosexuality somewhere along the line, and I didn't want to go to bed with the kid and then be in for an agonizing morning of remorse." He knew all too well the power shame had over some men. But he also knew there were other, less tortured souls to pursue—men who, like the writer and his friends, took more unreserved pleasure in their sexual experiences.

Indeed, the correspondence and diaries produced by gay men in the mid-twentieth century, supposedly the heyday of homosexual abjection, often contain astonishingly detailed, exuberant, uninhibited, and unashamed accounts of their sexual experiences of a kind that it is hard to imagine many of their heterosexual contemporaries committing to paper. Even W. H. Auden praised Constantine Cavafy's unashamed celebration of his homosexual experiences in his 1961 introduction to a collection of the Greek poet's work. "He refuses to pretend that his memories of moments of sensual pleasure are unhappy or spoiled by feelings of guilt," Auden wrote, using the occasion to argue that "nobody, whatever his moral convictions, can honestly regret a moment of physical pleasure as such."

Many more gay men participated in a vast sexual underground of cruising areas and public sex venues in urban streets, parks, subway cars, and tearooms, not to mention the standing-room section of New York's Metropolitan Opera and well-known men's rooms in department stores and university buildings across the country. The post-Stonewall generation has usually proclaimed that all the men who participated in this underground must have been heterosexuals or tortured, shame-filled homosexuals who crawled there and back. Some of them were and others of them did (some of them reveling in being so close to the mud). But many gay-identified men participated in this public sex scene, and rather than treating it like a shameful secret, they talked with their friends and lovers about it, wrote about it, and delighted in it. Tearoom sex was such a pervasive phenomenon that it became a subject of debate and moral reflection. While some gay men joined in condemning such locales as shameful, others angrily denounced or simply dismissed those who condemned them, tried to police them, or otherwise tried to shame them. Among the men who had sex in such venues even though they found them shameful, some deliberately eroticized their shamefulness in ways that enhanced their sexual pleasure by making it seem even more transgressive. Some men, in other words, were paralyzed by shame, others rejected it, others reveled in it, and still others felt it not at all. To claim that all queers in the 1950s were the passive victims of shaming rituals or were governed or even incapacitated by an overwhelming sense of shame—as we typically do—is to misunderstand and condescend to them. It won't do to assert that they all lived in shame, that they all must have been governed by shame, no matter what they did or said about themselves, for that would reduce the state of shame to a tautology and give us no purchase on its manifold manifestations and dynamics.

I hope even these brief historical notes will serve a cautionary purpose. The growing theoretical and political interest in shame represented by the Michigan conference promises to reevaluate the forms, meanings, and effects of shame in the queer culture of the 1950s as well as in our own time. But it will only illuminate more than it obscures if it refuses to reinscribe the sharp distinctions drawn between the two eras by the partisans of gay pride. Queer culture of the 1950s was more complex and diverse than the usual portrayal allows. Our own era is too. If shame is to be a productive concept, we will need carefully to specify distinctive kinds of shaming processes and their effects, and above all to distinguish the latter from the former.

[MICHAEL WARNER]

Pleasures and Dangers of Shame

One of the interpretive puzzles of Walt Whitman's "Calamus" poems—the section in *Leaves of Grass* devoted to same-sex affections—is a persistent and conspicuous thematics of shame. From one point of view there should be nothing puzzling about this at all. Sodomy was a crime of infamy, homosexuals entered history wrapped in stigma, and modern sexual culture is structured around a repressive hypothesis for which shame is a practical medium. Whether we follow the progressive narrative, according to which modern gay culture emerges from centuries of repressive shame, or believe with Foucault that the rhetoric of shame has been intensified and redistributed in modern culture, the association of the homoerotic with the rhetoric of shame and disclosure is surely among the least surprising things about "Calamus."

But recent criticism has worked hard against that expectation. It has been said that the poems very often depict the kind of fluid public affection that we see in so many photographs of late nineteenth-century male friends, rather than the secretive and stigmatized eroticism of a deviant sexual minority. Not everything that looks queer to us now, we are reminded, would have looked that way in Whitman's time. "Calamus" was first published in the 1860 edition of *Leaves of Grass*, but it did not attract very much attention or controversy until thirty years later, when John Addington Symonds wrote to inquire if it represented Greek love, occasioning Whitman's famous denial. Meanwhile, what demonstrably provoked scandal was what we would call the heterosexual section, "Children of Adam." So we should certainly approach "Calamus" with some attention to the difference between its rhetoric and that which is familiar from gay culture a century later.

Both Jerome Loving and David Reynolds, Whitman's most recent biographers, have taken up a version of a social-constructionist argument as a way of cautioning against a gay reading of Whitman in general, and "Calamus" in particular. "In the free, easy social atmosphere of pre-Civil War America," Reynolds writes, "overt displays of affection between people of the same sex were common." (This, by the way, from the same David Reynolds who argues that the young Whitman was denounced, tarred and feathered, and driven out of town for sodomy in 1841, when he was teaching school on Long Island. Reynolds even sees evidence of this in "Calamus," especially "Trickle Drops." "Never would the purging of demons cease for Whitman," he writes, somewhat melodramatically.)

For most readers, I suspect, the language of shame that is so salient in "Calamus" will be taken prima facie as a sign that something queer is going on. "No longer abash'd," the speaker announces in "In Paths Untrodden," the opening poem of the sequence,

(for in this secluded spot I can respond as I would not dare elsewhere,)
Strong upon me the life that does not exhibit itself, yet contains all the rest,
Resolved to sing no songs to-day but those of manly attachment
. . . .
I proceed for all who are or have been young men,
To tell the secret of my nights and days,
To celebrate the need of comrades.

Given such language, it is not surprising that many readers have found "Calamus" somewhat equivocal. Is there a secret or not? If the theme is just "the need of comrades," why all the hand-wringing about being abashed and secluded? Gay readers have typically read such tensions as evidence of the kind of takes-one-to-know-one double coding typical of closet formations; as Whitman put it in "Among the Multitude," a later poem in the sequence, "I meant that you should discover me so by faint indirections." The poems, in this view, speak secrets to the initiated; only the blind majority will see in them nothing more than "the need of comrades."

The address of these poems is indeed extremely hard to locate. There is a rather conventional irony, for example, in the idea that a published poem will be understood as issuing from a "secluded spot" in which the speaker can dare an admission he would not make elsewhere. One way to understand the deictic gesture of this parenthesis is through the modern conventions of lyric reading, in which lyric speech is understood as an intimate emanation, overheard in an impossible privacy. In hearing this speech, we are recruited into a knowledge environed by shame even as we are told that there is no more need for shame. The speaker, insofar as he seems to address no one in particular, is on an intimate footing with us, an intimacy that is then broken by the unabashed—and rather unlyric—project of celebrating the need of comrades.

The famously shameless persona of Whitman's poems mounts in these poems a calvary of shame. I quote from "Scented Herbage of My Breast," the second poem in the sequence:

Grow up taller sweet leaves that I may see! grow up out of my breast!
Spring away from the conceal'd heart there!
Do not fold yourself so in your pink-tinged roots timid leaves!
Do not remain down there so ashamed, herbage of my breast!
Come I am determin'd to unbare this broad breast of mine, I have long enough stifled
    and choked;
Emblematic and capricious blades I leave you, now you serve me not,
I will say what I have to say by itself,
I will sound myself and comrades only, I will never again utter a call only their call,
I will raise it with immortal reverberations through the States,
I will give an example to lovers to take permanent shape and will through the States,
Through me shall the words be said to make death exhilarating.

Here, as in so many Whitman texts, we find what has become familiar as a transgressive impulse. In this case, however, that impulse also involves great care to repudiate his own verse and its symbols—"emblematic and capricious blades" being, of course, leaves of grass. "Emblematic and capricious blades I leave you" is a paradoxical claim, to be sure, in so emblematic and capricious a leaf as this. Such rhetoric can be read as gesturing toward an impossibly free and unshamed speech that has not yet arrived, and perhaps never quite arrives ("I will say what I have to say by itself"); but it can also be read more specifically as commentary on the public persona, already a matter of some notoriety by 1860, when "Calamus" was first introduced into *Leaves of Grass*. A great many of the poems that Whitman added in 1860 have the same gesture of self-revision, notably "As I Ebb'd with the Ocean of Life," where the speaker announces that "before all my arrogant poems the real Me stands yet untouch'd, untold, altogether unreach'd." In that poem as well, you might remember, the speaker is mocked and shamed by the "real Me." But it is in "Calamus" that the speaker of "Song of Myself" is most put in question.

In the "Calamus" poems, differences from the earlier poems are striking in form as well as theme. Where the poems of the 1855 version are loud and expansive, seemingly wanting to go on forever, the "Calamus" poems are short, some of them a mere three lines. Many of them end with an image of wordless intimacy, closing as rapidly as possible into an image of lovers' touch seen from the outside. Gone is the garrulous rough who sounds his barbaric yawp. In his place is a new Whitman, "charged with untold and untellable wisdom," initiating a chosen few into his mysteries by "faint clews and indirections," terse, reticent, silent. Although the sequence begins with the claim that it will broadcast the new theme of manly love, it continues to invoke an environment of danger and stigma, as in "Here the Frailest Leaves of Me," which I quote entire:

Here the frailest leaves of me and yet my strongest lasting,
Here I shade and hide my thoughts, I myself do not expose them,
And yet they expose me more than all my other poems.

The method of these poems cannot be understood apart from the rhetoric of the unspeakable construed as excruciating shame. Do they "shade and hide" something or "expose" it?

Because the play of the poetic enunciation seems to be at stake in such questions, I trust it is not just belaboring the obvious to insist on the centrality of a rhetoric of shame in Whitman's poetics, though I rather suspect that the pose of shamelessness distracts us, as it is meant to do, from the enframing dialectic.

I also take this problem in Whitman as historically and theoretically significant to queer studies, insofar as a narrative about shame and its overcoming has come to structure the self-understanding of the modern gay movement. In the public mythology of the gay movement, the fundamental political antagonism is not so much between classes of people—heteros and homos, straights and gays, normals and queers—as between affects: shame and pride. This mythology has many unintended effects. In an earlier phase of the movement the destigmatizing project of lesbians and gays imitated that of other social movements: "gay is good" self-consciously mirrored "black is beautiful," for example. Thus the idea of gay pride connoted a clash between systems of value, a whole realignment of judgment, a collective decolonization. Somehow the same rhetoric has come to signify the opposite: the movement of homosexuals individually out of abjection into maturity and, by a homologous movement at the aggregate level (rather than by collective action), out of stigma into acceptance. Cultural conflict has come to seem beside the point. Who, after all, could be against pride? Ironically, the answer can only be: queers.

Gay pride, and much of the movement organized around it, entails a theory of shame as a thing of the personal and collective past—shame about shame, if you will. For many, this picture has come to seem not only empirically false and subjectively thin, but worse: too safe to be sexy and too dishonest to be safe. A backlash can be seen in many quarters. One hears "postgay" rhetoric; there is an activist group called "Gay Shame"; ACT UP Paris marched a couple of years ago under the banner "Proud of What?" And in gay studies, there is a renewed attention to the productive force of shame. David Halperin's book *What Do Gay Men Want?* is the most recent example of a trend that began, if not with Jouhandeau, then at least when Eve Sedgwick observed in an influential 1993 essay that "queer" differed from the rhetoric of gay pride mainly in its naked refusal to repudiate shame.

The dialectical movement over the past few decades has undoubtedly been complex, and it would be a mistake to see the new conditions as a return of queer shame, just as it was a mistake to think of the movement as fundamentally an assertion of gay pride; the historic antagonism of queer struggles has to do with the whole range of the conditions of heteronormativity, of which the affect pairing of shame and pride is a somewhat tendentious metonym. In *The Trouble with Normal* I tried to outline some of the changing conditions in movement politics that lie behind the depoliticizing rhetoric of pride, acceptance, and inclusion. These include material conditions, such as the massive influx of capital into gay organizations and media that began with the 1992 election, and the way it intensified and distorted the stigmaphile/stigmaphobe dynamics of the social movement form. (Briefly: the stigmaphile world is where we find a commonality with those who suffer from stigma and in this alternative space learn to value the very things the rest of the world despises; the stigmaphobe world is the dominant culture, where conformity is ensured through fear of stigma. Political groups that mediate between queers and normals are internally structured by this tension, and because power lies almost exclusively on the normal side, any centralization of money and organization will favor those who resolve their own ambivalence in the stigmaphobe direction.) So I mean to be cautious; there is an inevitable tendency to allegorize when speaking of shame and pride in this context.

And yet the shame/pride affect pairing appears so frequently, and with such powerful effects, and with so many mutations over the past century or two, that we cannot help but wonder why. Many other social movements have agendas of destigmatization, including feminism and anticolonialism. Why did the queer movement come to be defined centrally by the opposition of shame and pride when these other political contexts did not?

Some obvious answers spring to mind. First, the antagonism of the heterosexual–homosexual relationship emerged out of what was primarily a set of moral injunctions and gender norms, only occasionally elaborated as a social taxonomy. To this day, the sense that sexual orientations identify different classes of persons remains confused by the sense that some of those persons should not exist. The behavior constitutes the class, as the U.S. Supreme Court put it. Shame and guilt therefore continue to resonate in queer politics in a way that has only inexact analogues in most other political formations. Insofar as the behavior (or the desire) constitutes the class, it will remain difficult to specify the constituency in any way that forecloses shame altogether. And because the stigma of a dominated group and the shame of proscribed behavior are overdetermined by the shame attending sexuality in general, it is easy to see that we are dealing with a potent mix. The rhetoric of gay pride plays on each of these levels, and more.

The same line of reflection soon discloses that "shame" is a fairly reductive analytic category. There is a tendency to treat shame as a constant, even in analyses that focus on the different role of shame in different cultures. In the anthropological literature, for example, so much has been said about honor and shame as a defining element of Mediterranean cultures that this is often advanced as a warrant for seeing the Mediterranean in area-studies terms, as a single formation. There is also a familiar if somewhat dubious distinction between shame cultures and guilt cultures, the source of shame being externalized in the former, internalized in the latter. (In a shame culture, the thought goes, people worry about their status in the eyes of others; in a guilt culture, they worry about their status when no one is looking.) A monotheistic god obviously plays a large role in distinguishing one from the other. In these traditions of argument, shame has different roles to play in the organization of different cultures, but the experience of shame is thought to be familiar and explanatory. Shame comes to seem a universal affect—more central to the mechanisms of social control in some cases than in others, sometimes externalized and sometimes internalized, but experientially the same whenever we see it.

Queer studies has been groping toward an alternative suggestion: that there is something distinctive about the queer experience of shame. Is there at least a special way of transmuting shame that the word "queer" connotes? To understand this intuition we will need to discriminate much more finely among the possible contexts and mediations of shame. Obviously, given the way I began with Whitman, I think there is something to this intuition. But I also think that to explore it requires skepticism about universal accounts of the mechanisms of shame, whether psychoanalytic or ego-psychological. It might in fact be difficult to develop much in the way of a general theory of shame.

As with sex and sexuality, shame involves a complex relationship between rhetoric and physiological reactions; those for whom the latter seem decisive tend to think that it is extracultural.[1] Some corporeal dimensions of affect—blushing, lowering of the head and eyes, a flooding sensation—are so common and widespread as to seem to warrant the sense that shame is a universal human constant. Sylvan Tomkins, for one, argues strongly for the place of shame as an elemental apparatus, hardwired into the human. "Shyness, shame, and guilt," he says, "are one and the same affect." "Shame," he writes elsewhere, "is the affect of indignity, of defeat, of transgression, and of alienation."[2]

A suggestive list, to be sure. The clustering of these different meanings suggests why the affect can be so complexly resonant in queer culture. Yet the heterogeneous meanings of the affect also suggest that we are no closer to understanding how it could be special to queer culture if it underlies so many social phenomena.

There are some suggestive themes in Tomkins's psychology of the self, many of which have been taken up by Eve Sedgwick, Douglas Crimp, and others. Shame is seen by them as foundational to the sense of self, but in a paradoxical way, for it is both individuating and obliterating. It is an essentially social affect—occasioned by the regard of another even if the other is internalized—yet it is fundamentally an experience of the separateness of the self, a broken exchange. It is essentially ambivalent: "In shame I wish to continue to look and to be looked at, but I also do not wish to do so." It summons elemental, infantile affect, but no one social relationship accounts for it, even the caregiver–child relationship. In fact the appearance of strangers seems to be a crucial trigger: "As soon as the infant learns to differentiate the face of the mother from the face of a stranger (approximately seven months of age), he is vulnerable to the shame response."[3]

For reasons I will bring up shortly, I do not believe that this psychological tradition can be a sure guide to the politics of shame, but I do not mean to dismiss this train of reflection out of hand. I find much of it suggestive. Take for example the notion that shame is an affect of defeated reciprocity. This very general pattern has a specifically sexual manifestation that can be overdetermined by the shame of the sexual body. As Tomkins puts it in his disarming way, "If I wish to suck or bite your body and you are reluctant, I can become ashamed."[4] This kind of shame is what I believe is called normal experience. But a related form of nonreciprocity-shame must be in-

trinsic to the idea of counternormative desire—not just because such desire is statistically less likely to be returned (an odd thought, supposing one
could imagine a random distribution of desired objects), nor because it is
expected to be unreturned, nor even because I expect that the object of my
desire ought to be reluctant, but because the entire possibility of a willing
partner has no place in the imagery and institutions of social belonging.
The reproduction of the world is indifferent to such desire; my wish to suck
or bite your body is waste, with no place in the motivating structures of reciprocity. In this way some experience of shame might be immanent to counternormative desire, and not just to derivative discourse about such desire.

Shame is a kind of social knowledge, even if only in the infant's discovery of strangers, and the social contextualization of shame is therefore not
extrinsic to the affect. But it is infinitely complex, perhaps especially in the
Anglophone North Atlantic cultures, where shame encompasses in some
sense guilt, degradation, abasement abashedness, bashfulness, shyness,
embarrassment, self-consciousness, modesty, dishonor, disgrace, humiliation, mortification, low self-esteem, indignity, ignobility, abjection, and
stigma. It's like having thirty-two words for snow: the fine discriminations
of the vernacular suggest something like a fascination. Modern culture has
created new forms of shame as well as new remediations of shame.

In understanding this we are obviously handicapped by any theory that
treats shame principally as an elemental affect, with a "logic" and a physi-
ology. Let me just be tedious for a moment by naming a few of the contexts
that make shame especially resonant for Whitman, Jean Genet, and contemporary queer culture—not to systematize a new theory of shame, but to
remind us how little we understand simply by calling it shame.

Gender. The scandal of masculine shame is such that we call it feminizing.
Drag queens, sissies, and bottoms are virtuosi of shame, in ways that are almost infinitely variable but have in common the background expectation of
masculinity as immunity to shame.

Sexual objectification. Shame is an experience of exposure, in which I become
suddenly an object through the eyes of another; it thus resonates powerfully
in situations of erotic objectification, visuality, and display. This of course
also has gendered meanings, and a special resonance in liberal culture,
which takes objectification to be an unethical indignity upon the human.

Privatization of affect. When we read that sixteenth-century Frenchmen were
in the habit of administering slaps and verbal abuse to the corpses of con-

demned men, we are reminded that practices of public shaming have not always been understood in terms of an affect that is thought to be actually experienced. Modern forms of discipline rely less on the kinds of public degradation that once were such a spectacular armature of shaming; the stocks have been dismantled. Indeed, modern liberal culture defines itself as more moral than other cultures partly because it avoids public rituals of shaming and abjection. The dignity of the human is asserted by screening criminals from public display. Thus we accustom ourselves to the expectation that shame is a problem, that it never has a normative application.

The visibility or invisibility of the racial body as another form of involuntary corporeal exposure through the eyes of the Other. This is in evidence in section 7 of "I Sing the Body Electric," where the speaker dramatizes the indignity of slavery by recoding the exposure of the slave's body as celebration—but where the exposure as "black" of the slave's body and the invisibility of the auctioneer's voice are part of the taken-for-granted frame for the performance.

Erotic idealization. The play of fantasy renders any physical actuality an occasion of unwonted and shameful visibility: fatness, thinness, freckles, baldness, hairiness, asslessness, whatever. In the environment of erotic idealization that is heightened by mass culture, any aspect of the body can be registered as actuality, and shame measures the gap.

Class shame, whether of bourgeois modesty and propriety, or the attendant indignity of working or outlying classes.

Normalization and deviant shame. In modern culture the statistical and demographic imagination has created a new variety of shame. Norms of health and physicality are no longer understood to stem from divine plan, or Platonic ideas, or an ordering of the world established in the time of myth. They are understood to be revealed in their lawfulness by standard distribution; the norms and averages of population disclose the natural laws, teleology, and healthy state of my own body. So I experience shame in the degree of my deviance from this imagined but essentially distributional norm. Queerness can be understood as the constitutive antithesis of the modern demographic imaginary, and therefore in a sense as its unanticipated by-product.

Provincialism. The shame of the rube, the bumpkin in the metropolis, the culture that discovers itself as belated and parochial from the cosmopolitan vantage. In Whitman's time this was the self-understanding of America in relation to Europe, and among the transmutations of shame he performed most effectively was the invention of shameless provincialism as the rhetoric of American nationalism. Writing apparently artless verse, sounding a barbaric yawp, was part of that transmuting performance.

The liberal language of dignity and its shame theory. We take it for granted that we should not be ashamed. The veil, as an objectification of shamefulness designed to introject modesty, scandalizes this sensibility.

Christian redemption. The narrative movement from shame to pride or dignity has a normative force for modern culture that stems in part from the resources of redemptive culture more generally. The queer embrace of shame thus has to combat—or adapt—the expectation of redemptive narrative.

The revaluing of the passions. During the long eighteenth century, pride and shame were systematically revalued, with the other passions. Pride was rehabilitated, moving from its place at the fount of all sins to a cardinal virtue, while shame was severed from its tight relationship to ethical virtue and the divine perspective.

Authenticity and expressivism. Involuntary corporeal affect acquires a new kind of value when it is recoded as evidence of authentic experience and therefore as a resource for expressivity. The flushed body of shame and the aroused body of sexuality have this in common, and Whitman's performances of shame are often the same passages in which he does so much to invent the modern vision of sexuality as an expressive capacity.

Secular confession. The literature of temperance and addiction has transformed the role of shame in confessional form, from something performed by confession to something overcome through confession.

Pariah parallelism. Insofar as dignity is understood not as a limited resource like honor but as intrinsic to the human, it becomes possible to see an essential homology among the outcasts of shame. Both Whitman and Genet were capable of carrying this into a kind of prophetic politics.

Circulatory norms of discourse. The norms of modernity, and especially the public sphere, include the metadiscursive norms of explicitation and extensive access. Secrecy and explicitation, intimacy and publicity, are very often overdetermined as shame and pride (as in "The Frailest Leaves"), so that the normative movement from shame to pride is also a rule for the production of discourse. This makes for some very strange and interesting effects in counterpublics, which constitute themselves by circulation among strangers, but also by setting bars to total accessibility and explicitation.

Translation. Shame is very often a recontextualization effect; something that plays invisibly in one context feels shameful when exposed to a more encompassing or powerful view. And the feeling of shame as separation is a discovery of the divided social field. The impulse of mass culture toward the suture of the social field—a mainstream—means that an embrace of shame feels socially perverse. This also is in play for counterpublics.

These last points help us to reevaluate a theme in the general self-psychological account of shame that might bear more particularly on queer life. The shame of the Other can have a peculiar shaming effect, not only because it directly inhibits mutual enjoyment, but also because it poses "an identification threat." The shame of the Other, insofar as I am interested in the Other, produces in me some shame as an affect of defeated interest, but also as an affect of self-repudiation. This opens onto a problem interestingly taken up in Crimp's essay on Warhol (this volume). Following Tomkins and Sedgwick, Crimp observes that there is no community in shame. It is an isolating, obliterating affect. In shame my exposure has witnesses (even if imaginary or internalized), but being witnessed separates me, abjects me. And the shame of the Other, as Crimp puts it, might flood me with a shame that I imagine to be analogous, but insofar as I am likely to be ashamed of my shame I repudiate my very identification with the shamed Other. Shame is a poor footing for sympathy. For Crimp, in fact, this is the basis of what he calls an ethical response in shame: a recognition of insuperable Otherness. Facing the shame of the Other, I understand the shame but am at the same time prevented from assimilating it to my own shame. And that's good.

As I have already indicated, I have misgivings about this argument and its construal of ethical virtue. At the very least, it seems to me to dodge, by the very generality of its phenomenological account of shame, a reckoning of what is queer about queer shame; shame is taken as a constant. And the current vogue for a theory of the ethical as deriving from the Otherness of the Other seems to me to be blind to the most interesting questions about ethical projects that Foucault and others have laid out. But I think Crimp is right to identify a problem in the collectivization of shame, at least as shame functions in contemporary North Atlantic culture. Persons shamed by the nature of their desires, in what they take to be their innermost privacy, are not drawn into commonality by the witnessing of each other's shame; quite the contrary. (There is an analogue to this insight in Goffman's analysis of stigma: "I'm not that," the stigmatized person says of her image.)[5] Perhaps the problem here lies in the reflexive layering of shame, the possibility of my not being ashamed of the shame that the shame of the Other provokes in me, a possibility that is very far removed from the idea of pride for either of us.

We might notice, in this connection, that queer preoccupations with shame tend not to be simply about intrasubjective registrations of shaming or its internalization as guilt. There is a distinct pattern or tradition of queer ethical practice in regard to the shame of the Other, an effort of imagination at a commonality not predicated on the erasure of shame. Remember, for example, that Genet's spit-and-roses fantasy is provoked by the sight of schoolboys spitting in another boy's mouth, not his own.[6] For all the transfixing isolation of shame in Genet's own experience, it is the witnessing of the transitive shaming of another that provokes his fantasy of transmutation. (Sartre, in *Saint Genet*, emphasizes that in such ways Genet differs quite sharply from Jouhandeau; he attributes the difference to Jouhandeau's Catholicism and Genet's secularization of abjection.)[7]

Indeed, in this light we might return briefly to the peculiar use of lyric convention in "Calamus":

Here I shade and hide my thoughts, I myself do not expose them,
And yet they expose me more than all my other poems.

"Here," on one reading, is the magnificently capacious and ambiguated deixis of lyric speech. Here we are, mysteriously present at the scene of enunciation, which is the scene both of the speaker's speaking and of our reading (but not of any possible relationship of alterity or address between the two). Here I shade and hide my thoughts. Well, am I here or not? Is this "my thought," or is the speaker's thought something shaded and hidden from me? Do I see him exposed? To imagine him as exposed "here," I must stand back, objectifying the utterance as exposing him to me, rupturing the miraculous immediacy of lyric speech (thus suggesting a less conventional reading in which "here" might really be there on the page, in the form of the book circulated among strangers in real situations of address). I am both inside and outside the scene of speech, both drawn into identification with the speaker (these are, after all, "my thoughts") and forced to recoil from that identification in order to make literal sense of what he says. And this oscillating movement makes real to me a sense both of shame and of a perversely defeated relationality that is one of the preoccupations of the series as a whole: "Are you the new person drawn toward me?" and so on.

This pattern can, I think, be shown to be fundamental to the distinctive cluster of the Calamus poems. But it leads to some more general recognitions about Whitman; to be attuned to this question is to rethink especially the standard image of Whitman as the poster boy of shamelessness. The "Calamus" lyrics can be taken retrospectively to gloss the famous opening—"I celebrate myself"—as an attempted overcoming of shame. That the perfect circle of happy subjectivity in that line continues to be interesting at all probably has to do with its paradoxes. How is it that "myself" stands in such need of celebrating? And where am I when I do this celebrating? The assumed need for the enunciation of the phrase, the implication in other words that it does not go without saying, makes us wonder whether it can ever felicitously perform—or, by the same token, fail to perform—the celebratory ritual it undertakes. The energy of this "I" contrasts suspiciously with myself, left alone in its mute, inglorious inexplicitness before I began making the noise of celebration. The opening can be taken to frame the work as a whole—all that follows being a specification of the self I purport to celebrate, and an ever-expanding test of my ability to celebrate it. The implied need for the remediation of shame is a metapragmatic gloss on the poetic enunciation itself.

More concretely, Whitman's rhetoric of dignity very often entails quite pointed performances of shamed subjectivity, from the masturbatory raving of section 28 in "Song of Myself" to the "O hot-cheeked and blushing" passage or the slave auction scene in "I Sing the Body Electric" to the confessional section 6 of "Crossing Brooklyn Ferry." When these are kept in mind, "Calamus" seems less eccentric, distinct mainly for the explicitness by which it codes itself as speech in a dialectic of shame and dignification of which the closure remains elusive. In describing the procession of the Carolines in Genet, Didier Eribon remarks that they are an incarnation of the poetic gesture, or, more precisely, an allegory of poetry; we could say the same about these displays of shame in Whitman.[8]

Queer culture has practiced in countless ways the complexities not just of shame but of performances of shame, of formally mediated imitations of shame that objectify counternormative experience, of squirm-making disturbances in the social field that bring counterpublics into a kind of public co-presence while also deploying shame to mark a difference from the public. Staging shame as disruptions of relationality, we paradoxically create new relationships insofar as we can school ourselves not to be ashamed of our shame—a project that of course disappears the second we persuade ourselves that not being ashamed of our shame requires us to be proud.

Notes

1. Many recent studies of the emotions insist, however, that the difference between what is physiologically "hardwired" and what is culturally variable is neither sharp nor exclusive. For a good discussion of this point see Jesse Prinz, *Gut Reactions: A Perceptual Theory of Emotions* (New York: Oxford University Press, 2004).

2. Sylvan Tomkins, *Shame and Its Sisters*, ed. Eve Kosofsky Sedgwick and Adam Frank (Durham, NC: Duke University Press, 1995), 133, 103.

3. Ibid., 140.

4. Ibid., 152.

5. Erving Goffman, *Stigma: Notes on the Management of Spoiled Identity* (Englewood Cliffs, NJ: Prentice-Hall, 1963), passim.

6. The scene, from Genet's *Miracle of the Rose* (trans. Bernard Frechtman [London: A. Blond, 1965]), is perhaps more familiar from the 1991 Todd Haynes film *Poison*.

7. Jean-Paul Sartre, *Saint Genet: Actor and Martyr*, trans. Bernard Frechtman (New York: George Braziller, 1963).

8. Didier Eribon, *Une morale du minoritaire: Variations sur un thème de Jean Genet* (Paris: Fayard, 2001), especially 9–11.

[JULIE HERRADA AND TIM RETZLOFF]

Shamefully Gay

DOCUMENTS FROM THE LABADIE COLLECTION

North Lobby, Harlan Hatcher Graduate Library, March 20–April 30, 2003; sponsored by the Lavender Information and Library Association in conjunction with the international Gay Shame Conference, University of Michigan

These selected materials from the Labadie Collection document a number of peoples, behaviors, and beliefs that commonly fall outside the strictures of contemporary gay pride.

Such artifacts reflect individual expression and real lives lived, however unpopular or unsavory. Those who do not conform to traditional gender conceptions of female and male, in particular, are and have been among the most ostracized persons in American society. Transgendered people, along with queer punks, sadomasochists, man-haters, radical faeries, and diseased pariahs all challenge the narrowing of viewpoints, the confining parameters of an increasingly corporatized gay culture.

The rubric of gay shame, in challenging such heteronormative values as monogamy, marriage, safe sex, and civil rights laws that promote simple inclusion, confronts the agenda of political and social acquiescence of such mainstream gay institutions as the Human Rights Campaign, the Gay and Lesbian Alliance against Defamation, the *Advocate*, and lesbian and gay studies.

When leaders, followers, and allies, in fear of jeopardizing presupposed goals of greater acceptance, marginalize individuals and groups within gay, lesbian, bisexual, transgender, queer communities, they raise crucial questions about identity and power: How do societies police transgression? How are marginalized people represented? How do perceptions of taboo change over time? In what ways are human behaviors politicized? What is the age of consent? What is consent? What is gender? Who decides?

We hope that showcasing these materials in conjunction with the international Gay Shame Conference will spur further reflection and perhaps even action.

Since 1911, when the Detroit anarchist Joseph Labadie donated his extensive archive to the University of Michigan, the Labadie Collection has been world renowned as a repository of radical materials from the Left and the Right. For the past century, sexual freedom has been an important theme documented by the rare resources preserved here.

Based on the materials amassed in the Labadie Collection, in 2001 the directors of the national organization Gender Education and Advocacy chose the University of Michigan Library from a pool of twelve competing institutions to house the National Transgender Library and Archive. The NTLA repository is believed to be the largest catalogued collection of transgender-related material in the world.

The materials referred to in this text can be found on the DVD included with this volume.

COMMUNITIES
OF SHAME

[BARRY D. ADAM]

How Might We Create a Collectivity That We Would Want to Belong To?

If gay shame is the necessary critique of gay pride, then where did gay pride go wrong? Pride celebrations, as the most publicly visible manifestation of lesbian, gay, bisexual, and transgendered people, have come to occupy a major part of the public imagery associated with LGBT communities, both for the communities themselves and for the public at large. Not surprisingly, not everyone likes what they see.

So what is wrong with pride? Pride's roots are in the commemoration of major activist events. New York's Pride, of course, still celebrates the Stonewall rebellion, and many others at least implicitly share this reference by being scheduled for the last week of June. Pride celebrations in Germany, for example, often go by the acronym CSD, for Christopher Street Days, an explicit reference to their New York roots. Pride events in their early years intended to communicate to the world around them that LGBT people were here to stay and still had many grievances to be resolved on the way to achieving full citizenship rights. Pride was also very much about coming out: it was a declaration that LGBT people were not going to hide any more, were not going to act straight any more, and were going to stake out a place for themselves.

Over the ensuing three and a half decades, pride, like the new social movements around it, gradually lost much of its political fury. In its place were left more purely celebratory aspects, often in the form of mass parties, until, by the turn of the twenty-first century, pride was rushing headlong down a trajectory taken by many popular cultural forms before it: professionalization, commercialization, bourgeoisification. In other words, LGBT people became the niche market of the decade, corporations became major sponsors of pride events, and events that had once been community mobilizations and protest actions turned into yet another sales event.

Pride, then, was just one symptom of a larger transformation of LGBT cultures, where active citizens were being converted into avid consumers and where the struggle for freedom and equality was somehow being reorganized into yet another occasion to define oneself though commodities. Pride was turning into entertainment, available to those ready to pay the price of admission. As Marie-Jo Bonnet remarks of Paris Pride, "Homosexual pride has been turned into a carnival in the service of sexual consumerism which values . . . one thing alone: the virile image exhibited by young, well-fed, tanned gay men, their heads shaved like soldiers, their muscles bulging, flaunting their genitals as if to reassure society as to their sexual identity by giving it proof of their masculinity."[1]

The invasion of pride by the marketplace advanced a process already well developed in other spheres of LGBT cultures where the gay liberation press had been displaced by fashion-and-glitz reviews such as *Out* magazine, community dances had given way to circuit parties, and protests had disappeared in favor of beer tents. And with the market inevitably comes the reassertion of the power of money, the consolidation of class hierarchy, and abandonment of the dispossessed. It also means the exacerbation of old divisions between those who seek equality through respectability and those who seek inclusiveness, the former tending to want to present the heterosexual public with a vision of LGBT people as simply a variant of the white middle class, the latter wanting to embrace the diversity of LGBT people, namely older people, poor people, nonwhite people, dykes on bikes, leathermen, drag queens, boy lovers, and so on, the sort of people whose appearance at Pride events occasions letters to the editor decrying perversion flaunted in the streets.

The commercialization of pride has not simply been a colonization of LGBT communities by outsiders but has come about as well because of internal developments. As pride celebrations have grown into some of the largest urban events of the year in such cities as San Francisco, Toronto, and Sydney, their reliance on volunteer labor and fund-raising has stretched to the breaking point. Corporate sponsorship has come about at a time when several major pride organizations have imploded through volunteer exhaustion and financial bankruptcy.

It is in this context that a keen sense of disillusionment and a fresh critique began in 2000 and 2001 to take the form of "gay shame" in San Francisco, New York, and a few other centers. The immediate context of the gay-shame critique of pride was a simmering turf war occurring on the very high-priced real estate market of San Francisco, fueled by the Silicon Valley boom of the late 1990s and resulting in a new wave of gentrification with the influx of a new moneyed class. With LGBT people on both sides of a widening class divide, the debate over the siting of a shelter for homeless youth in the Castro neighborhood pitted gay property owners and developers against those with few resources who had come to San Francisco in search of a gay-friendly community. San Francisco, which for decades had functioned as a beacon of freedom and site of refuge for LGBT Americans victimized or abandoned in other parts of the country, now had its own gay establishment, which, in the spirit of civic philanthropy, was seeking to raise capital to build some of its own institutions of permanence. Gay shame in San Francisco, then, sought to expose these contradictions and challenge the powers that be for having forgotten so many members of the community in whose name they so often spoke. As Matt Bernstein Sycamore told the Gay Shame conference in Ann Arbor, the gay shamers enlivened the traditionally leaden approach of the usual Left critique with a touch of queer genius by adding a fashion runway of the gay shameful to its counterpride event and bestowing "awards" upon a leading real estate developer and on Mary Cheney for "helping the right wing cope." In that, gay shame recovers, perhaps unwittingly, the lengthy history of the gay Left, from Harry Hay's Mattachine manifesto to Carl Wittman's gay-liberation tract "Refugees from Amerika" to Queer Nation. Although the term "gay shame" signals a readily understandable inversion of "gay pride," it is scarcely about embracing (or regressing to?) shame; it is, rather, an anticapitalist critique that resonates with many similar critiques before it. Perhaps most disconcerting about gay shame is not the novelty of its approach, but the apparent need in American political culture to reinvent the Left with each generation, ostensibly out of nothing, its architects having forgotten a venerable tradition of earlier leftist initiatives.

Despite this critique, it is still important to note that commercialization is just one trend, if a very powerful one, in the evolution of pride. Despite an increasingly strong presence of corporate actors in San Francisco pride, there remain a great many genuine community groups that are actively engaged in pride events. When I attended San Francisco Pride in 2000, the vigorous reassertion of one of the original messages of pride—that "I will not allow you to make me feel ashamed"—was embodied especially strongly in a contingent of breast cancer survivors who marched topless down Market Street. The Sydney Gay and Lesbian Mardi Gras, perhaps the largest event of its kind in the world, retained into the 1990s community ownership and a rich display of Australia's regional, ethnic, gender, and political constituencies without the corporate sector taking up a dominant presence—but then, Sydney has also struggled in more recent years with bankruptcy and reorganization. There are also many other pride celebrations, in the United States and elsewhere, that have yet to show the traits that have attracted the critical scrutiny of gay shame. In Detroit, for example, the Hotter than July celebration of African American LGBT pride remains a large grassroots event (though not averse to funders), as do many pride celebrations in smaller cities.[2]

Unraveling Pride

So if pride led us to a politics of respectability, do we unravel it "back" to gay shame in order to recover more innocent times? If LGB (but perhaps not yet transgendered) identities have become too bourgeois, too white, and too sold out, can they be stripped away? And if so, what lies underneath? Is shame that which underlies proud LGB identities and all that goes with them?

Despite the apparent attractiveness of shame as an antidote to the pretense and commercialism of pride, the pursuit of shame as an alternative to pride has pitfalls of its own. It slides toward postulating a new universal subject, as if shame were the fundamental experience of all LGBT people. As Judith Halberstam pointed out at the Gay Shame conference in Ann Arbor, the experience of butch lesbians growing up is scarcely the same as that of unmasculine boys, and indeed shame may not be at all a significant part of their experience, nor even of all gay men. If history is the path to be followed in tracing pride back to pre-pride, it may actually reveal, as George Chauncey and Esther Newton noted at the same conference, no lack of examples from earlier in the century of LGBT people who had definitively rejected shame. How central is shame, then, to either the ontogenesis or phylogenesis of LGBT peoples?

Shame, after all, is an effect induced externally by a powerful other. Although few LGBT people escape some degree of humiliation or degradation aimed in their direction, whether by family, school, work, the street, sport, religion, and so on, the degree to which would-be humiliators succeed in inducing shame is highly variable. Referring to another subordinated people in another era, Jean-Paul Sartre remarked, the Jew "has learned that modesty, silence, patience are proper to misfortune, because misfortune is already a sin in the eyes of men."[3] Shame is not an originary experience; it is an attitude demanded of the inferiorized.

Guilt, the persistent and interiorized version of shame, "is the crampedness of the powerless subject in dialectical relation with the powerful object. It is the symptom of the aborted project and frustrated intention."[4] Pride, then, is a name for that necessary and important remedy to oppression, of resisting the shamers' attempt to disempower and asserting one's right to be. It is a social dynamic that has found widespread resonance well beyond its origins. Now that the gay and lesbian cultural revolution has come so far that it has entered into the public imaginary, all sorts of people, entirely unconscious of the gay roots of the metaphor, are coming out of thousands of closets. As Mark Simpson noted at the Gay Shame conference, coming out from private shame to public self-affirmation has now been rendered almost banal as a widespread ritual and virtual article of faith of American culture, from twelve-step programs to daytime television.

The allure of the gay-shame idea, if indeed it is very attractive at all, may be its connection to a long-standing ambivalence toward having a marked identity. Hardly anyone outside the charmed circle of unmarked noncategories inhabited by those who can think of themselves as "just people" without a modifying adjective can fail to wish at times to be able to shrug off a particularized "limiting" category. Queer theory's deconstructionist efforts have always rested on this ambivalence, necessarily locating itself as lesbian or gay at the same time as it tries to challenge and dissolve "lesbian/gay" as a category. Gay shame raises again the question of the "underneath" of gay/lesbian identity. If pre-Stonewall nostalgia is a dead end, is there some other kind of "pregay" state of being that might be recaptured or reconstructed into something different from that which we have now? It is the kind of question D. A. Miller raises in *Place for Us* in his exploration of the oft-remarked "affinity" of gay men for the Broadway musical or opera,[5] even before they knew themselves to be, or anyone else thought they were, gay. Or the phenomenology of men meeting sketched by Henning Bech, referring to the diaries of historical figures unconscious of things gay but describing feelings and experiences that few contemporary gay men could fail to recognize.[6] Or why men, regardless of identity, seem able to recognize each other even across language and cultural frontiers in the vast international underground of cruising and fleeting encounters.[7]

None of these pregay subjectivities will ever acquire the status of a new universal. I, for one, am not alone in being left cold by the Broadway musical/opera complex that is undeniably an important facet of culture for many gay men, but I nevertheless recognize the subjective location Miller points to. Musical theater is one of a number of possibilities that speak to the sense of difference, desire to escape, and will to imagine alternatives that seems a widespread childhood experience of many pregay boys. Although there may be no single universal pregay experience, these works nevertheless indicate a range of core experiences with broad resonance among gay and potentially gay men that exceed the notion of "gay" as "just" a social construction or discursive effect.

We are now in a period when difference is the order of the day, and queer orthodoxy denies the search for, or assertion of, commonality now that the commonality posited by gay/lesbian identities has been exposed as never really having existed (which is why queer theory will never be able to account for why so many women and men defy the odds to affirm identity again and again.)[8] But a sense of mutual recognition, commonality, and—dare one say—identity endures despite the many fractures and assaults that try to undermine it.

In Other Worlds

So where does this leave us? One of the fundamental questions David Halperin posed to us in Ann Arbor is: how better can we produce a collectivity we might want to belong to? The gay/lesbian world, at least its best-known, commercial face, has scarcely delivered Whitman's aspiration for a community of adhesive comrades or feminist visions of sisterhood. I am struck, in interviewing gay and bisexual men in Toronto, how well one sector of men active in the commercial gay world has adapted itself to a neoliberal, marketized version of sex as a kind of fast-food consumerism.[9] While hardly a new phenomenon,[10] it is an orientation entirely consonant with current neoliberal ideologies that posit the ideal citizen as a rational, consenting, contract-making individual with no interest or concern for the well-being of community, no care for the vulnerable, and no relation to "unmasculine" realms of feeling. Yet perhaps it is a peculiarly Western article of faith to look to sexuality as a primary foundation for a better world, when sexuality is not a thing, but a potential, which requires social organization if its promise is to be realized. There is a queer (mis)reading of Foucault that thinks that deconstruction leaves freedom in its wake; it fails to remember Foucault's own assertions that new assemblages of power and knowledge generate new possibilities in sexuality as elsewhere.

On the question of alternatives, I want to offer a few reflections on Cuba, not to construct a romantic Other or to imply a utopian critique, but simply to delineate a different geography of (homo)sexual connection at once familiar and yet distinct. Cuban state socialism provides an interesting point of comparison because the Cuban state has attempted to hold off the power of corporate globalization by resisting both corporate control of the overall economy and its ideological agents in the media and advertising. This attempt is, at best, a partial success: Cuba cannot avoid engagement with global capitalism in international trade, and as the country has moved closer to the Chinese model of "market socialism," the Cuban state has constructed a sizable joint-venture sector with foreign corporations, primarily to manage the immense tourist industry. The dollarization of the Cuban economy in the 1990s gave rise to a tripartite economy: (1) a state infrastructure of health, education, housing, and basic nutrition along with a peso economy that provides a minimum standard of living, (2) a state engagement with corporate capital in the lucrative tourism sector and a dollar economy inside the country that markets imported goods, and (3) a vast informal economy. For most Cubans, with the peso economy providing so little and the dollar economy largely unaffordable, real survival and improvement of quality of life happens in the informal economy. Finally, it should be noted that despite a state monopoly over the mass media, the state's control over information flows is, at best, partial, for constant traffic in and out of the country by Cuban expatriates and foreigners, along with the dogged procapitalist stance of the U.S.-financed radio broadcaster Radio Martí, guarantee alternative information sources.

The Cuban state also embargoes the overt presence of anything gay by policing and suppressing public gatherings of gay men, incipient gay bars, or voluntary associations, and through a near blackout of gay-related information in the media. Still, the state sexuality education institute maintains an officially liberal position on the right of homosexual people to exist and be respected, and Cuba has at times voted in United Nations forums in favor of gay-related human rights issues.

So how does this very different political economy and absence of gay community, at least as understood in the north, translate into the lives of homoerotically inclined men and women? First of all, the informal economy engenders strong ties of mutual obligation, gift giving, and informal trade that extend across the island. Personal networks, grounded in kinship, and neighborhood networks are intensively cultivated, creating a robust sense of community that, in the north, lives more as nostalgia than reality for both left and right political rhetoric. These strong ties infuse sexual relations as well and are equally characteristic of personal networks formed through homosexual contact.[11] Out of these networks has grown a resilient, well-developed, well-networked, not-so-underground street culture with a strong sense of identity and commonality, an intense appetite for news about the gay world elsewhere, and a sense of connection with that world. Today there is sufficient popular interest in, and sense of commonality among, homosexual, bisexual, and transgendered people in Cuba that many thousands continually reconstruct the impromptu street venues that the police try to erase, and underground discotheques pop up guerrilla-style at unpredictable times and locations in an effort to elude police surveillance.

That "gay" and "lesbian" are well-understood terms in Cuba does not mean that homosexually interested Cubans necessarily understand themselves in terms similar to those used by North Americans, or that the expression of homosexual desire recognizes the same boundaries or contours. Like many other Latin American societies, indigenous gender-inscribed systems of sexuality (especially current among working-class and rural populations) coexist with the more egalitarian (at least in terms of sex roles) and "endogamous" forms typical of gay and lesbian models.[12] The indigenous Latin American sexual system gives large numbers of men permission to have (at least some) homosexual practice while splitting off other men for a distinctive, and often reviled, identity. (The Euro-American homo/hetero binary presses all men and women with homosexual practice toward identity while trying, without much success, to suppress it among everyone else.)[13]

In addition, it should be noted that the dollar economy has resulted in the proliferation of *jinoteros/as*, that is, women and men eager to sell sex in order to earn dollars, especially from foreigners. In this sector, the global marketplace has generated the conditions for sex tourism. (Perhaps the more interesting story here is the articulation of the two economies as *jinoteros/as* try to navigate both.)[14]

The Cuban example, then, gives some substance to queer fantasies that sexualities can be constructed in ways other than those employed by contemporary LGBT worlds in the advanced industrial countries. It also cautions against the utopian impulse implicit in the deconstructionist agenda that implies that a state of freedom or an end to hierarchy would be the result of the deconstruction of sexual categories. The Cuban political economy (perhaps as much despite as because of socialist ideology) creates conditions wherein individual advancement and self-sufficiency are hard to achieve or sustain, but personal well-being and quality of life are tied to intensely cultivated relationships with other people in networks. Whether these networks grow out of family, work, neighborhood, or heterosexual or homosexual starting points, what is valued and celebrated is the strength and extension of the social safety networks, which provide everything from food to emotional support.

The political economy of advanced industrial nations, on the other hand, tends to foster competitive individualism, personal autonomy, and privacy, creating a world where individuals are expected to provide for themselves and making extensive family and social networks less vital and human interactions more instrumental, specialized, and partial. The result in the north is a courtship model for gay men, where the single man plunges into a bar and bath scene that provides a wealth of sexual opportunities characterized by a sense of mutual personal consumption but no ongoing obligation. Out of this scene, he may extract a man with whom he can have a romantic and long-term relationship, an achievement made more despite than because of the structure of the gay scene itself. From my interviews with Toronto men, it seems the more successful players in the scene manage to become adept at both relationship modes, acquiring romantic partners with whom they may continue to engage in the scene as a supplemental pleasure.[15] Nevertheless, despite the dominance of the commercial scene, the development of LGBT communities and cultures has created (at least in large cities) multiple alternative sites where LGBT people may find and engage each other, and the anxiety about the direction of pride may spring from the desire to preserve and cultivate these alternatives. Some, however, adapt to a mode of recreational encounters with decreasing expectation of something more, or fear marginalization from the sexual marketplace with increasing age, or drop out altogether—with varying degrees of satisfaction. Many of these men, finding the gay scene inadequate in meeting their needs, express a sense of resignation or loneliness.[16]

Each of these social formations, then, offers a different range of opportunities, satisfactions, and drawbacks. Homoerotically inclined people in both cultures face legacies of homophobia and of shame induction; both have arrived at a historical era of self-assertion, if not pride, but under very different conditions and in social formations that provide different payoffs. Same-sex connections, whether labeled "gay" or not, are deeply embedded in the presumptions and expectations of the societies of which they are a part, but the emergence of LGBT communities especially in the metropoles of the global economy has created the conditions whereby their inhabitants now have greater opportunity to reflect on whether history has generated the kinds of relationships and institutions we now want to live in.

Poets and dreamers from Edward Carpenter to Audre Lorde have envisioned the homoerotic impulse as a charism out of which more caring alternatives to the status quo might be constructed. Comparisons of same-sex bonding in different cultures are an opportunity to glimpse other—sometimes better—ways to realize that charism. If pride has gone astray in advanced industrial nations and has been increasingly taken over by the marketplace, it is worth bearing in mind alternatives, both home and away, where this dynamic is not operative, because they raise the question of how we might innovate social alternatives and the conditions necessary to encourage them. The idea of gay shame at least reminds us that signing on to social relationships infused by the norms of the global marketplace is not the only possibility. The shame/pride binary can be just an opener for a much more complex conversation over what kind of LGBT communities we would want to live in, what they would "deliver," and how they might better provide support and care.

Notes

1. Marie-Jo Bonnet, "Gay Mimesis and Misogyny," *Journal of Homosexuality* 41, nos. 3-4 (2001): 276. Bonnet diagnoses the problem as one of male venality versus female community, contrasting this image of Paris Pride with a description of the lesbian pride forum, which "brings together lesbian and feminist associations, book signings, video projections, and poetry readings, followed by the actual festivities themselves: more than three thousand women dancing to music chosen to please women of all ages" (277). This assessment rather underestimates the degree to which lesbians are also swept up in consumerist iconography or how pride still embraces voluntary "associations, book signings," etc., with strong male participation.

2. See http://hotterthanjuly.com (accessed February 9, 2009).

3. Jean-Paul Sartre, *Anti-Semite and Jew* (New York: Schocken, 1948), 109.

4. Barry D. Adam, *The Survival of Domination* (New York: Elsevier, 1978), 73.

5. D. A. Miller, *Place for Us* (Cambridge, MA: Harvard University Press, 1998).

6. Henning Bech, *When Men Meet* (Chicago: University of Chicago Press, 1997).

7. One of the few books documenting this phenomenon is William Leap, *Public Sex/ Gay Space* (New York: Columbia University Press, 1999).

8. Barry D. Adam, "Love and Sex in Constructing Identity among Men who Have Sex with Men," *International Journal of Sexuality and Gender Studies* 5, no. 4 (2000): 325-39.

9. Barry D. Adam, "Constructing the Neoliberal Sexual Actor," *Culture, Health and Sexuality* 7, no. 4 (2005): 333-46.

10. See, e.g., Barry D. Adam, *The Rise of a Gay and Lesbian Movement* (New York: Twayne, 1995), 106-8, or Dennis Altman, "What Changed in the Seventies?," in *Homosexuality: Power and Politics*, ed. Gay Left Collective (London: Allison & Busby, 1980).

11. Ian Lumsden attempts to convey the strong communitarian spirit of gay Cubans in *Machos, Maricones, and Gays* (Philadelphia: Temple University Press, 1996). Reinaldo Arenas's *Before Night Falls* (New York: Penguin, 1993) documents his experiences in Cuba's vast underground of cruising and fleeting encounters.

12. Adam, *Rise of a Gay and Lesbian Movement*, 7.

13. I have explored the issue of the globalization of gay and lesbian identities further in Barry D. Adam, "Globalization and the Mobilization of Gay and Lesbian Communities," in *Globalization and Social Movements*, ed. Pierre Hamel, Henri Lustiger-Thaler, Jan Nederveen Pieterse, and Sasha Roseneil (New York: St Martin's/Palgrave, 2001), 166-79, and

"Theorizing the Globalization of Gay and Lesbian Movements," *Research in Political Sociology* 10 (2002): 123–37.

14. Perhaps one of the most interesting studies that transcends the usual parameters of the sex-tourism argument by exploring the articulation of sex work with traditional kinship and economic formations is Heather Montgomery's study of Thailand, *Modern Babylon?* (New York: Berghahn, 2003).

15. Barry D. Adam, "Relationship Innovation in Male Relationships," *Sexualities* 9, no. 1 (2006): 5–26.

16. James Murray and Barry D. Adam, "Aging, Sexuality, and HIV Issues among Older Gay Men," *Canadian Journal of Human Sexuality* 10, nos. 3–4 (2001): 75–90.

[DON KULICK AND CHARLES KLEIN]

Scandalous Acts

THE POLITICS OF SHAME AMONG BRAZILIAN *TRAVESTI* PROSTITUTES

In a small, dimly lit hotel room, a man and a *travesti*, a transgendered prostitute, have just had sex. The price of this transaction had been agreed on before the couple entered the room, and the man, now dressed and anxious to leave, removes his wallet from his back pocket.

The travesti straightens her bra straps and eyes the man. "No," she murmurs, as she sees him open the wallet and take out a few notes. "More. I want more."

The man is startled. "What do you mean, you want more?" he asks warily. "We agreed on thirty *reais*, and here's thirty *reais*. Take it."

The travesti slips towards the door in a swift, resolute gesture. "Listen, love," she says calmly, blocking the man's exit, "the price went up. You wanted me to fuck you. You sucked my dick. That's more expensive. That's not thirty *reais*. It's sixty."

The man growls that the travesti can go fuck *herself* if she thinks she can rob him like that. He flings the notes in his hand at her and moves towards the door.

But the travesti moves too. Practiced. Fast. She slams her purse on the floor and plants her feet firmly apart, in a stance that makes her seem thicker, stronger, more expansive. A pair of tiny nail scissors flashes in her hand. Suddenly afraid, the man stops in his tracks. He stands in front of the travesti, staring at her and wondering what to do next. He sees her coral-red mouth open and he hears her begin to shout, loud, harsh, venomous

A longer version of this essay was published in Barbara Hobson, ed., *Recognition Struggles and Social Movements: Contested Identities, Agency and Power* (Cambridge: Cambridge University Press, 2003). For this version, we are grateful to David Halperin for his editing skills.

screams that fill the room, the hotel, and, horrifyingly, it seems to the man, the whole neighborhood: "Have shame, you pig! You disgraceful faggot! You act like a man but you come in here and want to be fucked more than a whore! You sucked my dick and begged me to fuck you! Disgusting faggot! *Maricona* without shame! You're more of a woman than I am! You're asshole is wider than mine is! You're more of a *puta* than me!"

In travesti parlance, what is occurring here is *um escândalo*, a commotion, a scandal. A scandal is an example of what ethnographers of communication call a performative genre: it is a named act that has its own structure, dynamics, and intended consequences. Like all performatives, scandals have illocutionary force; that is, they announce a specific intention on the part of the speaker—in this case, the conferral of shame. Scandals also ideally produce a set of perlocutionary effects, namely, the surrender by the client of more money than he had agreed to pay in the first place.

Scandals as performatives can operate and make sense only within structures of shame. They work to the extent that they elicit shame and channel it into service that benefits travestis. What is the specific configuration of this shame? In this case, it hinges on widespread and violently upheld sanctions against male homosexual relations. The flame being fanned here is the fact that travestis are males. They are males who habitually consume estrogen-based hormones and who often have impressively feminine figures, owing to those hormones and to the numerous liters of industrial silicone that they pay their colleagues to inject into their bodies. But they are males nonetheless. They have penises. Those penises are usually kept tightly pressed against a travesti's perineum and well out of anyone's view. But in their professional lives as prostitutes, travestis remove their penis from concealment and frequently put it to use. And during a scandal, a travesti's penis is rhetorically unfurled and resoundingly brandished at anyone within hearing distance of her shouts.

The point of drawing dramatic attention to that part of the travesti's anatomy that she normally keeps concealed is to publicly reconfigure the social status of her client. The overwhelming majority of men who pay travestis for sex are married or have girlfriends, and they identify themselves as heterosexual. Even if these men are publicly revealed to have been in the company of a travesti (for example, on the relatively rare occasions when they go to the police to report that a travesti robbed them, or on the relatively more frequent occasions when police arrest them for having shot a travesti), the majority will steadfastly maintain that they were unaware that the prostitute they picked up was a travesti. Travestis, however, know better. They know that the men who pay them for sex come to the specific streets on which they work looking for a travesti, not a woman. They know that the sexual service requested by many of the men (travestis say "most of the men") is anal penetration, with the travesti assuming the role of penetrator. Finally, travestis know that the last thing one of these men ever wants revealed in public is that he has paid money to have a transgendered prostitute insert her penis into his ostensibly heterosexual ass.

So in order to blackmail her client and scare him into parting with more money than he would ever agree to, a travesti will "cause a scandal" (*dar um escândalo*). Scandals constitute one of the everyday, mundane means by which individual travestis see to it that they earn enough money to support themselves. They are not collective actions. Although scandals can turn into brawls, in which other travestis within hearing distance will come to the aid of their colleague and help attack a particularly violent or recalcitrant client, for the most part they are singular actions taken by individual travestis. Indeed, travestis actually prefer not to involve other travestis in scandals, because they know that they will have to split their takings with any travesti who helps them extract money from a client.

Despite their individualistic nature, scandals can be analyzed as a kind of politics—a micropolitics certainly, and one that produces only small-scale and temporary crinkles in the overall social fabric. But these little crinkles are not altogether without interest. Or irony. For note: in excoriating their allegedly heterosexual clients for being effeminate homosexuals, *travestis are drawing on the exact same language that is habitually invoked by others to condemn travestis and to justify violence against them.* What is perhaps most striking about scandals is that they do not in any way correspond to the noble "hidden transcripts" of resistance that liberal scholars like James Scott expect to find among oppressed groups.[1] Scandals do nothing to contest or refute the sociocultural basis of travestis' abject status in contemporary Brazilian society. Quite the opposite—instead of challenging abjection, scandals cultivate it. And with a skill that is nothing short of dazzling, travestis use scandals as a way of extending the space of their own abjection. A scandal casts that abjection outward like a sticky web, one that ensnares a petrified client, completely against his will.

But scandals do not only compel their recipient to explicitly acknowledge his relationship to a travesti (and listen as his own ontological distance from travestis is challenged and mocked); scandals also force the client to part with more of his money than he had intended. In this way, they can be seen as resolutely political actions that result in both recognition *and* redistribution—to use the two terms continually bandied about and debated in philosophical and political science debates about recognition struggles.

Furthermore, despite their locally managed nature, scandals draw on large-scale structures for their intelligibility and efficacy. The existence and salience of these structures suggests that scandals could be tapped and extended into larger, more organized, and more collectivized spheres.

Our contribution to this volume on gay shame concerns the relationship between scandals and the emerging political activism of Brazilian travestis. Since the early 1990s, Brazilian travestis have been forming activist groups and making demands for recognition and rights. These demands—which include protection from brutal police violence, the ability to use their female names on certain official documents, and the right to appear in public space unharassed—may seem to us modest and even self-evident. However, we want to argue that there is something fundamentally *scandalous* about travesti demands. In emerging as a public voice and asserting entitlement to equal citizenship rights with others, we see travesti activism as building on the same kinds of principles as those that structure scandals. In both cases, travesti politics is a politics anchored in shame. It is a politics that invokes and activates specific structures of shame not in order to contest them, but, instead, in order to extend their scope, to imbricate others. In both scandals and their more recognizably activist registers of political action, travestis transgress public decorum and civil society not by rejecting shame (and championing something like "Travesti Pride"), but by inhabiting shame as a place from which to interpellate others and thereby incriminate those others. Travestis are deploying what Eve Kosofsky Sedgwick has called a "shame-conscious" and "shame-creative" vernacular, one that inflects the "social metamorphic" possibilities of shame.[2] This means, in turn, that travesti demands for more money from clients or for uninhibited access to public space are not what Nancy Fraser has dubbed "affirmative" demands for redress.[3] They are not demands that build upon and enhance existing group differentiation in order to claim additional recognition. Instead, travesti demands are transformative, in Fraser's terms—they work to undermine group differentiation (between normal, upstanding citizens and low-life, perverse travestis) by foregrounding and challenging the generative structures that permit that differentiation to exist in the first place.

Travestis in Brazil

The word *travesti* derives from *transvestir*, or cross-dress. But travestis do not only cross-dress. Sometimes beginning at ages as young as eight or ten, males who self-identify as travestis begin growing their hair long, plucking their eyebrows, experimenting with cosmetics, and wearing, whenever they can, feminine or androgynous clothing such as tiny shorts exposing the bottom of their buttocks or T-shirts tied in a knot in above their navel. It is not unusual for boys of this age to also begin engaging in sexual relations with their peers and older males, always in the role of the one who is anally penetrated. By the time these boys are in their early teens, many of them have already either left home or been expelled from their homes because their sexual and gender transgressions are usually not tolerated, especially by the boys' fathers. Once they leave home, the overwhelming majority of travestis migrate to cities (if they do not already live in one), where they meet and form friendships with other travestis, and where they begin working as prostitutes. In the company of their travesti friends and colleagues, young travestis learn about estrogen-based hormones, which can be purchased inexpensively over the counter at any of the numerous pharmacies that line the streets in Brazilian cities. At this point, young travestis often begin ingesting large quantities of these hormones. By the time they reach their late teens, many travestis have also begun paying their colleagues to inject numerous liters of industrial silicone into their bodies in order to round out their knees, thighs, and calves, and in order to augment their breasts, hips, and, most important (because this is Brazil), their buttocks.

Despite irrevocable physiological modifications such as these, the overwhelming majority of travestis do not self-identify as women. That is, despite the fact that they live their lives in female clothing, call one another "she" and by female names, and endure tremendous pain to acquire female bodily forms, travestis do not wish to remove their penis, and they do not consider themselves to be women. They are not transsexuals. They are, they say, homosexuals—males who feel "like women" and who ardently desire "men" (i.e., masculine, nonhomosexual males). Much of a travesti's time, thought, and effort is spent fashioning and perfecting herself as an object of desire for those men.

Travestis occupy an unusually visible place in both Brazilian social space and the national cultural imaginary. They exist in all Brazilian cities of any size, and in the large southern cities of São Paulo and Rio de Janeiro, they number in the thousands. They are most exuberantly visible during Brazil's famous annual carnival, but even in more mundane contexts and discourses, travestis figure prominently. A popular Saturday afternoon television show, for example, includes a spot in which female impersonators, some of whom are clearly travestis, are judged by a panel of celebrities on their beauty and their ability to mime the lyrics of songs sung by female vocalists. Another weekly television show regularly featured a well-known travesti named Valéria. *Tieta*, one of the most popular television *novelas* in recent years, featured a special guest appearance by Rogéria, another famous travesti. Another widely watched novela featured a saucy female lead whose speech was peppered with words from travesti argot and who sounded, everybody agreed, just like a travesti.[4] But most telling of all of the special place reserved for travestis in the Brazilian popular imagination is the fact that the individual widely acclaimed as most beautiful woman in Brazil in the mid-1980s was—a travesti, Roberta Close. She became a household name throughout the country, appeared regularly on national television, starred in a play in Rio, posed nude (with strategically crossed legs) in an issue of *Playboy* magazine that sold out its entire press run of 200,000 copies almost immediately, was continually interviewed and portrayed in virtually every magazine in the country, and had at least three songs written about her by well-known composers. Although her popularity declined when, at the end of the 1980s, she left Brazil to have a sex-change operation and live in Europe, Close remains extremely well-known. A book about her life appeared in the late 1990s,[5] and in 1995 she was featured in a nationwide advertisement for Duloren lingerie, in which a photograph of her passport, bearing her male name, was juxtaposed with a photograph of her looking sexy and chic in a black lace undergarment. The caption read "Você não imagina do que uma Duloren é capaz" (You can't imagine what a Duloren can do).

As it happens, famous individuals such as Valéria, Rogéria, and Roberta Close are not representative of Brazil's travestis. They are more like exceptions that prove the rule. And the rule is harsh discrimination and vituperative public prejudice. The overwhelming majority of travestis live far from the protective glow of celebrity, and they constitute one of the most marginalized and despised groups in Brazilian society. Most travestis (like most Brazilians) come from working-class or poor backgrounds, and many remain poor throughout their lives—even though some, these days, also travel to Europe and earn enough money working there as prostitutes to return to Brazil and secure their own futures and those of their mothers. In most Brazilian cities, travestis are harassed so routinely that many of them avoid venturing out onto the street during the day. And at night, while they work, they are regularly the victims of violent police brutality and random assassinations by individuals or gangs of men who take it upon themselves to "clean up the streets," as local governments periodically order their police forces to do—despite the fact that neither cross-dressing nor prostitution is criminal under the Brazilian legal code.

So the nature of the relationship between the Brazilian populace at large and travestis is hot-cold and love-hate: hot and loving enough to propel a handful of travestis to national celebrity and to sustain a thriving market in which tens of thousands of travestis are able to support themselves through prostitution; cold and hateful enough to ensure that the majority of those travestis live in continual anxiety that their right to occupy urban space will be publicly challenged and perhaps violently denied. Jovana Baby, founder and president of Brazil's first travesti activist organization, Grupo Astral (Associação de Travestis e Liberados de Rio de Janeiro), provided a pithy summary of popular Brazilian sentiments towards travestis when she remarked in an interview with Kulick that "Brazilians love travestis, as long as they stay on television or on the covers of magazines. A travesti on the street or, God forbid, in the family—that is another story altogether."

Misrepresentation, Shame, and Power

Ambivalent public sentiments toward travestis are mirrored in ambivalent public perceptions about the precise composition of travesti identity. One of the most striking dimensions of the Brazilian preoccupation with travestis is that despite the habitual presence of travestis in both what we might see as the "high" contexts of popular culture and the "low" contexts of city streets and the crime pages of the local newspaper (frequently in lurid close-ups as murdered corpses), there appears to be no clear consensus about what exactly travestis are. In the press, travestis are sometimes referred to as "he" and sometimes as "she." Some commentators insist that travestis want to be women; others maintain that they self-identify as men. Still others, especially those commentators influenced by postmodernist ideas, claim that travestis reject identity altogether. They are usually depicted as homosexuals, but occasionally this identity is elided and they are identified instead as transsexuals. Expressed in structuralist terms, the result of these various depictions of travesti identity is that the signifier "travesti" is continually deferred and never finally coalesces with a specific signified. This means that the Brazilian public can never be certain that it knows what "travesti" means from one context to the next.

The ambivalence about travestis produces what scholars such as Charles Taylor and Axel Honneth would call the "misrecognition" of travestis.[6] And such a lack of recognition is not trivial or merely insulting—both Taylor and Honneth argue at length that it is pernicious and profoundly harmful.

When it comes to travestis, these scholars are, of course, in a sense, right. One politically significant example of the harmful nature of travesti misrecognition was a 1997 interview with the then-mayor of Rio de Janeiro,

Luis Paulo Conde, in the monthly gay magazine *Sui Generis*. In an otherwise generally affirmative and sympathetic interview about homosexuality, the mayor suddenly announces that he finds travestis "offensive" ("O que agride é o travesti"). The reason? "A travesti doesn't admit to being gay. He dresses in women's clothes to be accepted by society. When he puts on the clothes, it's to be accepted by society. Since society doesn't accept homosexuality, he creates a woman so that he will be accepted." Now, leaving aside the mayor's intriguing suggestion that Brazilians might be more tolerant of men in dresses than they are of homosexuals, here we have a case of misrecognition in which mayor Conde denies the homosexual component of travesti identity, thereby necessarily disqualifying them from any of the rights or protections that he might eventually be willing to grant homosexuals.

But although public ambivalence about travestis is indeed harmful in many of the ways discussed by Taylor and Honneth, it is not *only* harmful. This is a point that seems likely to be missed by the analytical frameworks elaborated by those scholars. For besides constituting damage, public uncertainty about the precise nature (and hence the precise boundaries) of travesti identity also generates a space of ambiguity that travestis can use to their advantage. If travesti identity remains fuzzy, it becomes possible to suggest that the identity (or at least key dimensions of it) is not specific to travestis but is instead shared by others who do not self-identify as travestis. Hence, ambivalence provides travestis with a wedge that they can use to insert themselves into the identificatory constellations of others and, in doing so, compel a reconsideration and perhaps even a reconfiguration of those constellations.[7]

A forced realignment of identity is what we believe travesti scandals accomplish. Scandals publicly accuse a travesti's client of being a depraved effeminate homosexual, one who is so pathetically abject that he actually pays money to be abased at the hands of a person who herself is at the very nadir of sociocultural hierarchy.

The reason scandals work (that is, the reason they nine times out of ten produce the desired result of more money) is that travestis are right. Or rather, scandals work because travestis *might* be right. The great majority of a travesti's clients would hotly disagree with travesti assertions that they are depraved, effeminate perverts. However, because the boundaries of travesti identity are not neatly demarcated or entirely clear-cut for most people, the possibility remains open that travesti ontology does not occupy the place of the absolute Other in relation to the public at large. On the contrary, because the contours of travesti identity are ambiguously outlined in relation to others, there is a distinct possibility that travestis might be right when they point a finger and assert affinity with a particular individual. Especially if that individual did what the travesti says he did (and he may or may not have—who can know for sure?), public perception of the man will change, and he will be resignified by whoever hears (or hears about) the scandal as someone who does indeed share an (until that moment) secret affiliation with his travesti accuser.

So travesti scandals raise a specter of ontological similarity between the travesti and her client. But they depend for their effectiveness on the simultaneous assertion of the shameful nature of that ontology ("Have shame, you pig! You disgraceful faggot!"). Shame here becomes the channel through which identification flows, the contours within which it takes form. Eve Sedgwick has addressed this identity-delineating power of shame in her essay on the politics of performativity. Sedgwick argues that whereas guilt is an affect that focuses on the suffering of another (and the self's blame for that suffering), shame concerns the suffering of the self at the hands of another.[8] Furthermore, while guilt is a bad feeling attached to what one does, shame is a bad feeling attaching to what one is. "One therefore is *something*, in experiencing shame," Sedgwick explains.[9] But that is not all. For conferred by another, shame always responds. It *performs*, as Sedgwick phrases it. Often, embarrassment, a blush, an aversion of eyes, a turning away— these are the responses, the performances, of shame. In the case of scandals, shame performs by compelling acquiescence to the travesti's demands for more money.

Sedgwick suggests that this performative dimension of shame has overtly political consequences. In order to better understand the import of this suggestion, it might be useful to contrast it with the way in which shame has figured in the work of another scholar who has recently discussed shame and politics. The philosopher Axel Honneth, in his writings on recognition struggles, identifies shame as the "missing psychological link"[10] that allows us to understand how economic privation or social repression can motivate people to engage in political struggle.[11] Shame, in other words, explains how a subject can be moved from suffering to action. Honneth argues that shame is raised when one's interactional partners refuse to grant one the respect to which one believes oneself entitled. When this occurs, the disrespected subject is brutally brought up against the normally unreflected-upon fact that it is dependent on the recognition of others for its own sense of self. The affronted realization that the other's view of the self is, in Honneth's terms, "distorted," constitutes the motivational impetus to identify specific others as the source of oppression, and, hence, as the target of political struggle. In Honneth's framework, shame is thus the psychological bedrock of political action. And the psychological goal of political struggle is the elimination of shame.

Sedgwick's view is different. Like Honneth, Sedgwick argues that shame in the self is conferred by others, and that the experience of shame is a constitutive dimension of the identities of oppressed people. Unlike Honneth, however, Sedgwick stresses that shame is a crucial component in *all* identity formation. "One of the things that anyone's character or personality is," she insists, "is a record of the highly individual histories by which the fleeting emotion of shame has instituted far more durable, structural changes in one's relational and interpretive strategies toward both self and others."[12] In other words, all of our socializing experiences in which our behavior and expression were or are controlled with sharp reprimands such as "People are looking at you!" are important nexuses in the construction of our identities. This implies that forms of shame cannot be considered "distinct 'toxic' parts of groups or individual identity that can be excised" through consciousness raising or recognition struggles.[13] Instead, shame is integral to the very processes by which identity itself is formed; which means that the extinction of shame would be, in effect, the extinction of identity itself. Therefore, instead of fantasizing about the end of shame, Sedgwick proposes that shame be acknowledged, embraced, and put to transformative political use. In this framework, the goal is not the end of shame. The goal is the refiguration of shame as "a near inexhaustible source of transformational energy" and its creative deployment in political struggles.[14]

Shame's creative deployment can occur in a variety of registers, many of them, Sedgwick speculates, as yet unimagined. But travestis certainly hit on one of them when they began to claim shame as a place from which they might speak and hail others, asserting power to resignify those others, and compelling them to respond in wished-for ways. In scandals, what gets redesignated is the public (and sometimes perhaps also the privately felt) identities of a number of individual men. For a long time this seemed to be enough for travestis. Nowadays, though, some travestis have decided that they have bigger fish to fry. Instead of contenting themselves with redefining the public perceptions of a few men who pay them for sex, these travestis are turning their attention to redefining the public perceptions of more consequential entities, such as the concept of Brazilian citizenship and the nature of human rights. These are the targets that are the focus of travestis' more recognizably activist modes of political activism, and it is to these forms of political struggle that we now turn.

Travesti Political Activism

The emergence of travesti political struggles in Brazil can be understood only in the context of the rise of Brazilian gay and AIDS activism during the past three decades, for these movements, although they have not always welcomed travestis or responded to their concerns, have heavily influenced the content and organizational structures of travesti activism.[15] Brazilian gay and AIDS organizing in turn have been strongly shaped by two larger political processes, namely the redemocratization of Brazilian society during the late 1970s and 1980s and the rapid expansion of nongovernmental organizations (NGOs) during the 1980s and 1990s.[16] The following discussion traces the development of Brazilian gay and AIDS activism and highlights the various interconnections between the two movements. We then turn our attention to contemporary travesti political struggles and their complex blend of AIDS, gay, and specifically travesti-related issues.

In 1964 the Brazilian military staged a coup d'état and forced João Goulart, a leftist president, to flee the country. Over the next few years an authoritarian regime was gradually institutionalized.[17] Repression was particularly strong from 1968 to 1973, and many who actively opposed the dictatorship were imprisoned or forced into political exile. In the mid-1970s, a more "moderate" wing of the military assumed power and instituted the *abertura* (political opening), thereby beginning Brazil's lengthy redemocratization, which was finally completed in 1989 with the first direct presidential elections in more than twenty-five years.

The *abertura* generated an intense surge of political and social mobilization. In the late 1970s movements such as worker's organizations, neighborhood associations, ecclesiastically based communities, women's organizations, environmental groups, and Afro-Brazilian groups sprang up throughout Brazil. Building on democratic principles and grassroots mobilization, this "revolution in everyday life" represented a break from traditional Brazilian politics and its history of clientelism, hierarchy, and populism.[18] Given the continued dangers of directly confronting the legitimacy of an "opening" but still authoritarian regime, the new social movements served as an important organizing arena for social and political sectors that opposed the dictatorship.

It is within this context of widespread political and social mobilization that the Brazilian homosexual movement arose.[19] In 1979 Brazil's first homosexual newspaper, *Lampião*, was launched in Rio de Janeiro. That same year, SOMOS—Grupo de Afirmicão Homosexual (We Are—Homosexual Affirmation Group) was established in São Paulo. During the same period, homosexual liberation groups were established in several other Brazilian states, and in April 1980 representatives from these organizations met in São Paulo at the first Brazilian Congress of Organized Homosexual groups. The movement achieved particular public notoriety several months later through a historic protest march against police violence in São Paulo that brought together nearly one thousand people, including many travestis.[20]

In terms of its sexual politics, the early Brazilian homosexual movement stressed the subversive dimensions of sexuality, including sexual freedom, androgyny, and what today is often referred to as "gender fucking." Rather than decry the social marginality of homosexuals, movement leaders argued that outrageous and "shameful" dimensions of homosexuality, such as camp, gender bending, and promiscuity, should not only be celebrated at the personal level; rather, those phenomena also constituted a creative, antiauthoritarian force that could work against the dictatorship and transform society. Although they focused on gender and sexual politics, the homosexual liberation activists also worked with the opposition movement more generally, and with movements such as those developed by feminists, Afro-Brazilians, and indigenous peoples. In these political alliances, homosexual leaders adopted a discourse that emphasized citizenship and democracy.[21]

It did not take long, however, for the marked gender, class, racial, and political differences among group participants to threaten the cohesion of the young gay liberation movement. For example, internal tensions within the São Paulo–based SOMOS group, which had become the most influential Brazilian homosexual liberation organization, reached crisis proportions in May 1980, when nearly all of its female members left en masse to form the Lesbian-Feminist Action Group. The remaining men then largely divided into anarchist and Trotskyite factions. Similar schisms occurred at Lampião. By the end of 1981, with SOMOS in tatters and Lampião having closed its doors, the first wave of Brazilian homosexual mobilization had more or less ended. As Edward MacRae has argued,[22] this decline resulted from a combination of the internal conflicts noted above and a more general shift in political energy from social movements to party-oriented electoral politics in the multiple-party democratic electoral system implemented in the early 1980s. These conflicts and the changing political landscape were compounded by significant transformations in the organization of Brazilian homosexuality during this period, including the rapid growth of gay identity politics and gay consumer culture, neither of which was easily reconcilable with the movement's anarchism and anticonsumerism.[23]

The beginning of the AIDS epidemic in Brazil in the early to mid-1980s raised new challenges for an already fragile and fragmented movement.

Was AIDS a gay issue? If gay groups worked on AIDS, would they be reinforcing the public perception that AIDS was (only) a gay disease, thereby
potentially reinforcing the shame and stigma associated with AIDS and increasing discrimination against gay Brazilians?[24] Given governmental apa-
thy in response to an increasingly out-of-control epidemic, would taking
on AIDS issues overwhelm gay groups and prevent them from working on
specifically gay issues (e.g., fighting antigay discrimination and violence,
supporting gay rights legislation, building a gay community)? Facing these
dilemmas, Brazilian gay groups in the 1980s made different choices—
some, such as the Grupo Gay da Bahia (Gay Group of Bahia) in Salvador and
the Grupo Atobá de Emancipação Homosexual (Atobá Group for Homosexual Emancipation) in Rio de Janeiro were among the first groups, gay or
otherwise, to develop AIDS prevention and education activities in Brazil.[25]
Others, such as Triângulo Rosa (Pink Triangle) in Rio de Janeiro, initially
declined to work extensively on AIDS-related issues.[26]

Not surprisingly, given the significant impact of the Brazilian AIDS epidemic on men who have sex with men, throughout the 1980s and well into
the 1990s many of the leaders and active participants in the AIDS NGOs
were gay-identified men, including some who had participated in the first
wave of the Brazilian homosexual movement. Yet despite the involvement
of many gay-identified men, these organizations did not consider themselves to be gay groups, and until the mid-1990s most AIDS NGOs primarily directed their prevention activities toward the "general population."
This is not to say that gay-related issues were of no interest to AIDS NGOs,
as can be seen in the work of Herbert Daniel,[27] a noted writer and activist
for leftist and gay political causes. In 1987 Daniel began working at Brazil's
second-oldest AIDS NGO, the Brazilian Interdisciplinary AIDS Association
(ABIA) in Rio de Janeiro. There he played a leading role in developing some
of the first sexually explicit and culturally sensitive AIDS-prevention materials directed toward men who have sex with men. In early 1989 Daniel discovered that he was HIV positive.[28] Recognizing the need for an organization focused primarily on the political dimensions of living with HIV/AIDS,
Daniel formed the Grupo Pela VIDDA (Group for the Affirmation, Integration, and Dignity for People with AIDS) in Rio de Janeiro later that year.[29]

Grupo Pela VIDDA represented an epistemological and practical break in
Brazilian AIDS activism and served as a critical reference for AIDS-related
programs and politics throughout the 1990s.[30] Unlike its counterpart AIDS
NGOs in the late 1980s and early 1990s, Pela VIDDA did not provide direct
services to people with HIV/AIDS or focus on developing educational materials and activities. Instead, under Daniel's leadership, Pela VIDDA articu-

lated a political project that emphasized citizenship and solidarity in the face of the *morte civil* (civil death) experienced by people living with HIV/ AIDS in Brazil. By civil death, Daniel referred to the then-prevalent practice in Brazil—and indeed throughout the world—of treating people living with HIV/AIDS as already dead. This civil death was often internalized by people with HIV/AIDS. Facing the various shames associated with AIDS (e.g., its rhetorical links to promiscuity, contagion, and homosexuality), many individuals became either socially invisible or the passive subjects of sensationalist media coverage.[31]

A significant dimension of Daniel's political project was to openly assume the "shame" of AIDS and use it to formulate political goals. From the position of a person living with the stigma of HIV, Daniel asserted that *everyone* in Brazil was living with AIDS. This argument was not a new one; it had been powerfully formulated by gay groups in the United States and the United Kingdom as soon as the magnitude of the epidemic—and also the magnitude of government inaction—became evident. What was important about it, however, was that it reterritorialized shame, relocating it not so much in individual bodies as in the political structure of society. It also importantly refigured people associated with AIDS as active articulators, rather than passive recipients, of shame. In other words, arguments like those deployed by Daniel and Pela VIDDA fashioned shame as a powerful position from which individuals could speak and demand hearing.

Despite the vitality and political possibilities of Daniel and Pela VIDDA's vision of "living with HIV/AIDS" and its explicit incorporation of both (homo)sexuality and AIDS within a broader political discourse, throughout the 1980s and into the early 1990s the relationship between AIDS NGOs and gay groups—and gay and AIDS activists—remained complex and often antagonistic.[32] Part of this antagonism resulted from different approaches to sexual politics, for during this period most of the more visible Brazilian gay groups, such as the Grupo Gay da Bahia, adopted a vision of sexual politics that focused on promoting gay identities and eliminating— rather than reterritorializing—the shame associated with homosexuality. But equally important were questions of money, expertise, and representativeness, particularly as AIDS-related organizations came to outnumber and in many respects eclipse gay groups in the late 1980s and early 1990s.

These tensions between AIDS and gay organizations diminished throughout the 1990s. One critical factor in this rapprochement was Brazil's receiving a loan of more than $150 million from the World Bank in 1992 to develop and implement a comprehensive national AIDS program.[33] As part of this so-called World Bank Project, from 1993 to 1998 more than $9 million was distributed to nearly two hundred community-based organizations who worked on AIDS-related issues—not only AIDS NGOs, but also gay, travesti, sex-worker, and women's organizations that previously had been largely outside of AIDS-related funding circles.

These shifts in the content of AIDS prevention programs and the patterns of AIDS industry funding must be situated alongside the changes in the landscape of same-sex sexuality that have been occurring in Brazil over the course of the AIDS epidemic.[34] For despite much hyperbole predicting the demise of homosexuals and their supposedly "contaminated" ghettos in the early years of the epidemic, Brazilian gay-oriented commercial establishments expanded in both number and type during the 1980s and especially the 1990s, and male homosexuality—including travestis—became everyday topics within the mainstream media. This increased gay visibility has been complemented by gay-oriented national magazines (e.g., *Sui Generis, G*), which have been critical nodes in the emergence of a vital and media-oriented national gay culture.[35] At the same time, gay political activism grew dramatically in Brazil during the mid- to late 1990s. From a handful of groups at the end of the 1980s to sixty groups in 1995, there are now nearly one hundred gay groups in the Associação Brasileira de Gays, Lésbicas and Travestis (Brazilian Association of Gays, Lesbians, and Travestis [ABGLT]). In addition, gay rights issues are being seriously considered in the national political arena. For example, a domestic partnership proposal was introduced in the national legislature in 1998, where it initially faced little organized opposition. More recently, opposition to the measure from conservative and religious sectors (e.g., Protestant fundamentalist groups and certain sectors of the Catholic church) has intensified, and gay rights activists have been working with legislators to mobilize political and popular support around these and other gay rights issues.

How do travestis fit within these emerging gay communities and the resurgence of the Brazilian gay movement? As discussed above, travestis occupy a complicated and shifting position within Brazilian (homo)sexual worlds. Although travestis are sometimes admired and desired for their beauty and sensuality, many Brazilians—including a sizable number of gays and gay leaders—consider travestis a shameful group whose ostentatious presence and frequently scandalous behavior discredits gay Brazilians and the gay political movement. This marginalization of travestis within gay worlds is further demonstrated by the relatively low levels of travesti involvement in (non-travesti-specific) gay activism. For example, despite the existence of a travesti-led "department of travestis" at the ABGLT, the overall presence and influence of travestis within the organization is quite limited. Travestis are absent from the organized Brazilian gay movement at regional levels as well: at the 1994 meeting of the Encontro dos Grupos Lésbicos e Gays da Região Sul (Southern Regional Meeting of Lesbian and Gay Groups) in Porto Alegre, only one of more than the thirty participants who attended was a travesti. Nor are travestis generally active participants in the growing Brazilian "pink market,"[36] for its costs, middle-class cultural values (e.g., respectability), and emphasis on masculine gay male aesthetics present an inaccessible and often hostile environment for most travestis.

Facing these barriers to participation in Brazil's emerging gay culture and gay political movement, over the past decade and a half travestis have grounded their political organizing around AIDS-related issues. Jovana Baby of ASTRAL observed in an interview with Kulick that travesti activism has "ridden on the back of the AIDS." In other words, to the extent that travestis have established formal organizations, programs, and venues, it has been entirely through AIDS-related funding, usually from the ministry of health. This kind of funding has placed specific limits on how travesti activism is articulated and how it is perceived. However, Baby and other travestis have made sure that those limits have been enabling ones.

Scandalous Citizenship

As sex workers, travestis were particularly hard hit by the AIDS epidemic. It is difficult to estimate the number of travestis who have died of HIV-related illness because statistics on AIDS in Brazil do not report on travestis—travestis are subsumed under the category "men" and "homosexual transmission." Travestis are agreed, however, that they have lost innumerable friends and colleagues to AIDS, and they are emphatic that the transmission of HIV continues to constitute a profound threat.[37]

Travesti involvement in the Brazilian response to AIDS dates to the mid-1980s, when the travesti Brenda Lee founded a support house/hospice for travestis living with HIV and AIDS in São Paulo. In most cases, travesti-focused AIDS-related projects and the travesti organizations they support have been established by charismatic leaders such as Brenda Lee and Jovana Baby, although several important travesti groups are ongoing programs within AIDS NGOs and gay organizations (e.g., GAPA/Belo Horizonte, GAPA/RS, and Grupo Gay da Bahia). With the expansion of the National AIDS Program in the early 1990s and its commitment to the distribution of condoms and safer-sex education within "special populations" such as men who have sex with men and sex professionals,[38] the number of travesti-led and travesti-related programs in Brazil has grown from a handful in the early 1990s to approximately twenty today.

Since 1993 the ministry of health, at times in collaboration with international philanthropic agencies who fund AIDS-related programs, has underwritten an annual national conference called the Encontro Nacional de Travestis e Liberados que Trabalham com AIDS (National Meeting of Travestis and Open-Minded People who Work with AIDS"). These meetings, which usually attract about two hundred participants, have developed into crucial arenas where politically conscious travestis meet one another and discuss strategies and demands.

However, one of the effects of conferences such as the Encontro Nacional de Travestis e Liberados que Trabalham com AIDS is that they cement an association in the public mind between travestis and AIDS, an association that dates to the beginnings of the Brazilian AIDS epidemic. One of the first published reports about AIDS in Brazil, for example, reported the research of a Brazilian clinician who claimed that the recently discovered epidemic could be traced to the injection of female hormones and "infected" silicone by travestis.[39] As a result of this history, an already well-established connection between travestis and AIDS is reinforced every time a travesti group receives government funding, for these resources are inevitably tied to HIV prevention work. In political-activist contexts, this continually foregrounded link between travestis and AIDS is restricting in some ways, as the travestis who want to talk about such issues as police violence at the annual conference regularly point out. However, the fact that travesti claims are channeled and heard through an AIDS discourse gives travesti political actions a particular character and potential in which shame emerges as a key position from which travestis speak and demand to be heard.

Much like Daniel and Pela VIDDA's politics of "living with AIDS," travesti political strategies have been centered upon highlighting and reterritorializing shame. Whenever travestis organize a protest march, which they do at the conclusion of every Encontro Nacional de Travestis e Liberados and which local groups occasionally do in their home cities to protest police brutality,[40] many of the protestors take care to wear their most outrageous attire—revealing lingerie-style clothing that they would normally display only while working the street late at night. In other words, in these contexts travestis play up, rather than down, their difference from others and fill public space with their most scandalous avatars. Just as a scandal turns space inside out by making the most intimate interactions public, travestis walking down a city's main street in broad daylight in tight bodices and minuscule shorts resignify that space and saturate it with an intimacy that refuses to be contained by normative notions of privacy. This kind of public manifestation of normally concealed persons and intimacies is a striking example of what the sociologist Steven Seidman called "queer politics."[41] "Queer politics is scandalous politics," Seidman argued, writing generally, but in language highly pertinent to the point we are making here; "Queers materialize as the dreaded homosexual other imagined by straight society that had invisibly and silently shaped straight life but now do so openly, loudly, and unapologetically."[42]

In travesti protest marches, this loud, unapologetic body of the homosexual Other is significantly juxtaposed with a particular kind of linguistic form. What is interestingly absent from travesti street demonstrations is language and placards bearing such assertions as "Travesti Pride" or "Proud to be a Travesti." On the contrary, on the surface of things, the language of travesti public protests is not particularly outrageous: "Travestis are Human Beings," a placard might propose, modestly. "Travestis are Citizens," a chant might proclaim. Nothing seriously scandalous here, one might think. However, the scandal in this case lies precisely in the very straightforwardness and simplicity of the message. For if travestis are human beings, they deserve to be accorded respect and human rights, like other human beings. And if they are citizens, then the very concept of citizenship has been revised. Linguistically, what is foregrounded in these activist manifestations is sameness with non-travestis. Nonlinguistically, however, stark differences from non-travestis are conveyed through dress, demeanor, and the sheer fact that so many travestis gather together in one place at one time. So what is happening here is that at their most different, their most shameless, travestis assert that they are most *like* everyone else.[43]

Once again, this brings us back to scandals. Just as they do when they challenge the ontological difference between their clients and themselves by shouting that the client is as abject as they are, travesti political activism refuses what Nancy Fraser calls "affirmative" demands for redress. That is, travesti activism refuses to build upon and enhance group differentiation in order to claim additional recognition without disturbing the underlying framework that generates it. Instead, travesti demands pressure group differentiation by declaring sameness from a position of difference, thereby disclosing and challenging the generative structures that produce particular configurations of hierarchically ranked differentiation in the first place. In Slavoj Žižek's terminology, this is a "political act proper."[44]

Conclusion

The question that remains to be asked is whether the scandalous acts of travesti activists constitute a politically effective strategy. Are travesti assertions of shared ontology politically transformative? Do they produce desirable results? Do they work?

That, alas, is difficult to say. Travesti political activism is still nascent in Brazil, and it is still far too bound up with the initiatives and actions of charismatic individuals like Jovana Baby to constitute anything even approaching a coherent political movement. The overwhelming majority of travestis have little political consciousness, and they are much more concerned with being beautiful, earning money, and traveling to Italy to become what they call *europêias* (that is, rich and sophisticated "European" travestis) than they are in participating in activist protest marches or travesti political organizations. Furthermore, despite the enormous visibility accorded them in the Brazilian press (which is sometimes positive, even though it does remain heavily slanted towards images of travestis as vaguely comic, but hard-nosed and dangerous criminals),[45] travestis continue to face grave discrimination from politicians like the mayor of Rio de Janeiro, who, it will be recalled, is of the opinion that travestis are confused cowards who dress in women's clothes only to be accepted by society. Travestis are also openly disparaged and discriminated against by Christian churches of all denominations, and by large segments of the Brazilian population who find them scary and shameless.

Equally problematic for travesti political organizing is the discrimination travestis experience from one of their seemingly most likely political allies, gay men and lesbians. Not only are travestis at the margins of Brazil's emerging gay culture, pink economy, and gay political movement, but, as we have mentioned previously, many Brazilian gay men and lesbians are hostile toward travestis because they think travestis give homosexuals a bad name. In their formal political statements, however, travestis disregard this, and they typically position themselves alongside—if not within—gay rights discourses. For example, the 1995 Constitution of the National Network of Travestis, Transsexuals and Open-minded People defines itself as "a non-profit, civil organization fighting for the full citizenship of female and male homosexuals in Brazil, giving priority to travestis and transsexuals, encompassing as well sympathizers and friends who we call open-minded people."

This 1995 Constitution also identifies at least one political strategy through which to work toward this objective, namely, the promotion of "actions together with groups that suffer discrimination and social prejudice, with the intention of guaranteeing Travestis, Gays and Transsexuals the right to exercise their full citizenship, always respecting the autonomy of their organizations."

Given the often antagonistic nature of travesti/gay interactions described above, it remains to be seen whether the realities of travesti difference and the goal of political sameness (i.e., full citizenship) can be reconciled. If travestis face major challenges in working with gay groups with whom they share certain affinities and previous collaborations, what is the likelihood that they will be able to reach out and form new partnerships with other socially oppressed groups, many of whom hold travestis in even more disdain? And even if these political alliances could be formed in ways which respect the autonomy of travestis and travesti activist organizations, might they not require travestis to renounce—or at a minimum downplay—the very qualities (i.e., gender and sexual ambivalence, scandalous acts) that are central to travesti social identities and scandals?

Despite all these challenges, there is some indication that travesti political activism might be making some headway, at least in some contexts and in some circles. For example, at a July 2000 meeting in Brasília (the country's capital) between travesti representatives and officials from the Ministry of Health, it was decided that all future material pertaining to travestis published by the Ministry would be examined by a travesti before it went to press.[46] It was also decided that in the future, the Ministry would break with Portuguese grammatical convention and employ feminine grammatical articles, pronouns and adjectives when referring to travestis—so instead of writing *o travesti* (sing.) or *os travestis* (pl.), using the grammatically prescribed masculine articles, future texts will write *a travesti* and *as travestis*, using the feminine forms. These may seem like purely symbolic concessions, but the travestis present at the meeting regarded them as significant victories.

And then there is Lair Guerra de Macedo Rodrigues, the former director of Brazil's National Program on Sexually Transmissible Diseases and AIDS. Guerra de Macedo Rodrigues is one influential individual who seems to have gotten and appreciated the message that travesti political actions strive to convey. In a speech delivered in 1996, the Director referred to travestis as model citizens. "Our society is one that can no longer live with fears and taboos that certainly only impede our objectives," she asserted: "[We must] involve ourselves in this ceaseless battle against discrimination and violence. Even if it means that we must fight against the intolerance of more conservative juridical and religious postures. *The organization of travesti groups*, especially following the advent of AIDS, *is evidence of the beginning of the arduous task of defending citizenship.*"[47]

Just as Brazil is one of the few countries in the world where a travesti could be declared the country's most beautiful woman, so it is perhaps the only one where travestis could be held forth as beacons of civic responsibility that other citizens ought to follow. In the eyes of those who do not like travestis and wish they would just shut up and disappear, this, perhaps, is the biggest scandal of all.

Notes

1. Scott, *Domination*.

2. Sedgwick, "Queer Performativity," 13, 14.

3. Fraser, *Justice Interruptus*, 23.

4. Browning, "The Closed Body."

5. Rito, *Muito prazer*.

6. Taylor, *Multiculturalism*; Honneth, *The Fragmented World* and *The Struggle for Recognition*.

7. Besides ambivalence—or rather, another dimension to ambivalence that makes it possible for travestis to interfere in the identity constructions of others—is the fact that they are taboo, in the Freudian sense of being rejected and prohibited by ideology, and, at the same time, therefore, desired. As Freud discusses, anyone who has violated a taboo becomes taboo himself "because he possesses the dangerous quality of tempting others to follow his example: why should *he* be allowed to do what is forbidden to others? *Thus he is truly contagious* in that every example encourages imitation" (Freud, *Totem and Taboo*, 42; first emphasis in original, second added). Georges Bataille's development of Freud's thoughts on taboo can also be mentioned here (Bataille, *Erotism*), for, according to Bataille, and with clear relevance for the dynamics of travesti scandals, the shame associated with the breaking of sexual taboos is engendered as female.

8. As Darwin noted in his discussion of shame and guilt, shame is raised not by one's sense of guilt, but, rather, by "the thought that others think or know us to be guilty" (*The Expression of the Emotions*, 332).

9. Sedgwick, "Queer Performativity," 12.

10. Honneth, *The Struggle for Recognition*, 135.

11. Honneth, *The Fragmented World*, 256-60; *The Struggle for Recognition*, 131-39.

12. Sedgwick, "Queer Performativity," 12-13.

13. Ibid., 13.

14. Ibid., 4.

15. Daniel, *Vida/Life*; Daniel and Parker, *AIDS*; Green, *Beyond Carnival*; Klein, "'The Ghetto Is Over'"; MacRae, *A construação* and "Homosexual Identities"; Parker, *A construação da solidariedade* and *Beneath the Equator*; Terto, "Homosexuality and Seropositivity"; Trevisan, *Perverts*.)

16. On redemocratization, see Alvarez, *Engendering Democracy*; Skidmore, *Politics of*

Military Rule. On expansion of NGOs, see Fernandes, *Privado porém público*; Landim, *Sem fins lucrativos* and *Para além do mercado e do estado.*

17. Skidmore, *The Politics of Military Rule*; Burns, *A History of Brazil.*

18. See Burns, *A History of Brazil*, for excellent summaries of these dimensions of Brazilian political history, and Scheper-Hughes, *Death without Weeping*, for a vivid account of their continued existence in contemporary Brazilian life. On the term "revolution in everyday life" see Scherer-Warren and Krischke, *Uma revolução no cotidiano.*

19. Although organized homosexual political organizations and movements are a relatively recent phenomenon in Brazil—as well as the world more generally—Brazil has a long history of homosexual subcultures and social spaces (Green, "Beyond Carnival" and *Beyond Carnival*; Mott, *O sexo prohibido*; Parker, *Beneath the Equator*; Trevisan, *Perverts*). It is interesting to note that during the late 1970s and early 1980s, most activists used the term "homosexual" rather than "gay" to describe their liberation movement. In the 1980s and 1990s, "gay" has been used increasingly by participants to describe themselves and their political movement. See also MacRae, *A construação* and "Homosexual Identities."

20. MacRae, *A construação.*

21. Ibid.; Trevisan, *Perverts.*

22. MacRae, *A construação* and "Homosexual Identities."

23. Green, *Beyond Carnival*; MacRae, *A construação* and "Homosexual Identities"; Parker, *Beneath the Equator.*

24. On the connection of the stigmas associated with AIDS and homosexuality in Brazil, see Costa, *A inocência e o vício*; Daniel, *Vida/Life*; Daniel and Parker, *AIDS*; Galvão, "AIDS: a 'doença' e os 'doentes'" and "AIDS e imprensa"; Klein, "AIDS, Activism"; Moraes and Carrara, "Um mal de folhetim" and "Um vírus só não faz doença"; Terto, "Homosexuality and Seropositivity."

25. See Daniel and Parker, *Sexuality*; Galvão, "As respostas das organizações"; Parker, *A construação da solidariedade*; Terto et al., "AIDS Prevention and Gay Community Mobilization."

26. Câmara da Silva, "Triangulo Rosa."

27. During the dictatorship, Herbert Daniel participated in the underground resistance before leaving Brazil as a political exile. Upon returning to Brazil, and before becoming a noted AIDS activist, he worked primarily on gay and environmental issues. Daniel died of AIDS-related complications in March 1992.

28. Daniel, *Vida/Life.*

29. Like many AIDS-NGOs during this period, and paralleling epidemiological realities (e.g., men who have sex with men were the largest category of people with HIV/AIDS in Brazil at this time), most of the participants at Pela VIDDA in its first years were gay-identified men.

30. Other Pela VIDDAs were established in São Paulo, Curitiba, and Goiania in the early 1990s. Pela VIDDA-Rio de Janeiro's National Conference of People Living with HIV/AIDS, which has been held annually since 1991, has also played a critical role in promoting visibility and political voice among people living with HIV/AIDS.

31. See Daniel, *Vida/Life*; Daniel and Parker, *AIDS*; Galvão, "AIDS e imprensa"; Klein, "AIDS, Activism"; Terto, "Homosexuality and Seropositivity."

32. Câmara da Silva, "Triangulo Rosa"; Vallinoto, "A construação de solidariedade."

33. Galvão, "As respostas das organizações."

34. Klein, "'The Ghetto Is Over'"; Parker, "Empowerment" and *Beneath the Equator*; Parker and Terto, *Entre homens*; Terto, "Homosexuality and Seropositivity"; and Terto et al., "AIDS Prevention."

35. Parker, *Beneath the Equator*.

36. Klein. "'The Ghetto Is Over'"; Parker, *Beneath the Equator*.

37. There are several reasons for this. One is that even though the overwhelming majority of travestis do use condoms with their clients, condoms can burst or slip off and remain inside a travesti's anus after intercourse. There are also travestis who are less careful about using condoms, either because they know or suspect themselves to be HIV positive, or because they are desperate for money and a client offers to pay them more if they agree to be penetrated (or even to penetrate him) without a condom. Astonishingly, these kinds of clients remain common (for some interesting analysis and interviews with clients who say they do not use condoms when they visit male prostitutes, see Veneziani and Reim, *I mignotti*, 199–252). A final reason HIV remains a grave threat to travestis is that condoms are almost invariably dispensed with entirely in a travesti's private relationship with her boyfriend(s). Using a condom with a man one loves would be like treating him like a client, and it is well documented that one of the ways prostitutes (not just travestis) mark the status of their partner as special is to not use condoms during sex (see Kulick, *Travesti*, 242 n. 3, for a discussion).

38. Larvie, "Managing Desire," has argued that international and national governmental agencies that work on AIDS issues (e.g., the World Health Organization, the Brazilian National AIDS Program) have played a critical role in the very creation of categories (e.g., sex professionals, men who have sex with men, transgendered people, street youth) around which travestis and other disempowered groups often organize.

39. Daniel, "Bankruptcy," 33.

40. For example, in August 1994 approximately thirty travestis and fifty of their "Open-Minded" supporters staged a protest march through the streets of downtown Porto Alegre in response to the killing of the travesti Cris Loira (a GAPA group participant) by a client on the streets of Porto Alegre's main travesti prostitution zone (Klein, "AIDS, Activism" and "From One 'Battle'").

41. Seidman, *Difference Troubles*.

42. There is a substantial and growing literature, mostly by geographers, on "queering public space." All scholars who write on this make the point that the mass appearance of gays, lesbians and/or transgendered persons in public space "queers" it: i.e., it (a) reveals that public space thought to be unmarked or neutral in regard sexuality is in fact heavily saturated with *heterosexuality* (hence the common reaction to such manifestations as scandalous and unseemly), and (b) it reterritorializes the space to be space that can host queers (see, e.g., Bell and Valentine, *Mapping Desire*; Duncan, "Renegotiating Gender and Sexuality"; Hubbard, "Sex Zones"; Nast, "Unsexy Geographies").

43. We are indebted to Roger Lancaster's formulation of a similar point in his discussion of this ethnographic data, which comes from Klein, "From One 'Battle'" (Lancaster, "Transgenderism in Latin America," 270). We have augmented Lancaster's observations with our own to foreground the notion of shame.

44. Žižek makes a useful distinction between political acts that "remain within the

framework of existing social relations," and what he calls the "political act proper." A political act or intervention proper "is not simply something that works well within the framework of existing relations, but something that *changes the very framework that determines how things work*" (*The Ticklish Subject*, 199; emphasis in original)

45. The anthropologists Hélio Silva and Cristina de Oliveira Florentino estimate that the Rio de Janeiro equivalents of daily tabloids like the British *Sun* or *Daily News* feature articles about travestis on the average of twice a week ("A sociedade dos travestis," 107).

46. This had been a major bone of contention between travesti groups and the Brazilian Ministry of Health ever since the ministry financed and published a text called *Manual do Multiplicador—Homosexual* (The Manual for Multipliers—Homosexuality); a "multiplier" is the ministry's term for engaged persons who develop educational methods and practices in specifically targeted communities. The manual explained homosexuality for people who work with HIV prevention programs. The part of the manual that concerned travestis, authored by the then-president of the Gay Group of Bahia, Luiz Mott, discussed travestis in ways many of them found deeply offensive. For example, the text designates travestis as *rapazes de peito* (boys with breasts) and asserts in lurid language that they are part of "the same subculture [*subcultura*] of violence that dominates the subculture of prostitution" (Brazilian Ministry of Health, *Manual*, 26). This text led to heated protests from travesti groups and demands that future official texts about travestis be written in consultation with travesti representatives.

47. Quoted in Larvie, "Queerness," 539; emphasis added.

Works Cited

Alvarez, Sonia. *Engendering Democracy in Brazil: Women's Movements in Transition Politics*. Princeton, NJ: Princeton University Press, 1990.

Bataille, Georges. *Erotism: Death and Sensuality*. San Francisco: City Light Books, 1957.

Bell, David, and Gill Valentine, eds.. *Mapping Desire: Geographies of Sexuality*. London: Routledge, 1995.

Brazilian Ministry of Health. *Manual do Multiplicador—Homosexual*. Brasília: Ministério da Saúde, 1996.

Browning, Barbara. "The Closed Body." *Women and Performance: A Journal of Feminist Theory* 8, no. 2 (1996): 1-18.

Burns, E. Bradford. *A History of Brazil*. 3rd ed. New York: Columbia University Press, 1993.

Câmara da Silva, Cristina Luci. "Triangulo Rosa: a busca pela cidadania dos homossexuais." Master's thesis, Universidade Federal do Rio de Janeiro, 1993.

Costa, Jurandir Freire. *A inocência e o vício: estudos sobre o homoerotismo*. Rio de Janeiro: Relume-Dumará, 1992.

Daniel, Herbert. "The Bankruptcy of the Models: Myths and Realities of AIDS in Brazil." In Herbert Daniel and Richard Parker, *Sexuality, Politics and AIDS in Brazil: In Another World?* London: Falmer Press, 1993.

———. *Vida antes da morte/Life before Death*. Rio de Janeiro: Jabotí, 1989.

Daniel, Herbert, and Richard Parker. *AIDS: a terceira epidemia*. São Paulo: Iglu Editora, 1990.

———. *Sexuality, Politics and AIDS in Brazil: In Another World?* London: Falmer Press, 1993.

Darwin, Charles. *The Expression of the Emotions in Man and Animals*. Chicago: University of Chicago Press, 1985.

Duncan, Nancy. "Renegotiating Gender and Sexuality in Public and Private Places." In *Bodyspace: Destabilizing Geographies of Gender and Sexuality*, ed. Nancy Duncan. London: Routledge, 1996.

Fernandes, Rubem Cesar. *Privado porém público: o terceiro setor na América Látina*. Rio de Janeiro: Relume-Dumará, 1994.

Freud, Sigmund. *Totem and Taboo*. New York: W. W. Norton, 1950.

Fraser, Nancy. *Justice Interruptus: Critical Reflections on the "Postsocialist" Condition*. London and New York: Routledge, 1997.

Galvão, Jane. "AIDS: a 'doença' e os 'doentes.'" *Comunicações do ISER* 4 (1985): 42–47.

———. "AIDS e imprensa: um estudo de antropologia social." Master's thesis, Universidade Federal do Rio de Janeiro, 1992.

———. "As respostas das organizações não-governamentais brasileiras frente à epidemia de HIV/AIDS." In *Políticas, instituições e AIDS: Enfrentando a epidemia no Brasil*, ed. Richard Parker. Rio de Janeiro: Jorge Zahar Editor/ABIA, 1997.

Green, James N. "Beyond Carnival: Homosexuality in Twentieth-Century Brazil." Ph.D. diss., University of California, Los Angeles, 1996.

———. *Beyond Carnival: Homosexuality in Twentieth Century Brazil*. Chicago: University of Chicago Press, 1999.

Honneth, Axel. *The Fragmented World of the Social: Essays in Social and Political Philosophy*. Albany: State University of New York Press, 1995.

———. *The Struggle for Recognition: The Moral Grammar of Social Conflicts*. Cambridge, MA: MIT Press, 1996.

Hubbard, Phil. 2001. "Sex Zones: Intimacy, Citizenship and Public Space." *Sexualities* 4, no. 1 (2001): 51–71.

Klein, Charles H. "AIDS, Activism, and the Social Imagination in Brazil." Ph.D. diss., University of Michigan, 1996.

———. "From One 'Battle' to Another: The Making of a Travesti Political Movement in a Brazilian City." *Sexualities* 1, no. 3 (1998): 329–43.

———. "'The Ghetto Is Over, Darling': Emerging Gay Communities and Gender and Sexual Politics in Contemporary Brazil." *Culture, Health, and Sexuality* 1, no. 3 (1999): 239–60.

———. "Para onde caminham as NGOs na luta contra a AIDS." *HIVeraz* 2 (1994): 7–8.

Kulick, Don. *Travesti: Sex, Gender, and Culture among Brazilian Transgendered Prostitutes*. Chicago: University of Chicago Press, 1998.

Lancaster, Roger. "Transgenderism in Latin America: Some Critical Introductory Remarks on Identities and Practices." *Sexualities* 1, no. 3 (1998): 261–74.

Landim, Leilah, ed. *Para além do mercado e do estado? Filantropia e cidadania no Brasil*. Rio de Janeiro: ISER/Série Textos de Pesquisa, 1993.

————, ed. *Sem fins lucrativos: as organizações não-governamentais no Brasil*. Rio de Janeiro: ISER, 1988.

Larvie, Sean Patrick. "Managing Desire: Sexuality, Citizenship and AIDS in Contemporary Brazil." Ph.D. diss., University of Chicago, 1998.

————. "Queerness and the Specter of Brazilian National Ruin." *GLQ* 5, no. 4 (1999): 527–58.

MacRae, Edward. 1990. *A construação da igualdade: identidade sexual e política no Brasil da "abertura."* Campinas, Brazil: Editora de UNICAMP.

————. 1992. "Homosexual Identities in Transitional Brazilian Politics." In *The Making of Social Movements in Latin America*, ed. Arturo Escobar and Sonia Alvarez. Boulder, CO: Westview Press.

Moraes, Cláudia, and Sergio Carrara. "Um mal de folhetim." *Comunicações do ISER* 4 (1985a): 20–27.

————. "Um vírus só não faz doença." *Comunicações do ISER* 4 (1985b): 5–19.

Mott, Luiz. *O sexo prohibido: virgens, gays e escravos nas garras da inquisção*. Campinas, Brazil: Papirus, 1989.

Nast, Heidi. "Unsexy Geographies." *Gender, Place and Culture* 5, no. 2 (1998): 191–206.

Parker, Richard. *Beneath the Equator: Cultures of Desire, Male Homosexuality and Emerging Gay Communities in Brazil*. New York: Routledge, 1999.

————. *A construação da solidariedade: AIDS, sexualidade e política no Brasil*. Rio de Janeiro: ABIA, IMS-UERJ, and Relume-Dumará, 1994.

————. "Empowerment, Community Mobilization, and Social Change in the Face of HIV/AIDS." *AIDS* 10, suppl. 3 (1996):S27–S31.

Parker, Richard, and Veriano Terto, Jr., eds. *Entre homens: homossexualidade e AIDS no Brasil*. Rio de Janeiro: ABIA, 1998.

Rito, Lucia. *Muito prazer, Roberta Close*. Rio de Janeiro: Editora Rosa dos Tempos, 1998.

Scott, James. *Domination and the Arts of Resistance: Hidden Transcripts*. New Haven, CT: Yale University Press, 1990.

Scheper-Hughes, Nancy. *Death without Weeping: The Violence of Everyday Life in Brazil*. Berkeley and Los Angeles: University of California Press, 1992.

Scherer-Warren, Ilse, and Paulo J. Krischke, eds. *Uma revolução no cotidiano: os novos movimentos sociais na América Latina*. São Paulo: Editora Brasiliense, 1987.

Sedgwick, Eve Kosofsky. "Queer Performativity: Henry James's *The Art of the Novel.*" *GLQ* 1, no. 1 (1993): 1–16.

Seidman, Steven. *Difference Troubles: Queering Social Theory and Sexual Politics*. Cambridge: Cambridge University Press, 1997.

Silva, Hélio R. S., and Cristina de Oliveira Florentino. "A sociedade dos travestis: espelhos, papéis e interpretações." In *Sexualidades brasileiras*, ed. Richard Parker and Regina Maris Barbosa. Rio de Janeiro: Rene Dumará, 1996.

Skidmore, Thomas E. *The Politics of Military Rule in Brazil, 1964–85*. New York: Oxford University Press, 1988.

Taylor, Charles. *Multiculturalism and the "Politics of Recognition."* Princeton, NJ: Princeton University Press, 1992.

Terto, Veriano, Jr. "Homosexuality and Seropositivity: The Construction of Social Identities in Brazil." In *Framing the Sexual Subject: The Politics of Gender, Sexuality and Power*, ed. Richard G. Parker, Regina Maria Barbosa, and Peter Aggleton. Berkeley and Los Angeles: University of California Press, 2000.

Terto, Veriano, Jr., Edgar Merchán-Hamann, Kátia Guimarães, Maria Eugênia Lemos Fernandes, Murilo Mota, Vagner de Almeida, and Richard Parker. "Projeto Homossexualidades: a prevenção de AIDS de homens que fazem sexo com homens no Rio de Janeiro e São Paulo." In *Entre Homens: Homossexualidade e AIDS no Brasil*, ed. Richard Parker and Veriano Terto Jr. Rio de Janeiro: ABIA, 1998.

Terto, Veriano, Jr., Richard Parker, Murilo Mota, Katia Guimarães, and Renato Quemmel. "AIDS Prevention and Gay Community Mobilization in Brazil." *Development* 2 (1995): 49–53.

Trevisan, João Silvério. *Perverts in Paradise*. London: GMP, 1986.

Vallinoto, Tereza Christina. "A construação de solidariedade: um estudo sobre a resposta coletiva à AIDS." Master's thesis, Escola Nacional de Saúde Pública, 1991.

Veneziani, Antonio, and Riccardo Reim. *I mignotti: vite venduti e storie vissute di prostitute, gigolò e travestiti*. 2nd ed. Roma: Castelvecchi, 1999.

Žižek, Slavoj. *The Ticklish Subject: The Absent Center of Political Ontology*. London and New York: Verso, 1999.

[N E I L   B A R T L E T T]

"Plunge Into Your Shame"

Neil Bartlett is a novelist, theater and opera director, playwright, translator, performance artist, historian, and sometime gay civil rights and HIV/AIDS activist. The recipient of an O.B.E. for services to the British theater, he first came to prominence in the late 1980s as a founding member of Gloria, a groundbreaking theatrical collective that created thirteen original works of performance and music-theater from 1988 to 1998 and collaborated with (among others) the National Theatre, the Royal Court, and the New York Theatre Workshop. From 1994 to 2004 Bartlett was the artistic director of the Lyric Hammersmith and established its reputation as one of London's most adventurous and best-loved theaters. At the Lyric he translated, adapted, and directed many plays, from classic works by Shakespeare, Molière, and Marivaux to lesser-known dramas by Dumas, Labiche, and Kleist; he staged the English-language premiere of Jean Genet's Splendid's *as well as adaptations of Dickens's* A Christmas Carol *and* Oliver Twist *and Wilde's* The Picture of Dorian Gray. *Many of his adaptations have been restaged in such theaters as the Goodman Theater in Chicago and Arena Stage in Washington, D.C. In 2005, he directed Marlowe's* Dido, Queen of Carthage *for the American Repertory Theater in Cambridge, and in 2007, an American revival of his* Oliver Twist *for the A.R.T., Theatre for a New Audience in New York, and the Berkeley Repertory Theatre. Neil Bartlett's own plays include* A Vision of Love Revealed in Sleep, In Extremis, *and* Night After Night, *and his prose works include a remarkable study in gay male history (or meta-history),* Who Was That Man? A Present for Mr Oscar Wilde; *three novels,* Ready to Catch Him Should He Fall, Mr Clive and Mr Page *(published in the United States as* The House on Brooke Street *and shortlisted for the 1996 Whitbread Prize), and* Skin Lane; *and a collection of dramatic monologues,* Solo Voices. *He gave an interview to David Halperin on Friday, September 30, 2005, in Ann Arbor, during a visit to the University of Michigan, and the remarks of his that follow are based on an edited transcript of that conversation.*

Neil Bartlett (NB): About the relations between shame and theater: By "the-ater" I mean a huge range of kinds of public performance, from drag acts in working-class pubs to opera at the London Coliseum to West End the-ater to subsidized art theater (all the kinds of work that I go and see, really, and some of the kinds of work that I make)—but whatever the gig, I *always* ask myself the same question: what are we paying those people who appear up on that stage to *do?* Because we always do pay them—none of these art forms is free. It seems to me that we pay them to do the things that we *don't* do, sometimes in a very simple sense: we pay people because they're more beautiful than we are, or because they can sing better than we can (that's why gymnastics and sports are sister arts to theater, because they're also about simple *skill*), and some of the things that performers do—the things that we can't do, or don't do, or we *pretend* that we don't do—are shameful things. I mean, theater is basically about misbehaving, isn't it? You never pay good money to sit there in the dark and watch people *behave*. Drama could be defined as people misbehaving in public for wages.

I've always loved and been drawn to those art forms in which people mis-behave *spectacularly*—the kind of costume drama which centers on a heroine who misbehaves so badly that she must be severely punished, for instance, whether that's Somerset Maugham's *The Letter* or Racine's *Bérénice*: specta-cles where the heroine suffers for our pleasure. I suppose what we're pay-ing for *there* is to watch performers act out either things that we've dreamt of doing but don't dare do, like kill people or fuck people, or things that we think on some subliminal level that we *have* done or have been accused of doing. As we watch them, we share their crime; we share their shame.

People say that shame prevents communication. In the theater there is a very particular kind of communication: the actors talk and perform and wave their arms around and dance and sing (depending on the art form), but the audience's role is to be silent, to simply *listen*, to a greater or lesser degree. Of course, there are some other art forms where the audience joins in the chorus, for instance in the music hall, or where applause becomes an intrinsic part of the performance, as in grand opera, but in the theater it's precisely because everything is done in silence that the sharing of shame, the sharing of the shameful act is very potent. There is a joke that theater, like sex, is best done in the dark. You know the old joke, "Is sex dirty? Only if you're doing it right." Is theater dirty? Only if they're doing it right. As I say all this, I'm quite aware that there are other kinds of theater which are *not* about these things, but there *is* an enormous amount of theater which *is* about performing shameful actions. And as we watch them per-formed, in this strange, heightened silence, we don't think what we're *sup-*

posed to think, which is, "Oh my God, I'm so ashamed; this is showing me that I must never do that again," or "I never should have done that," or "My mother was right, that's dreadful." In general, I think it would be true to say our response is, "Oh, isn't she fabulous!" Certainly, in my work that is often the case. I think somewhere in *Ready to Catch Him Should He Fall*, when the lovers O and Boy are going out for the evening, the narrator says, "They preferred either operas or farces; anything in which men were reduced to tears or a woman was forced to sing."

David Halperin (DH): How does shame work in the case of the performer, especially a queer performer?

NB: Well, let me talk about my own experience. There are moments when you have an absolutely concrete sense of negotiating with the audience around the issue of shame, when you *know* you are about to do a shameful action. This happens microscopically, from second to second, in the performance—and this goes for singing a song or doing a drag number at a benefit or performing a performance-art monologue—when you say to the audience, or you imply by the way you prepare to perform something, "I am now going to do something that I *know* you do not want to watch me do, I am going to go too far, I'm going to embarrass you, because I'm doing something shameful." For instance, I'm going to be too effeminate, I'm going to be too loud, I'm going to be too obscene. Or watch me, I'm being *too* tender, I'm being *too* sincere—I'm sorry but I'm going to talk *not* dirty for a moment. I'm going to really get down to the common emotional reality of our shared experience. That can be *very* shaming, very embarrassing. Especially for men.

Sometimes, as a performer, you know there's a difficult bit coming up in the show; you think, I'm about to turn a tricky corner in the material, and this is going to be difficult for me to do. Say it's something a bit too dirty, or a bit too close to the bone in one way or another. What you then do is somehow *use* the audience's expectation of the moment: you reverse the relationship between the shamer and the shamed; you blame them. You play that bit as if to imply, "You all want me to do this. OK, then, I'll do it, and it's *your* fault, because *you* asked me to do it. It's not really me that's responsible." For instance, I've appeared in some of the *most* terrible outfits on stage, really shaming things, and I've always felt, "This is *your* fault! *You* wanted me to dress like this, and so I am, and now you're going to applaud me for it!" There's a real conversation going on in these moments, and the reason why the conversation can be so powerful, and also so malleable, so flexible from second to second in the performance, is that we have such incredibly well-developed ideas about what is shameful and what is not.

DH: What is the connection between the social shame of being different, deviant, queer, and the determination, often from an early age, to perform in public, to take performance as a birthright?

NB: Well, it's a mysterious process, but since so many of us do it, there must be some kind of truth universally acknowledged lurking in there. When they tell you—"they" being in my case conservative, small-town, white, south-of-England culture, as exemplified by my parents, my neighbors, my school—when they tell you that little boys *don't do that*, you just obey—up to a certain point; then, when you get to be a teenager, you spend more time on your own at school; then, when you get to college, you're really unsupervised, so now they can't stop you doing it. You still probably don't really know *what* they're trying to stop you doing, exactly. You may know that, for instance, being girly (whatever that means: vocal or physical mannerisms, dressing up, wearing makeup, whatever)—you know that being girly is something you're not supposed to do, but you will also suspect that being girly is only a symptom of *something else*, some unnamed thing. It's not being girly in itself that's dreadful, it's because *if* you're girly, that "means" something else. I think I knew that as a child, and as a teenager I certainly knew it, and later on as an artist I exploited this strange sense that you don't know what *the thing itself* is—which gives rise to that strange, exploitable instinct that "if I adopt the symptom, maybe I'll discover, or catch, or *become* the disease." Certainly, that was true in my case.

When I was at college, I was wearing semi-drag a lot of the time, and a lot of makeup. I hadn't entered into the world of drag yet, I didn't know any drag queens at that point, and I hadn't ever seen a drag performance as such. Pantomime, theater, yes; but not gay drag; I didn't know about it. For me, my early forays into dressing up were coming from punk, where you could dye your hair and wear makeup and weird clothes on the street; in fact, it was expected. But I somehow divined that by taking those symptoms and by effeminizing them even more and by starting to "gay" them—I was clearly a fairy, not a punk, because I had a shirt on my back that said, "Now do you believe in fairies?"—I divined somehow that that would help to turn me into a homosexual, or a gay man, or whatever this *thing* was that no one could tell me about, but which I had an instinct I was. Performing is *pretending* to be something, it's *dressing up as* something, it's *disguising yourself as* something, but the trick is, by performing it, you *become* the thing.

At the same time as I was doing this, in different arenas I was starting to make my first forays into butch drag, where I was doing something that wasn't deemed to be shameful in the same way—in other words, dressing in a very masculine way, and having facial hair, and lowering my voice, and trying to look "Masculine" with a capital M. As it turned out, I found that *much* more mortifying. I can remember going to Heaven, *the* big gay night-club in London, in butch drag, in my checked shirt and my tight jeans, and spending the evening in an agony of shame, thinking, "I am *so* embarrassed, no one believes that I'm butch, everyone can see that I am pretending." Then someone came on to me and picked me up and I haven't looked back since. As a student I never found the draggy-faggy-fairy thing humiliating—I loved it, I took to it like a duck to water—but the butch thing. . . . Oh, I can remember the first time I bought a jock strap, I can remember trying it on. For me, and I'm blushing now just talking about this, that was for me like when Quentin Crisp in *The Naked Civil Servant* dances in his mother's clothes in front of the mirror as a child; that was me, trying to be an athlete, trying to be butch—that was deeply, deeply shaming. But I made it. I made it, I came through; by performing it, I became it.

All children dress up—I'm not an anthropologist but I think all children dress up. I think all children play mummies and daddies, I think all children masquerade. I think performing alternative versions of yourself in the subconscious hope that you'll arrive at yourself—I think that is absolutely normal.

I can't remember my parents ever policing my desire to perform. I went to the Edinburgh Festival with some friends from school. This is when I was fourteen or fifteen. I was, unbeknownst to my parents, already a fully fledged queer. I was having an affair with my religious knowledge teacher, I was regularly having sex with men on the way home from school in tearooms. And the show I did in Edinburgh with my school friends. . . . We did a street-theater performance based on the characters of the Commedia dell'Arte, and I played the lover in the troupe, the unmasked character, which was basically just me in fabulous Renaissance drag which I'd made for myself, and this wonderful elaborate makeup, walking around making up sonnets and waving my hands in the air. I must have been *totally* faggy, but I didn't really realize that at fifteen. As soon as I began to make the connection between the dressing up and the gayness, then I knew I could only do it in special places. I knew I could do it in college, which was odd; I felt safe there. OK, it was pushing the envelope a bit—my tutors never formally objected, but one or two of them were not very happy about the fact that I would wear makeup according to the century we were studying that term.

But still I knew I had to take that makeup off on the train before I got back home to visit the parents; that was not a safe space in which to perform myself in that way.

DH: A recurrent theme in the current thinking about gay shame is that shame is not necessarily something to be got rid of. The dictates of gay pride require us to overcome and jettison our shame, but now we are being told (by Eve Sedgwick and others) that you can't just excise your shame from the rest of you.

NB: I think a lot of this has to do, in my experience, with the butch/femme argument. Getting rid of your gay shame, in London in 1982, was about getting rid of the negative, effeminate stereotype, butching up, dressing like a real man, pretending to be American, becoming a confident, sexually active gay man—*that* was getting rid of your shame. It was rejecting the Church, rejecting Europe even, rejecting Englishness, rejecting the small town. You were going to dress up like The Village People and be one of the guys—not even one of the *boys*: one of the *guys*—and *that* was rejecting shame. Equal and opposite to that movement, culturally, it now turns out for me, was the performance world, and my first meetings with drag queens, particularly Bette Bourne and the Bloolips, and through them encountering the repercussions of the first wave of gay liberation in London. There it wasn't a question of avoiding the shame of effeminacy; the advice I was getting from all my newfound drag-queen surrogate mothers and aunties was, "No, plunge *into* your shame, hook, line, and sinker. And, in fact, do the most shameful thing which any man can do, which is, put on a frock, walk down the street in the frock, so that you will be abused—worse than women, even, are abused—so that you will be threatened with physical assault. Go forth and make it clear to the world that the two things that you love more than anything else in Western Civilization are taking it down the throat and up the ass!" Because, you see, masculinization was all about saying, "I'm a fucker." (I know, I know, this is such a parody of our history, and I hope everyone who's reading this knows that it was and is more complicated than that!) And the femme response, the radical gay liberation movement response, the radical drag response, was, "I love to get fucked. I'm like a woman— I'm the one who gets fucked socially, politically, and physically. I'm the one who gets fucked." That tactic of saying, "Don't give up your shame," "Go *into* your shame" ("Go into the light, children; *all* are welcome, cross over," as the clairvoyant says in *Poltergeist*, oh god I love that scene so much where she says that, sorry—carried away there—you'll have to leave that out of the transcript!): I think that the idea is that you can go *into* your shame, and, by performing your own shame *to excess*, you heal yourself. Empower yourself. And for me this is not a theory, this is an absolutely physical sensation.

An example: there's a moment in my performance piece *The Seven Sacraments of Nicolas Poussin* where I impersonate Mary Magdalene, and I scramble fragments from some of the confessional psalms, and from the gospel account of the moment where the Magdalene anoints Christ's feet with her tears, with a sex rap of me as the passive partner in a public sex scene.[1] It was very hard to write, and even harder to perform. I can remember the first time I read it, in front of my colleagues in a private read-through, and I had to stop. These were two men who were very dear colleagues, straight men (but that's irrelevant), I know them very well, I trust them with everything about my work, and I had to say, "I'm going to have to stop, I just don't think I can say these words in public, I feel I'm blaspheming, I'm mixing the words of the Bible with obscenity; I can't do it."

Now, everyone in the world knows Neil loves to get fucked, but when it came to standing up there and saying those words, it was very hard. When I did it in performance, the sensation of confession, of "I confess my shame, I enact my shame in public, I say, *this is me—I am Mary at the feet of Christ, I am filth and I need forgiveness*," was amazing. Because it *was* a performance: I wasn't in church, I wasn't saying to a Higher Power, "I want you to forgive me." I was *enacting* that moment on my own terms, and it was extraordinarily powerful for me, and, more to the point, it was very powerful for all the people who watched me do it. I'd never made that connection with that Bible story before, but it was a very powerful moment.

DH: Isn't it still disgraceful, even in queer circles, to identify oneself as a bottom?

NB: Yes. There's a very dangerous thing in current pornography—there are very many dangerous things in pornography—where the bottom is always a kind of cheerful joke. "I'm a pig! I'm a slut!" Bottoms aren't often shown as real people in pornography. They don't have personalities; too often in gay men's culture they're either a joke in the way that we talk about them or they're peculiarly absent as people, as performers. That's a whole other conversation. We need to be talking about specific pieces of work, I think, but I agree with you by and large about that.

DH: What did you mean about "healing yourself" of shame, then?

NB: Well, in some simple way, a sense of, "It is all right for me to be like this. I've confronted my own worst fear, and it didn't hurt; in fact, it was fabulous." That's the feeling. They tell you, "If you do this thing, terrible things will happen: someone will beat you up, or your mother will find out, or people will laugh at you," or whatever—and, hey presto, you do it, and then find yourself saying, "Actually that was one of the best nights I've had out in years! That was fantastic, thank you, I feel much better." So, in very concrete, simple ways, it can be exhilarating and liberating.

My experience of gay culture has been that you find other people who share your shame. That whole tactic through which, by making you ashamed of things, the straight world tries to isolate you and make you introverted—boy, is that their big mistake! Because what happens, when we then find each other—whether that's finding one other person or whether that's walking into a nightclub where there are a thousand other people or going to a demonstration where there are a hundred thousand other people—what happens is that that very powerful edict completely backfires, and precisely because we are now doing together what we were told would isolate us. We're doing it together—enacting our shame together. The liberating potential of that is kind of exponential. That's what being on a big demonstration or on a crowded dance floor is like. It's like queer fission. Some sort of chain reaction goes on, and everyone's transgression multiplies everyone else's.

But, because we're talking about performance, the tension around our shame never resolves. It's never a question of, "I've done that and now I'm a real, complete man, and I don't need to do that anymore." No, I need to do it—or watch it—again next weekend! And not because I'm a profoundly sick person and I need help—not because what I *should* do is stop all this and just go into therapy, where someone would really get me to work through my shame and then I wouldn't need to do this anymore—no, that isn't it at all, thank you very much. But because the world I live in means that I need constant reaffirmation.

Of course one reason why we choose to constantly reenact or rewitness our shame—and are we even allowed to broach this subject?—is that performance, the performance of transgression, is intensely pleasurable. Could that be the reason? That we don't just go to discos and drag shows and sex clubs because we are helpless consumers of late Western decadent gay culture, but because pleasure is necessary. . . .

DH: Does that imply that whether or not we are healed, or healing, we need to take our shame along with us? We need to retain it, if we want there to be hundreds of thousands of other people at the demonstration?

NB: Maybe. Maybe. Yes, because otherwise, if we're saying shame can be "worked through," then in some idiotic way we're proposing that this wonderful bit of our lives is going to end, and this time next Wednesday we'll all be "cured," so really we ought to leave all of this behind. We're talking about (and some of us *are* talking about this, people have argued for this very strongly) choosing to end the traditional forms of gay culture. And I don't choose that.

I have one other thing I'd like to throw into our conversation. I can't talk very intelligently about it, but it must be screamingly obvious to anyone who's reading this transcript that the deep model, in my culture at least, of this need to reenact shame on a weekly basis is religion. It can't be an accident that I spent my childhood going through a weekly ritual where you perform shame in public. In the Anglican rite, before you approach the Table for communion, you say out loud, kneeling next to your parents and your grandmother and neighbors, in my case, "We are not worthy so much as to gather up the crumbs under your table," and you then confess your sins. In the Anglican rite, you do it privately, you have a little quiet moment, where the vicar says, "We will now confess our sins." You don't recite them in public, but I used to kneel there and, in silence, I would think about the bad things I had done—perhaps that is the true origin of the silence in which I now want to perform shameful acts in public. . . . Anyway, then you go up to the Table and you're given the treats and you feel better. It's a wonderful thing. Of course, that ritual takes place under an image of the most beautiful man you've ever seen, not wearing any clothes, who wants you to tell him that you love him as much as he loves you, so there's also *that* old chestnut to be dealt with. . . .

DH: Is theater, then, for you, the anti-church?

NB: In a very simple way it's deeply anti-church because it's so much more fun. It's so much more fun, it's so loud and splendid. The Church of England was pretty tacky and timid, aesthetically speaking, the version that I grew up in.

DH: As a performer, you do it night after night, but for so many people theater is more like a weekly thing, like going to church, or instead of going to church.

NB: No. No, I don't really think so, because theater is public and commercial—no, I don't see the theater as being defined by or replacing the church in that way. I think this working out of religious roots I've talked about is a very interior, private thing with me. Perhaps the religious dimension comes out in my performance work, because that's a very private, singular, small-scale kind of theater. But Theater with a capital T is a big, public, commercial business.

Your question does remind me of one thing though. When I was in Toronto in the mid-'80s, performing and having a fabulous affair, I got to hang out with a bunch of guys who called themselves The Family. I only spent about ten days with them, but they turned my head around—I'd never seen people living like that. Their terminology was, "Are you going to Church?," which meant, "Will we see you in thse bar on Friday, or on Saturday? Are you going to *Church*?" So in that sense, yes, a certain sort of subcultural or marginal theater is like church because when you get there, you know the rest of the congregation. When you go to the West End, to the commercial theater, you're in a room full of strangers. For me, you see, one of the defining aspects of church ritual is that you know your fellow celebrants and they know you. So, yes, bar culture and drag culture can be very like going to church. Absolutely. Going to see Regina Fong at the Black Cap, or going to see Lily Savage at the Vauxhall Tavern back in the early '80s, that was like going to church—we were the congregation and she was the celebrant. Absolutely. Yes, absolutely, I would say. Especially in Regina's case; there was an order of service, certain specified hymns (show tunes), of which the congregation knew all of the words, and a kind of final celebratory, transfigurative ritual, involving a final punch line. Yes, definitely, when Regina Fong and the congregation at the Black Cap all screamed, "Jungle Red!" in unison at the end of the night, she might as well have been saying, "Go in peace and serve the Lord." You had to be there. Believe me, it was that good.

Note

1. See the appendix for the complete text of this passage.

Appendix

Excerpted from Neil Bartlett's performance piece "The Seven Sacraments of Nicolas Poussin," in his Solo Voices: Monologues, 1987–2004 *(London: Oberon Books, 2005), 95–128.*

The third slide: **Marriage.**

Dearly Beloved, the third painting depicts the sacrament of Marriage, and shows us **gathered together here in the sight of the congregation and in the face** of considerable public opposition **to join this man and this woman in holy Matrimony, which is an holy estate and is commended to be honourable among all men, and therefore is not by any to be enterprised, nor taken in hand, unadvisedly or lightly; to which the celebrant shall reply:**

How every true.

There are twenty-four figures in this painting. The priest, in the centre, is in a yellow robe. There are ten guests with the groom, including a woman on the far right of the picture standing behind a pillar whose face you can't actually see, and ten with the bride, including that man standing right over there by the door, who I see has chosen to wear black, which I think is a very funny thing to wear to a wedding; he looks very unconvinced by the whole proceedings. And the twenty-fourth guest . . . is me. I'm here to provide the ring. Because I'm not fourteen any longer; and I choose to wear a ring. (*He takes off and holds up his wedding ring.*) And Poussin has placed it here so that the light from a window here on the left hand side of the painting falls exactly on it. Everyone is exactly placed. So that everyone can see. That's the point, after all; you can't do this sort of thing in private.

I was sixteen the first time I saw two people actually doing it.

They made me an usher; I had to say to everyone, *Bride, or Groom?*—meaning, are you with the Bride, in which case you have to sit on the left hand side of the aisle, or are you with the Groom, in which case you have to join the figures on the right hand side of the composition. They ought to ask you that on the door of the club, really. You know; *Have you been here before, and are you Bride or Groom?* It's a very good question: bride or groom, left or right, we haven't got all night dear, we close at two. . . .

When I went to get the ring, the woman in the shop was very brusque. Rather forward, actually. The thing is, according to the brochure, many people now find the traditional plain gold band frankly outmoded, and so I thought, well, let's not be outmoded, let us not: tradition?—ha! . . . Well, it was bewildering. The choice, I mean. And there you are again you see, first of all you have to choose between *his* and *hers*. Which as several of you here tonight will I am quite sure be able to testify, can be such a tricky choice to make, especially before the wedding night—but choose you must, because apparently *hers* start at £750, *his* at £2100, because *his* are chunkier. Men generally prefer it chunkier, I was told. It was all I could do to silently nod my head in agreement. We moved on to the next tray. "Modern Simplicity" . . . well Modern, yes; Simple, I don't think so. Something a little more showy?, she said; So my friends are always telling me, I said. White gold interlocking with matching gypsy-set pink tourmaline was suggested. Well somebody had to speak up. Seems a little *ostentatious*, I said. Seems like someone feels the need to raise their voice, I said. Newfangled, I said; what on earth would I be trying to prove? Which is also a very good question. . . . Engraved?, she said. Engraved?, I said—Engraved, Tattooed, Scarred for Life!—Bruised. . . . On the surface or on the inside, she said. Quite, I said. Time, date, names? Very important, I said; so easily forgotten. A few choice words?, she said. How long have you got, I said. Something basic, like "Everlasting Love," was suggested. Something basic like full civil rights in the lifetime of this parliament was what I had in mind, not that I'm feeling particularly civil, I said, and she said, *Are you taking the piss?*

No.

Though that is also quite a good question.

"Make of our hearts one heart?" she suggested; which seemed to me to be pushing things a little too far once again—and it did raise the whole issue of his and hers again I felt, I mean it's a lovely sentiment, lovely, in fact I think in a way those are some of the most effective lyrics Stephen ever wrote, but look what happened to Maria and Tony—"Even death can't part us now . . .": yeah, right, *in your dreams*, I mean you do find yourself thinking, don't you, are they the only two people in the entire cinema who've never read *Romeo and Juliet*, don't they know what happens? There is a place, somewhere, absolutely, but really, George Chakiris maybe, Natalie Wood I don't think so—she said could I just remind you **that no person whatsoever shall in any interludes, plays or by other form of open Words declare or speak any thing in Derogation, Depraving or Despising of the Form or Manner of the Sacraments,** *The Book of Common Prayer*, 1642, and I quote—I said *please*; please don't tell me that you think I'm joking. Not with the life I've led. Not with the life I'm planning on leading. The life we're owed.

Hmmm . . . traditionalist, are we?, she said. Assimilationist. "Virtually Normal," Southwark Cathedral, all that sort of thing. Something in Latin then, perhaps, she said.

Well, **to speak darkly is a kind of silence,** John Donne, 1627, I said—and I quote. No, I said. So how about this one . . . it was my Mother's. It fits me; and inside, it says: If any one here knows cause or just impediment why these two persons should not be joined together, let him now speak or else hereafter for ever hold his peace.

And then:

The minister shall cause the Man with his right hand to take the woman by the right hand and say after him: I take thee . . . And then the priest, taking the ring, shall deliver it unto the man, to put it upon the fourth finger of the woman's left hand, and the Man holding the ring shall say: With this ring I thee wed . . . and all the guests lean forward, because this is the good bit, the bit they came to see; and the woman behind the pillar, whose face we can't see, that is in fact my grandmother, and I'm so glad she's here to see this. And the man in black watches, very intently; he stares—but not at the ring, but at another man whose face says I know; I know. But people do say them, they say them all the time, these words—and they let other people hear them say it . . . and wouldn't you? Can't you imagine what it's like to want to say those words—even in secret, when it's late, and you're tired, and you can't even see his face, and it's filthy what you're doing, really filthy. Or amongst the faithful, when of course no one in here minds if you kiss him—but you two mind how you go on the way home tonight . . . . Or right in the middle of town, in the middle of the afternoon, right in the midst of the congregation, when **the priest shall then say—**

Notice how in this composition the sun is about to shine down through an archway which is seen through the window which is directly above their hands as they are joined, and the window is garlanded with flowers . . . ; take a step closer . . . can everybody see? . . . See, as the sunlight comes through the arch, and through the window and through the flowers and now exactly strikes the third finger of her left hand—

Oh God I hate weddings. Somebody always comes up to us and says *Hello, is this your friend?* Well, I haven't seen you since—well since you were kneeling down there in that yellow robe in the second painting! "To have and to hold . . ." ah—it's such a lovely service, isn't it—"With my body I thee worship," aren't they just the lucky couple—and look at you now, all these years later, still going to other people's weddings. . . . I see you've chosen to wear black—funny thing to wear to a wedding, I see you've placed yourself as close to the door as you can, but you haven't left, have you—

And he hasn't.

And we can have no idea of what he is thinking, that man over there by the door. We should make no assumptions at all about what he is feeling as he listens very carefully, not unadvisedly, or lightly, as the priest says

Those whom God has joined together
Let no man—
Nobody—
Let no man put asunder.

Don't even *touch* them.

As he slides the ring onto his finger, a flash photograph is taken.

> **I will give thanks**
> **With my whole heart;**
> **Secretly, among the faithful; and in the**
> **congregation.**
> *Psalm 111*

The fourth slide: Penance.

. . . lovely the sun coming out like that. Needn't have used my flash I suppose really. Lovely. And lovely flowers I thought. I do like a good photo. And a video's not the same thing at all in my opinion, because with a video you can't put it in the book, can you? With all your other photos. Turn the pages over and see the people from one photo in another. There you are in your christening robe, there you are at Audrey's wedding and now look at you. And of course we all missed Grandma but there she is on the beach. Nice to have something to look back on. Nice to have people with you.

On the wards here, you'll often see that people have a photograph or two on the little bedside cabinet—well they can be very impersonal these wards, can't they? And when somebody dies they say it's a good idea for the first few months to have a picture of them up in every single room so that you can talk to them whenever you need to ask them a question or something. Also that way they can be watching you the whole time, you don't have to worry about ever being out of their sight. It's nice to have one of them by the side of the bed.

Every night when I go to bed and as soon as I get up in the morning.

Funny though, but anything on the TV with someone dying, I can't watch. Can't watch it at all. Can't look at it.

—I'm sorry. I always cry at weddings. Actually I don't know about you but I cry a lot these days. I was watching this film this afternoon it was ridiculous I—

Oh
I'm sorry
I try and only do it when I'm on my own. Never in public, I—
Oh I'm sorry. I try never to actually let myself go you see because once I've started I'm afraid I'd never stop you see, I don't know—
Oh I'm sorry. Excuse me.
Catch me walking down the street crying! I decided to give all that up almost nine years ago now. It was getting embarrassing. I used to be just walking down the street and then I'd—
Oh!

Sorry. You see what I mean? Embarrassing. Now I try and do it just when I'm indoors. Not in front of other people. Obviously I have to practise not making too much noise when I do it, even then—I find having the television on helps, and also a towel. Sort of on my face. I mean you don't want people to pass the house and think oh dear what on earth is that woman crying for do you? I mean someone might come and knock on the door and ask you if you were—yes, fine, really, no thank you . . . I'm sorry. Oh dear, could you? I'm sorry, it's not as if I haven't practised believe you me. I don't want to upset anybody you see. I mean I wouldn't ever make a point of it. I wouldn't ever, I mean I just wouldn't, I wouldn't ever walk into a room, I wouldn't ever go into a dark room, full of men, because. . . . Because all the men there would stop and turn and watch me doing it. That's my absolute nightmare, I—

Oh.

Oh I want it to stop. This . . . sadness.

(*Beginning to sound drunk.*)—God I get myself into such a state!!

The fourth of the paintings, portraying the sacrament of Penance, depicts the passage in the Gospel of St Luke in which an unnamed woman—What did you just say? What did you call me?—traditionally identified as Mary Magdalen, who is shown in this picture with her right shoulder exposed—oh I'm sorry—but I hadn't let myself go all evening, and I—and they were all bloody watching me—I went right up to him, and I took hold of his foot in my right hand and I—I couldn't think about anything else—I—I was . . .

. . . a woman who was a sinner, when she knew Jesus sat at meat at the Pharisee's house, she stood at his feet behind him, weeping, and began to wash his feet with her tears, and did wipe them with the hairs of her head, and kissed his feet, and annointed them. And when the Pharisee which had bidden him saw it, he spake within himself, saying, This man, if he were a prophet, would have known who, and what manner of woman, this is, that toucheth him; for she is a sinner. And Jesus answering him said unto him, Thou gavest me no water, but she hath washed my feet with tears; my head with oil thou didst not anoint; but this woman hath anointed my feet. Thou gavest me no kiss, but this woman since the time I came in hath not ceased to kiss me feet; let her alone. She hath done what she could. This she hath done shall be spoken of; wherever this gospel shall be preached, this that she hath done shall be spoken of for a memorial of her. And he said to the woman: Go; go in peace . . .

. . . I'm sorry? Peace? What's that then? Is that what you call what I've never 'ad?

He opens a can of beer.

She had no bloody shame—she did it right there in front of all those men. She bent over—*and I've done that*—she took 'is foot in 'er 'and—*and I've done that*—she opened 'er mouth, and she . . .

Pardon me. No, really.

Go on; pardon me. Pardon me for exposing the back of my neck to a stranger's gaze. Pardon me for saying you've got no idea how much I need this. Forgive me. Shut me up. Push me down with one hand on each shoulder, go on, *make me*. Forgive me, for I have sinned right down there in the very back of my throat, with three fingers down there, with the heel of a boot, with how bloody *thick* it is, with the whispers, the noise, the sounds I let out, I can't believe the words I say sometimes, *Jesus!*

Make me forget my own name
Make me not care, *come on, make me!*
Make me do it again, and slower.
Turn the light on.
Make me do it for money.
Make me do it in public places.
Make me do it in my parent's house.
Make me do it with your son.

Tell people all about me—and then forgive me.
Flood me; dissolve me; wash me away;
Scatter me in drops, spill me, pour me out;
Make me despair.
Wear me out, wring me out, beggar me;
Wither me,
Spend me,
Waste, enervate, destroy and demolish me;
Make me despair—and then forgive me.
For I acknowledge my faults; make me a clean heart, *break me* . . .
And then forgive me.
Excuse me.
Pardon me.

Pardon?
Pardon me?
Catch me being one of those people who do it in public.
Cry, I mean.
I can't stand that sort of thing.

The Magdalen is not depicted alone with Christ. Six of the other guests at the feast are staring at her and four of them are pointing at her, they include a man having a drink who has no idea what she is talking about and who obviously doesn't need forgiving for anything, that's probably because he's got nothing to confess; two men saying to each other, did you see that?—did you *see* that?—and a man looking out of the picture straight at the viewer (the only one in all of the seven canvases who does that) and raises his left eyebrow; and his left eyebrow says: I expect you all saw that.

And at the very front of the picture, a young man, who has heard and seen nothing, kneels, and very carefully, pours out a pitcher of red wine, as she pours out her heart . . . without . . . spilling . . . a . . . drop.

Red wine is poured from the beer can.

In the third painting, the Bride has her hair covered, and in this fourth painting the Magdalen lets her hair down; the Magdalen's skin is exposed, and the Bride's is covered. One has a name, and the other doesn't. Everyone is looking at them, that's the same in both pictures, but don't tell me you haven't noticed the difference; I noticed it even when I was sixteen. The difference is in the third finger of the right hand. Even if the ring has been taken off an X-ray will still reveal the characteristic callous just below the first joint of the third finger thus enabling us to distinguish between the accepted, and the unacceptable.

There are no women at all in the next picture.

Thank you.

[J E N N I F E R   M O O N]

Gay Shame and the Politics of Identity

In Jonathan Tolins's play *The Last Sunday in June*, a gay male couple about to move to the suburbs reluctantly observes New York's annual Gay Pride parade from their apartment on Christopher Street while friends, ex-lovers, and tricks drop by to stir up trouble. The play is self-consciously "meta," with the characters repeatedly joking about how they seem like typical figures in the standard gay play, doing what gay characters in gay plays generally do: attempting to assuage their feelings of self-loathing through bitchiness and humor. Alternately envious and disdainful of the shirtless muscle boys in the parade, the men feel disillusioned and alienated by the spectacle below, yet are unable to pry themselves away from the window. A collective crisis ensues when James, an ex-boyfriend of two other characters and the critically panned author of *Circuit Boy*, reveals that he is marrying a woman because he is tired of unsuccessfully fitting into the gay scene. His disclosure forces the other characters to acknowledge their own ambivalence toward the sex-driven, image-obsessed gay community, but by the time the men decide to band together, be proud of their status as average homosexuals in a world of gay supermen, and march in the parade, the festivities have ended and the cruising has begun. The play concludes with the painful breakup of Tom and Michael alone in their apartment, after learning of each other's infidelities during the course of their seven-year union. Traumatized by James's compromised decision to marry, Michael tearfully refuses a similarly sexless, companionate arrangement with Tom and thereby denies the audience the happy ending this "typical gay play" had earlier promised.

Thanks to David Halperin, Valerie Traub, Brendan Sanchez, and Heather Seltzer for their valuable suggestions and much-needed encouragement.

The vision presented in *The Last Sunday in June* is a stark one, and though the play deliberately deals in gay stereotypes and clichés, it offers a compelling critique of gay community and the concept of pride. As standard figures in the "typical gay play," the men are positioned as representative spokesmen for the white gay male community, and the tensions and conflicts dramatized in the play serve as powerful allegory. Reluctant to claim the gay community as their own, many of the men feel little affinity toward the perfectly chiseled or rainbow-bedecked participants outside, and their alienation and disdain suggest how far removed the celebration of pride is from their everyday lives. For them, this annual display of gay community simply reinforces their sense of marginalization from an already marginalized population. Only Charles, the aging opera queen who participated in the first Pride march, and Joe, the flamboyant newbie excited to be in a room full of gay men, provide perspective on the benefits and necessity of gay community. Ironically, what unites these men on Gay Pride Weekend is the news of James's engagement and their shared defensiveness at his betrayal of "the cause," not the official celebration of gay culture going on outside. James's feelings of shame and self-loathing evoke the others' own insecurities, but rather than attempting to eliminate these troubling emotions by switching teams, the men in the play instead recognize in their shared marginalization a basis for community and a unifying force. For although the men remain divided and apathetic toward the Pride festivities, they stage an impromptu intervention for James and his fiancée upon hearing of his decision to go straight. Despite this display of solidarity, the play ends with the dissolution of a seven-year partnership and the implication that not even the poster children of gay pride—the monogamous, middle-class couple—are immune to alienation, self-loathing, and shame, even on Gay Pride Weekend.

The Last Sunday in June opened at New York's Rattlestick Theatre and ran there from February 9 to March 16, 2003, after which the play moved off Broadway to the Century Center for the Performing Arts. The performance I saw was on May 14, 2003, nearly two months after the University of Michigan's Gay Shame conference, hosted March 27–29, 2003. Witty and moving, *The Last Sunday in June* demonstrates the potentially mobilizing and productive aspects of shame, the very concepts the conference sought to explore. In its dramatization of the tensions surrounding gay identity, the play exposes the limitations of a politics and culture centered on gay pride and lends support to the assertion that David Halperin made in his opening remarks at the conference: "Before there was Gay Shame, there was already gay shame." The play suggests, like the concept of gay shame itself, that as long as sexuality is policed and viewed in moralizing terms by the mainstream, those of us with deviant desires and gendered self-presentations will be excluded and marginalized. In such a context, shame and alienation cannot be eliminated and might instead form the basis of a new, collective identity and a radical queer politics.

As an alternative to the utopian celebration of pride, an exploration of shame seems both timely and relevant. Douglas Crimp, whose paper on the shaming of Mario Montez in Andy Warhol's *Screen Test #2* initiated the discussion of shame at the conference, argues that shame has "the capacity for articulating collectivities of the shamed": "[The contemporary politics of gay and lesbian pride] sees shame as conventional indignity rather than the affective substrate necessary to the transformation of one's distinctiveness into a queer kind of dignity."[1] Though profoundly individualizing, shame affectively unites the already marginalized. Crimp's vision of "collectivities of the shamed" derives from Eve Sedgwick's writings on queer performativity: "Shame interests me politically, then, because it generates and legitimates the place of identity—the *question* of identity—at the origin of the impulse to the performative; but does so without giving that identity-space the standing of an essence."[2] As Crimp and Sedgwick suggest, shame, as a discourse of Otherness, provides an antidote to identity politics, yet without ignoring the fact that certain identities are irredeemably marked. Whereas the men in *The Last Sunday in June* remain divided on the meaning of gay identity and are unwilling to celebrate the version embodied by Gay Pride, they do agree on one thing: shame is an inescapable part of gay identity.

Shame distinguishes the queer from the normal, not because there is anything inherently shameful about having deviant desires or engaging in deviant acts, but because shame adheres to (or is supposed to adhere to) any position of social alienation or nonconformity. Shame thus seems especially useful to a radical queer politics for three main reasons: (1) it has the potential to organize a discourse of queer counterpublicity, as opposed to the mainstream discourse of pride; (2) it provides the basis for a collective queer identity, spanning differences in age, race, class, gender, ability, and sexual practice; and (3) it redirects attention away from internal antagonisms within the gay community to a more relevant divide—that is, between heteronormative and queer sectors of society.

Throughout the course of the conference, these potentially productive aspects of shame were articulated sporadically, but discussion was repeatedly impeded by narrower claims about the relevance of shame to particular categories of identity. These issues of identity-based representation, while certainly important, functioned as a form of shaming of others. Instead of exploring the possible alliances and affinities between disparate queer communities, conference participants, during both formal presentations and informal discussion periods, used shame to police group boundaries, which had the effect of exacerbating existing divisions within the community and limiting cross-identifications between groups. In making this claim and detailing it more fully in what follows, I hope to be read neither as making a naive plea for camaraderie, nor as attempting to deny the specific forms of oppression and intolerance that different groups face. Rather, I wish to emphasize that outside of some academic circles and a few major metropolitan centers, these distinctions of identity make little difference. In a world where same-sex couples, regardless of race or gender, can feel completely safe holding hands only during Gay Pride events and where a conference on gay shame requires precautionary security guards, much more is to be gained in finding productive uses for our already existing shame than in trying to shame others like us.

In the second issue of the queer activist zine *Swallow Your Pride*, the organizers of the Gay Shame events in Brooklyn set forth their political stance: "We are ashamed of Chelsea homogeneity, 'community' as a corporate target market, giuliani in the 'pride' parade, foaming-at-the-mouth praise for anti-feminist 'pro-gay' beer advertising, and reactionary 'we're just like you' gays and lesbians who ally themselves with straight, racist conservatives." As the members of the activism panel—Stephen Kent Jusick, Mattilda (aka Matt Bernstein Sycamore), and Oakie Treadwell—made clear on the first day of the conference, Gay Shame, in its original, activist form, is a queer-radical, anti-assimilationist, anticorporate, antiglobalization, pro-sex movement committed to exposing the hypocrisies of the mainstream gay and lesbian movement and to creating a radical outsider queer culture. It provides a radical queer alternative to consumerist pride parades and as such helps constitute a queer counterpublic. Nancy Fraser defines "subaltern counterpublics" as "parallel discursive arenas where members of subordinated social groups invent and circulate counterdiscourses to formulate oppositional interpretations of their identities, interests, and needs."[3] A specifically queer counterpublic would, following Michael Warner and Lauren Berlant, reject a politics of assimilation and instead foster an independent, sexually rebellious ethos of antinormativity. The concept of a queer counterpublic encompasses much more than merely commitment to a particular political agenda:

By queer culture we mean a world-making project, where world, like public, differs from community or group because it necessarily includes more people than can be identified, more spaces than can be mapped beyond a few reference points, modes of feeling that can be learned rather than experienced as birthright. . . . World-making, as much in the mode of dirty talk as of print-mediated representation, is dispersed through incommensurate registers, by definition unrealizable as community or identity.[4]

Queer counterpublicity is a celebration of exclusion and marginality; it is the conscious development of print and visual cultures, private institutions and occupied public spaces, and personal styles, affects, and politics that collectively seek to modify or subvert heteronorms.

Emma Crandall's presentation during the "Fuck Activism?" panel aptly demonstrated what one version of queer world-making or counterpublicity might look like. In describing her feelings of shame at not being activist enough, Crandall playfully proposed an alternate term, "activity-ism," to describe the everyday acts of queer resistance in which she and her friends engage on the streets of Ann Arbor. Crandall suggested that she and her friends, who "look weird and do weird things," challenge heteronormativity and suburban conventionality by being publicly, visibly queer: they have tattoos, piercings, and funky hair; they have an androgynous punk style; they spray-paint queer-radical and feminist slogans on walls and T-shirts; and they take over Ann Arbor during Punk Week with homemade go-cart racing. What these disparate behaviors amount to is a queer occupation of public space, a demand for recognition without the compromise of assimilation. Like the concept of gay shame itself, activity-ism is a form of queer counterpublicity in its celebration of the marginal, its rejection of the mainstream, and its articulation of a discourse of Otherness.

Throughout the conference, this potential for shame to function as a vehicle for queer mobilization was overshadowed by questions regarding the degree to which shame marked different configurations of identity. In an early and influential presentation, Judith Halberstam criticized the notion that shame applies equally to bodies differently marked by race and gender, and, like Sedgwick, she focused on the childhood origins of shame. Drawing on Sedgwick's influential proclamation—"If 'queer' is a politically potent term, which it is, that's because, far from being detachable from the childhood scene of shame, it cleaves to that scene as a near-inexhaustible source of transformational energy"[5]—Halberstam warned of possibly negative implications of a politics of shame: that it might glorify a pre-Stonewall past and overlook newer discourses of transgenderism, race, and immigra-

tion; that it idealizes youth; and that it focuses on the too psychically invested subject. She pointed out the traditional associations of shame with
femininity and rage with masculinity, and she argued that "the childhood
scene of shame" applied only to the white gay man humiliated by his deviant femininity and symbolic castration. She further asserted that the butch
lesbian does not experience her masculinity as shameful, in childhood or
in adulthood.

Although I appreciate Halberstam's warnings against overidealizing
shame, as well as her careful attention to differences of race and gender, I
find the rest of her argument a bit problematic. First, why doesn't the butch
lesbian experience her masculinity as shameful? If it's because she has
something that the gay man doesn't have—namely, masculinity—doesn't
the denial of butch lesbian shame merely reify masculinity as presence and
femininity as lack? The assertion that the butch lesbian is merely proud of
and empowered by her masculinity leaves the femme lesbian, the straight
woman, and the gay man at a loss, literally. Halberstam's argument depends
on the notion that femininity is inherently less desirable and more shameful than masculinity; but although this may be true in our society, not all
types of masculinity are therefore equally valued, as she herself argues in
Female Masculinity. At the conference, however, Halberstam's implication
that masculinity in any form, even when routed through a female body, is
socially validated seems to align butch lesbians with straight men as inher-
itors of a normative masculinity. Second, why *doesn't* the butch lesbian experience her masculinity as shameful? It seems that any position of gender dissonance, whether of male femininity or female masculinity, would
be met with social disapproval and ostracism. Although there may be mar-
ginally more acceptance of tomboys than of sissy boys, butch lesbians
surely do not experience less public harassment, condescension, or hatred
than gay men. Like effeminate men, butch lesbians and mannish women
are visibly marked and subjected to scorn and mockery. They are supposed
to feel ashamed, and if they don't, it's because they've developed the self-
confidence needed to protect themselves.

Third, the projection of shame from butch lesbians onto gay men polar-
ized the conference, making it into a queer battle of the sexes. Halberstam's
remarks brought to the forefront existing tensions within the queer community, and her denial that butch lesbians experience any sort of shame
magnified the differences between lesbians and gay men, rather than the
affinities. In projecting shame onto gay men alone, rather than exploring
how shame might similarly inform the butch lesbian experience of social
nonconformity, Halberstam in effect reprimanded gay men for being un-

comfortable with their gender deviance and implied that their shame was in some way invalid. In the context of the conference, such implications limited productive dialogue between these two groups and became part of a recurring pattern of shaming and identity policing.

The shaming of conference participants took a number of different forms, but in each instance, shame functioned to mark off one group from another and to bring into play questions regarding authenticity and the right to speak. For example, members of the activism panel began their presentation by accusing academics of appropriating queer culture to further their own careers and by suggesting that "Gay Sham" would be a more fitting title for the conference. In positing a clear divide between queer activists and queer academics, the members of the activist panel not only overlooked the history of LGBT activism and the biographies of conference participants, but also asserted that only one group had a legitimate perspective on the topic of gay shame. By criticizing the ivory tower for its ostensible lack of political engagement, the activists cast academics as too bourgeois for gay-shame activism. Their shaming of the audience was an attack on academic privilege that fell along lines of class and age, with the implication that those who were not marginalized enough did not have the authority to speak about radical politics and social justice.

Halberstam's denial of butch lesbian shame and the activists' critique of academia, though certainly quite different, were both made from positions of identity and directed against those with power and privilege. During the conference the other major identity marker—besides gender, age, and class—that provoked shaming and confrontation was race, an area of inquiry that seemed initially overlooked in the opening discussions. *Screen Test #2*, the Andy Warhol film that kicked off the Gay Shame proceedings and formed the basis of Douglas Crimp's essay on shame, featured Miss Montez, a Latina drag queen humiliated in front of the camera by Ronald Tavel and Warhol, the white master manipulators offstage. In his article Crimp fails to address the racialized overtones of Montez's shaming and during the discussion period devoted to the essay expressed little interest in analyzing the racial politics of the film. Although Crimp attempted to keep sexual shaming separate from racial shaming, race, gender, and sexuality can never be understood independently of one another, as feminists have understood for years and as commentators such as Hiram Perez rightfully pointed out. Furthermore, the screening of Warhol's film was followed by "Intimacy and Tomorrow," a loosely knit, multimedia performance by Vaginal Davis, an African American drag queen. Since drag queens and people of color form some of the most underrepresented and disenfranchised sectors of the queer community, it seemed anything but coincidental that performances by two drag queens of color opened the conference. Although the inclusion of these two performances does not mean that white shame is always mediated by brown bodies, an attention to race is essential to ensure that this is not the case.

Failure to consider questions of race is a form of racism, just as inattention to gender perpetuates sexism. At the same time, attempting to acknowledge all forms of difference—whether of race, gender, class, ethnicity, ability, or sexual practice—is simply not feasible at all times. When taken to its logical extremes, the decentering of the universal white male subject, one of the major accomplishments of postmodernism, has the potential to slide into a narrow identity politics, in which it becomes impossible to meet every minority demand for recognition and equitable representation. These tensions surrounding the degree to which difference can and should be acknowledged pose a theoretical and political problem, one that was made manifest during the conference by the conflict between Perez and Ellis Hanson.

In his presentation Ellis Hanson analyzed the erotics of pedagogy in Plato's *Symposium* while a pornographic slide show of Kiko, a man of color, played in the background. Hanson briefly introduced Kiko, noted that he himself was wearing the same outfit as Kiko (white polo shirt and khaki shorts), and continued with his presentation, without further explanation. Meanwhile, the slides featured Kiko in a classroom setting, becoming progressively more naked and exposed, until he was finally shown in a variety of explicit shots. The following day, during the final discussion session, Perez, one of the panelists, responded passionately to Hanson's presentation. Acknowledging that he might be considered "hysterical," Perez described his sense of shame and outrage upon viewing the slides of Kiko. As a man of color, he felt as if he could not view such images, whatever their context, without being reminded of specific histories of racial oppression, and he publicly shamed Hanson as a white gay man who *could* ignore such implications. Like many of the presenters at the conference, Perez spoke of his shame in highly personal terms, beginning with his nervousness around white gay men and academics in general. During the following question-and-answer period, Hanson and Perez reached a stalemate, with Hanson maintaining that he had deliberately tried to provoke a shame dynamic with his presentation and Perez asserting that such negative minority representations should never be publicly displayed.

Hanson might have better contextualized his slideshow and presentation; at the same time, Perez's justifiable outrage illustrates some of the potential problems with identity politics, and particularly with its relation to shame as a vehicle of queer mobilization. First, in casting himself as the man of color and Hanson as the white gay man and by couching his critique in highly personal terms, Perez made race into something that could only be individually experienced, with the implication that people should therefore speak only from positions of identity. Like the lesbian-versus–gay man and the academic-versus-activist divides, the white subject–versus–person of color dynamic limited productive dialogue and was based on the erroneous assumption that one's identity necessarily determines one's politics. White gay men do not all share the same politics any more than lesbians, people of color, academics, or activists do. Second, although differences of race, class, gender, ability, and sexual practice must be acknowledged, there is also the possibility that time spent focusing on differences within the queer community takes away from antihomophobic work. If the point of gay shame is to forge a new collective identity resistant to the normalizing discourse of pride, then the real enemy is religious and social conservatives, not white gay men. Attention to specificities of gender and race does not necessarily fracture collective thinking, but it is important that differences between groups not define the totality of the analysis. Third, the demand for specific histories and accounts of shame simply cannot be met for all minority groups. It is impossible to elaborate exactly how bisexuals, gay Asians, disabled femmes, or butch Chicanas, for example, experience shame. Not only does such elaboration have the potential to be endless and thereby to fragment the larger movement, but it also poses the danger of devolving into a comparative ranking of experiences of shame. The question should not be which groups feel more or less shame than others—another version of the "who's more oppressed?" game—but rather how systems of power intersect to mark off the queer from the normal.

Finally, the demand for specific histories of shame is an individualizing move, one that was reflected throughout the conference by the prevalence of personal anecdotes and confessional moments. Conference participants recounted their personal histories of shame, which, though entertaining and sometimes poignant, cannot form the basis of a collective identity or movement. Narratives of shame are often coming-out stories differently inflected, and though they may have therapeutic value and contribute to a history and culture of shame, they are not generalizable within groups. And this is where my critiques of Halberstam, the activists, and Perez come together: in trying to demonstrate how differences in identity produce varying experiences of shame, they each claimed to speak as representatives of a particular minority group. Yet shame is a profoundly individual experience, even for people who share particular features of identity, which is why attempts to define specific group experiences of shame may come across as defensive or overly simplistic. As evidenced by the conference, the tendency exists for different levels of shame—individual experiences, minority-group experiences, and collective gay experiences—to be conflated. Shame is a provocative emotion that elicits personal histories, but its greater value, as Crimp and Sedgwick suggest, lies in its general appeal as a marker of social nonconformity. In order to effectively mobilize a constituency held together by something so elusive as sexual preference, gay shame needs to move away from individually felt, subjective experiences of shame and toward shame as a collective identity defined by alienation and exclusion; in this case, the personal does not always make for effective politics.

Let me conclude by describing one final shaming confrontation that occurred during the first day of the conference. Responding primarily to Amalia Ziv's presentation on lesbian pornography featuring gay men, one of the panelists, Patrick Moore, noted that his writings on gay men have always been particularly well received by women and was appreciative that so many lesbians were doing work on gay men. During the question-and-answer session, an audience member, Elisabeth Ladenson, rhetorically challenged the panel, inquiring as to whether any gay men were doing work on lesbians. Although Michael Warner, another panelist, was able to provide one example of a gay male porn film featuring a lesbian with a dildo, the rest of the room was shamed into silence. After an awkward pause and Judith Halberstam's ironic suggestion that conference participants go back to talking about gay men, conversation turned to a discussion of barebacking, with the male panelists responding to Barry Adam's questioning on HIV transmission rates. The extended discussion was interrupted when a male conference participant rose to ask, "Is there *lesbian* barebacking?" Pleased at the taunting question, many audience members applauded, while the panelists once again sat in shamed silence. The panel chair, Carolyn Dinshaw, reluctantly responded that as far as she knew, there wasn't, and the conference adjourned for the day.

I include the preceding exchange in some detail, not only because I myself was a (mostly silent) member of the panel, but because I felt particularly implicated in the discussion. There I was, surrounded by five academic celebrities, four of whom also happened to be white gay men: what was *I* doing writing about white gay men too? Why wasn't I writing about lesbians? Or even Asian lesbians? And how could I respond to the question about lesbian barebacking, when I was not only shamed by the question, but also *shy?*[6]

This essay began as an attempt to think through these questions, and perhaps my own defensiveness at their implications colored part of my argument. However, in asserting that claims about gay shame made from positions of identity only exacerbate existing tensions within the community, I do not mean to justify the centrality of white gay male culture. Instead of hoping for fair and accurate representations of all different kinds of queer peoples, might it not be productive to explore the cultural fascination that white gay masculinity holds within our culture and to examine the complicated identifications across lines of race, gender, and sexuality that take place as a result? If representations of white gay men are the dominant forms in which homosexuality is currently imagined, and if these representations play a large role in our understanding of what constitutes collective gay identity, then how do these images of gay men shape *other* queer identities? What role do cross-identifications play in the construction of individual queer identities, especially for those of us whose identities tend not to be represented in popular culture?[7]

Darieck Scott, in an essay on the politics of interracial gay sex, attempts to describe the appeal of white masculinity:

White dick is socially and historically represented to us as potency; it is power, and power is sexy, just as sex can be the exercise of power—or rather, just as sex can be the interplay of relatively empowered and relatively disempowered roles, roles that can become all the more erotically charged when the markers of different kinds of power, gender/race/sexuality, are acknowledged. The sexiness of power (and the fears of and revulsion from it) is, perhaps, the sexiness of white men.[8]

For Scott, who is African American, white men embody not only power, but also eroticized difference, and he argues that black men's desire for white men might mean more than one thing, more than internalized self-hatred and racial disloyalty. Similarly, I would argue that queer identifications with white gay masculinity do not reflect a straightforward wish to be like white gay men, with whatever advantages that might entail. Rather, I suggest that white gay masculinity is a complex "interplay of relatively empowered and disempowered roles," to use Scott's words in a different context, and that it is this unique combination of autonomy and ostracism, of privilege and shame, that makes representations of white gay men such a potent force within our culture. Even though "white dick" may be traditionally associated with power and authority, its meaning necessarily changes when moved from a heterosexual to a homosexual context. White gay masculinity represents a normative masculinity under siege; it registers the effects of sexual stigma without succumbing to that burden; and it demonstrates that social marginalization need not preclude the development of autonomous sexual publics. In short, white gay masculinity might provide a compelling model for other queer identities because it makes clearly visible the inconsistencies, contradictions, and inadequacies that are central to *all* identities, especially those marked by sexual deviance and shame.[9]

Notes

1. Douglas Crimp, "Mario Montez, For Shame," this volume, 72.

2. Eve Sedgwick, "Shame and Performativity: Henry James's New York Edition Prefaces," in *Henry James's New York Edition: The Construction of Authorship*, ed. David McWhirter (Stanford, CA: Stanford University Press, 1995), 239.

3. Nancy Fraser, "Rethinking the Public Sphere," in *Habermas and the Public Sphere*, ed. Craig Calhoun (Cambridge, MA: MIT Press, 1992), 123.

4. Michael Warner and Lauren Berlant, "Sex in Public," in Michael Warner, *Publics and Counterpublics* (New York: Zone Books, 2002), 198.

5. Sedgwick, "Shame and Performativity," 210.

6. Ibid., 238: "Some of the infants, children, and adults in whom shame remains the most available mediator of identity are the ones called (in a related word) shy. ('Remember the fifties?' Lily Tomlin asks. 'No one was gay in the fifties; they were just shy.')"

7. These questions have been undertheorized within queer studies, although there are a few notable examples of critics engaging with issues of lesbian cross-identification with queer masculinity: Eve Sedgwick, *Epistemology of the Closet* (Berkeley: University of California Press, 1990); Eve Sedgwick, "Willa Cather and Others," in *Tendencies* (Durham, NC: Duke University Press, 1993), 167–76; Judith Halberstam, *Female Masculinity* (Durham, NC: Duke University Press, 1998); Stephen Maddison, *Fags, Hags, and Queer Sisters: Gender Dissent and Heterosocial Bonds in Gay Culture* (New York: St. Martin's Press, 2000); Anne Herrmann, *Queering the Moderns: Poses/Portraits/Performances* (New York: Palgrave, 2000); José Esteban Muñoz, *Disidentifications: Queers of Color and the Performance of Politics* (Minneapolis: University of Minnesota Press, 1999).

8. Darieck Scott, "Jungle Fever? Black Gay Identity Politics, White Dick, and the Utopian Bedroom," *GLQ* 1, no. 3 (1993): 310.

9. For further analysis of this claim, see Jennifer Elizabeth Moon, "Cruising and Queer Counterpublics: Theories and Fictions," Ph.D. diss., University of Michigan, 2006.

[G A Y L E R U B I N]

A Little Humility

The Limits of Resistance

Where there is power, there is resistance. . . . There is no single locus of great Refusal, no soul of revolt, source of all rebellions, or pure law of the revolutionary. Instead there is a plurality of resistances, each of them a special case. . . . They are the
odd term in relations of power; they are inscribed in the latter as an irreducible opposite. Hence they too are distributed in irregular fashion: the points, knots, or focuses of resistance are spread over time and space at varying densities, at times
mobilizing groups or individuals in a definitive way, inflaming certain points of the
body, certain moments in life, certain types of behavior. Are there no great radical
ruptures, massive binary divisions, then? Occasionally, yes. But more often one is
dealing with mobile and transitory points of resistance, producing cleavages in a society that shift about, fracturing unities and effecting regroupings, furrowing across
individuals themselves. . . . It is doubtless the strategic codification of these points
of resistance that makes a revolution possible.

Michel Foucault, *The History of Sexuality,* vol. 1

Foucault's comments on resistance and revolution are a reminder of
the transitory quality of pretty much every group, idea, or stance that is
anointed as the agent of history or the source of social upheaval. Much of
this conference has been devoted to exploring the ways that gay pride has
lost its critical edge, and to the potential of gay shame to reignite a less commercial and more vibrant form of gay activism.[1] However, I can recall when
"gay pride" was saturated with all that sense of passion and power of cultural insurrection. Like Carroll Smith-Rosenberg, I remember with considerable nostalgia the time when radical lesbianism was similarly vibrant—
fun, erotic, rebellious, redolent of feminism and gravid with critique. But
much of that lesbian feminism I recall with such pleasure eventually de-

volved into a dictatorship of prudish bullies who loved nothing better than to condemn everyone—especially other lesbians—whose beliefs or behavior differed from their own.

Many of the problems that have been identified for gay pride or lesbian feminism, however, come from the expectation that their generative and world-shattering moments are supposed to be permanent conditions. As Foucault cautioned, this is unrealistic. Various formations of power, as they develop historically and in particular social contexts, animate certain moments, movements, persons, practices, places, and things with sensibilities of resistance, rebellion, or transgression. But these are generally transient. Some sites of resistance are more durable or recurrent than others, but most change eventually, as the social structures of domination shift and develop. It is an exercise in futility to anoint any particular critical stance or political movement with permanent transgressive or revolutionary status. Gay pride may be exhausted; gay shame will have its day. But this too shall pass. Some day gay shame will seem just as tired.

We have a kind of long hangover from Marxism, in which there is a constant search for the next movement or group whose activities will bring about a better society for all. This expectation of a final perfectibility owes a good deal as well to millennial Christianity and its watchful expectation of an imminent return to a heavenly version of the garden of Eden. Various constituencies want to claim the mantle of the industrial proletariat and the status as the chosen agent of social change and revolutionary upheaval. This quest produces two sorts of problems. The first is that temporary inflammations are mistaken for permanent potencies. The second is that the legitimacy of various groups is articulated in terms of whether or not they are "revolutionary" or transgressive or oppositional or embody some critique of whatever is the prevailing system of power (capitalism, gender, binarism, categories, etc.). It should not be necessary to justify gay populations, or transgendered individuals, or movements for civil equality for all citizens regardless of whom and how they fuck by arguing that they possess some special quality and power to bring about economic utopia or recreate an earthly paradise.

Meg Conkey, an archaeologist at Berkeley, likes to tell her students that "today's solutions are tomorrow's problems." A corollary is that today's problems are often yesterday's solutions. If there are problems now with gay pride, these are collateral consequences of activism that seemed like a good idea at the time. In fact, gay pride was a great idea, one that should be credited with many profoundly important positive results. But no good idea goes unpunished by shifting conditions and the passage of time. Such considerations lead me to suggest that along with pride and shame, we should be giving due consideration to humility: humility about the inevitability of change; humility about the imperfection of our formulations; and humility toward the decisions of the past, which were made in different circumstances and under different conditions to meet a different set of needs. Moreover, whatever we do today will be critically assessed when it becomes part of the past (if not before). History makes fools of us all, sooner or later. We can only hope that it is later, and do our best to ensure that the positive contributions outweigh the collateral damage.

The Schools and the Streets

A recurrent theme of the Gay Shame conference was the relationship—often a troubled one—between academy and community, activism and scholarship, those who do and those who think. I do not want to underestimate these troubles or dismiss these tensions. However, it worth recalling that at least in the case of sexual politics, the movements for sexual freedom and equality and the academic study of sex have been deeply entangled with one another for the better part of the last century or so.

First, there has been considerable overlap of personnel. An emblematic figure in this regard is Magnus Hirschfeld, the pioneer German sexologist and early homosexual activist. Hirschfeld produced a vast body of scholarly work on homosexuality whose importance was eclipsed by the destruction of his life's work and legacy by the Nazis. Hirschfeld was also one of the founders of the early German movement to decriminalize and destigmatize homosexuality.[2]

Even when individual scholars are not themselves activists, academic work on sexuality is still an interactive site where research and communities have repeatedly been mutually engaged. Communities of sexual deviants (homosexuals, etc.) have become material for scholars, and scholarship has provided resources to build community and political mobilization. Homosexual men, for instance, actively used Krafft-Ebing's work as a vehicle to promote their views, as a means of personal identification, and as a resource for moral and psychological justification.[3] In fact, sexology as an enterprise from its beginnings in the late nineteenth century provided vast symbolic resources not only for gay men, but also for lesbians and other assorted sexual perverts. Havelock Ellis is another example. In contrast to Carroll Smith-Rosenberg and other feminists who find his work distasteful, I (like Paul Robinson) consider his work to have been a huge force in the destigmatization of homosexuality for both men and women, as well as the de-demonization of masturbation, among other things.[4] Similarly, the work and views of Alfred Kinsey and Evelyn Hooker—particularly their assertions that homosexuality was not intrinsically unhealthy and the reclassification of homosexuality as nondiseased—were widely discussed and disseminated in homophile publications and were mobilized at a more authoritative level in the project of getting homosexuality out of the *DSM*.[5]

Disability and Dildos

My favorite sex invention over the past two decades? The silicone dildo, of course. No more of the ugly hard plastic dong of yesteryear, our silicone are all about heat and pleasure served up with the dignity and beauty we deserve.

Felice Newman, *On Our Backs*, 2004

I want to conclude with some comments on the recent history of the dildo, inspired by the fabulous panel on disability at the conference. About twenty years ago there was a great dildo divide. In the 1970s, most of the dildos available in the United States were made of a particular type of relatively stiff rubber and were shaped like more or less anatomically correct penises (although they tended toward anatomically unrealistic sizes). These were sold mainly in seedy sex shops that catered mostly to a straight male clientele (or, less frequently, to gay men). They were thus rather intimidating and relatively inaccessible to many female customers. Moreover, the low status and marginal legality of such shops tended to make customers of all kinds feel ashamed. Shopping for dildos was thus part of the furtive and socially stigmatized world of sex shops and porn.

All of this began to shift with the emergence of feminist, woman-oriented sex shops such as Good Vibrations in San Francisco and Eve's Garden in New York City. Both shops began to sell a limited supply of a new kind of dildo. These were made of silicone rubber, which had a softer feel than the older style of dildo, yet sufficient stiffness to "perform" admirably. These silicone rubber dildos were also made in many shapes; in addition to the realistically penile, many were available in more muted designs. These silicone rubber dildos quickly became the favorites among aficionados and standard equipment for lesbians who were interested in penetration.

What most of those who use these dildos do not realize is that the revolution of dildo design, production, and distribution began with a straight black male paraplegic. The silicone dildo was invented by a guy in a wheelchair who wanted to have a sexual relationship with his wife and who did not like the commercially available prosthetic penises. So he developed the silicone dildo and sold a few through Eve's Garden. Good Vibrations then brought the Scorpio dildo to the West Coast. When Susie Bright was managing Good Vibrations, she engaged in intensive discussions with the producer about dildo design; he made one to her specifications, which was called, in her honor, the Susie.

There are now several producers of these silicone dildos, and they come in a vast range of shapes, from dolphins to corncobs to goddesses to equipment that looks as if it belongs on the body of some kind of space alien. There is even a company called Divine Interventions that produces dildos for the blasphemous among us, including the Jackhammer Jesus, God's Rod, the Diving Nun, and the Baby Jesus buttplug. There is also the Buddha's Delight (for finding Nirvana) and the Moses (for parting the Pink Sea and getting to the Promised Land). But everyone who has ever used a silicone dildo—lesbians, bisexuals, women fucking their boyfriends—owes a great debt of gratitude to a straight black guy in a wheelchair who was trying to improve his marital sex life.

The story of the silicone dildo illustrates that much of what we assume without investigation can be wrong, that social life is infinitely complex, and that the social histories of sexual change are often full of surprising connections. This too should make us a little humble, and cautious about consecrating any group as the specially anointed agents of change.

Notes

1. It should be noted that there is no single temporal trajectory for these kinds of developments. The significance and valence of gay pride, or lesbian feminism, vary according to time and place. Somewhere, right now, for someone, gay pride and lesbian feminism are as electrifying as they ever have been anywhere. New York City and rural China are in different time zones, their difference measured not in hours but in years and decades.

2. See James D. Steakley, *The Homosexual Emancipation Movement in Germany* (New York: Arno Press, 1975).

3. See Harry Oosterhuis, *Stepchildren of Nature: Krafft-Ebing, Psychiatry, and the Making of Sexual Identity* (Chicago: University of Chicago Press, 2000).

4. See Paul Robinson, *The Modernization of Sex: Havelock Ellis, Alfred Kinsey, William Masters, and Virginia Johnson* (New York: Harper & Row, 1976).

5. See Ronald Bayer, *Homosexuality and American Psychiatry: The Politics of Diagnosis* (New York: Basic Books, 1981).

[DENNIS ALLEN, JAIME HOVEY, AND JUDITH ROOF]

Enactivism: The Movie

We made "Enactivism: The Movie" as a way to present ways of thinking about the pretexts of gay, lesbian, and queer activism through various modes of performance and enaction. We hoped the film would work enactively—that is, illustrate the ideas it presents via the ways it presents those ideas. "Enactivism" does offer a set of theses: (1) that activist activities are historical and contextual, (2) that effective activism strategically and enactively plays upon context, and (3) that to perform strategic activism we need to know what we are doing—activist activities must be theorized.

Context

Activism is always historical and contextual, both the product of and a response to a particular sociocultural moment. But the very concept of activism itself is also historically local, available only after a certain time. It is difficult to imagine Joan of Arc, for example, describing herself as a pro-France activist or the Luddites seeing themselves as engaging in "environmental terrorism," and, not too surprisingly, the word itself does not appear in the first volume (A–Ant) of the first edition of the *Oxford English Dictionary*, completed in January 1884. Activism would seem, then, to be a product of the twentieth century. One question we wanted to address in our film was whether activism is viable, either as a concept or a practice, in the twenty-first century, at least insofar as lesbians, gays, and bisexuals are concerned.

We wondered this because it seems like there's so much less of it than there used to be. The second wave of lesbigay/queer activism, which flourished under the aegis of organizations such as ACT UP and Queer Nation during the 1980s, began to dissipate rapidly in the second half of the 1990s. Perhaps this was because streamlined Food and Drug Administration pro-

cedures for approving the release of new AIDS drugs or the advent of pro-
tease inhibitors reduced the sense of urgency that had spawned ACT UP.
Perhaps, insofar as Queer Nation was concerned, the decline of activism
was simply because lesbigays *were* here and queer and everyone *had* gotten
used to it, including the queers themselves.

Another way to understand the latter point is to venture the speculation that, at least for queers, activism has always, finally, transcended whatever specific issue was involved. Ever since the days of the Mattachine society and the Daughters of Bilitis, there has always been another, overarching
goal in all lesbigay/queer activism: recognition. Typically, this recognition has been articulated and understood in terms of sameness and difference. Traditionally, it has focused on heterosexual acceptance of lesbigays
through the insistence, either overtly or implicitly, that we are really the
same as everyone else or that the ways in which we are different ("what we
do in bed") are minor and unimportant in comparison to the common characteristics we share with everyone else. The alternate approach, the queer
one, has been to insist that the difference is irreducible, that queers interrogate the very assumptions underlying heteronormativity. In this case, the
recognition that is demanded is not merely a recognition of gay difference
or of the political and personal validity of this difference but, finally, a recognition of the impossibility of sameness itself.

Now, as we understand it, activism is by definition oppositional. After
all, whatever the hegemony does or believes is not "activist" but just action
(or, more often perhaps, reaction). As such, the queer stress on difference,
which has been conceptually available in some form since Stonewall itself,
has always provided a much more fertile ground for political action than
the emphasis on sameness. And perhaps, we concluded, the apparent decline in lesbigay/queer activism is the result of a shift in focus from difference to sameness within the gay community in recent years, signaled by
the growing stress on civil unions and "gay marriage" as the issue that must
surely be of greatest importance to the communities united under the les-
bian/gay/bisexual/queer labels.

Taking marriage as the dominant goal of gay politics goes right to the
heart of sameness, of course, seeking integration into the core institution
underlying not only heterosexuality but also, arguably, Western culture
itself. And there does seem to have been a generational shift, a change in
lesbigay goals and ideals, in the past few years. Ten years ago many of the
students in introductory lesbian and gay studies classes self-identified as
queer; nowadays the word goes on the midterm because nobody in the class
is familiar with the term, much less the political stance it represents. In-

stead of shattering sexual identity categories, the goal now seems to be to find a partner at the age of twenty and settle down for good. Or, as one of the students put it during a discussion of Michael Warner's *The Trouble with Normal*, "Maybe I'm just heteronormativity's bitch, but I don't see what's wrong with gay marriage."

Increasingly, it seems, more and more of the hetero and the normative agree with him. The summer of 2003 was a heady one, with the Supreme Court's decision to strike down sodomy laws being widely taken as a major advance for lesbigay rights on a number of fronts and with both Canada and Massachusetts moving toward the legalization of gay marriage. And although the majority of public opinion is still against this, and although the Supreme Court decision produced something of a backlash, nonetheless, opposition to gay marriage has been declining in the last few years. According to a CBS News/*New York Times* poll released on July 30, 2003, 55 percent of those interviewed opposed gay marriage, while 40 percent supported it, numbers unimaginable even twenty years ago. Even more strikingly, age proves to be of some significance here: "Sixty-one percent of 18- to 29-year-olds favor [gay marriage]; that drops to just 18 percent among people 65 and older."[1] Increasingly, it begins to look like being able to list some hers-and-hers towels in the bridal registry is only a matter of time.

If the future thus seems clear, and if, in this not-too-distant future, recognition, acceptance, and sameness will have finally been achieved, then, we thought, most people would see no reason for gay activism, and even the concept of gay shame would be archaic. Maybe it already is. Always slaves to fashion, we were ready to give in and go along with the crowd and start publishing *Reluctant Bride* magazine.

Except for one thing. We couldn't help but wonder whether the insistence on lesbigay sameness by both the homo and the hetero wasn't itself a reflection of gay shame, a repression of the queer difference that it disavows but that must nonetheless exist for the argument for sameness to be raised (to have to be raised) in the first place. And this latent but insistent evidence of the continuation of gay shame seemed to us both to call for continuing lesbigay/queer activism and to imply new modes of activism itself.

To understand this requires a small shift in the metaphoric frame, however. Instead of seeing lesbigays in terms of sameness and difference, we prefer a conception that invokes the ideas of inside and outside—itself another binary, but one that expands infinitely in several directions. There is a queer history for this way of seeing things too, if only in the House Un-American Activities Committee panic over homosexuals as alien elements that had infiltrated the Department of State. And the first night of the Stonewall riots, during which the police barricaded themselves inside the bar while the mob outside tried to get in, can be taken as symbolically apt if we see the struggle for gay rights as a struggle to be included within the nation, to be acknowledged as part of America. The continuing relevance of such metaphorics was demonstrated as recently as July 2003, when President George W. Bush, affirming his opposition to gay marriage during a news conference, also made a plea for tolerance of homosexuals, asserting, "I think it is very important for our society to respect each individual, to welcome those with good hearts, to be a welcoming country," as if queers were the migrant workers of desire.[2]

Now, to be fair, we should note that the Bush administration tended to recycle its sound bites, and that the "welcoming country" trope was a favorite of Colin Powell's, who usually used it to refer to (literal) immigration by Muslims, so that the phrase became a standard formulation the White House employed to signal tolerance, perhaps because it avoids having to mention such notions as diversity and pluralism. Yet the obvious awkwardness and vague inappropriateness of the phrase in the present instance is highly telling, not simply because it frames recognition or acceptance in literally spatial terms (of the geographical country and of immigration), but also because it points to the central confusion that the inevitable literalization of the inside/outside metaphor always produces and then elides. Whether we speak of "the welcoming country" or of letting gays into the military, on the literal level, queers are always already inside these institutions. It seems entirely possible that there was a lesbian nurse at the hospital where Bush was born who very well might have welcomed *him* to the country. What is really at stake here is something else: not physical but conceptual space. What lesbigays and queers want, of course, is to be included in the *idea* of America.

And this is where we think things get interesting. From the standpoint of the inside/outside metaphor, activism has to be understood not as oppositional but as liminal. The activist must be conceptually inside the entity to the extent that he or she believes in it enough to feel it is worth changing, has to be inside it to the extent that he or she initiates protests that will be comprehensible to the other members, has to be inside it enough to be recognized as an activist in the first place rather than simply being seen as irreducibly Other. Yet the activist is always outside the entity to the extent that the ideas that it has are not entirely his or her ideas, or that the idea it has of itself does not include him or her.

Seen in this way, activism—queer activism—does not repress difference, nor does it deny gay shame. What it does do is to make clear that being inside—being recognized—is an ongoing conceptual and ideological struggle and that even when one is "inside," the possibilities for (and the necessity of) activism don't end. Instead, it suggests a new model of activism, one that focuses on the notion that, given the enduring fact of difference, queer inclusion has the power to modify and alter the ideas of the entities and institutions, those "countries," that welcome it. Gay marriage will include lesbigays/queers within a hegemonic structure, but that inclusion will itself begin to change the conception of what that structure is and what it means, revealing that "marriage" is not—has never really been—a monolith but was always already different from itself. This is what we mean when we speak of infiltration as a mode of activism. Because infiltration works from the inside rather than the outside, because it changes what our idea of that inside is, the exact form and shape that such activism will finally take remains to be seen, but our sense is that it will involve pixels more often than picket signs. Our film is thus an attempt to begin enacting what this new activism might be.

Actors

Activism implies an actor or actors. For lesbians, gays, and transgendered people, this actor is understood to be queer, to have a gender or a sexuality, or a gender and a sexuality, that deviates from the heterosexual norm (whatever *that* is supposed to be). The queer identity of activism's actors, though it results in various degrees of social stigma for most of them, has also been a source of strength, allowing people with perverse genders and sexualities to recognize each other and organize politically. At the same time, queer identity has also become interchangeable with queer activism: to be queer is to do the political work of deconstructing heterosexual normativity and privilege. With the rise of queer marketing strategies in consumer culture, identity, agency, presence, and visibility have all become interchangeable. To buy queer is to be queer is to do queer political work. Gay pride events have become about brand endorsements. Being queer, being visible as queer, and supporting queer products have become confused with political activism.

The importance of presence and recognition in queer activism helped contribute to the rise of queer academic "stars" in the 1980s and 1990s in many universities. Academic stardom sprang from the creation of big names to draw other scholars and students to the expanded graduate programs of this era. As Lauren Berlant points out in the film, the star was an important site of optimism about the kinds of activism that might be possible in colleges and universities, an optimism that included making connections between disciplines. As she also notes, one of the unfortunate side effects of academic stardom is the conflation of personality and intellectual ideas, to the point where an academic star's personality and the ideas he or she contributes begin to stand in for each other. The queer academic star system is made up of intellectuals who have become stars because their ideas are so compelling and important, and because many of them have created bodies of work that laid the foundation for thinking about queer genders and sexualities in ways that go way beyond both feminist and lesbian and gay studies models. The star system has helped create the notion of academics in general and queer academics in particular as fabulous, as possessing a value very similar to the star quality of film personalities. This notion of fabulousness, of star quality, has in turn helped create the notion that queer sexuality and gender, treated as shameful and worthless by those who make heterosexual normativity the gold standard of moral behavior, is actually a valuable and compelling way to be in the world. In a post 9/11 world of diminished state budgets, conference travel funds, and fear of travel, queer academic stars, like academic stars more generally, still draw people to conferences by means of celebrity as well as by virtue of their ideas and expertise, and so have remained an attractive way of organizing conferences and of assuring attendance.

But intellectual and personal value shouldn't be reified; it should be dynamic, in process, enactive. Limiting conferences to academic stars ossifies academic discourse and risks limiting the scope of what can be said to what has been said already. A case in point occurred at the Gay Shame conference, when we overheard one graduate student announce to another that only one person on a particular panel was worth hearing because the others were—in his opinion, at least—nobodies. It strikes us that gay shame is right there, in the feeling that we need celebrity scholars to make our conferences meaningful and important, rather than thinking or imagining that the work is enough. Enactivism might suggest not only that stars take the place of where political work should be, but that political work can occupy the space of stardom. Enactivism might imagine that everybody is a star, that stars are important, but that stars are no different from the rest of those of us who teach classes, grade papers, come out as queer to our students, make ourselves resources for them, model courage to our peers, and encourage political desire in our classrooms, our departments, and our colleges and universities.

Talking Activism

Getting away from such star-struck tokenism into another kind of activism—or any kind of activism—requires analysis that works through the assumptions of commodity culture and visibility to more subtle understandings of context and mechanism. Effective analysis, apart from being savvy about historical and cultural contexts, also considers the structures and assumptions underlying any phenomenon of oppression activist activities wish to redress.

It is never enough merely to talk about activism, nor is activism usually mere talk. When activism is mere talk, it is preaching, sanctimony, or opposition. Preaching convinces those who are convinced already. Sanctimony usually parallels the moralistic precepts of the systems and ideas that cause the trouble in the first place. Opposition reifies that which one opposes. Contemporary activism demands a set of changing strategies that reveal the relations and assumptions at work in oppressions and simultaneously demonstrate what is wrong with these relations. It is enactivism. For example, if 1990s talk-show appearances by gay citizens consisted mainly of talking, they still enacted a kind of representative visibility. The enactivist strain of their appearances was in relation to a notion of invisibility as oppression rather than necessarily the pleas such representatives might have been making.

The difference between activism and talking is that in order to alienate, activism needs to enact, to reveal through its very sites, strategies, and performance the relations it critiques. Activism that is enactive makes sociopolitical relations and assumptions visible. It alienates us from the obvious or the unconsidered ideological supports of culture by staging the very terms through which the obvious inflects lives. If the problem with a lack of support for AIDS care is that the number of victims is unknown and their plight has been depersonalized, then enactive activism makes the extent of the tragedy known by circulating an AIDS quilt testifying to the reality of AIDS victims' suffering, as well as memorializing individual victims. This kind of activism is different from protesting with signs which, though called a demonstration, is often really a form of talk.

Enactive activism is like good drama. (The theater, too, is a seeing place.) Drama that discusses what it should show is merely the rehearsal of ideas—mere talk. Drama whose action and shape play out and make visible the forms and circumstances of events produces crises of perception. Good drama makes the audience active. Such, too, is the wish of activism. Although activism, too, has sets of conventions (and the more conventional the convention, such as the placard-bearing demonstrator, the more likely the activism will be invisible), activist events can situate themselves more strategically than theater. Activist events can take advantage of geography, timing, and situation as sites of intervention. Activism must be opportunistic as a part of its strategy. What works next may not be what worked before. Circumstances always change. The purpose of enactive activism is always to use context to force insight. The method is to employ mobile and versatile forms to push the seams. And activist events may touch people, invite them in, force or inveigle participation, often unwitting, as when we unconsciously repeat commercial catchphrases or hum the tunes from advertisements.

We chose to use film as a mode of activism that comments on the assumptions of activist strategies because we wanted to enact rather than outline, to present rather than lecture, to use a conventional medium to reveal our stakes in media. We wanted the film to enact the very strategies we discuss here: to infiltrate opportunistically, not so much through what it said, but in the way it was organized, through infectious music, through humor and parodied conventions of documentary video. We wanted to see if there was any intrinsically lesbian, gay, or queer activism, so we played crudely with the tropes associated with those cultures. We wanted to critique the star system, which has borne the weight of activism far too long.

It may be that the film *Enactivism* itself is already too hackneyed and dismissible to enact and that its enactivism comes in discussions about it, even those which pan the film. In this sense, the film is bound to work.

Notes

1. CBS News, "Poll: Legalize Same-Sex Marriage?" http://www.cbsnews.com/stories/2003/07/30/opinion/polls/main565918.shtml, July 31, 2003 (accessed August 23, 2007).

2. Neil A. Lewis, "Bush Backs Bid to Block Gays from Marrying," *New York Times*, http://www.nytimes.com/2003/07/31/national/31BUSH.html, July 31, 2003 (accessed August 23, 2007).

ON THE DVD

Totally Kickball, or The Philosophy of Activity-ism
Emma Crandall

Tough
Terry Galloway

Enactivism: The Movie
Dennis Allen, Jaime Hovey, and Judith Roof

Shamelessly Gay: Documents from the Labadie Collection
Julie Herrada and Tim Retzloff

Figure 1. *Tranz: The World of Transvestism* (London), no. 1, n.d. (Labadie Uncatalogued)

Figure 2. *Transsexuals in Prison* (Pendleton, Ind.), vol. 2, no. 2, September–October–November–December 1993. (Labadie HV 8301 .T74)

Figure 3. *Transformatie: Opiniblad over travestie en transseksualiteit* (Amsterdam), vol. 16, no. 1, February 1999. (Labadie HQ 77.9 .T693)

Figure 4. *Trans-Talk* (Portland, ME), April 1998. (Labadie Uncatalogued)

Figure 5. *Powder and Pearls: Newsletter of the Memphis TransGendered Alliance* (Memphis, TN), vol. 2, no. 9, September 1994. (Labadie HQ 77.9 .P69)

Figure 6. *TransAction: The Newsletter of the Congress of Transgender Organizations* (Minneapolis, MN), July 1994. (Labadie HQ 77.9 .T67)

Figure 7. *She-Male Trouble* (San Francisco), no. 1, 1992. (Labadie PN 6728 .S54 S54)

Figure 8. *Willyboy: The Faboo New TransZine* (Portland, OR), issue 2, January 1998. (Labadie HQ 77.9 .W55)

Figure 9. FTM Newsletter (San Francisco), issue 30, April 1995. (Labadie HQ 77.9 .F86)

Figure 10. *Transvestia* (Los Angeles), no. 13, Summer 1962. (Labadie HQ 77 .T7)

Figure 11. *The Female Impersonator: A Special Magazine for Special People* (Belmar, NJ), vol. 4, no. 5, 1972. (Labadie HQ 77 .F15)

Figure 12a. *GenderFlex: A Polygenderous Publication* (Sacramento, CA), vol. 4, issue 22, July–August–September 1994. (Labadie HQ 77.9 .T18)

Figure 12b. *GenderFlex: A Polygenderous Publication* (Sacramento, CA), vol. 2, issue 13, September–October 1992. (Labadie HQ 77.9 .T18)

Figure 13. "82 Club Souvenir Program" (New York: 82 Club, 1969). (Labadie PN 2071 .I47 E44 1969)

Figure 14. *Drag* (New York), vol. 2, no. 8, 1972. (Labadie HQ 77 .D66)

Figure 15. *Christian Love Letter: A Letter of Spiritual Encouragement Published for Crossdressers, Transgendered, Transsexuals* (Jackson, MS), issue 5, December 1999. (Labadie HQ 77.9 .C47)

Figure 16. *Gender Trash from Hell* (Toronto), vol. 1, issue 1, April–May 1993. (Labadie HQ 77.9 .G487)

Figure 17. *Les "Girls": Boys Will Be Girls* (New York), vol. 1, no. 1, 1979. (Labadie HQ 77 .L47)

Figure 18a. *Girly: Transgender Scene 'Zine* (London), issue 1, Summer 1995. (Labadie HQ 77.9 .G57)

Figure 18b. *Girly: Transgender Zine* (London), issue 5, July 1996. (Labadie HQ 77.9 .G57)

Figure 18c. *Girly: Transgender Zine* (London), issue 7, Winter–Spring 1997. (Labadie HQ 77.9 .G57)

Figure 19. *Finocchio's: America's Most Unusual Night Club* [program] (Hollywood, CA: A Zevin-Present Publication, 196-). (Labadie PN 1969 .C3 F565 196-)

Figure 20. "Kim Christy and Female Mimics International Present the 1986 She-Male Calendar" (Studio City, CA: Leoram Productions, 1985). (Labadie HQ 77.2 .U5 K55 1985)

Figure 21. Kim Elizabeth Stuart, *A Guide for Male to Female Transsexuals Considering Shifting Gender Identity*, rev. 2nd ed. (San Francisco: Educational TV Channel, 1994). (Labadie HQ 77.9 .S78 1994)

Figure 22. *He, She, We, They: Partners of Cross Dressers* (Derby: Derby TV/TS Group, 1988). (Labadie HQ 77 .H412 1988)

Figure 23. Louis Sullivan, *From Female to Male: The Life of Jack Bee Garland* (Boston: Alyson, 1990). (Labadie HQ 77.8 .G37 S851 1990)

Figure 24. Esther Newton, *Mother Camp: Female Impersonators in America* (Chicago: University of Chicago Press, 1979). (Labadie HQ 77 .N56 1979)

Figure 25. Leslie Feinberg, *Transgender Warriors: Making History from Joan of Arc to Ru-Paul*, advance uncorrected proofs (Boston: Beacon Press, 1996). (Labadie HQ 77.9 .F451 1996)

Figure 26. Gilbert Oakley, *Sex Change and Dress Deviation: The Secrets of an Odd Sexual World Revealed* (London: Morntide, 1970). (Labadie HQ 77 .O34 1970)

Figure 27. Edw[ard] Podolsky and C. Wade, *Transvestism Today: The Phenomena of Men Who Dress as Women* (New York: Epic, 1960). (Labadie HQ 77 .P628 1960)

Figure 28. Dawn Langley Simmons, *Man into Woman: A Transsexual Autobiography* (New York: Macfadden-Bartell, 1971). (Labadie 828 S58960 A32 1971)

Figure 29. Larry Maddock, *Sex Life of a Transvestite* (Hollywood, CA: K.D.S., 1964). (Labadie HQ 76.98 .W494 M338 1964)

Figure 30. Amy Camus, *School for a Transvestite* (n.p.: n.d.). (Labadie PS 3553 .A538 S36 19–)

Figure 31. *Transvestites Guide* (San Diego, CA: Flag, 197-). (Labadie HQ 77 .T75 197–)

Figure 32. Peter Ackroyd, *Dressing Up: Transvestism and Drag: The History of an Obsession* (New York: Simon and Schuster, 1979). (Labadie HQ 77 .A251)

Figure 33. Eli Clare, *Exile and Pride: Disability, Queerness, and Liberation* (Cambridge, MA: South End Press, 1999). (Labadie HQ 1426 .C561 1999)

Figure 34. Samuel R. Delany, *Times Square Red, Times Square Blue* (New York: New York University Press, 1999). (Labadie HQ 146 .N7 D451 1999)

Figure 35. Joël B. Tan, ed., *Queer PAPI Porn: Gay Asian Erotica* (San Francisco: Cleis Press, 1998). (Labadie PS 648 .H57 Q441 1998)

Figure 36. Pat Califia, *Macho Sluts: Erotic Fiction* (Boston: Alyson, 1988). (Labadie PS 3553 .A37 M2 1988)

Figure 37. *Boys Speak Out on Man-Boy Love*, 3rd ed. (New York: North American Man/Boy Love Association, 1986). (Labadie HQ 71 .B7 1986)

Figure 38. "The Lavender and Red Book: A Gay Liberation/Socialist Anthology" (Los Angeles: Lavender and Red Union, 1976). (Labadie Pamphlets)

Figure 39. *Barebacking Boys* promotional flyer, 2002. (Labadie Vertical Files)

Figure 40a. House o' Chicks brochure, 1994. (Labadie Vertical Files)

Figure 40b. House o' Chicks publicity photograph, 1994. (Labadie Vertical Files)

Figure 41. Susan Raffo, ed., *Queerly Classed: Gay Men and Lesbians Write about Class* (Boston: South End Press, 1997). (Labadie HQ 76.3 .U5 Q445 1997)

Figure 42. Girth and Mirth Detroit flyer, 1992. (Labadie Vertical Files)

Figure 43. Gay-Male-S/M Activists Demo Flyer, 1984. (Labadie Vertical Files)

Figure 44. GMSMA Rope Tricks Flyer, n.d. (Labadie Vertical Files)

Figure 45. GMSMA Special Nights Leather County Fair/Mineshaft Flyer, 1984. (Labadie Vertical Files)

Figure 46. GMSMA Demo Flyer, n.d. (Labadie Vertical Files)

Figure 47. Coyote: A Loose Woman's Organization solicitation letter, January 1975. (Labadie Vertical Files)

Figure 48. Dyke-Faggot Anarchist Gathering, Buffalo, NY, flyer, n.d. (Labadie Vertical Files)

Figure 49. Gay Atheist League of America brochure, n.d. (Labadie Vertical Files)

Figure 50. International Association of Black and White Men Together brochure, n.d. (Labadie Vertical Files)

Figure 51. Geoffrey Erikson, "What Liberty Offers the Gay Community," brochure, [199-]. (Labadie Vertical Files)

Figure 52. Libertarians for Gay and Lesbian Concerns, "Toward Peace and Freedom" brochure, n.d. (Labadie Vertical Files)

Figure 53. *Outpunk* (San Francisco), no. 4, June 1995. (Labadie Uncatalogued)

Figure 54a. *Anything That Moves: The Magazine for the Bisexual-at-Large Covering Gender and Sexuality Prix Fixe to A la Carte* (San Francisco), no. 10, Winter 1996. (Labadie Uncatalogued)

Figure 54b. *Anything That Moves: The Magazine for the Working Bisexual* (San Francisco), no. 19, Spring 1999. (Labadie Uncatalogued)

Figure 55a. *Hothead Paisan: Homicidal Lesbian Terrorist* (New Haven, CT), no. 16, November 1994. (Labadie HQ 75 .H82)

Figure 55b. *Hothead Paisan: Homicidal Lesbian Terrorist* (New Haven, CT), no. 17, February 1995. (Labadie HQ 75 .H82)

Figure 55c. *Hothead Paisan: Homicidal Lesbian Terrorist* (New Haven, CT), no. 18, May 1995. (Labadie HQ 75 .H82)

Figure 55d. *Hothead Paisan: Homicidal Lesbian Terrorist* (New Haven, CT), no. 20, November 1995. (Labadie HQ 75 .H82)

Figure 56. *On Our Backs: Entertainment for the Adventurous Lesbian* (San Francisco), Summer 1984. (Labadie HQ 75 .O56)

Figure 57a. *RFD: A Country Gay Journal* (Grinnell, IA), no. 21, Fall 1979. (Labadie HQ 75 .R115)

Figure 57b. *RFD: A Gay Country Journal for People Everywhere* (Grinnell, IA), no. 35, Summer 1983. (Labadie HQ 75 .R115)

Figure 58. *Centaur* (Desert Hot Springs, CA), vol. 7, no. 3, May–June 1996. (Labadie Uncatalogued)

Figure 59a. *DPN: Diseased Pariah News* (Oakland, CA), no. 5 (1992). (Labadie RC 607 .A26 D58)

Figure 59b. *DPN: Diseased Pariah News* (Oakland, CA), no. 9 (1994) (Labadie RC 607 .A26 D58)

Figure 60. "The Transsexual Menace, New York City," T-shirt from the National Transgender Library and Archives. (Labadie Manuscripts)

Figure 61. Miscellaneous buttons from the National Transgender Library and Archives. (Labadie Manuscripts)

Figure 62. *Steam: A Quarterly Journal for Men* (Cazenovia, WI), vol. 2, issue 4, Winter 1994. (Labadie HQ 75 .S74)

Figure 63. *Spectre* (Ann Arbor, MI), no. 5, November–December 1971. (Labadie HQ 76 .S74)

Figure 64. Dangerous Bedfellows, eds., *Policing Public Sex: Queer Politics and the Future of AIDS Activism* (Boston: South End Press, 1996). (Labadie HQ 76.3 .U5 P641 1996)

Marlene Dietrich: Four Black-and-White Photographs (to accompany David Caron, "Shame on Me, or The Naked Truth about Me and Marlene Dietrich")

Figure 1. Cover of Michel Hermon's CD *Dietrich Hotel*.

Figure 2. Marlene on the set of *Morocco*, 1930: gender as image. (Photo: Don English; © Kobal Collection)

Figure 3. Marlene photographed by Nickolas Muray in the 1930s: layers of artifice. (Photo: Nickolas Muray; © International Museum of Photography, George Eastman House, Syracuse)

Figure 4. At the Olympia, Paris, in the 1950s: Jean Louis's notorious "naked gown." (© Paris Match)

Kiko: Five Color Photographs (to accompany Ellis Hanson, "Teaching Shame")

Figure 1. Shortly before I am tenured, a conservative talk-show host, "Dr. Laura," airs an opinion that my course on child sexuality "has crossed the threshold from the merely absurd to the potentially dangerous." The dean, the chair of my department, and the president of the university get angry letters from hundreds and hundreds of outraged people, including a minister in Maryland who claims I seek to "normalize criminal thought" and lead the university into "a quagmire of iniquity." Someone named "Pedo Hunter," evidently offended by the same course, writes to me to say, "All I can PROMISE you is I'll TRACK YOU DOWN FOR THE MANGY DOG YOU ARE!!!" Using his real name, an undergraduate circulates a fantasy on the Internet in which he takes me to a Brazilian leper colony and tortures me to death because I am teaching a course on lesbian fiction and am clearly a lesbian myself.

I have an unpleasant suspicion that these shaming tactics, not my views on Plato or Genet, make my teaching queer. With this improbable pornography of violence and moral panic, they expose me, they expose themselves, they expose teaching itself. Have they no shame?

Figure 2. Sudden twinge of shame, which sometimes takes the form of concern, amusement, or intellectual distraction, where a body or an affect, whether someone else's or my own, interrupts the smooth course of my lecture. Sleepiness, drunkenness, inordinate pulchritude, and hiccups, of course, in my own classes no less than in Plato's *Symposium*, where they pose a powerful challenge to the intellectualizing discourse on eros, but I have also witnessed helpless giggling, uncontainable enthusiasms, bursting into tears, bleeding, fainting, screaming, shouting, sneezing, spilling, stumbling, pencil-gnawing, gum-chewing, breast-feeding, wardrobe malfunctions, horniness, speechlessness, embarrassment, nausea, panic, and obstreperous bolting from the room for typically undisclosed forms of relief. I feel obliged to carry on with whatever train of thought still has tracks. Thinking is done with bodies, and as in Plato, they sometimes rewrite the pedagogical script.

Figure 3. When Ham sees Noah, his father, drunk and naked, he goes outside and blabs about it. But Shem and Japheth, also Noah's sons, approach their father with their faces turned away and lay a garment over his shoulders. Shame here is an act of judgment, but also a theatrical practice of love. I imagine Noah, one eye open, secretly enjoying this performance, which is arguably more absurd than his own.

Idiotic essence of professorial shame: wrong = naked. Truths can be naked, but it seems their professors cannot.

At MLA, Jane Gallop introduces me to her son, who is sitting with her. I remember a nude portrait she poublished in Living with His Camera: herself posed like Manet's Olympia on a sofa with her son, also nude. She had been concerned about what her colleagues might think. Cat's out of the bag, I guess.

Refreshing departure from biblical precedent.

Figure 4. I am lecturing to undergraduates on erotic domination and submission in the work of Genet, Reik, and Foucault. I am wearing leather fetish gear, and it feels more embarrassing than the usual jacket and tie, though not unpleasantly so. Some students ask if they can handle my whip. One of them, who likes my boots, sends me a very formal letter to ask if he can be my slave. The letter is oddly desexualized and businesslike, as if he were requesting that I be his academic advisor, and the gesture seems appropriate to me, even endearing. He writes of his shame in asking, and his rhetoric is impeccably pedagogical: he wants me to "train" him, he wants to read more on the subject. What to tell the registrar, I wonder. Independent study, perhaps? Or field work?

Figure 5. I use these images of Kiko as a digital chalkboard for my lecture notes on Plato. Undergraduates tell me they are "so into him," and sometimes they mean Plato too. Certain people at the Gay Shame conference also told me, though always in private, that they enjoyed these images. Judith Halberstam explained to me that only white gay men would say such a thing (shame on them!). Her formula certainly simplifies matters, but these people were not all white, they were not all gay, and they were not all men. She seemed to think I must be up to no good anyway. She said angrily that she hoped I liked being shamed in public and she was going to make sure it happened. Performative speech act, somewhat infelicitous.

Gay Shame meets Lesbian Piety. But have we accounted for the pleasure yet?

Nine Artworks
Dylan Scholinski

Every Good Boy Does Fine, from the Discharge Anniversary Series. Mixed media on paper, 22 × 30 inches. This and the next two pieces come from a series of paintings I create every year between my birthday, August 5, and the anniversary of my discharge, August 10. (© 2004 Dylan Scholinski)

mental (st)ealth, from the Discharge Anniversary Series. Mixed media on luan, 48 × 48 inches. (© 2005 Dylan Scholinski)

Blind, from the Discharge Anniversary Series. Mixed media on paper, 22 × 30 inches. (© 2003 Dylan Scholinski)

Fly American't. Mixed media on luan, 19 × 19 inches. This painting was created after an incident at the San Francisco Airport. I had been pulled aside for a "random" search, which had nothing to do with my baggage, since I had not set off any alarms with the X-ray, and everything to do with the question of what sex I was. (© 2004 Dylan Scholinski)

Self Portrait: Stand Up Straight. Mixed media on canvas, 48 × 56 inches. This painting was created while I was writing my memoir *The Last Time I Wore a Dress* (Penguin/Putnam, 1997). I was thinking about all the times I had been told to "stand up straight" while I was growing up, and about how my life might had been different if anyone had told me to "stand up queer." (© 1998 Dylan Scholinski)

Sweet Dreams. Mixed media on canvas, 5 × 7 feet. This painting was created while I was writing my memoir *The Last Time I Wore a Dress* (Penguin/Putnam, 1997). When I was in third grade, even at that early stage in life, I felt my life slipping from me. It was the love of my teacher that helped pull me through. I would frequently call her at night and she would tuck me in over the phone. I still remember her calm voice wishing me "sweet dreams." (© 1998 Dylan Scholinski)

Shame, from the Seclusion Room Window Series. Mixed media on canvas, 6 × 6 inches. This painting is from a series that consists of canvases the size of the windows in seclusion rooms. The image of the face up in the window sometimes refers to the patient looking out, sometimes to the staff looking in. Then a single word is placed on the work, symbolizing either how the patient is feeling or how he or she is being perceived in that space. (© 1994 Dylan Scholinski)

Outta My Mind, from the Thorazine (c)rush Series. Mixed media on paper, 22 × 30 inches. This piece and the next are from a series of paintings I originally created to convey the effects of Thorazine, a debilitating tranquilizer, on me as a teenager. Usually I began the painting by covering the surface with random colors and textures to visually duplicate the head rush. Then, as the painting dried, I watched and studied the surface. I waited until I saw a shadow of a figure intertwined within the colors. I would then pick a figure to "save," and pull it out of the surface by either blackening or whitening out the backgrounds. As the series progressed I would also start to play with the shadows of the chosen figures, often depicting the conflicts between what the figure was doing and what it wished to be doing. (© 1996 Dylan Scholinski)

Echo, from the Thorazine (c)rush Series. Mixed media on paper, 22 × 30 inches. (© 1996 Dylan Scholinski)

One wall of Sent(a)Mental Studios, my creative home, shown here in 2004. The studio is located above Townhouse Tavern in Washington, D.C. The artist's studio is currently located at The Other Side Arts in Denver, Colo. (© 2004 Dylan Scholinski)

Gay Shame conference poster

LIST OF CONTRIBUTORS

Barry D. Adam is University Professor of Sociology at the University of Windsor, Ontario, and the author of *The Survival of Domination* (1978) and *The Rise of a Gay and Lesbian Movement* (1995), co-author of *Experiencing HIV* (1996), and co-editor of *The Global Emergence of Gay and Lesbian Politics* (1999). He has published extensively on new social movement theory, gay and lesbian issues, and safer sex decision making among gay and bisexual men. His Web site is http://www.uwindsor.ca/adam.

Dennis Allen is a professor in the Department of English at West Virginia University, where he specializes in literary and cultural theory, gay and lesbian studies, and the history of sexuality. He is the author of *Sexuality in Victorian Fiction* (1993) and has published articles on the relationship of homosexuality and narrative, the emergence of lesbian and gay studies as a discipline, and the representation of desire in a variety of edited collections and in journals such as *Narrative*, *Genders*, and *SEL*. He is currently working on a book on the impact postindustrial material culture and globalization have had on contemporary gay identity.

Neil Bartlett is the author of *Who Was That Man? A Present for Mr Oscar Wilde* (1988), and of the novels *Ready to Catch Him Should He Fall* (1990), *Mr Clive and Mr Page* (1996), and, most recently, *Skin Lane* (2007). He also works as a theater director, most recently for the Royal Shakespeare Company. His Web site is http://www.neil-bartlett.com.

Leo Bersani's works include *The Freudian Body: Psychoanalysis and Art* (1986), *Homos* (1995), *The Culture of Redemption* (1990), and, in collaboration with Ulysse Dutoit, *Caravaggio's Secrets* (1998) and *Forms of Being: Cinema, Aesthetics, Subjectivity* (2004).

David Caron is professor of French at the University of Michigan. He has published essays on AIDS, the Holocaust, the family, and other topics. He is the author of *AIDS in French Culture: Social Ills, Literary Cures* (2001) and of *My Father and I: The Marais and the Queerness of Community* (2009).

George Chauncey is professor of history and American studies at Yale University and co-director of the Yale Research Initiative on the History of Sexualities. He is the author of *Gay New York: Gender, Urban Culture, and the Making of the Gay Male World, 1890-1940*

(1994) and *Why Marriage? The History Shaping Today's Debate over Gay Equality* (2004). He is currently completing *The Strange Career of the Closet: Gay Culture, Consciousness, and Politics from the Second World War to the Gay Liberation Era.*

Emma Crandall is a Marion L. Brittain Postdoctoral Fellow in the School of Literature, Communication, and Culture at the Georgia Institute of Technology. She received a Ph.D. in English and women's studies from the University of Michigan and writes on Gertrude Stein, queer ethics, and friendship.

Douglas Crimp is Fanny Knapp Allen Professor of Art History at the University of Rochester. He gave the 2007 David R. Kessler Lecture in Lesbian and Gay Studies for the Center for Lesbian and Gay Studies (CLAGS). He is a recipient of the College Art Association's Frank Jewett Mather Award for distinction in art criticism and has twice been the recipient of the Art Critics Fellowship from the National Endowment for the Arts. His books include *AIDS Demo Graphics* (1990), *On the Museum's Ruins* (1993), and *Melancholia and Moralism: Essays on AIDS and Queer Politics* (2002). He is currently writing a book on Andy Warhol's films and a memoir of New York in the 1970s.

Terry Galloway is a deaf, queer writer, performer, and director. She is currently the Head Cheese of the Mickee Faust Club, "a community theater for the weird community" in Tallahasee, Florida.

Rita Gonzalez is assistant curator of special exhibitions at the Los Angeles County Museum of Art. She is completing her doctoral dissertation in the Department of Film, Television and Digital Media at UCLA.

Deborah B. Gould is an assistant professor of sociology at the University of Pittsburgh. She was a member of ACT UP/Chicago from the late 1980s into the mid-1990s. Currently she is finishing a book on emotion and AIDS activism, *Moving Politics: Shifting Political Horizons in the Fight against AIDS.*

David M. Halperin is W. H. Auden Collegiate Professor of the History and Theory of Sexuality at the University of Michigan. He is the author of several books, including *Saint Foucault: Towards a Gay Hagiography* (Oxford University Press, 1995) and, most recently, *What Do Gay Men Want? An Essay on Sex, Risk, and Subjectivity* (University of Michigan Press, 2007).

Ellis Hanson is professor of English at Cornell University. He is the author of *Decadence and Catholicism* (1997) and the editor of *Out Takes: Essays on Queer Theory and Film* (1999).

Julie Herrada is the curator of the Labadie Collection at the University of Michigan Library, where she collects and manages holdings related to social protest movements from the nineteenth century to the present. She holds a master's degree in library science with a certificate in archival administration from Wayne State University.

Jaime Hovey has taught English and gender and women's studies at Rutgers University, the University of Miami, and the University of Illinois at Chicago. She is a second-year law student at the University of Illinois College of Law.

Nadine Hubbs is associate professor of women's studies at the University of Michigan, where she also serves as director of the Graduate Certificate Program in LGBTQ Studies and co-director of the Lesbian-Gay-Queer Research Initiative. Her work examines gender and sexuality in classical and popular music including Morrissey, disco, and Radiohead, and her book *The Queer Composition of America's Sound: Gay Modernists, American Music, and National Identity* (2004) dissects the nationalist triumph of gay American composers during the most homophobic period in U.S. history. Her current project analyzes intersections of gender, sexuality, and class in post-Hank country music.

Charles Klein is projects director at the National Sexuality Resource Center at San Francisco State University. His research has focused on AIDS activism, violence and transgender political mobilization, and the emergence of gay communities in Brazil. He has previously published in *Sexualities*; *Culture, Health and Sexuality*; *AIDS*; and the *NACLA Report on the Americas*.

Don Kulick is professor of anthropology in the Department of Comparative Human Development at the University of Chicago. His books include *Travesti: Sex, Gender and Culture among Brazilian Transgendered Prostitutes* (1998), *Language and Sexuality* (with Deborah Cameron, 2003), and *Fat: The Anthropology of an Obsession* (co-edited with Anne Meneley, 2005).

Elisabeth Ladenson is author of *Dirt for Art's Sake: Books on Trial from* Madame Bovary *to* Lolita (2007) and *Proust's Lesbianism* (1999). She teaches at Columbia University.

Heather K. Love is associate professor of English at the University of Pennsylvania, where she teaches gender studies, twentieth-century literature and culture, and critical theory. She is the author of *Feeling Backward: Loss and the Politics of Queer History* (2007) and is currently at work on a project on the source materials for Erving Goffman's 1963 book *Stigma: On the Management of Spoiled Identity* (The *Stigma* Archive).

Robert McRuer is an associate professor in the Department of English at George Washington University, where he teaches cultural studies, queer theory, and disability studies. He is the author of *Crip Theory: Cultural Signs of Queerness and Disability* (2007) and the co-editor, with Abby L. Wilkerson, of *Desiring Disability: Queer Theory Meets Disability Studies*, special issue, *GLQ: A Journal of Lesbian and Gay Studies* 9, 1-2.

Jennifer Moon received her Ph.D. in American culture from the University of Michigan in 2006. Her dissertation focused on gay male cruising and queer counterpublics. She currently lives in Brooklyn and is an editor for the dean at Weill Cornell Medical College in New York.

Frances Negrón-Muntaner is an award-winning filmmaker, writer, and scholar. She is the author of *Boricua Pop: Puerto Ricans and the Latinization of American Culture* (named 2004 Choice Outstanding Book); the editor of four academic books, including *None of the Above: Puerto Ricans in the Global Era* (2007); and the director of *Brincando el charco: Portrait of a Puerto Rican* (1994) and *Land of the Chamorros* (2007). Negrón-Muntaner is also a founding board member and past chair of NALIP, the National Association of

Latino Independent Producers. She currently teaches Latino and Caribbean literatures and cultures at Columbia University.

Taro Nettleton is a Ph.D. candidate in the Program in Visual and Cultural Studies at the University of Rochester. He is writing a dissertation on the relationship between subjectivity and spatial politics in underground performance-based art works and films of the 1960s in Japan.

Helmut Puff is an associate professor of German and history at the University of Michigan in Ann Arbor. His research focuses on German literature, history, and culture in the late medieval and early modern period, with particular interest in the history of sexuality and gender relations. He is the author of *Sodomy in Reformation Germany and Switzerland, 1400–1600* (2003).

Tim Retzloff is a doctoral student in history at Yale University. His research has appeared in *GLQ, Centro Journal*, in the *Encyclopedia of Lesbian, Gay, Bisexual, and Transgender History in America*, and in the anthology *Creating a Place for Ourselves*. He completed his undergraduate studies at the University of Michigan while working full-time at the Hatcher Graduate Library.

Judith Roof is a professor of English and film studies at Michigan State University. She is the author of five books, including most recently *The Poetics of DNA*. She is also a member of SteinSemble Performance Group.

Gayle Rubin teaches anthropology and women's studies at the University of Michigan. She is the author of many influential essays on sexuality. Her current research is focused on the spatial dynamics of urban sexual populations. She is also an occasional DJ, spinning tunes from the archives of danceology.

Born in a Chicago suburb, **Daphne Scholinski** was fifteen years old when she was locked up in a mental hospital, diagnosed as "an inappropriate female." She spent the rest of her high school years undergoing extreme femininity training. **Dylan Scholinski** now resides in Denver, Colorado, and is an artist, author, and public speaker whose books include (as Daphne Scholinski) *The Last Time I Wore a Dress: A Memoir* (Penguin/Putnam, 1997). He has appeared on *20/20, Dateline*, and *Today* and has been featured in a variety of newspapers and magazines.

Eve Kosofsky Sedgwick (1950–2009) was a Distinguished Professor in the Ph.D. program in English at the Graduate Center, City University of New York. Her books include *Between Men: English Literature and Male Homosocial Desire* (1985), *Epistemology of the Closet* (1990), *Tendencies* (1993), *A Dialogue on Love* (1999), *Touching Feeling: Affect, Pedagogy, Performativity* (2003), and *Shame and Its Sisters: A Silvan Tomkins Reader* (co-edited with Adam Frank, 1995).

Tobin Siebers is V. L. Parrington Collegiate Professor, a professor of English and of art and design at the University of Michigan. His *Disability Theory* appeared in 2008 from the University of Michigan Press.

Valerie Traub is professor of English and women's studies at the University of Michigan, where she chairs the Women's Studies Department. She is the author of *Desire and Anxiety: Circulations of Sexuality in Shakespearean Drama* (Routledge, 1992) and *The Renaissance of Lesbianism in Early Modern England* (Cambridge University Press, 2002).

Michael Warner teaches at Yale University, where he is a professor of English and American studies. His most recent books include *Publics and Counterpublics* (2002) and *The Portable Walt Whitman* (2003). He is also the author of *The Letters of the Republic* (1990) and *The Trouble with Normal* (1999). He has edited two literary anthologies: *American Sermons* (1999) and, with Myra Jehlen, *The English Literatures of America, 1500–1800* (1997). He is also the editor of *Fear of a Queer Planet: Queer Politics and Social Theory* (1993) and, with Gerald Graff, *The Origins of Literary Studies in America: A Documentary Anthology* (1988).

Abby Wilkerson lives in Riverdale, Maryland, and is the author of *Diagnosis: Difference: The Moral Authority of Medicine*, and a number of articles. Together with Robert McRuer, she co-edited *Desiring Disability: Queer Theory Meets Disability Studies*, special issue, *GLQ: A Journal of Lesbian and Gay Studies* 9, 1–2. Currently she is completing a book on the politics of obesity discourse. She teaches in the University Writing Program at George Washington University in Washington, D.C.

Amalia Ziv is a lecturer in literature and gender studies at Tel Aviv University. She wrote her Ph.D. dissertation on female sexual subjectivity in pornographic fiction by women. She has published articles on pornography, queer theory, and contemporary queer culture in Hebrew and English and co-edited the volume *Beyond Sexuality*, a reader in lesbian and gay studies in Hebrew translation (2003).